The Legal Power to Launch War
Who Decides?

The issue of who has the power to declare war or authorise military action in a democracy has become a major legal and political issue, internationally, and is set to become even more pertinent in the immediate future, particularly in the wake of military action in Syria, ongoing wars in the Middle East, and tense discussions between the United States and its allies, and Russia and China.

This book comparatively examines the executive and prerogative powers to declare war or launch military action, focusing primarily on the United States, Britain and Australia. It explores key legal and constitutional questions, including:

- who currently has the power/authority to declare war?
- who currently has the power to launch military action without formally declaring war?
- how, if at all, can those powers be controlled, legally or politically?
- what are the domestic legal consequences of going to war?

In addition to probing the extensive domestic legal consequences of going to war, the book also reviews various proposals that have been advanced for interrogating the power to commence armed conflict and explores the reasons why these propositions have failed to win support within the political establishment.

Michael Head is a professor of law at Western Sydney University, Australia.

Kristian Boehringer is a senior lecturer in business law at Torrens University, Australia.

The Legal Power to Launch War

Who Decides?

Michael Head and
Kristian Boehringer

Routledge
Taylor & Francis Group

LONDON AND NEW YORK

First published 2019 by Routledge

2 Park Square, Milton Park, Abingdon, Oxfordshire OX14 4RN
52 Vanderbilt Avenue, New York, NY 10017

Routledge is an imprint of the Taylor & Francis Group, an informa business

First issued in paperback 2020

British Library Cataloguing-in-Publication Data
A catalogue record for this book is available from the British Library

Library of Congress Cataloging-in-Publication Data
Names: Head, Michael, 1952- | Boehringer, Kristian.
Title: The legal power to launch war : who decides? / by Michael Head
    and Kristian Boehringer.
Description: Abingdon, Oxon ; New York, NY : Routledge, 2019. |
    Includes bibliographical references and index.
Identifiers: LCCN 2018036710| ISBN 9781138292086 (hbk) |
    ISBN 9781351965576 (adobe) | ISBN 9781351965552
    (mobipocket) | ISBN 9781351965569 (epub)
Subjects: LCSH: War and emergency powers. | War, Declaration of. |
    War and emergency powers—United States. | War and emergency
    powers—Great Britain. | War and emergency powers—Australia.
Classification: LCC K3344 .H435 2019 | DDC 341.6/2—dc23
LC record available at https://lccn.loc.gov/2018036710

ISBN: 978-1-138-29208-6 (hbk)
ISBN: 978-0-367-53413-4 (pbk)

Typeset in Galliard
by Swales & Willis Ltd, Exeter, Devon, UK

Contents

Preface

In war, truth is the first casualty.

Aeschylus, Greek tragic dramatist (525–456 BC)

As this book was being written, the clouds of trade war and war were looming. The United States was initiating tariff and investment measures against its rivals in Europe and China, proxy wars were raging in the Middle East, and geo-strategic flashpoints were smouldering in Korea, the Taiwan Strait, the South China Sea and elsewhere.

Under these conditions, there is an urgency to the two main questions we ask in this book: who holds the legal power to initiate wars; and who should have those powers? This volume is focused on three countries that have been in the forefront of most of the wars of the 20th and 21st centuries: the United States, Britain and Australia. Similar questions are posed internationally, however.

These questions have huge implications not only for the risk to human civilisation in the event of another world war, but also for fundamental democratic rights domestically, which are always among the first casualties of war, together with truth.

The conclusion we draw is that, despite the status of these three countries as democracies, the war powers are increasingly controlled by executive cabals, acting on behalf of corporate, military-intelligence and political establishments. This is not only an affront to democracy; it also escalates the danger of a third world war between major global powers battling for supremacy.

None of the numerous schemes proposed by scholars and commentators to prevent executive governments from taking their populations to war, via parliamentary or congressional votes or referenda, have proven feasible or effective. While referenda could provide a mechanism for popular hostility to war to be brought to bear, the forces driving toward war are deeply rooted in the socio-economic structure and social relations of the corporate profit system itself.

A common problem with previous works on war-making and related powers is that they take as their starting point the continuation of the existing economic, political and legal order, and they discuss how to accommodate the resort to war powers. They barely examine the actual measures, including propaganda, provocations and deception, that ruling elites adopt to trigger and prosecute wars. Nor do they probe the underlying implications for democracy.

We argue that, to prevent war, what is required is an end to the dictatorship of finance capital and the economic system that is the fundamental cause of militarism. That means abolishing the nation-state system as a whole, establishing instead a world based on equality and scientific planning. This would make possible the rational, planned development of global resources and, on this basis, the eradication of poverty and the raising of human culture to new heights that will render war unnecessary and obsolete.

For Michael Head, this book forms part of a four-part contribution. In *Emergency Powers in Theory and Practice: The Long Shadow of Carl Schmitt* (Ashgate, 2016), he examined the increasing use of emergency-type powers, as well as the promotion and even rehabilitation of Carl Schmitt, the best-known champion of 'exceptional' dictatorial powers during the post-1919 Weimer Republic and subsequent Nazi regime in Germany. In *Crimes against the State: From Treason to Terrorism* (Ashgate, 2011), he reviewed the range of criminal offences that governments use to protect themselves against perceived political or existential threats—subversion, rebellion, treason, mutiny, espionage, sedition, terrorism, riot and unlawful assembly. Previous writings, such as *Calling out the Troops* (The Federation Press, 2009), analysed measures to call out the military domestically to suppress civil unrest.

Michael Head's thanks, as always, go to his darling wife, Mary, and their four remaining children, Clayton, Tom, Daniel and Kathleen, for their understanding and forbearance during the researching and writing of this book. He is also grateful to his wonderful colleagues and students at Western Sydney University for their encouragement and intellectual insights, and to Alison Kirk, the wise and helpful law and legal studies publisher at Routledge, for her support and assistance.

Kristian Boehringer would like to express his deepest gratitude to his family for their support and sacrifice, and to Michael Head for his considered criticism and uncompromising motivation. He would like to express his appreciation to Dr Zelko Livaic for his lessons, his time and his endless compassion.

Sydney
4 July 2018

Introduction

What is at stake?

A decision to go to war, whether by formal declaration or not, is probably the most grave and potentially catastrophic decision a government can take. Millions of lives may be lost as a result, both combatant and civilian, not to speak of the devastating consequences for the lives of many millions more people who are likely to lose loved ones or be forced to flee their homes and countries. The future of human civilisation itself could be at stake.

World War II ended with two nuclear bombings by the United States on the cities of Hiroshima and Nagasaki, killing some 200,000 people, mostly women and children. Another world war would almost certainly involve far more powerful nuclear weapons, endangering the lives of billions of people and the planet's entire environment (Starr 2015).

More than 17 million people were killed during World War I, including 7 million civilians, and 20 million were wounded (Ellis 2001: 269–70). An estimated 80 million perished in World War II, counting those killed by war-related disease and famine, with the civilian death toll reaching 55 million (Somerville 2011: 5). Between 1955 and 1975, up to 3 million died in the Vietnam War (Lewy 1978: 442–53). Some half a million Iraqis died between 2003 and 2010 as a result of the US invasion of that country (Hagopian et al. 2013).

From 'coming to the aid of little Belgium' (World War I) to 'weapons of mass destruction' (the conquest of Iraq), each of these wars was instigated by lies, designed to overcome popular anti-war sentiment and foment nationalism. The longer these wars went on, with the human cost piling up, the more the popular opposition grew to them and the more onerous the means, such as conscription, imposed to fight them.

Despite the human costs involved, the power to go to war is exercised undemocratically, by 'the executive', with virtually no public, legislative or judicial scrutiny or accountability. Whether is it cloaked in the language of 'prerogative', 'presidential' or 'executive' powers, the legal authority to deploy armed forces for warfare is held in the hands of small cabals. The historical record shows that no parliamentary or congressional vote is necessary, let alone a public plebiscite, and no domestic court would uphold a legal challenge to a decision to launch a war.

In the three countries examined in this study, the United States, Britain and Australia, various efforts have been made to introduce forms of legislative control over war-making. Each has failed, underscoring the determination with which the ruling establishments insist that the power must remain free of limited or even token forms of democratic restraint.

Going to war also has far-reaching domestic political and legal consequences, including the extensive powers assumed by governments, the impact on the civil and political rights of their populations, and the implications for democracy.

In each of the countries examined, governments largely ruled by decree or regulations during the two world wars, invoking emergency powers, interning thousands of people and laying serious charges against anti-war dissenters. Wartime powers can include the internal mobilisation of the armed forces to deal with social unrest or anti-war opposition. The US Department of Defense's *Law of War Manual*, released in June 2015, asserts that the law of war supersedes other international and domestic law, as well as the US Constitution (Pentagon 2015: 7–16). It contemplates virtual martial law, including mass military detentions.

Why this book?

The issue of war, whether formally declared or not, has become a major and critical political and legal issue internationally. Public, parliamentary and constitutional debates have erupted since the turn of the century in Western countries, particularly after the declaration and adoption by many governments of the 'war on terror' and the US-led intervention into Iraq in 2003. The collapse of the lies propagated to justify that invasion, such as the alleged imminent threat of 'weapons of mass destruction', ignited popular opposition to war and led to efforts, universally unsuccessful, to hold those responsible to account and to curtail war-making powers.

Even more fundamentally, a century on from World War I, the underlying conflicts between the major capitalist powers that erupted in that terrible conflagration are re-emerging, with the United States—the hegemonic power since World War II—aggressively seeking to combat challenges from its rivals.

Today, the clouds of war hang over not only the Middle East, but also Ukraine, the Korean pensinsula and the South China Sea, raising the spectre of wider wars involving the nuclear powers of the United States, Russia and China. Both Germany and Japan, defeated in World War II, are remilitarising and seeking to rewrite their legal and constitutional restrictions on military action.

These developments have already generated considerable anti-war sentiment, although as yet there are no mass anti-war protests on the scale of the worldwide demonstrations against the invasion of Iraq in 2003. An NBC News/ Surveymonkey survey in 2017 reported that two-thirds of Americans were either 'very worried' or 'somewhat worried' about the possibility that the United States would become engaged in a major war in the next four years (NBC News 2017).

Such concerns have led to demands for democratic control over the commencement of military action. In response, however, governments have sought to develop new pretexts for going to war, while leaving the war powers essentially intact in the hands of executive authorities.

The ongoing wars in the Middle East and the mounting tensions between the United States, its post-war European and Japanese allies, and both Russia and China mean that the fundamental issues at stake will loom even larger in the years ahead. Decisive questions are raised, first and foremost politically, but also legally. Many of the key legal and constitutional questions have received insufficient attention, among them the following.

- Who currently has the power/authority to declare war?
- Who currently has the power to launch military action without formally declaring war?
- How and why have those powers arisen historically?
- Who *should* hold such powers?
- How, if at all, can those powers be controlled, legally or politically?
- What are the domestic legal consequences of going to war?
- What are the implications for basic legal and democratic rights?

None of these politico-legal issues can be realistically considered in isolation from the underlying causes and consequences of war, although a full examination of those geo-strategic, economic, political and other factors is beyond the scope of this book.

This book examines in detail the extraordinary executive and prerogative powers to declare war or launch military action, as well as any applicable constitutional conventions, legislation and legal doctrines, primarily focusing on the United States, Britain and Australia. Not only are these countries key examples of English-derived legal systems, but also they have been playing a leading role in the wars of the early 21st century, as well as in the informally declared indefinite 'war on terror'.

This book reviews and assesses various proposals advanced for scrutinising, limiting, transferring or holding to account the power to commence armed conflict, as well as the reasons for the general failure of these propositions to win support within the political establishment. Many attempts have been made, via parliamentary bills, litigation, official inquiries, public campaigns and academic contributions, to curtail the war powers, but with little or no success.

This book also probes the domestic legal implications of war. It does not examine in depth the international law of war, except in so far as it interconnects or overlaps with the national powers to launch warfare. One chapter, however, considers the degree to which international human rights law constrains war powers.

To some extent, this book further elaborates the legal picture presented by Michael Head's previous writings on emergency powers, military call-out powers and crimes against the state—the range of offences used to protect the state itself against perceived subversion.

- In *Emergency Powers in Theory and Practice: The Long Shadow of Carl Schmitt* (Ashgate, 2016), he examined the prevalence of emergency powers and the rehabilitation of theories of 'exception'.

- In *Crimes against the State: From Treason to Terrorism* (Ashgate, 2011), he reviewed in detail offences generally classified as crimes against the state or the nation—that is, rebellion, treason, mutiny, espionage, sedition, terrorism, riot and unlawful assembly.
- In *Calling out the Troops* (The Federation Press, 2009) and *Domestic Deployment of the Armed Forces* (with Scott Mann, Ashgate, 2009), he examined domestic military call-out powers, some of which rely on emergency powers.

This work examines, and places in historical context, the resort to war powers during the 20th century and the opening years of the 21st century in response to the the terrorist attacks known simply as 9/11, the interventions in Afghanistan, Iraq, Syria and Libya, and the rising tensions between the Western powers and Russia and China.

The book critically examines scholarly attempts to develop theoretical frameworks to justify or challenge the turn to war powers. A common problem with these works is that they take as their starting point the continuation or re-establishment of the existing political and legal order, and they discuss how to accommodate the resort to war powers. They barely examine the actual measures, including provocations, war propaganda and lies, adopted to prosecute war. Nor do they consider the underlying implications for democracy.

Intensifying war preparations

Amid escalating geo-strategic tensions, including threats of trade wars, preparations are being made for a new period of war, including by the major powers that fought World War II. The most aggressive in this planning is the United States. In January 2018, the US Department of Defense released an 11-page declassified summary of its *2018 National Defense Strategy* (Mattis 2018).

A longer, classified version of the strategy was circulated to members of the US Congress. It is likely to be more explicit and detailed. Nevertheless, the declassified synopsis was frank. It publicly signalled preparations for direct military confrontation with nuclear-armed Russia and China. The Pentagon document outlined an historic shift away from the ostensible justification for US global military operations of the last nearly two decades—the so-called war on terror; rather, '[i]nter-state strategic competition, not terrorism, is now the primary concern in U.S. national security' (Mattis 2018: 1).

The synopsis identified a new historic phase of 'increased global disorder' in which the hegemony of the United States—which resulted from the two world wars—was being challenged by rivals. In particular, it singled out China and Russia:

> China is a strategic competitor using predatory economics to intimidate its neighbors while militarizing features in the South China Sea. Russia has violated the borders of nearby nations and pursues veto power over the economic, diplomatic, and security decisions of its neighbors.
>
> (Mattis 2018: 1)

The document bluntly presented China and Russia as direct threats to the prosperity and 'global pre-eminence' of the United States, and insisted that intensified preparations had to be made to win military conflicts against them. The strategy required 'a more lethal, resilient and rapidly innovating Joint Force' that could 'prevail in conflict and preserve peace through strength' (Mattis 2018: 1). Even if peace could be achieved, it would be the result of US military supremacy. Moreover, the necessity for this 'pre-eminence' was put entirely in terms of US economic well-being, setting aside the claims of previous US governments justifying military interventions on the grounds of global peace, humanitarianism or the defence of democracy:

> The costs of not implementing this strategy are clear. Failure to meet our defense objectives will result in decreasing US global influence, eroding cohesion among allies and partners, and reduced access to markets that will contribute to a decline in our prosperity and standard of living.
>
> (Mattis 2018: 1)

China and Russia were depicted as threatening US economic wealth and the global order that rested on unchallenged US power:

> The central challenge to U.S. prosperity and security is the *reemergence of long-term, strategic competition* by what the National Security Strategy classifies as revisionist powers. It is increasingly clear that China and Russia want to shape a world consistent with their authoritarian model—gaining veto authority over other nations' economic, diplomatic, and security decisions.
>
> China is leveraging military modernization, influence operations, and predatory economics to coerce neighboring countries to reorder the Indo-Pacific region to their advantage. As China continues its economic and military ascendance, asserting power through an all-of-nation long-term strategy, it will continue to pursue a military modernization program that seeks Indo-Pacific regional hegemony in the near-term and displacement of the United States to achieve global preeminence in the future. The most far-reaching objective of this defense strategy is to set the military relationship between our two countries on a path of transparency and non-aggression.
>
> Concurrently, Russia seeks veto authority over nations on its periphery in terms of their governmental, economic, and diplomatic decisions, to shatter the North Atlantic Treaty Organization and change European and Middle East security and economic structures to its favour.
>
> (Mattis 2018: 2, emphasis original)

While the document spoke of 'non-aggression', the logic of these declarations was clear: China, as well as Russia, must accept the global dominance of the United States or face war. The synopsis insisted on the necessity of upholding the world order established after the US victories over Germany and Japan in World War II:

Another change to the strategic environment is a *resilient, but weakening, post-WWII international order.* In the decades after fascism's defeat in World War II, the United States and its allies and partners constructed a free and open international order to better safeguard their liberty and people from aggression and coercion. Although this system has evolved since the end of the Cold War, our network of alliances and partnerships remain the backbone of global security. China and Russia are now undermining the international order from within the system by exploiting its benefits while simultaneously undercutting its principles and 'rules of the road'.

(Mattis 2018: 2, emphasis original)

Even after the exposure of the lies about 'weapons of mass destruction' that provided the pretext for the 2003 US-led invasion of Iraq (see Chapter 2), the Pentagon continued to accuse 'rogue regimes' of seeking to acquire such weapons. The two countries specifically targeted as other threats to the 'post-WWII international order' were North Korea and Iran, both of which had links to China and Russia. Despite their relatively small size and the punishing impact of Western economic sanctions, they were both depicted as global dangers:

Rogue regimes such as North Korea and Iran are destabilizing regions through their pursuit of nuclear weapons or sponsorship of terrorism. North Korea seeks to guarantee regime survival and increased leverage by seeking a mixture of nuclear, biological, chemical, conventional, and unconventional weapons and a growing ballistic missile capability to gain coercive influence over South Korea, Japan, and the United States. In the Middle East, Iran is competing with its neighbors, asserting an arc of influence and instability while vying for regional hegemony, using state-sponsored terrorist activities, a growing network of proxies, and its missile program to achieve its objectives . . .

Rogue regimes, such as North Korea, continue to seek out or develop *weapons of mass destruction (WMD)*—nuclear, chemical, and biological—as well as long range missile capabilities and, in some cases, proliferate these capabilities to malign actors as demonstrated by Iranian ballistic missile exports.

(Mattis 2018: 2–3, emphasis original)

The document was blatant in asserting the goal of reversing the loss of unchallenged US military predominance:

Challenges to the US military advantage represent another shift in the global security environment. For decades the United States has enjoyed uncontested or dominant superiority in every operating domain. We could generally deploy our forces when we wanted, assemble them where we wanted, and operate how we wanted. Today, every domain is contested—air, land, sea, space, and cyberspace . . . In support of the *National Security Strategy,* the Department of Defense will be prepared to defend the homeland, remain the preeminent military power in the world, ensure the balances of power remain in our favor, and advance an international order that is most conducive to our security and prosperity.

(Mattis 2018: 2–4, emphasis original)

Another passage in the document, outlining the Pentagon's 'strategic approach', pointed to plans to provoke wars with identified enemies by conducting 'unpredictable' military operations and manoeuvres to 'frustrate' them and preclude their options. Behind a screen of displaying a commitment to deterring aggression, the intent would be to force targeted countries to 'confront conflict under adverse conditions':

> *Be strategically predictable, but operationally unpredictable.* Deterring or defeating long-term strategic competitors is a fundamentally different challenge than the regional adversaries that were the focus of previous strategies. Our strength and integrated actions with allies will demonstrate our commitment to deterring aggression, but our dynamic force employment, military posture, and operations must introduce unpredictability to adversary decision-makers. With our allies and partners, we will challenge competitors by maneuvering them into unfavorable positions, frustrating their efforts, precluding their options while expanding our own, and forcing them to confront conflict under adverse conditions.
>
> (Mattis 2018: 5, emphasis original)

In language reminiscent of George Orwell's *1984* doublethink, 'war is peace', the synopsis stated: 'The surest way to prevent war is to be prepared to win one' (Mattis 2018: 5). It was essential to '*[p]rioritize preparedness for war*', because '[a]chieving peace through strength requires the Joint Force to deter conflict through preparedness for war' (Mattis 2018: 6, emphasis original).

Central to this 'strategic approach' was the further development of nuclear weapons and the readiness to use them:

> *Nuclear forces.* The Department will modernize the nuclear triad—including nuclear command, control, and communications, and supporting infrastructure. Modernization of the nuclear force includes developing options to counter competitors' coercive strategies, predicated on the threatened use of nuclear or strategic non-nuclear attacks.
>
> (Mattis 2018: 6, emphasis original)

What emerged from the Pentagon synopsis was a vision of US imperialism in mortal danger of losing global dominance and a United States prepared to provoke new wars to restore it. The thrust of the document was a demand for an urgent build-up of the US war machine, which was already spending more on the military than the next eight countries combined, including nearly triple the military spending of China and roughly eight times the amount spent by Russia (see the next section).

The United States is not alone in preparing for war. Significantly, both of the imperialist powers defeated in World War II, Germany and Japan, are rearming. In part, they are responding to the growing unilateralism of the United States, epitomised by President Donald Trump's 'America First' programme. The Trump administration's offensive includes trade war measures against Europe and Germany, as well as other countries, on the grounds of protecting industries regarded as critical for US 'national security'.

During May 2018, German Chancellor Angela Merkel announced a major rearmament programme. Speaking at a Bundeswehr (Armed Forces) conference in Berlin, she referred to the growing conflicts between the United States and the European powers, including over Iran and climate change, and the 'rise in protectionism'. Under these conditions, Merkel said, it was important that Germany increase defence spending by 2024 to 2 per cent of its gross domestic product (GDP). That would amount to an increase from €37 billion to between €70 million and €75 billion. This would be the biggest expansion of German military spending since the end of World War II (Vandreier 2018).

At the same event, German Defence Minister Ursula Von der Leyen reported that Germany had already undertaken a significant military upgrade in the previous four years. The result was extensive new purchases, including 181 armoured personnel carriers, 51 armoured fighting vehicles, 31 combat helicopters, 16 transport aircraft, 2 submarines and 1,800 other military vehicles. In addition to this upgrade, armaments investments totalling €31 billion had already been launched. Over the ensuing four years, at least another 129 armoured vehicles, 5 new tanker aircraft, 15 marine helicopters, 50,000 suits of body armour, more than 33,000 modern digital radios and more than 70 armoured cranes were scheduled to be delivered to the German military. All this was still within previous budget planning, which the planned doubling of the military budget would greatly eclipse (Vandreier 2018).

Japan's remilitarisation was demonstrated in April 2018 when the country's military, still titled the Self-Defence Forces (SDF), activated its first marine unit since end of World War II. The ceremony was conducted at a base near Sasebo on the southwestern island of Kyushu. The 2,100-strong Amphibious Rapid Deployment Brigade (ARDB) was said to be a defensive force, but formed part of an ongoing rearmament and could be used far from Japan's shores (Symonds 2018).

As well as marines, the Japanese military is acquiring large helicopter carriers, which could function as aircraft carriers, amphibious ships, Osprey tilt-rotor troop carriers and amphibious assault vehicles. Prime Minister Shinzo Abe, who came to office in late 2012, actively campaigned to refashion the post-war Constitution of Japan to remove all restraints on the use of the military to prosecute the country's economic and strategic interests. The development of an offensive military capacity is a breach of the 'pacifist' Constitution, under which it renounced the right to wage war or to establish armed forces. Successive Japanese governments have circumvented the Constitution by claiming that its forces are purely for self-defence, but Abe went further in 2015 by pushing through so-called collective self-defence legislation that permitted Japan to join in military operations led by the United States or other allies (Symonds 2018).

In December 2017, the Japanese cabinet approved a record-high draft defence budget of US$46 billion, which included the purchase of two Aegis Ashore anti-ballistic missile batteries and Japan's first long-range cruise missiles, which could be mounted on fighter jets. While the Japanese defence budget remained substantially less than that of China, Japan has a substantial high-tech industrial base that could be used to expand its military capabilities rapidly (Symonds 2018).

Thus, amid growing global tensions, fuelled in large measures by the public turn to war preparations and aggressive trade war measures in Washington, Japan and Germany are rapidly building up military forces.

Rising military spending

Global military spending rose to more than US$1.7 trillion in 2017—the highest level since the Cold War, according to figures published in 2018 by the Stockholm International Peace Research Institute (SIPRI 2018).

With a budget totalling more than $610 billion in 2017, the United States remained by far the world's biggest military spender, dedicating a greater amount of money to the military than that of the next seven countries combined. The 2018 defence budget, signed by President Donald Trump, would push this figure to $700 billion (SIPRI 2018).

The United States still outspent China, the second largest spender globally, almost threefold, even though China increased its military spending by 5.6 per cent to $228 billion in 2017. China's spending as a share of world military expenditure has risen from 5.8 per cent in 2008 to 13 per cent in 2017, helping to manifest an arms race with ominous implications (SIPRI 2018).

Every major power has been rearming, pushing international military spending up by nearly 10 per cent since the 2008 global economic crisis. The particularly sharp rise in military spending over the last decade in Central Europe (20 per cent) and Eastern Europe (33 per cent) reflected the preparations by the alliance of the United States and the North Atlantic Treaty Organization (NATO) for war with Russia. The 29 members of NATO accounted for more than half of the world's military spending (SIPRI 2018).

Under Presidents Obama and Trump, the United States pressured its European allies to push their military spending higher. In 2018, Germany's grand coalition government pledged to nearly double military spending to 2 per cent of GDP by 2024, while French President Emmanuel Macron planned to increase military spending by 35 per cent.

Military expenditure in Asia and Oceania rose for the 29th successive year. India spent $63.9 billion on its military in 2017, an increase of 5.5 per cent compared with 2016, while South Korea's spending, at $39.2 billion, rose by 1.7 per cent between 2016 and 2017 (SIPRI 2018).

The SIPRI figures provided a glimpse of the global diversion of resources from social needs toward destructive ends. According to SIPRI, just 13 per cent of annual world military spending would be enough to end world poverty and hunger; 4 per cent would guarantee food security for the world's population; 5 per cent would meet health needs; 12 per cent would provide everyone with an education; 3 per cent would provide clean water and proper sanitation (SIPRI 2018).

An arms race is under way that finds its most acute expression in the arena of nuclear weaponry, delivery systems and associated technologies. Determined to maintain its supremacy in Asia and globally, the United States is planning to spend $1 trillion over the next three decades to develop a broader range of sophisticated nuclear weapons and the means of delivering them to their targets. The unstated aim of the Pentagon is to secure nuclear primacy—that is, the means of obliterating China's nuclear arsenal and thus its ability to mount a counterattack. The Chinese response, which is equally reactionary, is to ensure that it retains the ability to strike back in a manner that would kill tens of millions in the United States.

The intensifying military competition is an unequal one, which only heightens tensions and the danger of war. In the field of nuclear armaments, China is outgunned and outnumbered. While desperately seeking to catch up, the Chinese military is generations behind in the capability of its weaponry and fielded an estimated 260 warheads in 2016, compared to about 7,000 for the United States. The prime objective of the Chinese leadership is to ensure that a credible nuclear deterrent would survive a US first strike. Unlike Beijing, Washington has never ruled out the first use of nuclear weapons.

In June 2016, SIPRI published a report noting that the Obama administration was leading a global expansion of nuclear weapons programmes. It said that the United States 'plans to spend $348 billion during 2015–24 on maintaining and comprehensively updating its nuclear forces', adding that '[s]ome estimates suggest that the USA's nuclear weapon modernization programme may cost up to $1 trillion over the next 30 years' (SIPRI 2016: 1).

Hans Kristensen, a co-author of the report, noted that '[t]he ambitious US modernization plan presented by the Obama administration is in stark contrast to President Barack Obama's pledge to reduce the number of nuclear weapons and the role they play in US national security strategy' (SIPRI 2016: 1).

Given the enormous nuclear superiority of the United States over all other countries in the world, why the rush to pour ever more money into the development of new nuclear weapons and delivery systems?

The US nuclear arsenal, which is large enough to kill everyone on the planet many times over, is a remnant of a period in which the use of nuclear weapons was envisioned as a last resort, during which the launching of a nuclear weapon was assumed to mean 'mutually assured destruction'. During most of the Cold War, the theories of RAND Corporation military strategist Herman Kahn were pilloried—most famously in Stanley Kubrick's *Dr. Strangelove*.

But the thinking expressed by General Buck Turgidson in Kubrick's film—that the consequences of a nuclear exchange are 'modest and acceptable', even though the United States might get its 'hair mussed'—is becoming mainstream doctrine.

A report published in 2015 by Pentagon-linked think tank the Center for Strategic and International Studies (CSIS) noted that '[t]he scenarios for nuclear employment have changed greatly since the "balance of terror" between the two global superpowers' (Murdock et al. 2015: 12). The 'second nuclear age' involves combatants 'thinking through how they might actually employ a nuclear weapon, both early in a conflict and in a discriminate manner'(Murdock et al. 2015: vi).

The CSIS called for maximising 'flexibility and credibility' by moving to a 'smaller but newer responsive stockpile, lower and variable yields, and special effect weapons, a more diversified set of delivery systems, greater distribution and forward deployment, and greater integration with nonnuclear capabilities' (Murdock et al. 2015: 106).

Components of this plan include the stationing of missile defence systems on the borders of Russia and China, and the domination of key waterways, such as the South China Sea, Baltic Sea and Black Sea. These policies are intended to make it difficult for Russia and China to retaliate to a nuclear first strike, including by means of ballistic missile submarines.

A report published in 2016 by the Washington-based Center for Strategic and Budgetary Assessments (CSBS), titled *Rethinking Armageddon: Scenario Planning in the Second Nuclear Age* (Krepinevich and Cohn 2016), outlined a scenario in which the United States responds to an intervention by Russian forces in Latvia. The Joint Chiefs of Staff give the president four options, three of which involve the use of nuclear weapons (Krepinevich and Cohn 2016: 62–63).

Warnings of another world war

Increasingly openly, the prospect of another global war is being discussed in reports by official and semi-official think tanks. In September 2016, for example, the Atlantic Council, which plays an influential role in the formulation of US government policy, issued a document titled *The Future of the Army* (Barno and Bensahel 2016). It described the 'the world of 2016' as 'one in which strategic threats have returned and great power politics are once more at the fore (Barno and Bensahel 2016: 3). This threatening atmosphere was attributed to Russia and China, essentially identifying both as targets in a US war: 'The unrestrained aggressiveness of a resurgent Russia and a rising China threaten US allies in both Europe and the Pacific' (Barno and Bensahel 2016: 3).

Yet the report presented a scenario in which the United States would be permanently at war: 'In many ways, the United States has entered an era of perpetual war, since it will have to continue addressing the various manifestations of this threat for years and probably decades to come' (Barno and Bensahel 2016: 7).

Many of the battles ahead could be vague and amorphous, like the endless post-2001'war on terror'. The report spoke of 'an increasing number of conflicts in the gray zone, whose primary characteristic is ambiguity—about their objectives, participants, and even outcomes, since they clearly lack defined end points' (Barno and Bensahel 2016: 8). In addition to these undeclared wars, however, the army had to prepare for 'the "next big war"—involving very capable adversaries, high levels of death and destruction, and perhaps hundreds of thousands of US troops' (Barno and Bensahel 2016: 8–9).

The report emphasised the growing role of Special Forces contingents, especially in 'gray zone' conflicts, asserting that 'US special operations capabilities will continue to be required across a range of missions and theaters' and noting that, 'between 2001 and 2016, the number of US SOF [Special Operations Forces] more than doubled, from 28,620 to 63,150' (Barno and Bensahel 2016: 10).

Far bigger wars lay ahead, creating the need to prepare to rapidly expand the army, including by conscription:

> To fight much larger wars in the past, the Army had to expand massively and rapidly to deal with threats deemed existential. A future major war against a great power competitor might once again threaten national survival and require the Army to grow by several orders of magnitude in order to prevail. To fight and win the next big war, the Army must be able to absorb an enormous influx of dollars and tens of thousands of conscripted recruits, and rapidly turn them into an effective fighting force.
>
> (Barno and Bensahel 2016: 21)

There would also be massive casualties:

> Unpleasant as it is to contemplate, the Army must improve its capacity to sustain large numbers of casualties and keep fighting . . . Doctrine and training for this chilling eventuality must be revitalized, and leaders must be prepared to regroup and sustain operations and fighting spirit in the face of heavy losses. Training should expose units to mass rocket and artillery fires, chemical attacks, and even nuclear attacks in order to simulate the large-scale losses that would require reorganization to continue the mission.
>
> (Barno and Bensahel 2016: 31)

The reality of these dangers was underscored in May 2016 by the release of a report by the US-based Union of Concerned Scientists (UCS), which warned:

> Twenty-four hours a day, 365 days a year, the governments of the United States and the People's Republic of China are a few poor decisions away from starting a war that could escalate rapidly and end in a nuclear exchange. Mismatched perceptions increase both the possibility of war and the likelihood it will result in the use of nuclear weapons. Miscommunication or misunderstanding could spark a conflict that both governments may find difficult to stop.
>
> (Kulacki 2016: 1)

While appealing for the two sides to acknowledge the risks and heighten diplomatic efforts to prevent conflict, the UCS analysis offered not even the slightest hope that such steps would be taken. Instead, the report declared that:

Lack of mutual trust and a growing sense that their differences may be irreconcilable incline both governments to continue looking for military solutions—for new means of coercion that help them feel more secure. Establishing the trust needed to have confidence in diplomatic resolutions to the disagreements, animosities, and suspicions that have troubled leaders of the United States and the PRC [People's Republic of China] for almost 70 years is extremely difficult when both governments take every effort to up the technological ante as an act of bad faith.

(Kulacki 2016: 8)

Another 2016 study, conducted by the RAND Corporation and titled *War with China: Thinking Through the Unthinkable* (Compert, Cevallos and Garafola 2016), was devoted to assessing a US war against China. The study, commissioned by the US Army, provided further evidence that a war with China is being planned and prepared in the upper echelons of the American military-intelligence apparatus.

In advising the Pentagon and the White House, the RAND study called for 'prudent preparations to be able to wage a long and intense war with China' (Compert et al. 2016: 73). This was officially sponsored war planning. According to the study's preface:

This research was sponsored by the Office of the Undersecretary of the Army and conducted within the RAND Arroyo Center's Strategy, Doctrine, and Resources Program. RAND Arroyo Center, part of the RAND Corporation, is a federally funded research and development center sponsored by the United States Army.

(Compert et al. 2016: iv)

The RAND study considered four scenarios for a conflict defined by two variables: intensity (either mild or severe) and duration (from a few days to a year or more). It paid more attention to the outcomes of severe conflicts than those of mild ones. In both cases—a brief, severe war and a long, severe war—the study estimated that the economic and military impact on China would be far greater than that on the United States. At the same time, it concluded that the United States would suffer greater losses and costs in 2025 than in 2015. The unstated conclusion was that a war with China must be fought sooner rather than later:

As its military advantage declines, the United States will be less confident that a war with China will conform to its plans. China's improved military capabilities, particularly for anti-access and area denial (A2AD), mean that the United States cannot count on gaining operational control, destroying China's defences, and achieving decisive victory if a war occurred.

(Compert et al. 2016: ix)

For all the money and resources being poured into US nuclear dominance, the idea that a nuclear war against Russia or China is winnable, even with the most advanced weapons systems, is just as irrational as it was during the height of the Cold War. The use of low-yield 'tactical' nuclear weapons will very likely escalate into a conflict in which many millions of people will die.

At a certain point, such military fatalism becomes a significant contributing factor to the outbreak of war. As a specialist in international relations noted:

> Once war is assumed to be unavoidable, the calculations of leaders and militaries change. The question is no longer whether there will or should be a war, but when the war can be fought most advantageously. Even those neither eager for nor optimistic about war may opt to fight when operating in the framework of inevitability.
>
> (Rosencrance and Miller 2015: xi)

It should never be forgotten that the last world war ended with the catastrophic use of nuclear weapons, for which the United States has not apologised. During May 2016, US President Barack Obama took a side trip from a G7 summit meeting in Tokyo to visit Hiroshima's Peace Memorial, which documents the horrific human cost of the first use of nuclear weapons.

Overshadowing the visit was a muted public debate over whether, as the first sitting US president to visit Hiroshima, Obama should offer an apology for what was one of history's greatest war crimes. America's Nobel Prize-winning president and his aides made it abundantly clear that he would do no such thing.

It is not as if US officials have never acknowledged the criminal character of this closing act of World War II—the slaughter of hundreds of thousands of civilians, most of them women and children, in the back-to-back atom bomb attacks against Hiroshima and Nagasaki.

As the historical record makes abundantly clear, these acts of mass murder were not, as the American public was incessantly told, designed to bring a speedy end to the war and 'save lives'; rather, they were carried out with the aim of intimidating the Soviet Union and preparing for a potential third world war (Alperovitz 1965).

In 1963, less than three years after leaving office, Dwight Eisenhower, former World War II commander and president, acknowledged to *Newsweek* magazine that 'the Japanese were ready to surrender and it wasn't necessary to hit them with that awful thing' (Eisenhower 1963: 107).

Admiral William Leahy, who was chief of staff to Harry Truman, the US president who ordered the bombings, wrote in his memoir:

> It is my opinion that the use of this barbarous weapon at Hiroshima and Nagasaki was of no material assistance in our war against Japan. The Japanese were already defeated and ready to surrender because of the effective sea blockade and the successful bombing with conventional weapons . . . My own feeling was that in being the first to use it, we had adopted an ethical standard common to the barbarians of the Dark Ages.
>
> (Leahy 1950: 441)

Thus one of the most barbaric decisions of the 20th century was presented to the American and global public on the basis of a lie: that the atomic bombings were necessary to 'end the war' and 'save lives'. Likewise, decisions to go to war today, and to use nuclear weapons, will be based on fabrications designed to hide the truth about the causes of the war—both the immediate triggers and the underlying socio-economic driving forces. Any discussion about the war powers that ignores or brushes aside this historical record is falsely based.

What would a nuclear war look like?

Citing supposedly discredited science from the 1980s, US officials have adopted the policy that a nuclear first strike against Russia could be 'successful' and that the environmental dangers posed by multiple atomic or thermonuclear detonations—a so-called nuclear winter—have been disproven (Starr 2015).

The original nuclear winter research predicted that a war fought with the nuclear arsenals of the 1980s would create temperatures colder than those experienced at the height of the last Ice Age, some 18,000 years ago. This would leave the Earth virtually uninhabitable. More recent research has found that the original studies actually underestimated the consequences of nuclear war.

Peer-reviewed studies predicted that even a war fought between India and Pakistan, in which a total of 100 atomic bombs were detonated in their cities, would produce enough soot and smoke to create the coldest temperatures experienced in the past 1,000 years. This would significantly decrease production of rice, corn and grain crops for several years, and as many as 2 billion people would starve as a result.

Using modern climate models, scientists estimated that the entire globe could experience ten years of smoke clouds and a three-year temperature drop of approximately 2.25°F (1.25°C). The weapons would produce black carbon that would self-loft to the stratosphere, where it would spread globally, producing a sudden drop in surface temperatures and intense heating of the stratosphere. The calculations showed global ozone losses of 20–50 per cent over populated areas—levels unprecedented in human history. There would be summer enhancements in UV indices of 30–80 per cent over mid-latitudes, suggesting widespread damage to human health, agriculture, and terrestrial and aquatic ecosystems.

In sum:

> Killing frosts would reduce growing seasons by 10–40 days per year for 5 years. Surface temperatures would be reduced for more than 25 years due to thermal inertia and albedo effects in the ocean and expanded sea ice. The combined cooling and enhanced UV would put significant pressures on global food supplies and could trigger a global nuclear famine.
>
> (Mills et al. 2014: 161)

A larger-scale nuclear war would be even more catastrophic. Between them, the United States and Russia have 3,500 deployed and operational strategic nuclear weapons that they can detonate within an hour. They have another 4,600 nuclear weapons in reserve and ready for use, while China had an estimated 300 in 2015.

Moreover, the United States and Russia each have about 1,000 launch-ready nuclear weapons. In the United States, the solid-fuel engines of these intercontinental ballistic missiles are powered up 24 hours a day, awaiting the order to launch. It takes only minutes for a president to open the nuclear briefcase, which accompanies them at all times, and give the order to fire these weapons. A similar briefcase also follows the Russian president. There would be no time for a formal declaration of war, let alone a parliamentary or popular vote.

These launch-ready weapons are supposed to act as a deterrent, but this is meaningless with such short launch time frames. In effect, launch-ready nuclear weapons are essentially pre-emptive weapons. If the US early warning systems were to detect a missile launch, a president could order a retaliatory nuclear strike before incoming nuclear warheads took out communication systems and weapons. If this were to be a false warning of attack, the 'retaliatory' strike would become a first strike, starting a nuclear war.

Foreign Affairs published an article in 2006, written by Keir Lieber and Daryl Press, titled 'The rise of nuclear primacy' (Lieber and Press 2006). It basically claimed that the US weapon system had developed to the point at which it could undertake a first strike against Russia as a result of which Russia would lose any ability to retaliate. 'Nuclear primacy' conveys the chilling notion that the United States could 'win' a nuclear war against Russia should the United States attack first, but takes no account of the environmental and human consequences of such a first strike.

Given the vast numbers of mega-weapons held by the major powers, there is a strong chance that most large cities in combatant countries would be hit. By one estimate, 30 per cent of the US and Russian populations would be killed within the first hour. A few weeks later, radioactive fallout would kill another 50 per cent or more (Starr 2015).

High-altitude detonations could also trigger electromagnetic pulses (EMPs) that destroy electronic circuits over an area of tens of thousands of square kilometres, paralysing infrastructure and possibly causing nuclear power plants to melt down (Lenard and Mihelic 2008).

Some fundamental problems of analysis

This book seeks to clarify and counter common underlying problems of analysis. In general, examinations of war powers suffer because they:

- divorce the question of war powers from the underlying geo-strategic and economic causes of war, particularly in the present epoch, starting with World War I;
- take for granted the existence, and accept the legitimacy, of the current system of rival nation-states, based on competing economic interests;

- accept or understate the dominant role of major powers—above all, the United States—in seeking global hegemony;
- treat today's wars as a series of isolated events, each triggered by a separate incident, crisis or cause, rather than as part of an underlying pattern or trend;
- ahistorically examine wars in the abstract, without referring to the character of the warring parties, for example by making a distinction between a predatory or neo-colonial war waged by an imperialist power, such as the United States, and one fought by a country or population, such as Vietnam or Iraq, targeted by that aggression;
- suppose that countries referred to as 'modern liberal democracies' are inherently unable or unlikely to launch aggressive or expansionist military operations, and are likely to consider war only as a defensive necessity;
- assume that countries each make their own decisions to enter military conflict, when in fact they may be effectively compelled to do so by the demands or pressures imposed by other powers, or because their military forces or facilities are closely integrated into those of other powers;
- ignore the well-documented fact that every contemporary war has been launched on the basis of lies, such as 'coming to the aid of little Belgium' (World War I), responding to the attack on Pearl Harbour (World War II), the Gulf of Tonkin incident (the Vietnam War) or 'weapons of mass destruction' (the conquest of Iraq);
- brush aside the systematic whipping up of nationalist, patriotic, xenophobic and racist prejudices by governments and mass media to drum up support for war and to overcome prevailing anti-war sentiment among the population;
- bury the connection between war and the suppression of domestic opposition to war, including the accompanying sacrifices imposed on working people, such as the imprisonment of anti-war activists, the jailing or execution of resisters to conscription or deserters, and the mass internments of political opponents and 'aliens';
- fail to examine the domestic powers, usually of an authoritarian nature, assumed by governments during periods of war;
- whitewash the conflicting interests of the ruling financial, corporate and military elites, and the working-class members of society who invariably pay the highest price for war, not least by killing or being killed;
- dismiss the objective interests of the international working class, created by global capitalism, in unifying across national lines and overturning the nation-state system itself; and
- separate the 'legal' issues of war-making from all of these factors, as though law arises in a vacuum, guided by an 'internal' logic and history that is isolated from the political and economic driving forces and calculations involved.

Common political and socio-economic assumptions

One example of these defects is Rosara Joseph's *The War Prerogative*, a study of the war-making power in England from 1600 to 2012 (Joseph 2013).

Joseph's treatise was one of numerous works that appeared internationally in the wake of the 2003 US-led invasion of Iraq, in which both Britain and Australia played prominent supporting roles. That invasion defied massive anti-war demonstrations globally and was intensified by the subsequent exposure of the official lies that were perpetrated as pretexts for the military onslaught—most notably, the claims that the Iraqi government posed an imminent threat to the United States and its allies because it possessed 'weapons of mass destruction' and nuclear weapons capacity. Joseph's book can be seen as an attempt to restore public faith in government decisions to go to war.

In her introduction, she states:

> This monograph addresses issues fundamental to *modern liberal democracies.* The *state* must be able to *protect* itself, its citizens, and their ways of life. The executive has primary responsibility for protecting *national security* and the *welfare* of the community, based on its institutional competencies, expertise, and historical lineage. Although the executive has the primary responsibility, Parliament and the courts can and should contribute to the control and scrutiny of those powers. We must *enable* the executive to deploy the armed forces and wage war when it is *deemed necessary.* But we must also ensure that Parliament and (to a lesser extent) the courts are able to, and do, insist that the government makes *reasoned and justified* decisions about war. Relative institutional *competency* and *legitimacy* should condition the respective involvement of governmental institutions. The nature of armed conflict and international politics is becoming especially complex and contested. It is vital that decisions about these matters are subjected to reasoned and, *where possible*, public deliberation.
>
> (Joseph 2013: 5, emphasis added)

Many unstated and unsubstantiated political and socio-economic assumptions are made in this passage. They are worth probing because they are not unique to Joseph; similar assertions can be found in many writings on the war powers.

First, what are 'modern liberal democracies', and are countries such as Britain, the United States and Australia 'liberal democracies' in any meaningful sense? Are such countries democratic when handfuls of billionaires monopolise society's wealth, giving them an extraordinary grip over the economic, political and military levers of power?

In 2015, international charity Oxfam issued a report on social inequality showing that the gap between the super-rich and the majority of society was growing at an ever-faster pace. In 2013, the 92 richest multi-billionaires had as much wealth as the bottom 50 per cent of society combined. In 2014, this figure dropped to 80 billionaires. In other words, a group of people who could fit into a single train carriage controlled more wealth than 3.5 billion people— equivalent to the combined populations of China, India, the United States and the European Union. Inequality was growing at such a rapid pace that the richest 1 per cent would control more wealth than the bottom 99 per cent of society by 2016 (Oxfam 2015).

The combined net worth of the world's billionaires reached a new high in 2015 of US$7.05 trillion, according to *Forbes* magazine (Peterson-Withorn 2015). There were a record 1,826 billionaires, each with an average wealth of $3.8 billion. Not surprisingly, the United States—the home of Wall Street and the centre of global financial capital—had easily the highest number of billionaires: 536. Billionaires made up an estimated 0.000033 per cent of the world's population, yet this tiny social layer possessed about 4.5 times the total wealth of the bottom half of the population—some 3.5 billion people.

The reality is similar in Britain: in 2016, the richest 1 per cent of the population owned more than 20 times the total wealth of the poorest fifth, making the country one of the most unequal in the developed world, according to analysis by Oxfam (2016). Using data from Credit Suisse, Oxfam's report showed that the richest 10 per cent of the British population owned more than half of the country's total wealth (54 per cent), with the top 1 per cent owning nearly a quarter (23 per cent), whilst the poorest 20 per cent shared just 0.8 per cent of the wealth between them (Oxfam 2016).

Whatever the pretence of 'one person, one vote', the wealthiest 1 per cent dictates policy, assisted by a slightly broader, still highly privileged and small, section of the population—the top 5 or 10 per cent. The right to vote means little in political processes dominated by heavily funded corporate-backed political parties. Likewise, freedom of the press means little when the major media outlets are controlled by powerful corporate interests. Genuine democracy would require mass democratic participation in economic decision-making itself, including control over the transnational finance houses and corporations, as well as the military and state apparatuses.

Second, the world's leading 'democracies' have a record of supporting, and helping to impose, dictatorships in less-developed countries to further their own geo-strategic and economic interests. In 2013–14, for example, the US government quickly established cordial relations with, and resumed multibillion-dollar aid and arms supplies to, the military regime in Egypt in the wake of its coup, even as its courts sentenced hundreds of political opponents to be executed (BBC News 2014). This must be added to a long list of countries in which Washington has backed despotic and violent regimes, from the Shah of Iran to General Suharto in Indonesia, General Pinochet in Chile, Presidents Sadat and Mubarak in Egypt, and the Saudi royal dynasty (DeConde, Burns and Logevall 2001). These dictatorships are supported militarily and often they, or other essentially puppet governments, are installed or propped up by military means, as was the case with the pre-1975 South Vietnamese regimes and the post-2003 Iraqi administrations.

Third, Joseph identifies the 'state' with 'protecting' not only itself, but also 'its' citizens and their 'ways of life'. This takes no account of the social and class divisions wracking the political and legal order. How can a state based on yawning social inequality and domination of weaker and poorer countries be said to truly represent the interests of those people outside the wealthy elites? Might not the protection of the state itself, embodying and directed at furthering the agendas of the richest layers and most powerful corporations, be sought at the cost of the living standards, social conditions and basic rights ('ways of life') of the majority of the population? Whenever a whistleblower, such as Daniel Ellsberg, Chelsea Manning or Edward Snowden, or a publisher such as Julian Assange, seeks to alert the public to the war crimes or mass surveillance being conducted in their names, the response of the state is invariably one of repression, intimidation and demonisation designed to block citizens from any access to the information.

Fourth, the word 'protecting' projects an image of defensive actions by the state, rather than aggressive military actions that plunder other countries, secure resources, dominate markets or otherwise pursue corporate profit. The 2001 invasion of Afghanistan and the 2003 conquest of Iraq were both presented as acts of 'self-defence' by the United States and its allies, supposedly to 'protect' their citizens from terrorism or 'weapons of mass destruction' (WMDs). To do so, US military doctrine was proclaimed in 2002 to be 'preventive warfare'—a doctrine that violated the prohibition under international law of aggressive war. This doctrine decreed that the United States could attack any country in the world judged to pose a potential threat—not only of a military, but also of an economic character—to American interests. The George W. Bush administration justified the invasion of Iraq as a 'pre-emptive' war in response to the imminent threat posed by the country's WMDs to the people of the United States. That threat was as non-existent as were Saddam Hussein's WMDs.

The terrorist attacks in New York and Washington of 11 September 2001, now known simply as 9/11, were criminal and politically reactionary. There is ample evidence that they provided the pretext for the implementation of plans prepared in Washington political circles during the 1990s for the conquest of Afghanistan and Iraq (Bacevich 2002). The Middle East and Central Asia, as is well known, contain the largest proven concentrations of oil and natural gas reserves in the world. For all their claims to be exporting democracy to the Middle East, Washington and its allies have, for decades, financially, diplomatically and militarily supported dictatorial regimes such as the Saudi monarchy and the Gulf kingdoms (and previously the Shah of Iran), all in the interests of dominating this resource-rich and strategically critical region (Shalom 1993: 63–88).

Moreover, for all of the claims of the United States and its allies to be protecting their citizens from terrorism, the alleged primary 'terrorist' targets—groups linked to Al Qaeda—were 'freedom fighters' that the United States had assisted in the guerrilla warfare of the late 1980s and early 1990s against the Soviet-backed regime in Afghanistan (Blum 2002: 155). Likewise, Saddam Hussein was once a close ally of Washington and had been supplied with American weapons—particularly during the fratricidal Iran–Iraq war of the 1980s (Blum 2002: 133–34, 145–46).

Fifth, the terms 'national security' and 'welfare' are vague and laden with unstated political values. 'National security' is a notoriously expandable concept (Gross and Aolain 2006: 214–20). In the words of one international relations scholar, it is increasingly identified with corporate interests:

National security is an amorphous and elastic concept. Security may be conceptualised in a narrow way, restricted to military threats, which remains valid if safety from military attack is the primary consideration of national security. However, the modern world demands a re-conceptualisation of security to include, at least, economic considerations.

(Wyllie 2008: 78)

Judges, among others, are amenable to adjusting the boundaries of 'security' to meet the exigencies of war or emergency asserted by the executive. For example, in a leading Australian High Court case on the powers of the intelligence agencies, Justice Anthony Mason described security as a 'fluctuating concept, relying on circumstances as they exist from time to time—not unlike the issue of defence' (*Church of Scientology v Woodward* (1982) 154 CLR 25, 60). During times of war, the Australian High Court has validated draconian executive powers, including mass detention (*Lloyd v Wallach* (1915) 20 CLR 299; *Little v Commonwealth* (1947) 75 CLR 94; *Ex parte Walsh* [1942] ALR 359), as consistent with constitutional principle and the rule of law. After 9/11, a majority of the Australian Court accepted the proposition that to strike down the use of control orders—a form of detention without trial—would display 'September 10 thinking' (*Thomas v Mowbray* [2007] HCATrans 76, 78). Similar rulings, during both world wars and in the 'war on terror', have been handed down by the highest courts in the United States and Britain, as is discussed in the chapters that follow.

Sixth, to insist that parliaments and courts must 'enable' the executive to 'deploy the armed forces and wage war when it is deemed necessary' reduces them to facilitators of war. This overturns any notion of the legislature and the judiciary acting as a check on the power of the executive. To reduce the role of members of Parliament (MPs) and judges to simply trying to ensure that 'the government makes reasoned and justified decisions about war' leaves unchecked power in the hands of an inner sanctum. Parliaments and courts become rubber stamps, lending political legitimacy—after the fact—to the unleashing of military violence.

Finally, to propose that public deliberation be permitted only 'where possible' is to leave all decisions about public participation in the discretionary hands of the executive. Who decides what is 'possible'? By implication, the executive itself. In practice, this will ensure that no public involvement is tolerated, or that purely cosmetic consultation occurs. What is ruled out is any conception of the population holding the war powers—or even having the right to know what decisions about war are being made.

References

Alperovitz, G. 1965. *Atomic Diplomacy: Hiroshima and Potsdam—The Use of the Atomic Bomb and the American Confrontation with Soviet Power*. London: Pluto Press.
Bacevich, A. 2002. *American Empire: The Realities and Consequences of US Diplomacy*. Cambridge, MA: Harvard University Press.

Barno, D., and Bensahel, N. 2016. *The Future of the Army*. Washington DC: The Atlantic Council, www.atlanticcouncil.org/publications/reports/the-future-of-the-army (accessed 15 January 2017).

BBC News. 2014. 'US unlocks military aid to Egypt, backing President Sisi', 22 June, www.bbc.com/news/world-middle-east-27961933 (accessed 18 March 2015).

Blum, W. 2002. *Rogue State: A Guide to the World's Only Superpower*. London: Zed Books.

Compert, D., Cevallos, A., and Garafola, C. 2016. *War with China: Thinking Through the Unthinkable*. Santa Monica, CA: RAND Corporation, www.rand.org/pubs/research_reports/RR1140.html (accessed 15 December 2016).

DeConde, A., Burns, R., and Logevall, F. (eds). 2001. 'Dictatorships'. In *Encyclopedia of American Foreign Policy, Vol. 1*. New York: Simon & Schuster.

Eisenhower, D. 1963. Interview, *Newsweek*, 11 November.

Ellis, J. 2001. *The World War I Databook*. London: Aurum Press.

Gross, O., and Aolain, F. 2006. *Law in Times of Crisis: Emergency Powers in Theory and Practice*. Cambridge: Cambridge University Press.

Hagopian, A., Flaxman, A., Takaro, T., Al Shatari, S., Rajaratnam, J., Becker, S., . . . Burnham, G. 2013. 'Mortality in Iraq Associated with the 2003–2011 War and Occupation: Findings from a National Cluster Sample Survey by the University Collaborative Iraq Mortality Study', *PLoS Medicine*, 10(10): e1001533.

Joseph, R. 2013. *The War Prerogative: History Reform and Constitutional Design*. Oxford: Oxford University Press.

Krepinevich, A., and Cohn, J. 2016. *Rethinking Armageddon: Scenario Planning in the Second Nuclear Age*. Washington, DC: CSBS, http://csbaonline.org/research/publications/rethinking-armageddon (accessed 15 January 2017).

Kulacki, G. 2016. *The Risk of Nuclear War with China: A Troubling Lack of Urgency*. Cambridge, MA: Union of Concerned Scientists, www.ucsusa.org/sites/default/files/attach/2016/05/Nuclear-War-with-China.pdf (accessed 25 May 2017).

Leahy, W. 1950. *I Was There*. New York: McGraw Hill.

Lenard, R., and Mihelic, F. 2008. 'Healthcare vulnerabilities to electromagnetic pulse', *American Journal of Disaster Medicine*, 3(6): 321–25.

Lewy, G. 1978. *America in Vietnam*. New York: Oxford University Press.

Lieber, K., and Press, D. 2006. 'The rise of nuclear primacy', *Foreign Affairs*, March/April, www.foreignaffairs.com/articles/united-states/2006-03-01/rise-us-nuclear-primacy (accessed at 20 June 2018).

Mattis, J. 2018. *Summary of the 2018 National Defense Strategy of the United States of America*. Washington, DC: US Department of Defense.

Mills, M., Toon, O., Lee-Taylor, J., and Robock, A. 2014. 'Multidecadal global cooling and unprecedented ozone loss following a regional nuclear conflict', *Earth's Future*, 2(4): 161–76.

Murdock, C., Brannen, S., Karako, T., and Weaver, A. 2015. Center for Strategic and International Studies. *Project Atom: A Competitive Strategies Approach to Defining U.S. Nuclear Strategy and Posture for 2025–2050*. Washington, DC: CSIS, https://csis-prod.s3.amazonaws.com/s3fs-public/legacy_files/files/publication/150601_Murdock_ProjectAtom_Web.pdf (accessed 10 February 2016).

NBC News. 2017. 'SurveyMonkey Poll Results', 22 February, http://media1.s-nbcnews.com/i/MSNBC/Sections/NEWS/NBC%20News%20SurveyMonkey%20Toplines%20and%20Methodology%202.22.pdf (accessed 25 February 2017).

Oxfam. 2015. 'Richest 1% will own more than all the rest by 2016', Press release, 19 January, www.oxfam.org/en/pressroom/pressreleases/2015-01-19/richest-1-will-own-more-all-rest-2016 (accessed 20 June 2016).

Oxfam. 2016. 'Richest 1% owns 20 times more than UK's poorest 20%', Press release, 13 September, www.oxfam.org.uk/media-centre/press-releases/2016/09/richest-one-percent-owns-twenty-times-more-than-uks-poorest-twenty-percent (accessed 22 June 2017).

Pentagon. 2015. *Department of Defense Law of War Manual.* Washington, DC: Office of General Counsel, Department of Defense.

Peterson-Withorn, C. 2015. 'Forbes Billionaires: Full List of the 500 Richest People in the World, 2015' *Forbes,* 2 March, www.forbes.com/sites/chasewithorn/2015/03/02/forbes-billionaires-full-list-of-the-500-richest-people-in-the-world-2015/#518 64c6145b9 (accessed 15 April 2016).

Rosencrance, R., and Miller, S. 2015. *The Next Great War: The Roots of World War I and the Risk of U.S.–China Conflict.* Cambridge, MA: MIT Press.

Shalom, S. 1993. *Imperial Alibis: Rationalizing US Intervention after the Cold War.* Boston, MA: South End Press.

SIPRI (Stockholm International Peace Research Institute). 2016. 'Global nuclear weapons: downsizing but modernizing', Press release, 13 June, www.sipri.org/media/press-release/2016/global-nuclear-weapons-downsizing-modernizing (accessed 30 June 2016).

SIPRI (Stockholm International Peace Research Institute). 2018. *SIPRI Military Expenditure Database,* www.sipri.org/databases/milex (accessed 23 May 2018).

Somerville, D. 2011. *The Illustrated History of World War Two.* London: Southwater.

Starr, S. 2015. 'Turning a blind eye towards Armageddon: U.S. leaders reject nuclear winter studies', *Federation of American* Scientists, 9 January, https://fas.org/2017/01/turning-a-blind-eye-towards-armageddon-u-s-leaders-reject-nuclear-winter-studies/ (accessed 30 June 2016).

Symonds, P. 2018. 'Japan activates first Marine brigade since World War II', *World Socialist Web Site,* 10 April, www.wsws.org/en/articles/2018/04/10/japa-a10.html (accessed 21 April 2018).

Vandreier, C. 2018. 'German Chancellor Merkel announces major rearmament program', *World Socialist Web Site,* 17 May, www.wsws.org/en/articles/2018/05/17/germ-m17.html (accessed 20 May 2018).

Wyllie, J. 2008. 'Force and security'. In T. Salmon and M. Imber (eds), *Issues In International Relations.* 2nd edn, London: Routledge.

1 War and democracy

Formally speaking, as will be examined in Chapters 3–5, the war-making powers are exercised by 'the executive', with virtually no public, legislative or judicial scrutiny or accountability. Whether they are 'prerogative', 'presidential' or 'executive' powers, the legal authority to deploy armed forces for warfare is held in the hands of small cabals. The historical record shows that no parliamentary or congressional vote is necessary, let alone a public plebiscite, and no domestic court would uphold a legal challenge to a decision to launch a war.

Almost invariably, however, efforts to introduce parliamentary or congressional checks on war powers have been motivated by concerns to provide war-making decisions with a cloak of democratic legitimacy, so as to generate or bolster public support for military mobilisation. Suggestions of mass popular participation in decisions to go to war, such as via referenda, have generally been dismissed out of hand.

Even proposals for plebiscites take no account of the underlying economic and political power held in the hands of the corporate, military and political elite, or of the capacity of that elite to shape, poison or overwhelm public opinion, with the help of a complicit corporate media.

In fact, real doubts surround the formal exercise of war powers by the office formally endowed with those powers, whether it be a president, prime minister, cabinet or vice-regal representative. For one thing, the very notion of the 'executive' itself has shifted throughout history, according to the prevailing nation-state and socio-economic power structures.

In Britain, the war prerogative has morphed from being held by the absolute monarchy, in the name of the theory of the divine right of kings, to being exercised by the executive government—in effect, the prime minister and a perhaps a cabinet subcommittee (Joseph 2013: 22–41). In the United States, the executive has increasingly usurped the war powers—based on the president's constitutional power to command the military—from Congress, to which the US Constitution allocated the power to declare war (Zeisberg 2013: 1–53). In Australia's case, reflecting its unclear evolution from a British colony to an independent state, the major decisions to enter military conflict since Federation in 1901 have gone from being made in the name of the British king via the governor-general (still the constitutional 'commander-in-chief' of the armed forces) to the prime minister and cabinet, without any consultation with the governor-general (Sampford and Palmer 2009: 350–52).

The only common thread running through these histories is that the war powers must be kept in a small number of hands, far away from public scrutiny or control.

Who actually exercises the power?

Several further questions must be asked, however. To what extent is the person wielding the power functioning as a figurehead, conduit or even cypher for others in the corporate, media, political, military, intelligence and bureaucratic establishment? How are divisions within these circles resolved—and by whom? The titular head of government alone? Can that official be overruled or effectively countermanded by forces within the state apparatus? Can forces within the military trigger confrontations with other countries that make war inevitable?

Is it possible that economic ties, strategic dependence or treaty obligations can give governments no real choice but to join military operations? Or can the stationing of vital military-intelligence facilities (such as the US–Australian communications base at Pine Gap in central Australia) make involvement in war unavoidable?

These are not academic questions. To take the American case, there have been well-documented clashes between presidents and the military chiefs, including over General Douglas Macarthur's proposal to use nuclear weapons against China during the 1950–53 Korean War (Lowitt 1967), as well as demands by the military, including General Curtis LeMay, for an attack on Cuba during the Cuban missile crisis (Axelrod 2009: 332, 335). Both conflicts were ultimately resolved in favour of the president, as the constitutional civilian commander-in-chief. However, President John Kennedy was subsequently assassinated in circumstances that remain unclear. In more recent times, Pentagon officials pushed for more aggressive US deployments in Syria in 2013, the South China Sea in 2015–16 and Syria again in 2016, publicly adopting stances at odds with the official line of the White House.

In Britain, during 2016, a military commander openly called into question whether the armed forces would accept a decision by a government led by Labour Party leader Jeremy Corbyn to discontinue the Trident nuclear weapons programme. Chief of the Defence Staff Sir Nicholas Houghton, asked by the BBC's Andrew Marr about Corbyn's statement that he would never authorise the use of nuclear weapons, replied: 'Well, it would worry me if that thought was translated into power' (Payne 2015). Houghton had earlier told the media that Britain was 'letting down' its allies by not participating in bombing missions in Syria. These comments violated the supposed principle of military non-interference in civilian politics and raised concerns about the prospect of a military mutiny against a government led by Corbyn. Rather than censure Houghton, the Conservative-led government rushed to support him, with a spokesperson for Prime Minister David Cameron stating that, 'as the principal military adviser to the government', it was 'reasonable' for Houghton 'to talk about how we maintain the credibility of one of the most important tools in our armoury' (Payne 2015).

More than 55 years ago, US President Dwight D. Eisenhower, who had been a five-star general during World War II, used his farewell address to the nation on 17 January 1961 to warn of the unprecedented power of what he termed the military-industrial complex:

> This conjunction of an immense military establishment and a large arms industry is new in the American experience. The total influence—economic, political, even spiritual—is felt in every city, every statehouse, every office of the federal government. We recognize the imperative need for this development. Yet we must not fail to comprehend its grave implications. Our toil, resources and livelihood are all involved; so is the very structure of our society. In the councils of government, we must guard against the acquisition of unwarranted influence, whether sought or unsought, by the military–industrial complex. The potential for the disastrous rise of misplaced power exists, and will persist.
>
> (Eisenhower 1961)

The power of the military-industrial complex has only grown over the past six decades. As shown by whistleblower Edward Snowden's revelations in 2013, programmes run by the Pentagon-based National Security Agency (NSA) spy on the US and world's populations on a daily basis, capturing hundreds of millions of Internet communications, including emails, chats, videos, photos and credit card receipts.

The secret collaboration of the military, the intelligence and national security agencies, as well as gigantic corporations, in the systematic and illegal surveillance reveals the true wielders of power. Telecommunications giants, such as AT&T, Verizon and Sprint, and Internet companies, such as Google, Microsoft, Facebook and Twitter, provide the US military, the Federal Bureau of Investigation (FBI) and the Central Intelligence Agency (CIA) with access to data on hundreds of millions of people that these state agencies have no legal right to possess.

The US Congress and both of the major political parties serve as rubber stamps for the confluence of the military, the intelligence apparatus and Wall Street that really runs the country. The so-called Fourth Estate—the mass media—essentially functions as an arm of this ruling troika.

Similar webs of economic, political and military-intelligence exist in Britain and Australia. Moreover, they are linked to the US establishment by formal alliances, informal networks, the hosting of US bases and the integration of military forces. If the United States goes to war, these two allies are necessarily involved in many ways.

The US president can—and does—unilaterally order the extrajudicial assassination of people deemed to be enemy combatants, including US citizens.

The government can seize the phone records and emails of investigative journalists; those who expose US war crimes, such as Private Chelsea Manning, are jailed or, like WikiLeaks editor Julian Assange, are threatened with imprisonment. And the president can order alleged terrorists to be detained indefinitely and without trial in military prisons.

The massive scale of the spying—targeting every man, woman and child in the country—raises the question: what is the corporate-financial-military elite afraid of? The capitalist ruling class is haunted by the sense that it is socially and politically isolated, that the policies it is pursuing lack any serious base of support and that war can provide an impulse to social revolution, as it did in Russia in 1917 and Germany in 1918.

Is democracy compatible with war?

One of the United States' most influential geo-political strategists suggested that democracy was an obstacle to going to war. In his book, *The Grand Chessboard*, Zbigniew Brzezinski, security adviser to Democratic President Jimmy Carter and a long-time proponent of an aggressive strategy for asserting US global hegemony, wrote:

> America is too democratic at home to be autocratic abroad. This limits the use of America's power, especially its capacity for military intimidation. Never before has a populist democracy attained international supremacy. But the pursuit of power is not a goal that commands popular passion, except in conditions of a sudden threat or challenge to the public's sense of domestic well-being. The economic self-denial (that is, defense spending) and the human sacrifices (casualties even among professional soldiers) required in the effort are uncongenial to democratic instincts. Democracy is inimical to imperial mobilization.
>
> (Brzezinski 1997a: 35–36)

Four years later, on 11 September 2001—9/11—the 'sudden threat or challenge to the public's sense of domestic well-being' that the former national security adviser saw as a necessary precondition for launching a global campaign of American militarism was served up by Islamic fundamentalist forces that he and the CIA had promoted in Afghanistan during the 1970s. Al Qaeda, with its historic ties to US intelligence, claimed credit for the attacks on New York City and Washington, DC, which were carried out by individuals who were able to move remarkably unhindered in and out of the United States.

During his four-year tenure in the Carter White House, Brzezinski was involved in many criminal operations carried out in the name of US imperialism around the globe, from support for the Shah's attempts to suppress the Iranian Revolution, to the initiation of a US policy in Central America that led to bloody counterinsurgency campaigns that claimed the lives of hundreds of thousands (Andrianopoulos 1991).

Perhaps the greatest of these crimes, and one for which Brzezinski una-shamedly took credit, was the orchestration and support of a dirty war waged by Islamist mujahedeen against the Soviet-backed government of Afghanistan at the end of the 1970s. This war, which sowed the seeds for decades of catastrophe in that country and across the Middle East, is another devastating illustration of the unbridled exercise of war powers by the United States and its allies.

In an interview with the French news magazine *Le Nouvel Observateur* in January 1998, Brzezinski acknowledged that he had initiated a policy under which the CIA had covertly begun arming the mujahedeen in July 1978—six months before Soviet troops intervened in Afghanistan—with the explicit aim of dragging the Soviet Union into a debilitating war.

Asked whether he regretted the policy he championed in Afghanistan, given the catastrophe unleashed upon Afghanistan and the subsequent growth of Islamist terrorist groups such as Al Qaeda, Brzezinski replied:

> Regret what? That secret operation was an excellent idea. It had the effect of drawing the Russians into the Afghan trap and you want me to regret it? The day that the Soviets officially crossed the border, I wrote to President Carter: We now have the opportunity of giving to the USSR its Vietnam War. Indeed, for almost 10 years, Moscow had to carry on a war unsupport-able by the government, a conflict that brought about the demoralization and finally the breakup of the Soviet empire.
>
> (Gibbs 2000: 241–42)

Asked specifically whether he regretted the CIA's collaboration with, and arming of, Islamist extremists, including Al Qaeda, in fomenting the war in Afghanistan, Brzezinski responded contemptuously: 'What is most important to the history of the world? The Taliban or the collapse of the Soviet empire? Some stirred-up Moslems or the liberation of Central Europe and the end of the cold war?' (Gibbs 2000: 241–42).

In the four decades of nearly uninterrupted fighting that flowed from Brzezinski's 'excellent idea', more than 2 million Afghans have lost their lives and millions more have been turned into refugees.

In the aftermath of the Moscow Stalinist bureaucracy's formal dissolution of the Soviet Union in December 1991, Brzezinski refocused his attention on a strategy to assert undisputed US hegemony over Eurasia. In an article pub-lished in the September–October 1997 issue of *Foreign Affairs*, Brzezinski argued:

> Eurasia is the world's axial supercontinent. A power that dominated Eurasia would exercise decisive influence over two of the world's three most eco-nomically productive regions, Western Europe and East Asia. A glance at the map also suggests that a country dominant in Eurasia would almost auto-matically control the Middle East and Africa. With Eurasia now serving as

the decisive geopolitical chessboard, it no longer suffices to fashion one policy for Europe and another for Asia. What happens with the distribution of power on the Eurasian landmass will be of decisive importance to America's global primacy and historical legacy . . . In a volatile Eurasia, the immediate task is to ensure that no state or combination of states gains the ability to expel the United States or even diminish its decisive role.

(Brzezinski 1997b)

Brzezinski was among the more influential strategists in shaping a policy of attempting to offset the long-term decline in the world position of American capitalism by resorting to Washington's unchallenged supremacy in terms of military might. This turn would lead to unending wars in the Middle East and Central Asia designed to assert undisputed American dominance in the regions containing the lion's share of the world's oil and natural gas reserves.

The driving forces of war

Even more fundamental questions can be posed. The history of the 20th century, during which two calamitous world wars were fought, suggests that the essential cause of militarism and war does not rest in the personalities of the political, corporate and military leaders involved. Nor does it rest even in the immediate profit calculations of the military-industrial complexes of the rival powers.

Rather, it lies in the deep-seated contradictions of the world capitalist system, none of which were resolved by two world wars—contradictions primarily between:

- a globally integrated and interdependent economy and its division into antagonistic national states; and
- the socialised character of global production and its subordination, through the private ownership of the means of production, to the accumulation of private profit by the ruling capitalist class.

Powerful capitalist banks and corporations utilise 'their' states to wage commercial and ultimately military struggles for control of the raw materials, oil and gas pipelines, trade routes, and access to cheap labour and markets that are critical to the accumulation of profit. They also regard such struggles—and war itself—as necessary to quell the social discontent generated by the ever-greater inequality produced by the capitalist accumulation of wealth, and they divert the disaffection along nationalistic, jingoist and patriotic channels.

Politicians and historians from the conflicting powers in the first 'Great War', World War I, have long sought to cover over these driving forces. The devastating four years of war arose almost inadvertently, according to wartime British Prime Minister Lloyd George. The war was something into which the great powers 'glided, or rather staggered and stumbled' and nations 'slithered over the brink into the boiling cauldron of war' (quoted in Hamilton and Herwig 2004: 19).

One historian encapsulated this claim in the title of a book, *The Sleepwalkers: How Europe Went to War in 1914* (Clark 2012).

In reality, the war was the result of the deepening tensions produced by the rise of German capitalism, whose very growth since German unification in 1871 became a threat to the global interests of the then hegemonic power, Britain.

In 1907, an official in the British Foreign Office, Eyre Crowe, produced an extensive memorandum for Foreign Secretary Lord Grey. Crowe was tasked with making an assessment of whether, in conditions under which its economy and influence were rapidly expanding, Germany's intentions were peaceful or militaristic. In his *Memorandum on the Present State of British Relations with France and Germany*, Crowe concluded that, in the end, it did not matter because the very development of Germany and its expanding global interests threatened the British Empire; therefore, whatever assessment was made of Germany's intentions, Britain had to prepare for war (Dunn 2013: 247).

That war broke out just seven years later.

While the immediate event that triggered the Great War of 1914 was the assassination by a Serbian nationalist of Austrian Archduke Ferdinand in Sarajevo, Bosnia, that shooting set off long-fermenting conflicts between the major powers and their alllies, inexorably leading to war between the two primary rivals: Britain—the established hegemonic global empire—and Germany—the aspiring challenger.

The war in the Balkans might have been restricted to a local skirmish had it not been for the fact that the threat to the Austrian regime was intertwined with the economic and strategic interests of all of the European great powers.

Looking back in 1917, German politician Gustav Stresemann summed up the view in the powerful industrial circles for which he spoke. Germany had seen '*others* conquer worlds'—a world 'under the sceptre of others' in which 'our economic breath of life' was becoming increasingly restricted (quoted in Fischer 1975: 449, emphasis original).

As German historian Fischer established meticulously in his works *Germany's War Aims in the First World War* (1961) and *War of Illusions: German Policies from 1911 to 1914* (1975), the Germany ruling elite's conduct was driven by two interrelated factors. One was that 'when Germany finally entered the age of world policy and world trade it did so at a relatively unfavourable moment when most of the world had already been divided between the established powers' (Fischer 1975: viii). The other factor was domestic: 'The aim was to consolidate the position of the ruling classes with a successful imperialist foreign policy, indeed it hoped a war would resolve the growing social tensions' (Fischer 1975: viii).

Britain was likewise confronted with vital strategic and economic issues. Its policy was based on preserving the balance of power in Europe to ensure that no single power or group of powers was able to challenge Britain's global hegemony, based on its empire—above all, the plunder of India. In a remarkably candid assessment, then First Lord of the Admiralty Winston Churchill summed up Britain's position during a 1913–14 debate on naval expenditure:

We have got all we want in territory, and our claim to be left in unmolested enjoyment of vast and splendid possessions, mainly acquired by violence, largely maintained by force, often seems less reasonable to others than to us.
(Quoted in Kennedy 1987: 467)

The real war aims, of course, were never stated. How can a government declare to its population that it is sending the flower of its youth to die and be maimed on the battlefields in the interest of profits and the acquisition of resources, colonies and markets? The great powers sought to cover over the real motivations with an unending stream of lies issued through the mass media.

In Germany, the war was proclaimed to be for the 'defence of the fatherland', to maintain German culture and economy against the barbarism of Russia, Britain's ally. The British government declared that it entered the war to defend the neutrality of 'little Belgium', so grossly violated by the 'Huns'.

A new period of contested hegemony

Today, the danger of another world war is centred in the efforts of the United States to maintain its position as the global hegemonic power—a position that it gained as a result of the defeat of Germany and Japan in World War II. The dissolution in 1991 of the Soviet Union was seen by Washington's ruling circles, Wall Street and the Pentagon as an opportunity to assert unrivaled US economic and strategic domination throughout the world. They hailed the end of the USSR as creating a 'unipolar moment' in which the unchallengeable power of the United States would dictate a 'New World Order', in the words of President George H. Bush. The Soviet Union had encompassed a vast expanse of the globe, stretching from the eastern boundaries of Europe to the Pacific Ocean. Thus the vast regions of Eurasia, occupied by a debilitated Russia and newly independent Central Asian states, were again 'in play', open for corporate exploitation and plunder.

However, the drive to war is not confined to the US ruling class. European and Japanese imperialism are pursuing the no less predatory and reactionary interests of their own ruling elites. All are attempting to secure their stakes in a ferocious battle for the global redivision of world economic and political power.

Seventy years after the fall of Hitler's Third Reich, the German ruling class is again demanding that its state assert itself over Europe and as a world power. In the face of deeply felt anti-war sentiments within the German population, Berlin is deploying military force to assert its interests in the Middle East and Africa. It is pouring money into rearmament, while apologetics for the crimes of the Nazi regime are being advanced in the political establishment, media and academia, with the aim of justifying the revival of German imperialist ambitions.

British imperialism, for its part, sees, in the relative US decline, an opportunity to expand the still significant global operations of the banks and finance houses based in the City of London. France is striving to regain its grip over its former colonial dominions in North and West Africa. Italy has plans to re-establish its influence in Libya. In 2015, led by Britain, the ostensible 'special' US ally, the major European powers signaled their defiance of Washington by joining with China to establish the Asian Infrastructure Investment Bank and they are looking to China's 'One Belt, One Road' project to forge links across Eurasia to China.

At the same time, growing antagonisms among the European powers—in particular, hostility in Britain and France toward the growing assertiveness of Germany—are fracturing the European Union (EU). The delusion that the continent could be unified on the basis of capitalist relations was shattered by the 2016 referendum in Britain on exit from the EU (known as Brexit), which could set in motion the disintegration of the EU and the resurgence of the unresolved national antagonisms that led to two world wars.

While Japan still vows allegiance to a post-war order dominated by the United States, the country's ruling elite is repudiating the post-war restraints on its armed forces and building up its military for the assertion of its own ambitions. In 1941, the question of which power would control Asia ultimately drove US and Japanese imperialists to war.

The support for US militarism by lesser imperialist powers, such as Canada, Australia and New Zealand, flows from their mercenary decision that, at present, it remains the best means of preserving their economic and strategic interests.

Just as the Wall Street crash of 1929 set into motion the geo-political tensions that erupted a decade later in World War II, the crash of 2008 has fuelled imperialist militarism. The past decade has witnessed an escalating and increasingly bitter struggle over declining market share and profits among rival transnational conglomerates.

Escalating US-led wars

The United States had been at war on an almost continuous basis since the first US–Iraq War of 1990–91. The dissolution of the Soviet Union in December 1991, combined with the restoration of capitalism in China, was regarded by the American ruling class as an opportunity to restructure global geo-politics, with the aim of establishing the unchallenged hegemony of the United States.

The *Defense Planning Guidance*, drafted by the US Department of Defense in February 1992, unambiguously asserted the hegemonic ambitions of US imperialism:

> There are other potential nations or coalitions that could, in the further future, develop strategic aims and a defense posture of region-wide or global domination. Our strategy must now refocus on precluding the emergence of any potential future global competitor.
>
> (US Department of Defense 1992)

The strategy document outlined an 'American grand strategy' to 'discourage advanced industrial nations from challenging our leadership or even aspiring to a larger regional or global role' (US Department of Defense 1992). This strategy committed the United States to an unceasing use of military power.

Political developments in every part of the world were seen in relation to how they impacted American dominance. The American ruling class was compelled to intervene even where it might not have direct and immediate economic interests. Any step back, let alone defeat, would be seen as a sign of weakness, with global consequences.

As noted earlier, in *The Grand Chessboard*, Brzezinski (1997a: 30) explained the imperative to control Eurasia, the vast land mass that stretches from Western Europe to China and which includes the Middle East, Central Asia, Russia and the Indian subcontinent: 'America's global primacy is directly dependent on how long and how effectively its preponderance on the Eurasian continent is sustained.'

The 1990s saw a persistent use of US military power—most notably, in the first Gulf War, followed by its campaign to break up Yugoslavia. The restructuring of the Balkan states, which provoked a fratricidal civil war, culminated in the US-led 1999 bombing campaign to compel Serbia to accept the secession of the province of Kosovo. Other major military operations during that decade included the intervention in Somalia, which ended in disaster, the military occupation of Haiti, the bombing of Sudan and Afghanistan, and repeated bombing attacks on Iraq.

The events of 9/11 provided the opportunity to launch the 'war on terror', a propaganda slogan that provided an all-purpose justification for military operations throughout the Middle East. The second President Bush used the phrase 'wars of the 21st century' and, in 2002, US military strategy was revised in line with the new doctrine of 'preventive warfare'. This doctrine, which violated existing international law, decreed that the United States could attack any country in the world judged to pose a potential threat—not only of a military, but also of an economic character—to American interests.

The Bush administration justified the invasion of Iraq as a *pre-emptive* war, undertaken in response to the patently non-existent imminent threat posed by the country's 'weapons of mass destruction' to the national security of the United States. In effect, the United States asserted its right to attack any country, regardless of the existence or non-existence of an immediate threat to American national security.

The scope of military operations continuously widened. The cynical invocation of human rights was used to wage war against Libya and overthrow the regime of Muammar Gaddafi in 2011. The same hypocritical pretext was employed to organise a proxy war in Syria. The consequences of these crimes, in terms of human lives and suffering, are incalculable.

The academics, much like the journalists, who work within the framework of the official narrative of the defence of human rights and the 'war on terror', cannot explain the progression of conflicts. In the words of a prominent Marxist:

The last quarter century of US-instigated wars must be studied as a chain of interconnected events. The strategic logic of the US drive for global hegemony extends beyond the neocolonial operations in the Middle East and Africa. The ongoing regional wars are component elements of the rapidly escalating confrontation of the United States with Russia and China . . . But this latest stage in the ongoing struggle for world hegemony, which lies at the heart of the conflict with Russia and China, is bringing to the forefront latent and potentially explosive tensions between the United States and its present-day imperialist allies, including—to name the most significant potential adversary—Germany. The two world wars of the twentieth century were not the product of misunderstandings.

(North 2016: xix)

Domestic factors

The strategy of global domination posed several problems for the American ruling class. First, the plan for global empire, entailing incredible human, economic and social costs, ran up against public opposition. None of the wars that the United States launched after the fall of the USSR were popular. The ruling class was plagued by what it referred to as 'Vietnam War syndrome'—namely, the deep scepticism of the American people toward military intervention abroad. As Brzezinski (1997a: 35) noted: '[T]he pursuit of power is not a goal that commands popular passion, except in conditions of a sudden threat or challenge to the public's sense of domestic well-being.'

At the same time, glaring inequality, mounting social and class tensions, and growing political disaffection provided an impetus for military interventions as a means of diverting the discontent into nationalist and patriotic channels, as illustrated by Donald Trump's aggressive 'America First' programme.

Legislatures as a legitimising factor in war-making

Following the eruption of widespread public opposition to the 2003 invasion of Iraq, numerous efforts were made to provide a more 'democratic' framework for war-making. Although appeals were made to democratic conceptions and claims were made that more parliamentary or congressional involvement in the process would lessen the likelihood of war itself, the thrust of many of these proposals were to provide political legitimacy to decisions to deploy military forces. Indeed, a veneer of democratic legitimacy may make military action more likely, not less. In fact, in some instances, the arguments were directly linked to assisting the executive to overcome popular anti-war sentiment.

In her treatise on the war prerogative, Joseph (2013: 107) argued—on the basis of a brief review of four centuries—that the British House of Commons has played a 'varying, but influential, role in the exercise and scrutiny of' decisions to go to war. She said that this was contrary to the 'orthodox view', which asserted the executive's exclusive control over war.

Joseph's historical claim will be examined later in this chapter. For now, it must be noted that she reached her conclusion despite admitting that the effectiveness of Parliament's involvement in the decision-making process leading up to the 2003 invasion of Iraq was 'questionable' (Joseph 2013: 105). As she recounted, the case that the British governments presented to Parliament for deployment was not only 'selective and misleading' in relation to false claims of supportive legal advice, but also based on an intelligence 'dossier' that was subsequently discredited (Joseph 2013: 105). Moreover:

> The timing of the Commons' debate and vote on a substantive motion of support for the deployment reduced the Commons' input to essentially a rubber stamp of a fait accompli: 40,000 British troops had already mobilised into the region. Britain could not withdraw without a massive loss of credibility and authority, a factor which influenced many of the MPs speaking in the debate.
>
> (Joseph 2013: 105)

Joseph also recounted how, in 2011, then Prime Minister David Cameron brushed aside a supposed convention that the Commons be given the opportunity to debate the matter before troops were committed. The government had claimed only a few months earlier that such a convention existed, while reserving to itself the power to ignore the convention in what it judged to be 'an emergency'.

When it came to sending troops to Libya to participate in the ouster of the Gaddafi government, there was no debate until three days after the deployment began. Cameron claimed that there was no time for consultation before military action because of the urgency of avoiding the 'slaughter of civilians' (Joseph 2013: 106). That humanitarian pretext was just as false as those offered for the Iraq invasion just eight years earlier, as demonstrated by the overthrow and murder of Gaddafi and the subsequent descent of Libya into brutal internal wars in which thousands of civilians were indeed slaughtered.

Despite what these military interventions revealed about the cosmetic character of Parliament's role, Joseph (2013: 107–08) attributed to Parliament four highly political functions. The first was a 'legitimation function'—the attachment of a 'stamp of approval' of 'initiatives taken elsewhere'. This was an 'overt and conscious action' that consisted of members of Parliament (MPs) expressing their support for the war, voting in favour of it and granting financial supply for the war effort. In other words, Parliament's service is needed to lend political legitimacy to a war.

Secondly, Parliament performed a 'mobilising consent function' of building public acceptance of the war effort and the 'coercions placed on the citizen by the government'. Joseph (2013: 107–08) subscribed to the view that 'public processes of policy and decision-making can be shaped as a means of winning consent to those policies and decisions'. This amounts to Parliament operating to condition or manipulate public opinion to overcome popular opposition to the war or the accompanying 'coercions' imposed on the population—which could be conscription or the abrogation of civil liberties.

A third function was a 'scrutinising' one, which Joseph described as Parliament exerting influence on the conduct of an ongoing war. It could modify or reject government measures, but it could not substitute a policy of its own.

This envisages MPs acting as potentially useful advisers on the war, but without any power of veto.

The fourth function was 'expressive'—to express public opinion and sentiment. Joseph (2013: 107–08) characterised this as a 'tension-release' function, providing an outlet for different views and thus playing an 'important part in the dissipation of tension'. This means Parliament acting as a political safety-valve to channel opposition and dissent back into the safe waters of the political elite's parliamentary framework.

To sum up, Parliament serves as an indispensable cog in the war-making. It attaches a fig leaf of democratic legitimacy to the war, drums up public support, combats or manipulates public opinion, serves as an advisory body and diverts popular opposition.

In justifying her conclusions, which proposed that legislation require the government to obtain a vote in the House of Commons before deploying armed forces, except in certain circumstances, Joseph (2013: 160) outlined an anti-democratic view of democracy: 'Democratic decision-making, as used here, goes beyond a formal aggregative version of democracy, which centres on the idea of "majority rule". Democratic governments should be based on reasons and justification, not just votes and power.'

This conception fundamentally overturns the very core of democracy, which is majority rule. In the famous words of US President Abraham Lincoln's Civil War Gettysburg Address, democracy is 'government of the people, by the people, for the people'. Joseph eschewed 'elitist' theories of public decision-making that reject the capacity of most ordinary people to decide on matters, such as war, that supposedly require skill, expertise and experience. But she argued for a limited role for the House of Commons, not for any form of popular vote or participation in decisions to go to war. In keeping with the 'functions' she assigned to Parliament, she argued that the Commons' involvement would 'strengthen public trust' in the decision (Joseph 2013: 179). At the same time, the vague and ancient royal prerogative would remain the source of the powers, kept in the hands of the executive, to deploy the armed forces (Joseph 2013: 186). Her proposed legislation would place only limited conditions on the exercise of the royal prerogative.

Joseph criticised as inadequate the various proposals advanced by the British Labour government in the wake of the exposure of the lies told by the Blair administration about the 2003 invasion of Iraq. Those proposals, reviewed in Chapter 3, revolved around establishing a 'convention' that a parliamentary vote was necessary to sanction a decision to deploy armed forces. Ultimately, despite a series of official reports, the Labour government abandoned the idea (Joseph 2013: 184–85) and the subsequent Conservative–Liberal Democrat coalition government effectively swept aside any such convention when it joined the military onslaught on Libya in 2011 (Joseph 2013: 106).

As Joseph noted, there is an extensive literature on the 'democratic peace' argument that democratic involvement in war decisions makes conflict less likely. Two claims are advanced. One is that democracies are unlikely to fight each other because of shared democratic values and culture, and a shared commitment to the peaceful adjudication of disputes; the other is that democratic institutions inherently constrain resort to war, either because of public opinion or the alleged greater reluctance of legislatures, compared to executives, to go to war (Weart 1998).

Joseph acknowledged that other studies cast doubt on these propositions. The Iraq invasion of 2003 is only one example of supposed democracies conducting unprovoked wars of aggression, including against countries with elected governments (Layne 1994; Chan and Safran 2006). Nevertheless, Joseph (2013: 179) concluded, without substantiation:

> In democratic systems, where decisions about war are debated openly, both the public and policy-makers are sensitized to the costs of waging war, and it makes it more likely that war really is a rational response to a perceived threat.

This conclusion contradicted Joseph's earlier advocacy of Parliament's 'legitimation', 'mobilising consent' and 'expressive' functions.

Parliamentary involvement in promoting war

Other arguments in favour of a parliamentary voice clearly assigned to the legislature the task of helping to build a constituency for war.

In his 2016 essay, 'Firing line: Australia's path to war', James Brown (2016) explicitly connected the quest for a parliamentary role in war decision-making with the need to prepare public opinion for war and to provide a veneer of democratic legitimacy for going to war.

Brown, a former military officer, argued that Australians were dangerously resistant to, or politically and psychologically unprepared for, war—particularly one against China. Having been twice deployed to Iraq since the 2003 US-led invasion, he deplored the fact that the Iraq 'disaster' fuelled anti-war sentiment. One means of overcoming that problem was to seek to restore 'public trust' in war-making by involving Parliament in the process:

> In Australia's bright and blessed circumstances today, we rarely think of war: it is something we go to, not something that comes to us. It seems we often shrink from talking about war in any detailed way, as if to speak of evil might set us on an inevitable path towards it . . . As the Australian Defence Force spends billions of dollars on new equipment and facilities, building a grander military to insure against an uncertain future, the public remains largely mired in the past, blind to the new realities of strategic rivalry between our friends and allies. Our mechanisms for going to war lack the institutional rigour necessary to navigate a more complex world, and our decisions about conflict are not grounded by public trust and democratic legitimacy. We need urgently to re-engage with the problems of war, and to rethink just how it is that we choose whether we fight or not.
>
> (Brown 2016: 5)

Brown (2016: 33) invoked the necessity to 'consider deeply the possibility of war with China', most likely through a request from the United States. He extolled the American alliance as a 'distinctively close relationship—closer to a marriage' (Brown 2016: 33), underscoring Australia's strategic and military reliance on the United States since World War II. He complained that the 'disastrous' war in Iraq 'hangs in our national consciousness, a spectre looming over every discussion of war' (Brown 2016: 14), that 'Australians are worried about what it might means to support the United States in a conflict within the region' (Brown 2016: 36) and that 'our universities still view war as a morally tainted activity' (Brown 2016: 57).

For those reasons, Brown proposed a mechanism for proving parliamentary scrutiny over military deployments. He asserted, without any substantiation, that 'full parliamentary approval' over any 'substantial military action by the prime minister' would 'inhibit an effective response to a crisis' and that 'successive prime ministers have rightly resisted this' (Brown 2016: 58). There was, however, 'a compelling case for parliament to review whether a military deployment is in the national interest within a period of, say, ninety days' (Brown 2016: 58).

Many comments could be made about this proposal, not least the fact that once a war was under way, there would be little prospect of a parliamentary vote, by either house, to veto and withdraw from it. What is most revealing about this proposal, however, is not the absence of any supporting evidence or argumentation, or its cosmetic and easily flouted character, or its lack of any detail whatsoever; rather, it is the nakedness of its purpose—to erect a facade of parliamentary consultation to help to overcome public opposition to war.

Significantly, Brown had influential connections and his suggestions were part of a wider push to redirect public opinion. He was not only the son-in-law of Australian Prime Minister Malcolm Turnbull, but also research director of the United States Studies Centre (USSC), based within the University of Sydney. The Centre's specific function is to formulate the strategic conceptions underlying Australian involvement in US-led military interventions and to promote the US–Australia alliance, particularly among young people.

Formed in 2007, with the backing of leading business and political figures, the USSC's founding aim was to overcome the deep-seated hostility of broad layers of the population to Australia's participation in the invasion of Iraq. At a meeting of the American-Australian Association (AAA) in 2006, media magnate Rupert Murdoch had pointed with concern toward polling results from the Lowy Institute think tank, which showed that the majority of the Australian population—some 57 per cent—viewed American foreign policy as a potential threat. Murdoch reportedly declared: 'This is ridiculous, what are you blokes going to do about this?' (Lane 2007).

In 2006, the Liberal–National coalition government of John Howard announced it would provide AUS$25 million to finance the USSC, if the figure could be matched by funds from other sources. The sponsors and leading personnel of the USSC are intimately tied to the military and corporate elite. Sponsors have included Rupert Murdoch's News Limited and US arms conglomerate

Northrup Grumman, as well as Dow, the manufacturer of Agent Orange during the Vietnam War and a continuing supplier to the US nuclear and chemical warfare industry. Its board of advisers included former Prime Minister Bob Hawke, who dispatched Australian forces to the 1991 Gulf War, former Prime Minister John Howard, who committed Australian troops to the invasions of Afghanistan and Iraq, and former US ambassador to Australia Jeffrey Bleich, who was based in Australia during 2011, when there was a significant intensification of the US–Australia relationship.

The Centre's ideological function was further underlined in that year, when the Labor government of Julia Gillard provided it with $2 million to establish a research group entitled 'Alliance 21', which would function from 2011 to 2014. The group was established less than a year after Gillard had ousted her predecessor Kevin Rudd, who had called for the United States to make a limited accommodation to the rise of China. Upon being installed as prime minister, Gillard immediately pledged her unconditional allegiance to the United States. In November 2011, the Gillard government hosted US President Barack Obama as he announced the US military and strategic 'pivot', or 'rebalance', toward Asia, directed against China, from the floor of the Australian Parliament. Gillard signed a military agreement with Obama that provided for increasing numbers of US Marines to be based, on a rotational basin, in Darwin, along with other measures to integrate the Australian military into the US armed forces.

The purpose of Alliance 21 was twofold. One aim was that it would serve as the centre for discussions among the military, political and intelligence establishment regarding the US military build-up in Asia and the preparations for war. The other was to promote the US alliance, as it was stepped up in line with Washington's 'rebalance' toward Asia. Many of Alliance 21's publications advocated policies to prepare for war.

In 2014, Alliance 21 presented its report, *The Australia–US Partnership*, to the Australian government. As well as calling for a deepening of the US alliance and 'even greater investment in Australia–US interoperability and defence procurement cooperation', it warned that '[d]emographic and generational changes in the two countries mean young and immigrant populations are less attached to the alliance in historical, cultural, and emotional terms' (Alliance 21 Project 2014: 7).

The report concluded: 'Careful attention to the relationship is needed across government, business and social sectors in both countries, with an eye to demonstrating the value of Australia–United States ties and the mutual benefits they bring' (Alliance 21 Project 2014: 31). To that the end, the report called for the introduction of 'educational components at schools and institutions of higher learning on the history of shared values and commitments between Australia and the US, as well as the meaning of the alliance today' (Alliance 21 Project 2014: 32).

Again, this was not an independent report. It was funded by companies with substantial profit interests in bolstering the US–Australia partnership, expanding military spending and, if necessary, going to war with China. Among them were Raytheon, a major US arms manufacturer and supplier, Chevron and ConocoPhillips, two large US-based global oil and energy companies, and

Morgan Stanley, one the biggest surviving American transnational financial services corporations. As the report explicitly acknowledged:

> In particular, we wish to thank our principal sponsor, the Australian government, and eight corporate sponsors: Dow, Chevron, ConocoPhillips, GE, Visy, Raytheon and Morgan Stanley. These supporters have not only been financially generous, but their officials and experts have given generously of their time and insights as well.
>
> (Alliance 21 Project 2014: 4)

In 2016, amid mounting demands from the Pentagon that Australia conduct incursions into Chinese-claimed territories in the South China Sea, a USSC report warned that the alliance between the two countries 'is driven too much by policy elites in both countries . . . There is low public support in Australia for joining the United States in an Asian contingency' (Fontaine 2016: 10). By an 'Asian contingency', the report meant a military clash—or war in Asia. The report further called for the US–Australian alliance to become 'more enmeshed in the emerging regional web of relationships' that the United States was developing against China (Fontaine 2016: 10).

Britain's historical record: overturning democratic constraints

Far from becoming more democratically exercised, the war powers have become less so over the past four centuries, since the 17th- and 18th-century revolutions in England, France and the United States. Having overthrown the old monarchic and feudal orders, and consolidated economic and political power in their own hands, the capitalist classes have increasingly arrogated to themselves also the powers to go to war, overturning somewhat democratic constraints that were initially generated by those revolutions. This process will be explored in Chapters 3, 4 and 5 on the expanding executive war powers in the United States, Britain and Australia.

In her treatise, *The War Prerogative*, Joseph (2013) argued the opposite with regard to Britain. She contended that an examination of 'the war prerogative in practice' over the past four centuries demonstrates that the House of Commons has played 'an active and influential role', despite the common assumption of an exclusive executive power. She asserted that what she labels the civil wars period, from 1642 to 1651, during which the previous absolute monarchy was overthrown, laid the foundations for this parliamentary engagement. It was an 'extraordinary historical period' in which the House of Commons assumed responsibility for the war and foreign policy powers, with lasting legacies (Joseph 2013: 44–45).

Part of the problem with Joseph's thesis flows from her methodology, which she described as a 'lawyer's legal history' or 'internal legal history' (Joseph 2013: 8). This approach—predominantly based on legal sources, such as statutes, court cases and 'lawyers' literature'—divorces law from the underlying socio-economic and geo-political factors that more fundamentally determine the location of political power, as well as the struggles against the holders of that power. Joseph even eschewed supposed 'external legal histories' that 'typically look at the political, social and economic impact of people and events on legal institutions and rules, and vice versa' (Joseph 2013: 8).

In fact, Joseph cast doubt on the study of history and on historical truth itself. She insisted that 'historical analysis is the product of the research and interpretation of the individual historian' and that, therefore, 'history is made by historians' (Joseph 2013: 11). After briefly canvassing the scepticism advanced by post-modernist and critical legal studies advocates in any objective meaning in history, she contended that her approach avoids the ideological presumptions and biases that interpret history from the standpoint of contemporary issues and institutions.

Despite acknowledging methodological challenges, Joseph (2013: 13) hoped that her framework would make a 'unique and useful contribution' to understanding the war prerogative. Unfortunately, this narrow prism masks essential processes. In particular, it covers over the economic and class interests involved in the English Revolution and the subsequent concentration of power, via the restoration of the monarchy on new terms, in the hands of the rising capitalist class at the expense of the emerging working class—the majority of the population.

From 1642 to 1649, as Joseph (2013: 45) noted, the English Parliament assumed powers that included the raising and control of the armed forces, the raising of funds for the armed forces, the conduct of war, and the conduct of foreign affairs and relations. The forces led by Oliver Cromwell sought to justify their seizure of power by referencing previous constitutional theory, arguing that exceptional circumstances required them to assume the kingly powers of war and foreign policy (Joseph 2013: 45–46).

In reality, however, the exercise of these powers was based on the revolutionary overthrow of the old absolutist regime, which involved the trial and execution of Charles I, the abolition of the monarchy and the House of Lords, and the declaration of a Commonwealth. Militarily, too, the new order was revolutionary: Parliament proclaimed by ordinance the establishment of the New Model Army, which enlisted and paid plebeian members of society.

The mid-17th-century crisis was essentially a capitalist revolution, which overthrew the rule of the landed aristocracy and brought another to power: the budding merchant and financial class. Cromwell's New Model Army was not merely an army, but a party with which he repeatedly purged Parliament until it reflected the needs of his class, suppressing the Levellers, who represented the plebeian elements who wanted to take the revolution further than was necessary for capitalist society to thrive. Cromwell ruthlessly pursued the interests of the class he represented—such as when he had the leaders of the Levellers executed and, in Ireland, when he sacked the towns of Drogheda and Wexford, executing the captured garrison and civilian population (Hill 1970).

Both the overthrow of the king and the subsequent restoration of the monarchy in 1660 were accompanied by pitiless exercises of power in the interests of definite economic interests. Placing Charles I on trial raised innumerable legal problems, not least the rewriting of the law of treason to allow for the prosecution of the monarch (Robertson 2005: 135–50). Nevertheless, having conducted a revolutionary war for seven years and defeated the king on the battlefield, the forces of Parliament were not deterred by legal niceties. The 1649 indictment, headed 'A Charge of High Treason and Other High Crimes' and drafted by prosecutor John Cooke, impeached Charles Stuart as a 'tyrant, traitor, murderer and a public and implacable enemy to the Commonwealth of England'. He was 'the occasioner, author and continuer of the said unnatural, cruel and bloody wars, and therein guilty of all the treasons, murders, rapines, burning, spoils, desolations, damages and mischiefs to this nation' (Robertson 2005: 148–49). When Charles refused to plead to the charge and objected that the 70 judges empanelled to try him lacked any power to do so, his claim was simply overruled (Robertson 2005: 152–59).

Eleven years later, Cooke (who had prosecuted the king) and the others were summarily tried, convicted, and hung, drawn and quartered by the restored British monarchy in 1660 for their part in the 1649 trial. Pleas that the court lacked jurisdiction over acts commissioned by Parliament were quickly dismissed. The grand jury was instructed that 'the King can do no wrong: that is a rule of law' (Robertson 2005: 295). The jurors were warned that if they were to refuse to indict the men guilty of shedding the king's blood, they would themselves be guilty of treason (Robertson 2005: 296). Parliamentary privilege was overturned so that MPs could be executed for words spoken in the House of Commons (Robertson 2005: 306).

The 'Glorious Revolution' of 1688–89 established a new relationship between the monarchy and the Parliament, in which the monarchs essentially became figureheads for the ascendant capitalist class. The prerogative powers of the Crown were retained for purposes of war and the suppression of domestic unrest. Anxious to secure its position, the new regime under William III and Mary adopted a harsh policy toward political dissent, and the courts followed suit by holding, in 1704, that it was a crime to defame the government, as well as to libel an individual figure associated with the establishment. In effect, in the case of *Tutchin* (1704) 91 Eng Rep 1224, the judges reversed a century of common-law precedents that confined seditious libel to the defamation of some particular person (Hamburger 1985: 725–53).

A century later, in response to the French Revolution of 1789 and rising demands for political reform in Britain, the authorities responded with political repression, featuring the sedition trials of 1792 and 1793 and the treason trials of 1794. These were particularly directed against calls for democracy in the wake of the French Revolution—most notably, Thomas Paine's *Rights of Man*. Paine's pamphlet ended by proposing: a written constitution composed by a national assembly, in the American mould; the elimination of aristocratic titles, because democracy is incompatible with primogeniture, which leads to the despotism of the family; a national budget without allotted military and war expenses; lower taxes for the poor and subsidised education for them; and a progressive income tax weighted against wealthy estates to prevent the emergence of a hereditary aristocracy. As a result of the publication of *Rights of Man*, radical associations began to proliferate. The government issued a royal proclamation against seditious writings in 1792 and there were more than 100 prosecutions for sedition in the 1790s alone (Barrell and Mee 2006: xiii). Paine, who fled to France, was found guilty in absentia (Barrell and Mee 2006: xix).

There was a similar political evolution in regard to the war powers. Rather than demonstrating any continuity from the Cromwellian period, Parliament's role was always limited. Even that degree of participation in war-making decisions diminished by the end of the 19th century, as parliaments became more democratically elected in the wake of the growth of the working class and the demands for popular suffrage issued by the mass Chartist movement. Despite the bloody suppression of the Chartists (Head 2011: 28–29), the right to vote was eventually extended, ultimately to both men and women.

A cabinet of selected MPs initially emerged in the 1690s to administer the monarch's powers, with major decisions on war and foreign policy made in conjunction with the monarch and their Privy Council. After the installation of the House of Hanover on the throne in 1714, the monarchs continued to play a hidden, but material, role in foreign policy. The actual political power lay increasingly with governments of ministers who were formally accountable to Parliament (Joseph 2013: 58–59). As Joseph (2013: 59) admits, however:

> The development of parliamentary government altered the relationship between the Commons and the government. MPs still tried to influence the direction and conduct of foreign policy through debate in the House. However, as parliamentary governments became stronger and more coherent, the capacity of the Commons as an institution to initiate policy or influence decisions made about foreign policy became increasingly limited. The cabinet was where the real power lay.

By the end of the 19th century, the prominence and frequency of parliamentary debates on foreign policy had declined markedly. According to Joseph (2013: 78), one constitutional historian referred to the debates as 'tactical scrimmages', with Parliament providing only the illusion of debate: 'MPs were largely restricted to noisy criticism and censure, and there were few instances of real interference.'

During the first six decades of the 19th century, there were several examples of governments and ministers resigning or being defeated on questions of foreign policy, but that had become 'very rare' by the early 20th century (Joseph 2013: 95–96). Already, by 1857, when Prime Minister Henry Palmerston's government waged war against Persia without informing Parliament, let alone seeking its consent, despite the public antipathy to the calamitous and brutal Crimean War of 1854–56, Palmerston had rejected any constitutional requirement to consult Parliament. If a government became involved in a war with one of the 'great powers' with 'serious consequences', it had a duty to call Parliament together to 'state the grounds of the quarrel, and to ask for the means of carrying on the contest', he said; for a war on Persia that was 'not likely to entail upon us any considerable efforts', convening Parliament would be 'a burlesque on our constitutional forms' (quoted in Joseph 2013: 100–01).

By the latter part of the 19th century, governments would assemble Parliament only once they had already committed the country to war. That was the case in both the Boer Wars to annex South Africa in 1880–91 and 1899–1902, and World War I (Joseph 2013: 101–02). As a plethora of academic, parliamentary and government reports documented after the outcry over the 2003 invasion of Iraq, Parliament's role had been marginalised in the 20th century (Joseph 2013: 79).

As will be seen in the ensuing chapters, there were parallel processes of democratic reversal in the United States after the American Revolution that overthrew British rule, while Australia's record resembles that of Britain, except that its federal Parliament, established under British tutelage in 1901, always played an even more subservient role.

References

Alliance 21 Project. 2014. *Alliance 21: The Australia–US Partnership*, www.ussc.edu.au/analysis/alliance-21-the-australia-us-partnership1 (accessed 15 December 2015).

Andrianopoulos, G. 1991. *Kissinger and Brzezinski: The NSC and the Struggle for Control of U.S. National Security Policy*. New York: Palgrave Macmillan.

Axelrod, A. 2009. *The Real History of the Cold War: A New Look at the Past*. New York: Sterling.

Barrell, J., and Mee, J. (eds). 2006. *Trials for Treason and Sedition 1792–1794*. Eight vols. London: Pickering & Chatto.

Brown, J. 2016. 'Firing line: Australia's path to war', *Quarterly Essay*, June, www.quarterly essay.com.au/essay/2016/06/firing-line (accessed 11 May 2017).

Brzezinski, Z. 1997a. *The Grand Chessboard: American Primacy and Its Geostrategic Imperatives*. New York: Basic Books.

Brzezinski, Z. 1997b. 'A geostrategy for Eurasia', *Foreign Affairs*, Sept–Oct, www.foreign affairs.com/articles/asia/1997-09-01/geostrategy-eurasia (accessed 11 November 2016).

Chan, S., and Safran, W. 2006. 'Public opinion as a constraint against war: democracies' response to Operation Iraqi Freedom', *Foreign Policy Analysis*, 2(2): 137–56.

Clark, C. 2012. *The Sleepwalkers: How Europe Went to War in 1914*. London: Allen Lane.

Dunn, J. 2013. *The Crowe Memorandum: Sir Eyre Crowe and Foreign Office Perceptions of Germany, 1918–1925*. Cambridge: Cambridge Scholars.

Eisenhower, D. 1961. 'Farewell address'. In *The Annals of America, Vol. 18: 1961–1968— The Burdens of World Power*. Chicago, IL: Encyclopaedia Britannica.

Fischer, F. 1961. *Germany's Aims in the First World War*. New York: W.W. Norton & Co.

Fischer, F. 1975. *War of Illusions: German Policies from 1911 to 1914*. London: Chatto & Windus.

Fontaine, R. 2016. *Against Complacency: Risks and Opportunities for the Australia–US Alliance*, Sydney: Alliance 21 Program, www.ussc.edu.au/analysis/against-complacency-risks-and-opportunities-for-the-australia-us-alliance (accessed 1 December 2016).

Gibbs, D. 2000. 'Afghanistan: the Soviet Invasion in retrospect', *International Politics*, 37(2): 233–45.

Hamburger, P. 1985. 'The development of the law of seditious libel and the control of the press', *Stanford Law Review*, 37: 661–775.

Hamilton, R., and Herwig, H. 2004. *Decisions for War, 1914–1917*. Cambridge: Cambridge University Press.

Head, M. 2011. *Crimes against the State: From Treason to Terrorism*. London: Ashgate.

Hill, C. 1970. *God's Englishman: Oliver Cromwell and the English Revolution*. London: Weidenfeld & Nicholson.

Joseph, R. 2013. *The War Prerogative: History Reform and Constitutional Design*. Oxford: Oxford University Press.

Kennedy, P. 1987. *The Rise of Anglo-German Antagonism*. London: Ashfield Press.

Lane, B. 2007. 'Beazley signs on to US studies centre', *The Australian*, 23 August.

Layne, C. 1994. 'Kant or Cant: The Myth of the Democratic Peace', *International Security* 19(2): 5–49.

Lowitt, R. 1967. *The Truman–MacArthur Controversy*. Chicago, IL: Rand McNally.

North, D. 2016. *A Quarter-Century of War: The US Drive for Global Hegemony, 1990–2016*. Detroit, MI: Mehring Books.

Payne, N. 2015. 'Downing Street backs Sir Nicholas Houghton in Corbyn row', *The Spectator*, 9 November, https://blogs.spectator.co.uk/2015/11/downing-street-backs-sir-nicholas-houghton-in-corbyn-row/# (accessed 11 October 2016).

Robertson, G. 2005. *The Tyrannicide Brief*. London: Chatto & Windus.

Sampford, C., and Palmer, M. 2009. 'The constitutional power to make war: domestic legal issues raised by Australia's action in Iraq', *Griffith Law Review*, 18(2): 350–84.

US Department of Defense. 1992. *Defense Planning Guidance*, as published in *New York Times*, 8 March, http://nsarchive.gwu.edu/nukevault/ebb245/doc03_extract_nyt edit.pdf (accessed 10 April 2017).

Weart, S. 1998. *Why Democracies Will Never Fight One Another*. New Haven, CT: Yale University Press.

Zeisberg, M. 2013. *War Powers: The Politics of Constitutional Authority*. Princeton, NJ: Princeton University Press.

2 Vietnam, Iraq and the 'war on terror'

Deception, war propaganda and legislative approval

Many instances can be cited of governments and intelligence agencies systematically deceiving the populations whose interests they claimed to be defending, aiming to create the conditions for war. Not only were legislators fed distortions and fabrications to ensure their approval of the military interventions, but also—and more importantly—the people were misled in concerted efforts to manipulate public opinion and generate a pro-war atmosphere. Numerous examples are outlined in the ensuing chapters of this book, dealing with the records of governments in the United States, Britain and Australia. Almost invariably, these cases involve complicity by mainstream media outlets, which readily propagated misleading claims.

Two well-documented experiences of deceit, both of which had calamitous consequences for millions of people, are the long war in Vietnam, from the 1940s to the 1970s, and the 2003 invasion and ongoing military operations in Iraq. Both wars aroused intense popular opposition, leading to the ultimate exposure of many of the lies told to launch them, but this did not prevent the carnage from continuing for many years. In neither case have those responsible been held to account, despite irrefutable evidence of fraud and illegality.

Invariably, official inquiries into such crimes have resulted in whitewashes that have been readily accepted by governments, the mass media and legislatures. In the case of Iraq, the British government's Chilcot Inquiry provided an example of how, even when documented evidence is produced of deliberate deception, those responsible are excused, depicted as unwitting and innocent, if willing, dupes of 'intelligence failures'. Subsequent academic studies of the Iraq War, however, demonstrated the opposite: a campaign of intentional deception and propaganda designed to overcome widespread popular opposition to going to war, and to engineer the conditions for a parliamentary rubber stamp on a predetermined decision to join the US-led invasion of Iraq.

This evidence further sheds light on the underlying geo-strategic interests driving the ongoing US and allied military operations in the Middle East and globally. It also has wider implications for the current framework of parliamentary democracy. While the facade of democracy has largely been maintained, the documented record points to the deliberate undermining of democratic norms through the manipulation of public opinion, with the complicity of the mass media and legislators.

Vietnam and the Pentagon Papers

In June 2011, the US National Archives officially released the 'Pentagon Papers', 40 years after they were first leaked and published (National Archives 2011). The long-delayed authorised publication served only to underscore the degree to which the people of United States and the world were systematically deceived by a long succession of US administrations about the decisions taken by the United States and its allies to go to war in Vietnam, Cambodia and Laos.

On 13 June 1971, the publication by the *New York Times* of the first instalment of the top-secret documents played a significant role in galvanising mass opposition to the Vietnam War. The documents served as an indictment not only of the Republican administration of Richard Nixon, but also of the Democratic administrations that had preceded it—particularly those of John F. Kennedy and Lyndon B. Johnson.

Commissioned by then-US Secretary of Defense Robert McNamara in 1967, the 7,000-page study, officially known as the *Report of the Office of the Secretary of Defense Vietnam Task Force*, represented an exhaustive internal study of the policies that led to the US war in Vietnam and its progressive escalation.

The report's principal impact was its exposure of the systematic lying by successive administrations about the reasons for, and the conduct of, the US intervention in South East Asia.

The report exposed as a fraud the so-called Gulf of Tonkin incident of 1964, an alleged attack by Vietnamese patrol torpedo boats on a US destroyer that was the pretext given by President Johnson for obtaining a congressional resolution granting a virtual blank cheque to wage war in the region.

The report further established that Johnson, while campaigning for election in 1964 on the claim that he would not seek a wider war in Vietnam, had already drawn up plans to send in more troops and bomb North Vietnam.

The report also revealed previously unreported secret bombings of Cambodia and Laos, as well as coastal raids against North Vietnam. And it exposed the plot of Kennedy's administration to overthrow South Vietnamese ruler Ngo Dinh Diem in the run-up to his assassination in a 1963 military coup.

In sum, the report showed that successive US governments had repeatedly lied to the American people, carried out secret illegal operations in Vietnam, militarily intervened on blatantly false pretences and killed tens of thousands of Vietnamese civilians. It demonstrated that Washington had consistently violated international law and committed the most serious of war crimes.

These crimes went back to the 1940s. The 47-volume study commissioned by McNamara documented, for example, that:

- at the end of World War II, President Truman had rejected urgent appeals from Vietnamese leader Ho Chi Minh for US assistance;
- while the 1954 Geneva Peace Conference was in session, the United States was planning paramilitary operations against North Vietnam;
- President Kennedy's 'advisers' in Vietnam had participated directly in military operations;

- the US government had knowingly publicised false South Vietnamese intelligence reports about the extent of Communist infiltration;
- the Gulf of Tonkin resolution that officially justified US military intervention had falsely accused North Vietnam of attacking a US warship; and
- the US government had concealed from the American public the fact that extensive bombing of North Vietnam had done little to impair its military capacity, but had killed tens of thousands of civilians (Stone 2004: 500).

The impact of these revelations was magnified many times over by the response of the Nixon administration, which obtained a court injunction to halt the publication of further instalments of the document by the *New York Times* and the *Washington Post*. This marked the first time in US history that the federal government had intervened to restrain the publication of a newspaper. Within barely two weeks, the injunction was overturned by the US Supreme Court.

The Nixon administration invoked the Espionage Act of 1917, alleging that, by publishing previously secret contents of the leaked documents, the newspapers had violated the Act by wilfully communicating information 'it knew or had reason to believe . . . could be used to the injury of the United States . . . to persons not entitled to receive such information' (Stone 2004: 507).

By the time the Supreme Court considered the Nixon administration's injunction, some 20 newspapers had published material from the Pentagon Papers (Stone 2004: 508). In that context, the Court ruled 6–3 that the government had not met the 'heavy burden of showing justification' for a prior restraint on the press (Stone 2004: 511).

Far from any moves to hold responsible those, particularly in the Kennedy, Johnson and Nixon administrations, who had deceived the public and orchestrated the barbaric war, it was the whistleblower who alerted the people to the crimes who was harassed, demonised and prosecuted.

Daniel Ellsberg, the former Pentagon and RAND Corporation official who had leaked the report to the *Times*, was singled out for persecution. The so-called plumbers unit, whose Watergate break-in led to Nixon's downfall three years later, was ordered to break into the offices of Ellsberg's psychiatrist, in the hope of finding incriminating information with which to smear Ellsberg and the anti-war movement in the media.

In the meantime, Ellsberg and an associate, Anthony Russo, were indicted on a range of charges, including conspiracy to violate the Espionage Act, carrying possible total sentences of 125 years in prison. These charges were never put to the test, however: two years later, they were dismissed as a result of the Watergate burglary. The administration had organised a gang of Cuban CIA 'assets' for the purpose of 'incapacitating' or assassinating Ellsberg. In 1973, the trial judge ruled that the 'unprecedented' government misconduct had 'incurably infected the prosecution of this case' (Stone 2004: 515).

Nixon eventually resigned from office in August 1974, facing possible impeachment by Congress over his cover-up of the Watergate operation and actions to thwart an investigation of it, but he was immediately pardoned for his crimes by his replacement, Gerald Ford.

The circumstances surrounding the 2011 National Archives release highlighted the even greater suppression of efforts to expose government deception and halt wars in the 21st century than had occurred four decades ago. In an interview with CNN, Ellsberg, then in his 80s, noted that the crimes committed by the Nixon administration against him four decades earlier could now be carried out under the cover of law by the White House:

> That includes burglarizing my former psychoanalyst's office . . . warrantless wiretapping, using the CIA against an American citizen in the US, and authorizing a White House hit squad to 'incapacitate me totally'. But under George W. Bush and Barack Obama, with the PATRIOT Act, the FISA Amendment Act, and (for the hit squad) President Obama's executive orders, they have all become legal.
>
> (CNN Wire Staff 2011)

Indeed, former Army Private Chelsea Manning—who is alleged to have carried out acts similar to those of Ellsberg, providing WikiLeaks with hundreds of thousands of documents exposing US war crimes in Iraq and Afghanistan, as well as worldwide US diplomatic conspiracies—was sentenced to 35 years' imprisonment. Manning was subjected to solitary confinement and conditions tantamount to mental torture before finally being released in mid-2017.

Similarly, Julian Assange, the founder of WikiLeaks, was under virtual house arrest in Ecuador's embassy in London for years, under threat of extradition to face trial in the United States for conspiracy to commit espionage and other crimes against the state that could bring him life in prison or even the death penalty.

And Edward Snowden, the former National Security Agency (NSA) contractor who exposed the Agency's wholesale collection of data around the planet, was turned into a man without a country, living in forced exile in Moscow.

Iraq and the Chilcot Report

The report of the official Chilcot Inquiry into the role of the British government in the 2003 US-led invasion of Iraq, released in July 2016, provided further evidence of how governments deceive their populations about the reasons behind, and the need for, a decision to go to war.

The report shed some light on the machinations and manipulations involved in launching wars, and the fact that decisions are taken on the basis of alliances and geo-strategic calculations, not the publicly stated justifications. It also pointed toward the illegal character of that war, based on lies, and the criminal role of those officials, both British and American, who organised and led it.

The conclusions of the investigation headed by Sir John Chilcot were issued seven years after the Inquiry was first convened. The 2.6-million-word, 13-volume report covered the policy decisions made by the British government, military and intelligence services between 2001 and 2009.

While any finding on the legality of the invasion was specifically ruled out by the Labour Party government of Prime Minister Gordon Brown, which had established the Inquiry, the report nonetheless provided proof that those responsible for the war have the blood of hundreds of thousands of people, if not millions, on their hands.

This applies not only to then Prime Minister Tony Blair, who features heavily in the report; by extension, it is also an indictment of the principal architects of the war in the United States—that is, former President George W. Bush, Vice President Dick Cheney, Defense Secretary Donald Rumsfeld and others—as well as the leaders of other governments that participated, including that of Australia, and the politicians in every country who supported the invasion.

Personal testimony, confidential documents and private memos demonstrated that Blair opted to support a US war for regime change in Iraq that had been in preparation at least from the start of 2002, all while publicly claiming there were no such plans. Chilcot's report stated that Blair decided to join the war knowing that 'President Bush decided at the end of 2001 to pursue a policy of regime change in Iraq' (Chilcot 2016: executive summary, 6).

In his official media statement, Chilcot summed up his report's central finding as follows: 'We have concluded that the UK chose to join the invasion of Iraq before the peaceful options for disarmament had been exhausted. Military action at that time was not a last resort' (Iraq Inquiry 2016).

The Inquiry concluded that Iraq's Saddam Hussein did not present an 'imminent' threat at the time and that claims that Iraq possessed 'weapons of mass destruction' (WMDs) were 'not justified' (Chilcot 2016: vol. 11, 2). The invasion was launched on the basis of 'flawed intelligence and assessments' that were not challenged when they should have been (Iraq Inquiry 2016).

It was clear that 'the assessed intelligence had not established beyond doubt either that Saddam Hussein had continued to produce chemical and biological weapons or that efforts to develop nuclear weapons continued' (Chilcot 2016: executive summary, 116).

The Chilcot report published a declassified version of the so-called Downing Street Memo, memorialising a July 2002 meeting between Blair and other top officials in which the head of British intelligence explicitly acknowledged that President Bush 'wanted to remove Saddam, through military action, justified by the conjunction of terrorism and WMD. But the intelligence and facts were being fixed around the policy' (Chilcot 2016: vol. 4, 118).

In other words, all those involved knew that a false pretext was being manufactured to justify an unprovoked war. Moreover, the UN Security Council, which failed to sanction the invasion, was subverted:

> In the absence of a majority in support of military action, we consider that the UK was, in fact, undermining the Security Council's authority.
>
> Second, the Inquiry has not expressed a view on whether military action was legal. That could, of course, only be resolved by a properly constituted and internationally recognised Court.

We have, however, concluded that the circumstances in which it was decided that there was a legal basis for UK military action were far from satisfactory.

(Iraq Inquiry 2016)

Parliament was permitted to vote on the invasion and it did so overwhelmingly, with the backing of both the Labor government and the official Conservative Party opposition, with the assistance of deliberately misleading information: 'At the time of the Parliamentary vote of 18 March, diplomatic options had not been exhausted. The point had not been reached where military action was the last resort' (Chilcot 2016: vol. 7, 614).

The Inquiry also found that the leaders of the invasion had been warned in advance of the likely disastrous outcome: 'The risks of internal strife in Iraq, active Iranian pursuit of its interests, regional instability, and Al Qaida activity in Iraq were each explicitly identified before the invasion' (Iraq Inquiry 2016).

These anticipated dangers had immense consequences in terms of human lives and suffering:

The invasion and subsequent instability in Iraq had, by July 2009, also resulted in the deaths of at least one hundred and fifty thousand Iraqis—and probably many more—most of them civilians. More than a million people were displaced. The people of Iraq have suffered greatly.

(Iraq Inquiry 2016)

This appears to be an understatement. Not only were 179 British soldiers killed, along with 4,491 US troops, and many thousands more horribly wounded, but also, according to the most reliable estimates, the number of Iraqi lives lost as a result of the war stands at roughly half a million (Hagopian et al. 2013). By UN estimates, nearly 4 million more people were driven from their homes. The country remains embroiled in bloody sectarian conflict and extreme economic and social hardship.

Representing the interests of the ruling establishment, the report by Lord Chilcot and a committee of fellow Privy Counsellors carefully avoided accusing Blair and other government leaders, as well as the military and intelligence chiefs, of any conscious deception that could inform criminal charges. But among Blair's acts of duplicity were listed the following.

- In July 2002, 'Mr Blair told President Bush that the UN was the simplest way to encapsulate a "casus belli" in some defining way, with an ultimatum to Iraq once military forces started to build up in October. That might be backed by a UN resolution' (Chilcot 2016: executive summary, 16).
- 'The Assessments issued by the Joint Intelligence Committee (JIC) reflected the uncertainties within the intelligence community about the detail of Iraq's activities' (Chilcot 2016: executive summary, 115).

- 'The statements prepared for, and used by, the UK Government in public from late 2001 onwards conveyed more certainty than the JIC Assessments about Iraq's proscribed activities and the potential threat they posed' (Chilcot 2016: executive summary, 115).
- 'The tendency to refer in public statements only to Iraq's "weapons of mass destruction" was likely to have created the impression that Iraq posed a greater threat than the detailed JIC Assessments would have supported' (Chilcot 2016: executive summary, 116).
- The government's 'dossier', published in September 2002 to try to counter public opposition to the war, 'was designed to "make the case" and secure Parliamentary and public support for the Government's position that action was urgently required to secure Iraq's disarmament' (Chilcot 2016: executive summary, 116).
- 'The assessed intelligence had not established beyond doubt either that Saddam Hussein had continued to produce chemical and biological weapons or that efforts to develop nuclear weapons continued' (Chilcot 2016: executive summary, 116).
- In relation to the formal advice issued by Attorney-General Lord Goldsmith, in March 2003, on the legality of the war, 'Cabinet was not provided with written advice which set out, as the advice of 7 March had done, the conflicting arguments regarding the legal effect of [UN Security Council] resolution 1441 and whether, in particular, it authorised military action without a further resolution of the Security Council' (Chilcot 2016: executive summary, 120).

No one was held to account for these decisions. Despite its whitewash character, however, the Chilcot Inquiry represented an indictment of the predatory policy pursued in the name of US and British imperialism, and by US and British partners, in the Middle East since 2000. The catastrophes inflicted on Afghanistan, Iraq, Libya and Syria served only to strengthen sectarianism and Islamic fundamentalism.

Significantly, the Chilcot findings included previously secret memos from Blair to Bush (those sent from Bush to Blair were kept secret at Washington's request), which show that the real motive behind the war was not the threat of WMDs or terrorism, but global domination. Within days of the invasion, Blair exulted in the act of military aggression, declaring it a chance to establish 'the true post-Cold War world order', and he added: 'That's why, though Iraq's WMD is the immediate justification for action, ridding Iraq of Saddam is the real prize' (Chilcot 2016: vol. 9, 139).

The Nuremberg Trials convened following World War II were unequivocal in their principal conclusion: the use of war to achieve political ends that cannot be justified by imminent threat of attack constitutes the most heinous of war crimes. By this standard, Bush, Blair and their associates are war criminals, no less than the Nazi defendants who were sentenced to death by hanging.

Moreover, the collapse of the reasons used to justify the invasion of Iraq—'weapons of mass destruction', supposed nuclear war capacity and Saddam

Hussein's alleged links to terrorism backed by Al Qaeda—indicate that lies were told to divert attention away from the real motives of the 'war on terror'. As discussed in the Introduction, the attacks on New York and Washington of 11 September 2001 (that is, 9/11) provided the pretext for the implementation of plans prepared much earlier—during the 1990s—for the conquest of Afghanistan and Iraq, key strategic locations near the largest proven concentrations of oil and natural gas reserves in the world.

The Chilcot Inquiry's failure, as intended by the Brown government, to hold Prime Minister Blair or anyone else to account for the lies, war crimes, deaths and devastation caused by the war had been foreshadowed in 2004. A group of members of Parliament (MPs) attempted to bring impeachment proceedings against Blair for his conduct in the Iraq War. The motion for impeachment was drafted and tabled for debate in November 2004, but the three main parties— Labour, Conservative and Liberal Democrats—joined forces to forbid MPs from signing the motion and it was never selected for debate (Joseph 2013: 91). This outcome was a revealing demonstration of the readiness of legislative bodies to block political challenges to war-making.

Deception and war propaganda

Both the Vietnam and Iraq experiences raise wider questions about the use of official and media deception and propaganda to mislead, confuse and disorient the population for the purposes of overcoming opposition to going to war. Such concerted propaganda campaigns, involving governments, the military and intelligence agencies, as well as corporate media outlets, also seek to ensure congressional or parliamentary approval of executive war-making decisions. These manipulative operations expose the fig leaf of democracy, under cover of which the executive supposedly acts in the name of the people and is accountable to them via elected legislatures.

Several detailed academic studies have systematically refuted the conclusions reached by the Chilcot Inquiry, and earlier official reports, that the Blair government was not guilty of conscious deception in joining the 2003 US-led invasion of Iraq. It is beyond the scope of this volume to review all the official reports and academic literature. However, three rigorous works by British scholars Eric Herring and Piers Robinson established conclusively that the Blair government, acting in close collaboration with the George W. Bush administration, conducted an intensive campaign of deliberate deception and misleading propaganda for more than a year, which campaign included mis-stating, manipulating or doctoring intelligence reports, in an effort to overcome popular and international opposition to the conquest of Iraq. The official 'dossiers' produced in Washington and London to justify the 2003 invasion were designed and intended to mislead, alarm and agitate public opinion, not to provide honest, accurate or complete information (Herring and Robinson 2014a, 2014b; Robinson 2017).

Herring and Robinson listed multiple inquiries that examined these questions (House of Commons Foreign Affairs Select Committee 2003; Intelligence and Security Committee 2003; Hutton Inquiry 2004; Butler Inquiry 2004; Chilcot 2016), as well as a number of academic studies. One threshold weakness common to these examinations was a failure to place the intelligence and political record in context. By contrast, Herring and Robinson, first of all, drew on previous studies to document the fact that the policy of removing Iraqi President Saddam Hussein from power had been a component of conservative US thinking throughout the 1990s and that the terrorist attacks of 9/11 provided an opportunity to realise these aspirations.

In the immediate aftermath of 9/11, some in the Bush administration advocated attacking Iraq. However, the Bush administration decided to invade Afghanistan first. From late 2001, however, effecting regime change in Iraq through military force was back on the agenda. Leaked British documents from March 2002 show that the British government told the US government that it backed regime change through military force, but would need a strategy to sell military action to the public, the press and Parliament by wrong-footing Iraq on weapons inspections. It would also need a public document to help to make the case on the basis of disarming Iraq of WMDs. By late July, the internal British assessment of the US position was that war was inevitable. However, because of public opposition, the Blair government was anxious to secure at least a semblance of UN Security Council authorisation to buttress the claim that the war was legal. It also faced greater public pressure to justify any military action. This contributed to an emphasis on imminent threat from chemical weapons (Herring and Robinson 2014a: 559–60).

For their analysis of what then unfolded, Herring and Robinson employed a conceptual approach that distinguished between non-deceptive and deceptive persuasion campaigns. As they explained, the terms 'organised political persuasion' (OPP) or 'organised persuasive communication' (OPC) had been developed to capture the essence of an array of euphemisms used to describe persuasion and influence campaigns. These included words and phrases such as 'propaganda', 'public relations' (PR), 'strategic communication', 'political communication', 'public diplomacy', 'psychological operations' (pys ops), 'perception management' and 'information management'.

Their analysis drew upon academic literature on deception, propaganda and persuasion. It distinguished between non-deceptive and deceptive persuasive communication through the use of the categories of *deception through lying* ('making a statement one knows or suspects to be untrue in order to mislead'), *deception through omission* ('withholding information to make the viewpoint being promoted more persuasive') and *deception through distortion* ('framing a statement in a deliberately misleading way to support the viewpoint being promoted').

Alternatively, *non-deceptive* OPC referred to persuasion conducted honestly and with no effort to deceive—in particular, by avoiding, lies, distortion and omissions. Herring and Robinson employed the widespread and common definition of the term 'propaganda' as a form of manipulative persuasion that violates rational or free will. They noted that not all propaganda involves deception; other forms include communicative strategies involving incentivisation and coercion (Robinson 2017: 49–50).

From February 2002, internal discussions began in the Blair government about the need to prepare a dossier, ostensibly drawn from classified intelligence material, to provide the pretext for joining the planned US invasion of Iraq. For several months, work on the dossier and the strategy of publishing intelligence to mobilise public opinion continued, in both Britain and the United States. On 23 April, Alastair Campbell, Prime Minister Blair's director of strategy and communications, met with Sir John Scarlett, chair of the Joint Intelligence Committee (JIC), 'to go through what we needed to do communications wise to set the scene for Iraq, e.g., a WMD paper and other papers about Saddam' (quoted in Herring and Robinson 2014a: 563). On 8 May, Bush commissioned the CIA White Paper that would ultimately be published in October 2002, titled *Iraq's Weapons of Mass Destruction Programs*—the White House equivalent of the Blair government's dossier.

A memo from Jonathan Powell, Blair's chief of staff, dated 19 July, reiterated the need to construct a legal and public case for war based on alleged Iraqi WMDs:

> We need to establish a *legal base*. More difficult for us than for them [the United States]. It needs to be based on WMD rather than terrorism or regime change . . . We need to *make the case*. We need a plan and a timetable for releasing papers we have prepared on human rights abuses, WMD etc. We need to have the sort of Rolls Royce information campaign we had at the end of Afghanistan before we start in Iraq.
>
> (Herring and Robinson 2014a: 564, emphasis original)

Herring and Robinson concluded that this proposed 'Rolls Royce' campaign was not about informing the public about a serious threat posed by WMDs or about responding to a public clamour for information; rather, it was about presenting a defensible rationale for war as part of a campaign of organised political persuasion. By late July, the prime minister's office was being briefed that US military action was inevitable, even though existing intelligence on Iraq fell far short of establishing either that there was a significant threat from Iraqi WMDs or that Iraq was in clear breach of UN resolutions. To overcome this problem, a White House Information Group was formed in August to coordinate a media campaign regarding Iraqi WMDs. Documents released in Britain show the continued drafting of intelligence material, as well as coordination with the United States. They include an email dated 9 August from a Defence Intelligence Staff (DIS) official, who wrote 'further to your request to make the public paper more exciting and/or more like the slightly iffy claims about big buildings in [REDACTED] please see the following' (quoted in Herring and Robinson 2014a: 564–65).

This email confirms that the government asked the intelligence agencies to 'sex up' the material in order to deceive the public. On 4 September, John Williams, Foreign and Commonwealth Office (FCO) Head of Communications, wrote a memo titled 'Iraq Media Strategy', setting out the work that needed to be done:

The media siege should now be challenged regularly by the Prime Minister and the Foreign Secretary: to reinforce the broad case, so that it strikes a chord with more and more people, as opposed to journalists; and to create the right environment for the dossier . . . The tone of the launch will be critical . . . Our target is not the argumentative interviewer or opinionated columnist, but the kind of people to whom ministerial interviewers are a background hum on the car or kitchen radio.

(Quoted in Herring and Robinson 2014a: 565)

Williams acknowledged the weakness of the dossier in relation to this task:

The evidence dossier is unlikely to be enough . . . to win the argument . . . There is no 'killer fact' . . . that 'proves' that Saddam must be taken on now, or this or that weapon will be used against us.

(Herring and Robinson 2014a: 565).

For this reason, the Labour government set about concocting a scare campaign, featuring a false claim (regarded by the DIS as old and dubious) that Iraq could launch WMDs within 45 minutes of an order being given. Although received from an established source, the claim was subsourced and had been deemed unreliable in 2004. The report containing the 45-minute claim was vague and warranted little prominence in a JIC assessment dated 9 September. Despite this, it ended up in the executive summary of the dossier, and it was highlighted in Blair's Foreword and his statement to the House of Commons on 24 September. Throughout the drafting of the dossier, objections had been raised by DIS officials over the strength of the wording attached to the 45-minute claim. One such official stated: 'I have been making this point in comments on every draft of the dossier . . . but we are just being ignored.' At a drafting meeting on 17 September, DIS analysts challenged the prominence of the 45-minute claim and restated the fact that there was no firm evidence that Iraq was producing, or even had available, chemical weapons (Herring and Robinson 2014a: 574–75).

In his statement to the House of Commons on 24 September, Prime Minister Blair nevertheless repeated his assertions of certainty about Iraq's continued WMD production:

His [Saddam's] WMD programme is active, detailed and growing . . . It [the dossier] concludes that Iraq has chemical and biological weapons, that Saddam has continued to produce them . . . On chemical weapons, the dossier shows that Iraq continues to produce chemical agent for chemical weapons . . . In respect of biological weapons, again production of biological agents has continued.

(Herring and Robinson 2014a: 579)

None of these statements accurately reflected the available intelligence. Even before the Chilcot Inquiry, Herring and Robinson (2014a: 579–80) concluded:

In stark contrast to the claims by Blair and Campbell set out at the start of the paper, the dossier published in September 2002 was not an accurate reflection of the available intelligence penned by the intelligence services, designed only to inform public understanding. The dossier presented, in quite dramatic terms, the claims that Iraq was actively producing WMD, that they could be launched within 45 minutes of an order to do so, and that the intelligence was 'beyond doubt' . . . That the dossier ended up presenting such an inaccurate picture was not due to errors in the drafting process, but because it was the core component of a campaign of deceptive organized political persuasion which involved communications officials working closely with politicians and intelligence officials. As documented here, this campaign involved presenting the intelligence on Iraqi WMD in such threatening terms that it would serve to persuade and mobilize support. Hence, distortion of the intelligence was intentional. Contrary to the findings of the official inquiries to date, this study shows that the campaign involved deceptive organized political persuasion in which deception through distortion and omission occurred.

After the release of the Chilcot report, Robinson (2017) concluded that it confirmed that the Iraq dossier was the end product of a lengthy process designed to 'prepare' public opinion for military action in Iraq. Following President Bush's 'axis of evil' State of the Union Address on 30 January 2002, when Bush identified North Korea, Iran and Iraq as key threats as a result of their alleged sponsorship of terrorism and WMDs, Blair commissioned a set of papers on WMD proliferation in February 2002. Robinson cited an early memo from Williams, the FCO official, dated March 2002, in which Williams described the government's strategy as follows:

> The process of preparing media and public opinion for possible action on Iraq is underway . . .
>
> [. . .]
>
> We should exploit this interest by feeding newspapers and broadcasters with information on WMD, diversion of imports for military use, and human rights abuse: all of it presented as evidence from the Government's forthcoming dossier. By doing so, we can build momentum.
>
> (Chilcot 2016: vol. 4, 77–78)

In March 2002, a leaked 'Options Paper' on Iraq stated that UK policy was to 're-integrate a law-abiding Iraq which does not possess WMD or threaten its neighbours', but that this 'implicitly . . . cannot occur with Saddam Hussein in power' (quoted in Robinson 2017: 57). It concluded that 'the use of overriding force in a ground campaign is the only option that we can be confident to remove Saddam'. Sent only to some members of Blair's cabinet, the Options Paper indicated the emergence of a regime-change policy as the only way of dealing with Iraq. As Robinson (2017: 57, emphasis original) noted: 'Because of the way in which some members of the Cabinet, and indeed the public, were kept in the dark about its existence, it can be understood as an instance of *deception through omission.*'

Further important evidence that regime change, not disarmament, was the British government's goal comes in the form of a memo sent by Blair to his adviser Jonathan Powell in March 2002. In this memo, Blair acknowledged that the 'immediate WMD problems don't seem obviously worse than 3 years ago', then went on to discuss other justifications for action:

> So we have to re-order our story and message. Increasingly, I think it should be about the nature of the regime. We do intervene—as per the Chicago speech. We have no inhibitions—where we reasonably can—about nation-building i.e. we must come to our conclusion on Saddam from our own position.
>
> (Quoted in Robinson 2017: 57)

Robinson (2017: 58) noted that the Chilcot report continued to 'paint a picture of regime change being pursued whilst misleadingly presenting UK strategy as based on the objective of disarmament and maintaining that there was a realistic possibility of a peaceful outcome via Iraqi compliance'. But further records cited by the Chilcot report show that Blair and his advisers cynically sought to use the United Nations, and demands for UN-mandated inspections in Iraq, as a cover for joining a US invasion to overthrow the Iraqi government, occupy the country and install a new regime. Powell's advice to Blair in late July 2002 was explicit:

> I think we need a road map to getting rid of Saddam, drawing parallels as far as possible with his [President Bush's] success in Afghanistan, including the following elements: We will be there when the US takes the decision to act, but . . . We need to set an ultimatum as we did to the Taliban in Afghanistan. At a certain point we need to make it clear that unless Saddam agrees to inspectors on our terms—anyone, any time, anywhere—by a certain date we will act. We need to establish a legal basis. More difficult for us than for them. It needs to be based on WMD rather than terrorism or regime change . . .
>
> We need to make the case. We need a plan and a timetable for releasing the papers we have prepared on human rights abuses, WMD etc. We need to have the sort of Rolls Royce information campaign we had at the end of Afghanistan before we start in Iraq. We need a convincing military plan. What we know about so far is not convincing . . . And we need a plan for the day after . . . We need to be working on this now.
>
> (Quoted in Robinson 2017: 59)

Following this, Blair communicated his support directly to Bush. On 28 July 2002, he sent a note that started, 'I will be with you, whatever' (Robinson 2017: 59). The note said that getting rid of Saddam was the 'right thing to do', but that political support was weak. Blair set out the advantages of developing the UN route to create a *casus belli* by issuing Iraq with an ultimatum that Saddam would be unlikely to be able to satisfy. In a section of the note headed 'UN', Blair wrote:

> But we need, as with Afghanistan and the ultimatum to the Taleban, to encapsulate our casus belli in some defining way. This (the UN) is certainly the simplest. We could, in October as the build up starts, state that he must let the inspectors back in unconditionally and do so now, i.e. set a 7-day deadline. It might be backed by a UNSCR [UN Security Council Resolution] or not . . . I know there will be reluctance to this. But it would neutralize opposition around the UN issue. If he did say yes, we continue the build-up and we send teams over and the moment he obstructs, we say: he's back to his games. That's it. In any event, he probably would screw it up and not meet the deadline, and if he came forward after the deadline, we would just refuse to deal.
>
> (Quoted in Robinson 2017: 59)

Having advocated the use of the United Nations as a way of creating a war trigger, with no indication that there was any hope or expectation that this might lead to a peaceful resolution resulting from Iraqi compliance, Blair finished by suggesting an optimal date for an invasion: 'We would support in any way we can . . . On timing, we could start building up after the break. A strike date could be Jan/Feb next year. But the crucial issue is not when, but how' (quoted in Robinson 2017: 59).

The studies published by Herring and Robinson provided comprehensive empirical evidence that the British government pursued strategies of deception, acting in concert with the US administration, during the year leading up to the March 2003 invasion of Iraq. On 'weapons of mass destruction', a pattern of distortions and omissions fed official claims that went beyond the available intelligence. For political and legal purposes, the government also misleadingly claimed to make a genuine attempt at securing peaceful disarmament. Inside the political establishment, it was routinely acknowledged that the intelligence was weak, that Iraq was not an immediate threat, and that the 'UN route' was expected and intended to fail. As Robinson (2017: 68) noted, comments in the documentary evidence—such as 'obscuring the fact that Iraq was not the most serious WMD threat', going the UN route for 'optical reasons' and the need to 'appear reluctant to use force'—all indicate an intention to disguise the reality of what was going on.

Robinson concluded that, although avoiding deception through lying, officials were engaged in deception through exaggeration and omission. Chilcot, apparently working with a narrow definition of deception only in terms of lying (that is, telling falsehoods), thereby excluded deception via omission and distortion, absolving Blair of dishonesty. However, the evidence clearly shows Blair and officials working hard to manipulate public perceptions of both Iraqi WMD capability and threat, as well as the real purpose of the UN route. These manipulations involved deception via distortion/exaggeration and omission (Robinson 2017: 68).

Broader conclusions about the 'war on terror'

As Robinson (2017: 69) further concluded, section 3.1 of the Chilcot report 'provides highly significant new evidence regarding the "War on Terror" itself'. Robinson's analysis of section 3.1 pointed toward the underlying geo-strategic factors that drove the decision to invade Iraq, including the installation of a new regime and access to the country's oil wealth.

Section 3.1 provided indications of both the breadth and depth of the 'war on terror' and its geo-strategic objectives, both in the Middle East and more widely. First, it confirmed that the plans for invading Iraq were under way, on both sides of the Atlantic, even before the 9/11 terrorist attacks in New York and Washington. The Chilcot report cited a British embassy report from before 9/11 that noted 'the growing pressure to change course from containment to military action to oust Saddam Hussein' (Chilcot 2016: vol. 1, 318). This was in line with the US Iraq Liberation Act of 1998, which had made Saddam's removal official US policy.

Following 9/11, the removal of Saddam Hussein became a top priority. The Chilcot report quoted from the diary of Blair's adviser Alastair Campbell about a meeting on 20 September 2001 between Bush and Blair in which the focus on Afghanistan was emphasised, but Bush 'also talked about how they could go after Saddam's oilfields' (Chilcot 2016: vol. 1, 328). By mid-November 2001, Jonathan Powell advised Blair that 'only the removal of Saddam Hussein and a new regime would deal with the risks from Iraq' (Chilcot 2016: vol. 1, 345). In late November, a memo titled 'Iraq: Change of Heart or Change of Regime' specified UK objectives as 'the removal of Saddam and replacement by a new, more moderate regime'. This was to be achieved by the 'US, UK and others' setting 'up a UN 'demand for the return of inspectors', to be followed by 'a military plan, and if Saddam failed to meet the demands, there would be grounds to go ahead with the military plan' (the memo making reference to a possible coup). The memo outlined that the plan would be '[s]upported by air power and a small number of Special Forces in support roles', and that there was a '[n]eed to be clear with everyone that this time we are going all the way' (Chilcot 2016: vol. 1, 357).

Powell advised that officials should not publicly acknowledge that regime change was the goal; rather, that they should acknowledge that 'regime change would be desirable, but [is] not our formal objective for the moment'. He also stated that if 'Saddam did allow the inspectors in, there would be a "need to find a new demand to justify military action"' (Chilcot 2016: vol. 1, 357). Likewise, in a telephone conversation between Bush and Blair on 3 December 2001, Blair said first that 'it would be excellent to get rid of Saddam. But there needed to be a clever strategy for doing this', then repeated that he was 'not opposed to action against Saddam. But an extremely clever plan would be required' (Chilcot 2016: vol. 1, 367–68).

Blair detailed the elements of this 'clever plan' in a memo to Bush dated 4 December 2001. Blair wrote of a 'strategy for regime change that builds over time', involving 'softening up first' via demanding the return of weapons inspectors, and implying that military action would follow if Saddam were to fail to comply, as well as that the United States and Britain would engage in a raft of strategies aimed at weakening the regime. These included enforcing existing no-fly zones on 'a more intensive basis', supporting opposition groups, mounting 'covert operations with people and groups with the ability to topple Saddam', and backing any emerging rebellions. Blair summed up his covert action plan as follows:

> So: my strategy is to build this over time until we get to the point where military action could be taken if necessary: but meanwhile bring people toward us, undermine Saddam, without so alarming people about the immediacy of action that we frighten the horses, lose Russia and/or half the EU and nervous Arab states and find ourselves facing a choice between massive intervention or nothing.
>
> (Robinson 2017: 65)

Further information in section 3.1 of the Chilcot report indicated a much wider geo-strategic policy involving a belligerent strategy aimed at coercing 'enemy' states, including those uninvolved with Islamic fundamentalist terrorism. A cable sent by the British embassy noted that some in the US administration were seeking to concoct a 'war on terror' to pursue other objectives. Dated 15 September 2001, four days after 9/11, the cable stated: 'The "regime-change hawks" in Washington are arguing that a coalition put together for one purpose [against international terrorism] could be used to clear up other problems in the region' (Chilcot 2016: vol. 1, 324).

A 20 September 2001 note from Blair to Bush indicated that action was being planned against multiple countries. The British prime minister advised the US president to 'take our time to see whether we could build up the case against Iraq or other countries before acting' (Chilcot 2016: vol. 1, 327). Blair saw 9/11 as an opportunity to reshape the region and the entire world in the interests of the Western powers. The Chilcot report quoted the following line from his 2 October speech at the 2001 Labour Party conference: 'This is a moment to seize. The kaleidoscope has been shaken. The pieces are in flux. Soon they will settle again. Before they do, let us re-order this world around us' (Chilcot 2016: vol. 1, 335). Equally revealing was the 4 December 2001 memo from Blair to Bush in which Blair discussed the Middle East Peace Process (MEPP) and stated that '[t]he Middle East is set for catastrophe', before noting that the MEPP needs to be put back on track otherwise it will 'complicate everything in the Middle East for a wider struggle' (quoted in Robinson 2017: 65–66).

This indicates that a wider conflict was being prepared. On 17 September 2001, there was already discussion of 'Phase 2' of the 'war on terrorism', in which targets would be broadened out from the 'Phase 1' focus on Afghanistan and Osama Bin Laden. Blair's 4 December 2001 memo, titled 'The War against Terrorism: The Second Phase', discussed a total of seven countries—Iraq,

Philippines, Syria, Iran, Yemen, Somalia and Indonesia—and specifically identified Iran and Syria as targets for military action. Blair stated: 'If toppling Saddam is a prime objective, it is far easier to do it with Syria and Iran in favour or acquiescing rather than hitting all three at once' (Robinson 2017: 66).

Blair told Bush it was imperative to hide or camouflage the broader war aims and to conduct a significant propaganda campaign to deceive the public, as well as other governments. In a memo to Bush dated 11 October 2001, under the heading 'Extending War Aims', Blair wrote:

> [W]e know what you want; you can do it; but not whilst you are bombing Afghanistan. The uncertainty caused by Phase 2 seeming to extend to Iraq, Syria etc is really hurting them because it seems to confirm the UBL [Usama bin Laden] propaganda that this is West vs. Arab. I have no doubt we need to deal with Saddam. But if we hit Iraq now, we would lose the Arab world, Russia, probably half the EU and my fear is the impact of all that on Pakistan. However, I am sure we can devise a strategy for Saddam deliverable at a later date. My suggestion is, in order to give ourselves space that we say: Phase 1 is the military action focused on Afghanistan because it's where the perpetrators of 11 September hide. Phase 2 is the medium and longer-term campaign against terrorism in all its forms . . . We just don't need it debated too freely in public until we know what exactly we want to do, and how we can do it.
>
> (Robinson 2017: 66–67)

In this letter to Bush, Blair summed up his advice as follows: 'We need a dedicated, tightly knit propaganda unit for the war generally and for the Arab and Moslem world in particular' (Robinson 2017: 67). Robinson's study of this material concluded:

> These propagandistic OPC strategies would appear to be only the end product of critical decisions and opportunities seized in the immediate aftermath of 9/11. It was in this period that the initial 'clever' plan was set out to remove Saddam Hussein through a process of 'softening up' and pushing the issue of weapons inspections and WMD. In this period both Blair and his advisor Manning expressly stated the need for a 'propaganda' campaign to cover phase 2 of the 'War on Terror'. Moreover, whilst the public and academic perception of the 'War on Terror' has largely remained focused upon an interpretation of a campaign aimed at tackling Islamic fundamentalism, the evidence from Chilcot indicates that, in addition, there was a broader geo-strategic vision/campaign formulated in the immediate aftermath of 9/11.
>
> (Robinson 2017: 68–69)

The documents cited by the Chilcot report raise crucial questions about the subsequent military operations conducted or backed by the United States and its allies throughout the Middle East and internationally. If the US and British governments sought to exploit the events of 9/11 to topple or weaken 'hostile' governments, what does that indicate about the ensuing conflicts in Libya, Syria and Yemen? Blair's 4 December 2001 memo to Bush, asserting that '[t] he Middle East is set for catastrophe', proved accurate. In the name of fighting terrorism, governments in Afghanistan, Iraq and Libya were overthrown, while Syria and Yemen became engulfed in protracted and destructive regime-change battles and wars. Hundreds of thousands of people have died or been maimed in these conflicts, millions have been uprooted and Europe faces its largest refugee crisis since World War II.

Implications for democracy

Even more broadly, the material produced by the Chilcot report demonstrates the depths and lengths to which Western governments—supposedly the leading democracies of the world—are prepared to go to manipulate their populations into supporting wars over regional and global hegemony. The 'close-knit propaganda campaign' that Blair canvassed with Bush in 2001 makes a mockery of basic democratic conceptions. Deception, as a political strategy, is incompatible with democracy. As Herring and Robinson (2014a: 582) pointed out:

[I]n situations where organized political persuasion leads to a point where the British Prime Minister makes statements that are untrue or misleading, it becomes much more difficult for meaningful debate to occur. When a Prime Minister is declaring in Parliament that he knows for sure, based upon intelligence, that WMD exist in Iraq, journalists are then under strong pressure to accept the claims being made.

After examining and analysing the Chilcot report, Robinson (2017: 70) suggested that 'perhaps only now that we are beginning to understand the geostrategic underbelly of this war and the scale of the propaganda exercise needed to mobilize public and political support', and that it is 'a matter of urgency that much greater intellectual attention is paid to these issues'.

At the same time, the very scale of the propaganda exercise undertaken to try to justify the Iraq War indicates the growing difficulties that the ruling elites are experiencing in overcoming popular opposition. Certainly, further rigorous research and greater circulation of its results to the world's people can contribute to the development of a mass global anti-war movement. Already, despite the official campaign of lies and fabrications, in February 2003, millions of people around the world were marching against the impending invasion of Iraq. But the bitter experiences of Vietnam and the Middle East demonstrate the necessity of developing an even greater, and more politically conscious, movement to go beyond mass protest to overturn the governments and the ruling establishments that are responsible for such barbaric military interventions and wars.

References

Chilcot, J. 2016. *The Report of the Iraq Inquiry*. London: HMSO.

CNN Wire Staff. 2011. 'Hundreds protest treatment of alleged WikiLeaks whistle-blower', 21 March, http://edition.cnn.com/2011/POLITICS/03/21/wikileaks. protest/ (accessed 21 May 2018).

Hagopian, A., Flaxman, A., Takaro, T., Al Shatari, S., Rajaratnam, J., Becker, S., . . . Burnham, G. 2013. 'Mortality in Iraq Associated with the 2003–2011 War and Occupation: Findings from a National Cluster Sample Survey by the University Collaborative Iraq Mortality Study', *PLoS Medicine*, 10(10): e1001533.

Herring, E., and Robinson, P. 2014a. 'Report X marks the spot: the British government's deceptive dossier on Iraq and WMD', *Political Science Quarterly*, 129(4): 551–84.

Herring, E., and Robinson, P. 2014b. 'Deception and Britain's road to war in Iraq', *International Journal of Contemporary Iraqi Studies*, 8(2): 213–23.

Iraq Inquiry. 2016. *'Sir John Chilcot's public statement'*, 6 July, www.iraqinquiry.org.uk/the-inquiry/sir-john-chilcots-public-statement/ (accessed 20 May 2018).

Joseph, R. 2013. *The War Prerogative: History Reform and Constitutional Design*. Oxford: Oxford University Press.

National Archives. 2011. *Pentagon Papers*, www.archives.gov/research/pentagon-papers (accessed 15 March 2016).

Robinson, P. 2017. 'Learning from the Chilcot Report: propaganda, deception and the "war on terror" ', *International Journal of Contemporary Iraqi Studies*, 11(1–2): 47–73.

Stone, G. 2004. *Perilous Times: Free Speech in Wartime*. New York: Norton.

3 Increasingly unrestrained war powers in the United States

From Truman to Trump

The United States, the predominant global power since World War II, provides the clearest and most consequential example of the erosion of any semblance of democratic control over war powers. Despite the US Constitution explicitly vesting the power to declare war in the hands of Congress—as a result of the American Revolution—every US president, since Harry Truman launched the three-year Korean War in 1950, has gone to war without congressional approval, let alone any popular vote.

Equally, the US experience demonstrates the futility of any perspective based on legislative control, or even restraint, of executive war powers. The assertion of imperial presidential authority has been accompanied and facilitated by the complicit surrender by Congress of the war-making power. It was only in 1973, after US forces had already killed millions of people in Korea and Indochina, that Congress even passed the War Powers Resolution, purporting to place some limits on presidential war-launching. It stated that only a congressional declaration of war, 'a national emergency created by attack upon the United States, its territories or possessions, or its armed forces', or 'specific statutory authorization' by Congress could legally sanction the deployment of the armed forces to any conflict. Without such sanction, presidential military deployments would be subject to a 60-day limit.

This was a largely token resolution, adopted in the face of massive rising opposition to the illegal wars in Vietnam, Cambodia and Laos. It was full of loopholes, effectively allowing presidents to trigger wars by claiming to be responding to an attack upon the United States, its territories or its armed forces. In terms of any congressional enforcement, the resolution soon proved toothless as well. Every president since has flouted the Act, with the willing acceptance of both the Democrats and Republicans in Congress, and has essentially insisted, in one way or another, that it is unconstitutional. Year after year, Congress has approved multibillion-dollar defence spending bills, permitting one president after another to assert congressional agreement with each US military intervention.

On one occasion, in 1983, a Democrat-controlled Congress set an 18-month time limit for US troops already deployed as a so-called peacekeeping force in Lebanon by President Ronald Reagan's Republican administration. But the limit was never tested. Within two weeks of the president signing that timeline measure into law, a suicide bomb destroyed the US Marine barracks in Beirut, killing 241 military personnel. The Reagan administration withdrew its participation in the multinational force in Lebanon by the end of March 1984 (Friedman 1984).

Only once, during the 1990–91 Persian Gulf crisis, has Congress insisted on debate and hearings before rubber-stamping a war. Still acutely aware of deep public antipathy to war in the wake of the Vietnam defeat, a bipartisan congressional front required President George H. W. Bush to present an Authorization for the Use of Military Force (AUMF) before invading Kuwait and Iraq. Even so, Bush attached a signing statement asserting that his 'request for congressional support did not . . . constitute any change in the long-standing position of the executive branch on . . . the constitutionality of the War Powers Resolution' (Elsea and Weed 2014: 13). In other words, the White House continued to assert its right to go to war without explicit congressional approval (Glennon 1991: 84–101; Zeisberg 2013: 14).

Since 2001, each administration has relied on two further AUMFs to initiate and extend a series of military interventions. In 2001, Congress's support for the expansion of presidential power was demonstrated by the overwhelming votes in both houses for the sweeping AUMF proposed by the George W. Bush administration just three days after the terrorist passenger plane attacks on New York's twin towers and the Pentagon of 11 September 2001 (9/11). Without asking or waiting for any evidence as to who was responsible for the attacks, Congress gave the president carte blanche to use 'necessary and appropriate force' against anyone he determined had 'planned, authorized, committed, or aided' the attacks, or 'to deter and preempt any future acts of terrorism or aggression against the United States'. The vote was 98–0 in the Senate and 420–1 in the House of Representatives. A sole Democrat dissented, along essentially tactical lines, warning against embarking on 'an open-ended war with neither an exit strategy nor a focused target'.

Likewise, in October 2002, in the lead-up to the US-led invasion of Iraq, Congress endorsed a second AUMF permitting President Bush to use the armed forces 'as he determines to be necessary and appropriate' to 'defend the national security of the United States against the continuing threat posed by Iraq; and enforce all relevant United Nations Security Council Resolutions regarding Iraq'.

The 2002 AUMF (formally, the Authorization for Use of Military Force against Iraq Resolution of 2002) was passed by a vote of 296–133 in the House of Representatives and by 77–23 in the Senate. It was based on a series of false assertions, including that Iraq's 'continuing to possess and develop a significant chemical and biological weapons capability' and 'actively seeking a nuclear weapons capability' posed a 'threat to the national security of the United States and international peace and security in the Persian Gulf region', and that Iraq had the 'capability and willingness to use weapons of mass destruction against other nations and its own people'.

Administrations have since exploited the 2001 and 2002 AUMFs to send military forces into a range of countries, including Afghanistan (again), Iraq (again), Syria, Libya and Niger.

The judiciary too has proven complicit in this process, helping to clear the path for unfettered US militarism. No court has upheld a challenge to presidential war-making, invariably upholding White House submissions to block or strike down suits for one reason or another. One example occurred in 1999 during the sustained US bombing of Serbia, which the Clinton administration conducted without any UN authorisation, on the pretext of protecting Kosovo's right to secede from the former Yugoslavia. A few legislators sued President Bill Clinton, charging that he had violated the 1973 War Powers Act by keeping combat soldiers in the field past 60 days. Clinton pronounced the Act 'constitutionally defective' and a federal district court in Washington, DC, agreed, quickly ruling in the president's favour. The US Court of Appeals for the District of Columbia upheld the decision and the Supreme Court refused to hear an appeal (*Campbell v. Clinton*, 203 F.3d 19 (D.C. Cir. 2000)).

The violation of the Constitution and overturning of democracy—even of the facade of congressional rule—reached new heights under President Barack Obama. Despite being at war for his entire two terms in office, including in Afghanistan, Iraq, Libya, Syria and Niger, Obama never once went to Congress for authorisation to use military force and he defended his orders for drone assassinations of US citizens as part of the prerogatives of the commander-in-chief.

Obama was elected in 2007 on the pretence of being an anti-war candidate, having opposed the catastrophic 2003 invasion of Iraq, as well as promising to be a president of hope and change. Instead, his White House not only sidelined Congress so that it could to US militarism, but also blocked every attempt by citizens to hold the government to account via the courts. In doing so, the Obama presidency cleared the path for the even greater unilateralism and aggression of President Donald Trump's reign.

The unlawfulness and anti-democratic character of the presidential arrogation of war powers has long been recognised in many legal, media and political circles, yet it has only mushroomed unabated. One US legal scholar noted:

> This type of presidential power is dangerous, especially when presidents act unilaterally, in secret, and on the basis of false, deceptive, and unreliable information. Beginning with President Truman's use of military force against North Korea in June 1950, presidents have systematically circumvented Congress, violated statutes and the Constitution, and undermined democratic government. Even before Truman, presidents invoked threats to national security—sometimes real, sometimes exaggerated—to justify emergency power.
>
> (Fisher 2013: ix)

These far-reaching processes cannot be explained by the personalities or party politics of the presidents and administrations involved. The wars, invasions and other military interventions that escalated under the cover of the indefinite 'war on terror' proclaimed by President George W. Bush in 2001 are the product of a protracted evolution of US imperialism, which announced itself in 1945 as the dominant global power by incinerating the populations of Hiroshima and Nagasaki with nuclear weapons, even though Japan was already about to surrender. The United States subsequently waged wars of staggering violence in North Korea and Vietnam, killing millions of people.

Since the dissolution of the Soviet Union in 1991, for all the promises of a new period of peace and prosperity, the United States has been engaged in virtually perpetual war, starting with the first Gulf War pulverisation of Iraq. The American ruling class, represented by Democratic and Republican administrations alike, has sought to offset its declining economic position in the affairs of world capitalism by force of arms, relying on the vast size of the US military machine. This strategy has produced a string of disastrous failures, from Afghanistan and Iraq to Libya and Syria, but this has only intensified Washington's efforts to shore up its international hegemony.

This trajectory has become so blatant that calls have been made in the media establishment for some legislative measures to rectify the illegality of the military operations, in response to mounting public concern and opposition to the military aggression and fear of another world war. On 22 October 2017, for example, the *New York Times* published an editorial titled 'America's Forever Wars', which began with a fairly accurate sketch of the expanding operations of the US military on every continent of the globe:

> The United States has been at war continuously since the attacks of 9/11 and now has just over 240,000 active-duty and reserve troops in at least 172 countries and territories. While the number of men and women deployed overseas has shrunk considerably over the past 60 years, the military's reach has not. American forces are actively engaged not only in the conflicts in Afghanistan, Iraq, Syria and Yemen that have dominated the news, but also in Niger and Somalia, both recently the scene of deadly attacks, as well as Jordan, Thailand and elsewhere.
>
> (Editorial Board 2017)

The editorial added the extraordinary fact that the Pentagon publicly listed as 'unknown' the countries in which 37,813 of its troops were deployed, apparently referring to special operations units assigned to secret wars being waged entirely behind the backs of the American people (Editorial Board 2017). In part, the editorial appeared to be a response to a public debate that erupted in the wake of the deaths, on 4 October 2017, of four US Special Forces troops in a firefight in Niger. The episode revealed that some 1,000 US troops were deployed in the landlocked West African nation, reportedly without the knowledge or approval of Congress and behind the backs of the American people.

The editorial lamented the failure of Congress to debate the United States' multiple ongoing wars and to 'put the war against the Islamic State, which has broad popular support but no congressional authorisation, on a firm legal footing' (Editorial Board 2017). In effect, the editorial proposed the passage of another AUMF. Both Trump and Obama claimed that the AUMFs passed in

2001 in the immediate aftermath of the 9/11 attacks and in 2002 in advance of the Iraqi invasion provided them with all the power they have needed to wage war virtually anywhere on the planet.

The invocation of these old resolutions has been used to override both the US Constitution, which declares that only Congress can declare war, and the 1973 War Powers Act, passed in the midst of the political crisis over the US debacle in Vietnam. The latter placed limits and timetables on interventions ordered by US presidents, requiring that they either receive congressional authorisation or be terminated, but neither Democrat nor Republican congressional leaderships have sought to enforce it. That, in itself, is a telling indication of the impotence or unwillingness of legislatures to challenge executive war powers, pointing toward the need for genuine democratic means of halting the increasingly unrestrained resort to war and of ending the economic system responsible for it.

Indeed, the invocation of the 2001 and 2002 AUMFs has become increasingly absurd. The Obama administration utilised these measures, supposedly authorising a war against Al Qaeda and Iraq to eliminate 'terrorists' and 'weapons of mass destruction', to justify interventions in Libya and Syria, in which Washington-backed militias linked to Al Qaeda and the so-called Islamic State (or ISIS) sought to overthrow secular Arab regimes that, like the one in Iraq, had nothing to do with 9/11.

In the 2017 Niger affair, the Democratic Party and the Republican Party again showed no interest in challenging the arrogation of dictatorial power to the presidency on the issue of war, and no significant section of Congress displayed any inclination to debate the matter. All members of Congress are well aware that, for America's financial oligarchy, global military aggression is a critical instrument in its drive to secure profits, markets and resources.

Traditional legal scholars insist that US presidents have at least some unilateral authority to respond to crises, even though the US Constitution does not expressly grant such power. However, even in these circles, there is disagreement over the scope of such power, as well as the circumstances in which genuine emergencies exist (Head 2016: 175–79). Advocates of sweeping presidential power contend that presidents have 'plenary', or absolute, powers in defending the nation. Others conclude that while presidents can initially act unilaterally, they should subsequently obtain retroactive congressional approval and be subject to judicial review. However, the historical record demonstrates that presidents have increasingly exceeded even the most expansive doctrine.

US post-war hegemony and the soaring profits of the military-industrial complex

No discussion of US war powers can realistically ignore the power of the financial corporate elites, whose interests in waging war are bound up with two major factors. First and foremost, the military supremacy of the United States since World War II has been an essential aspect of its global economic hegemony. The United States spends more on its military than the next eight countries combined—China, Saudi Arabia, Russia, Britain, India, France and Japan. It also devotes a larger share of its government spending to defence—about 16 per cent of all federal spending (Peter G. Peterson Foundation 2018).

One *New York Times* columnist, Thomas L. Friedman, then an adviser to US Secretary of State Madeleine Albright, expressed the relationship between military power, economic domination and profit interests crudely in the *New York Times Magazine* at the end of 1999:

> The hidden hand of the market will never work without a hidden fist. McDonald's cannot flourish without McDonnell Douglas, the designer of the U.S. Air Force F-15. And the hidden fist that keeps the world safe for Silicon Valley's technologies to flourish is called the U.S. Army, Air Force, Navy and Marine Corps.
>
> (Friedman 1999)

Those words subsequently appeared in Friedman's 2000 book *The Lexus and the Olive Tree*, but the passage first surfaced, slightly edited, in the magazine. Filling almost its entire cover, a red-white-and-blue fist was captioned 'What the World Needs Now', the explanation in smaller type reading: 'For globalism to work, America can't be afraid to act like the almighty superpower that it is.' By the time the magazine reached the news-stands, US-led North Atlantic Treaty Organization (NATO) air attacks on Yugoslavia were under way, launching a bombing campaign that would last for 78 days.

The waning of the unchallenged economic dominance of the United States since the 1970s and the rise of new rivals, such as China, has intensified the drive by successive administrations—particularly those of George W. Bush, Barack Obama and Donald Trump—to escalate US militarism and preparations for war.

As discussed in the Introduction, the Trump administration's *National Defense Strategy* (NDS), released in 2018, signalled preparations for military confrontation with Russia and China, as well as the 'rogue states' of Iran and North Korea. It accused China of seeking 'Indo-Pacific regional hegemony in the near-term and displacement of the United States to achieve global preeminence in the future' (US Department of Defense 2018: 2).

'Great power competition—not terrorism—is now the primary focus of US national security', said US Secretary of Defense James Mattis in a speech that accompanied the release of an 11-page declassified document outlining the NDS in broad terms. A lengthier classified version was submitted to Congress, which included the Pentagon's detailed proposals for a massive increase in military spending.

Mattis insisted that the United States was facing a 'growing threat from revisionist powers as different as China and Russia, nations that seek to create a world consistent with their authoritarian models'.

The NDS summary document accused China of seeking 'Indo-Pacific regional hegemony in the near-term and displacement of the United States to achieve global preeminence in the future' (US Department of Defense 2018: 2).

It stated: 'China is a strategic competitor using predatory economics to intimidate its neighbors while militarizing features in the South China Sea.' Moreover, 'Russia has violated the borders of nearby nations and pursues veto power over the economic, diplomatic, and security decisions of its neighbors' (US Department of Defense 2018: 1).

A secondary, but interrelated, factor is the inexorable rise of the war-related sections of the American capitalist elite. As noted in the Introduction to this volume, more than 55 years ago, US President Dwight D. Eisenhower, who had been a five-star general during World War II, used his farewell address to the nation on 17 January 1961 to warn of the unprecedented power of what he termed the military-industrial complex. That 'complex' has magnified vastly since 1961, with Wall Street investing huge sums of money in the armaments industry.

During the first nine months of 2017, for example, the Standard & Poor's (S&P) Aerospace and Defense Industry subsector index climbed 31.5 per cent, in comparison with a rise of 12.9 per cent in the S&P index as a whole. This surge in the stock value of the weapons industry—at a pace two-and-a-half times that of the rest of the market—was an indicator of the profits being made, and anticipated, in the war industries. At the top of the list in growth were large companies such as Lockheed Martin, Northrop Grumman, Boeing and Raytheon. These companies remain responsible for the most-used and deadliest weapons of the US arsenal, including F-16 and F-22 fighter planes, B-2 bombers and Patriot missiles, as well as the lesser-known ammunitions, high-tech communication devices and vehicles essential for modern warfare.

Raytheon, the largest producer of guided missiles, was typical of the group, its stock price up 32 per cent during that period. That acceleration was part of a steep five-year climb in growth, trebling its stock price between 2013 and 2017. The growth in military industry stocks reflected the growth of US arms spending, as well as growing sales to allies such as Saudi Arabia, Germany and Japan, which were all making moves to increase their defence budgets and relied heavily on US armaments.

Roughly 10 per cent of the US$2.2 trillion in annual factory output in the United States goes into the production of weapons, sold mainly to the US Department of Defense for use by the armed forces (Uchitelle 2017).

The role of Congress in supporting militarism was underscored in 2018 when a bipartisan Republican–Democrat agreement called for $716 billion in military spending for that fiscal year—an increase of $80 billion. The military would get an additional increase of $85 billion in fiscal year 2019, as well as $140 billion in off-budget funding over the two-year period for 'overseas contingencies', such as the wars in Afghanistan, Iraq and Syria. The combined total fell short of the Obama administration's post-Cold-War peak of $691 billion in fiscal year 2010, which included $163 billion in war spending (Bloomberg 2018).

Under the agreement, missile defence spending would increase about 25 per cent over the Obama administration's last projected numbers for fiscal 2019, to $9.92 billion—that is, $1.91 billion more than previously planned. The increase would bankroll 20 new interceptor missiles and silos, a new 'homeland defence radar' in Hawaii and, for the first time, a 'salvo' test to fire two interceptors at once at an incoming target. According to Bloomberg (2018): 'The top contractors that would benefit from the proposed increase in missile-defense spending are Boeing, Raytheon Co., Orbital ATK Inc., Northrop Grumman, Lockheed and Aerojet Rocketdyne Holdings Inc.'

In relation to war planes, President Trump's plan called 24 Boeing Co. F/A-18E/F Super Hornet jets to be added in fiscal year 2019 and 110 jets through to 2023. The Pentagon requested funding for 77 F-35s for fiscal year 2019—three fewer than projected in the last Obama plan. The Trump plan projected 84 of the fighters for fiscal year 2020—the same as the last Obama plan—and 98 in 2021—that is, one fewer than under Obama. In addition, the US Air Force plans $16.8 billion in funding through to 2023 for the new B-21 bomber being built by Northrop Grumman Corporation, while the US Navy's five-year ship building plan called for 111 new vessels by 2023. As Bloomberg (2018) noted: 'The Navy's $58.5 billion fiscal 2019 procurement plan would benefit shipbuilders General Dynamics Corp., Huntington Ingalls Industries Inc. and combat system suppliers Raytheon, Lockheed and BAE Systems PLC.'

Constitutional conflicts

From World War II onward, presidents clearly have exceeded constitutional and statutory authority in exercising the war power. On the basis of the American Revolution to overthrow British colonial rule, the US Constitution expressly rejected the British model, which positioned exclusive authority over external affairs to the executive, and assigned the war-making power solely to Congress.

Debates at the Philadelphia Convention on 17 August 1787 underscored the determination of those drafting the Constitution to reject the British model. On the motion to vest in Congress the power to 'make war', Charles Pinckney suggested it would be better to vest that power in the Senate, it 'being more acquainted with foreign affairs, and most capable of proper resolutions' (Fisher 2013: 261). James Madison and Elbridge Gerry moved to insert 'declare' instead of 'make', leaving to the president 'the power to repel sudden attacks'. Roger Sherman remarked that the president 'shd. be able to repel and not to commence war'. Gerry said that he 'never expected to hear in a republic a motion to empower the Executive alone to declare war'. And George Mason was 'agst giving the power of war to the Executive, because not to be trusted with it . . . He was for clogging rather than facilitating war; but for facilitating peace' (Fisher 2013: 261).

The Madison–Gerry amendment passed. At the Pennsylvania ratifying convention, James Wilson expressed the prevailing view that the American system of checks and balances:

> . . . will not hurry us into war; it is calculated to guard against it. It will not be in the power of a single man, or a single body of men, to involve us in such distress; for the important power of declaring war is vested in the legislature at large.

> (Fisher 2013: 261)

Initiatives by President Abraham Lincoln at the start of the Civil War are at times cited to claim that, in a time of emergency, the president is empowered to invoke powers normally accorded to Congress. When Congress assembled in special session on 4 July 1861, however, Lincoln claimed neither exclusive or inherent powers nor executive prerogative. Instead, he admitted that he had used the powers of Congress: 'It is believed that nothing has been done beyond the constitutional competency of Congress.' In essence, he said that he had exceeded his powers and invaded those of Congress. For that reason, Lincoln asked lawmakers to pass legislation authorising what he had done. A bill providing retroactive authority for Lincoln's actions became law on 6 August 1861 (Fisher 2013: 264).

In 1966, in a bid to defend the presidential war power, the US State Department claimed that, since the adoption of the Constitution 'there have been at least 125 instances in which the President has ordered the armed forces to take action or maintain positions abroad without obtaining prior congressional authorization, starting with the "undeclared war" with France (1798–1800)' (Wormuth and Firmage 1989: 144). However, President John Adams did not assert that he could, on his own, go to war against France; rather, he urged Congress to pass 'effectual measures of defense' (Fisher 2013: 261). Congress passed several dozen bills to support the military action.

The State Department list included a number of minor actions. As noted by presidential scholar Edward Corwin (1951: 16), the examples of presidents unilaterally ordering military action consist largely of 'fights with pirates, landings of small naval contingents on barbarous or semi-barbarous coasts, the dispatch of small bodies of troops to chase bandits or cattle rustlers across the Mexican border, and the like'.

Pro-presidency commentators and scholars argue that the executive branch has the constitutional authority to engage in defensive military hostilities and that the president is the only judge of the practical meaning of this category. Truman made the claim prominent when he defended his actions in the Korean War as inherently authorised by the US Constitution's 'commander-in-chief' clause.

Since then, presidents have used blunt language to advance this claim and going far beyond purely defensive military action. Although President George H. W. Bush obtained authorisation for hostilities in the first Gulf War, he declared: 'I didn't have to get permission from some old goat in the United States Congress to kick Saddam Hussein out of Kuwait.' When Clinton sent troops to Haiti, he argued: 'Like my predecessors of both parties, I have not agreed that I was constitutionally mandated' to achieve congressional approval (Zeisberg 2013: 14).

Various scholars have elaborated and defended this line, which effectively supports positioning an almost limitless war-instigating power in the hands of a president. Increasingly, since the 1970s and even more so since the militarist response to the 9/11 attacks of 2001, academic opinion-writing has sought to justify the aggressive expansion of executive power. Eugene Rostow (1972: 854) argued that, although the executive's power to call the military into service is a limited power 'confined to cases of actual invasion, or of imminent danger of invasion', the president must be the 'sole and exclusive judge' as to when these cases have arisen (see also Yoo 2005; Emerson 1975; Commager 1974; Turner 1994).

Other scholars have since gone further. Some oppose any assessment of constitutional fidelity in the area of war powers at all. Both John McGinnis (1996) and Mark Tushnet (2007) contend that the constitutional text is consistent with, in Tushnet's words, 'whatever the political process produces' (Tushnet 2007: 1468).

Zeisberg (2013: 18) advanced an elastic approach, which she calls 'the relational conception of war authority', based on accepting presidential and congressional 'constructions of constitutional war powers that are well adapted to the security context of their own time'. She argued for a 'real politik' approach that essentially sweeps aside the US Constitution in favour of whatever institutional practices are established via exercises of political power, insisting that 'a too-rigid demand that the Constitution's "final word" be legally identifiable can crowd out space for other practices that support institutional consolidation' (Zeisberg 2013: 234). Revealingly, she asserted that Congress lacks the constitutional basis, not to mention the motivation, to scrutinise executive-branch war-launching processes, such as the role of the National Security Council or the military industrial complex (Zeisberg 2013: 235).

Zeisberg noted that successive presidents have seized upon precedents set by their forebears to generate 'ideological frames' that are then subject to broader use: 'Nixon cited Kennedy and the Cuban Missile Crisis as precedent for the Cambodian incursion, and the Obama administration cited Clinton interventions in Haiti and Bosnia as precedent for Libya (Zeisberg 2013: 215). However, she advocated an even more sweeping view of presidential power—one that is not constrained by previous precedents: her relational conception contended that 'good judgment' by the holders of political power must override 'consistency across cases' (Zeisberg 2013: 251).

Zeisberg's conception of constitutions themselves was a lawless one. She insisted that they are malleable documents that can be reinterpreted and exploited to deliver whatever outcomes are sought by those in power:

> Constitutions are law, but they are also resources with which political actors imagine themselves; ideological templates by which we imagine how to achieve in practice the goals we bring to and find in politics . . . It is in the practical pursuit of goals textured by the contingencies of the moment that the Constitution is made authoritative by those it empowers.
>
> (Zeisberg 2013: 261)

This is a truly limitless, authoritarian and militarist doctrine, but one that accords with the 'practice' of the Washington political, legal and security establishment, including Congress and the judiciary, since the United States acquired military and geo-strategic primacy in World War II.

Formal declarations of war

Initially, US presidents formally abided by the US Constitution. Since the first US administration, Congress and a president have enacted 11 separate formal declarations of war against foreign nations, covering five different wars—the War of 1812 with Britain, the War with Mexico in 1846, the War with Spain in 1898, World War I and World War II.

In each case, the formal declaration was preceded by a presidential request to Congress, either in writing or in person before a joint session of Congress, citing the reasons for requesting a war declaration. With one notable exception—that of the Spanish-American War, discussed below—these reasons were couched in defensive terms, although, as documented in the Introduction, US administrations have a historical record of provoking wars and then claiming the need for self-defence. The cited reasons included armed attacks on US territory or its citizens and attacks on or direct threats to US rights or interests as a sovereign nation. In the 19th century, all declarations of war were passed by Congress in the form of a bill; in the 20th century, the declarations took the form of a joint resolution. In each instance, the measures were adopted by majority vote in both the House and the Senate, and were signed into law by the president. The last formal declaration of war was enacted on 5 June 1942, against Romania during World War II (Elsea and Weed 2014: 1).

During the first half of the 20th century, presidential requests for formal congressional declarations of war were supposedly based on findings by the president that US territory or sovereign rights had been attacked or threatened by a foreign nation. President Wilson had pledged to maintain US neutrality after the outbreak of World War I, but he alleged that the German decision on 1 February 1917 to engage in unrestricted submarine warfare against all naval vessels in the war zone, including those of neutral states, was an unacceptable assault on US sovereign rights that the German government had previously pledged to respect. Wilson's request for a congressional declaration of war against Germany on 2 April 1917 stated that war had been 'thrust upon the United States' by Germany's actions. Congress passed a joint resolution declaring war, which the President signed on 6 April 1917. Wilson delayed requesting a war declaration against Austria-Hungary until 4 December 1917. He claimed that the state, a German ally in the war, had become an active instrument of Germany against the United States. Congress quickly passed a joint resolution declaring war, which the President signed on 7 December 1917. The real calculations behind the US entry into the final stages of the war, after benefiting economically from it, are discussed below.

Likewise, President Franklin D. Roosevelt used the Japanese attack on Pearl Harbor to enter World War II. He requested a declaration of war against Japan on 8 December 1941, ostensibly because of direct military attacks by that nation against US territory, military personnel and citizens in Hawaii, as well as other outposts in the Pacific area. The House and the Senate passed the requested declaration, and the President signed it into law that same day. After Germany and Italy each declared war on the United States on 11 December 1941, Roosevelt asked Congress to respond in kind by recognising that a state of war existed between the United States and those two nations. Congress passed separate joint resolutions declaring war on both nations, which the President signed on 11 December 1941. On 2 June 1942, President Roosevelt asked that Congress declare war on Bulgaria, Hungary and Romania, nations that were under the domination of Germany, were engaged in active military actions against the United States and had themselves declared war on the United States. Congress passed separate joint resolutions declaring war on each of these nations. The president signed these resolutions on 5 June 1942.

There is a striking similarity of language in the eight declarations of war passed by Congress in the 20th century. They all declared that a 'state of war' existed between the United States and the other nation. With the one exception of the declaration of war against Austria-Hungary on 7 December 1917, the other seven declarations characterised the state of war as having been 'thrust upon the United States' by the other nation. All eight of these 20th-century declarations of war stated in identical language that the president was authorised and directed to employ the entire naval and military forces of the United States and the resources of the government to carry on war against [the 'government' of the particular nation]; and to bring the conflict to a successful termination all of the resources of the country are hereby pledged by the Congress of the United States (Elsea and Weed 2014: 1–2).

Formal and informal declarations of war

The Spanish-American and Philippine-American wars marked the emergence of the United States as a global imperialist power. The one stated exception to the facade of formally declared defensive wars was President McKinley's request for a declaration of war against Spain in 1898. Made on 25 April 1898, McKinley's request was approved by a voice vote of both houses of Congress on that date. His request was made after Spain had rejected a US ultimatum that Spain relinquish its sovereignty over Cuba and permit Cuba to become an independent state. This ultimatum was supported by a joint resolution of Congress, signed into law on 20 April 1898, which, among other things, declared Cuba to be independent, demanded that Spain withdraw its military forces from the island, and directed and authorised the president to use the US Army, Navy and militia of the various states to achieve these ends (Elsea and Weed 2014: 1–2).

The war with Spain in 1898 was thus not based on attacks on the United States, but on a US effort to end the Cuban insurrection against Spain and restore order on the island—outcomes that were said to advance the interests of the United States. This war not only resulted in the installation of a pro-US regime in Cuba, but also led to the violent occupation of the Philippines, rendering it a semi-colony of the United States.

During the late 1890s, US public opinion had been agitated by anti-Spanish propaganda led by newspaper publishers such as Joseph Pulitzer and William Randolph Hearst, who called for war (Barnes 2010: 67).

After the US Navy armoured cruiser Maine mysteriously sank in Havana Harbour, the Democratic Party pushed McKinley into the war. On 20 April 1898, he signed a joint congressional resolution demanding Spanish withdrawal and authorising the president to use military force to help Cuba to gain independence. In response, Spain severed diplomatic relations with the United States the very next day. On that same day, the US Navy began a blockade of Cuba. On 23 April, Spain stated that it would declare war if the US forces were to invade its territory. On 25 April, Congress declared that a state of war between the United States and Spain had de facto existed since 21 April—the day on which the blockade of Cuba had begun. The United States sent an ultimatum to Spain, demanding that it surrender control of Cuba, but Spain did not reply soon enough, so the US government simply asserted that Spain had ignored the ultimatum and continued to occupy Cuba.

A ten-week war was fought in both the Caribbean and the Pacific, with US naval power soon proving decisive, as expected. The result was the 1898 Treaty of Paris, which nominally gave the United States temporary control of Cuba and ceded ownership of Puerto Rico, Guam and the Philippines, establishing outright US colonies (Beede 2013: 283–90).

The United States had sent a force of some 11,000 ground troops to the Philippines. Armed conflict broke out between US forces and the Filipinos when US troops began to take the place of the Spanish in control of the country after the end of the war, resulting in the Philippine-American War, which lasted from 4 February 1899 to 2 July 1902.

The war and the US occupation led to the deaths of an estimated 200,000–250,000 Filipino civilians, and to the introduction of English as the primary language of government, education and business (Foner 1972: 626).

Although the 1916 Philippine Autonomy officially declared the US government's commitment to eventually grant independence to the Philippines, it was delayed until 1946, after the Japanese occupation of the territory and World War II.

Wilson and World War I

In both world wars, US presidents consciously created the political and military conditions to enter the war to pursue the strategic and commercial interests of the corporate elite, after setting out to overcome, or simply to override, strong public opinion against going to war. President Woodrow Wilson won re-election in 1916 on the basis of the slogan, 'He kept us out of the war'—but he increasingly concluded that if the United States did not join the war, it would be denied a role in shaping the post-war world.

On 22 January 1917, Wilson delivered a presidential address to the Senate in which he called for 'peace without victory', posturing as a champion of global peace, self-determination and an open world without great power alliances. However, once Germany resumed submarine warfare in the Atlantic, targeting American ships carrying arms to Britain, and appealed to Mexico for an alliance, Wilson exploited the growth in anti-war sentiment to intervene. His main motive was to enter the conflict to guarantee the United States a voice in the post-war negotiations over colonies and reparations. When Emergency Peace Federation leaders visited Wilson at the White House on 28 February, he explained:

[A]s head of a nation participating in the war, the president of the United States would have a seat at the Peace Table, but that if he remained the representative of a neutral country he could at best only 'call through a crack in the door'.

(Stone and Kuznick 2013: 6–7)

On 2 April 1917, Wilson asked Congress for a declaration of war, saying that 'the world must be made safe for democracy'. Despite government appeals for 1 million volunteers, however, only 73,000 signed up in the first six weeks, forcing Congress to institute conscription. Reports of the horrors of trench warfare and poison gas fuelled the anti-war sentiment and resistance to recruitment. What followed was intense pro-war propaganda and repression of dissent, including the jailing of those who, like Socialist Party presidential candidate Eugene Debs, spoke out against the war. By the end of the war in November 1918, 2 million US soldiers had been sent to France, of whom more than 116,000 had died and 204,000 had been wounded (Stone and Kuznik 2013: 8–18).

The entry into the war almost immediately led the Wilson administration and Congress to resort to politically repressive measures to stifle and intimidate opposition. Less than three weeks after voting for war, Congress began debating what became the Espionage Act of 1917. Proposing the Act, Wilson declared that disloyalty was 'not a subject on which there was room for . . . debate' and asserted that disloyal individuals had 'sacrificed their right to civil liberties' (Stone 2004: 137).

The legislation was applied in an atmosphere of war hysteria stirred by government propaganda. At the government's direct instigation, vigilante groups accused thousands of people of disloyalty, often on the basis of hearsay, gossip and slander. The US attorney general boasted that, with the assistance of these volunteer groups, the government had 'scores of thousands of persons under observation' (Stone 2004: 156–58). Altogether, more than 2,000 dissenters were prosecuted for allegedly disloyal, seditious or incendiary speech (Stone 2004: 170).

The Supreme Court's embrace of the repression, particularly directed against socialists, was displayed in *Schenck v. United States* 249 US 47 (1919). Led by Justice Oliver Wendell Holmes, the Court unanimously upheld the conviction of Socialist Party supporters who had been charged with conspiring to obstruct the recruiting and enlistment service by circulating a pamphlet to men who had been conscripted. The pamphlet argued that the draft was unconstitutional and a 'monstrous wrong' designed to further the interests of Wall Street. It urged readers to join the Socialist Party, to write to their elected representatives in Congress and to petition for the repeal of the Act.

Likewise, in *Frowerk v. United States* 249 US 204 (1919), a publisher of anti-war, anti-draft articles in a German-language newspaper was sentenced to ten years' jail under the Espionage Act. One of the articles described the war as 'outright murder without serving anything practical'. Justice Holmes brushed aside the First Amendment issue, saying that the newspaper was circulated in quarters in which 'a little breath could be enough to kindle a flame' (*Frowerk v. United States* 249 US 204, 208–09 (1919)).

Even more anti-democratic was *Debs v. United States* 249 US 211 (1919. Debs was an internationally renowned figure, who had won almost 1 million votes as the Socialist Party's 1912 presidential candidate. He was sentenced to ten years in prison for making a speech near a prison after visiting three Socialist Party members who had been jailed for violating the Espionage Act. Debs defiantly ran his 1920 presidential campaign from prison, as 'Convict No. 9653', and again received nearly 1 million votes (Stone 2004: 198).

Equally instructive was *Abrams v. United States* 260 US 616 (1919). The Supreme Court upheld jail terms of up to 20 years imposed on socialists and anarchists who protested against the dispatch of US marines to Vladivostok and Murmansk as part of Western efforts to overturn the 1917 Russian Revolution. They distributed leaflets condemning the expedition as an attempt to 'crush the Russian Revolution' and calling for a general strike. One leaflet denounced the 'plutocratic gang in Washington', declaring that there was 'only one enemy of the workers of the world and that is CAPITALISM'. The defendants were arrested by the military police. Their trial featured anti-Semitic and anti-Bolshevik slanders by the judge, who declared: '[W]e are not going to help carry out the plans mapped out by the Imperial German Government, and which are being carried out by Lenine [*sic*] and Trotsky' (Stone 2004: 206).

The Supreme Court affirmed the convictions on two counts: one charging conspiracy 'to incite, provoke or encourage resistance to the United States'; the other alleging conspiracy to urge curtailment of production of war materials with intent to 'cripple or hinder the United States in the prosecution of the war' (Head 2011: 41–48).

In *Pierce v. United States* 254 US 325 (1920), four Albany socialists were punished for expressing opinions that pointed out the economic and strategic calculations behind Washington's entry into World War I. They were convicted of violating the 'false statement' provisions of the Espionage Act for distributing a pamphlet that asserted that, despite all President Wilson's rhetoric about democracy, 'this war began over commercial routes'. The Court held that 'common knowledge . . . sufficed to show' that the 'statements as to the causes that led to the entry of the United States into the war . . . were grossly false' (Head 2011: 45).

Roosevelt and World War II

In October 1939, a Gallup poll reported that 95 per cent of the American people wanted the United States to stay out of World War II (Stone and Kuznick 2013: 94). Before winning re-election for a third term, in 1940, President Franklin D. Roosevelt, like Wilson before him, had promised to keep the United States out of the world war. He told an overflow crowd in Boston Garden: 'I have said this before but I shall say it again. Your boys are not going to be sent into any foreign wars' (Stone and Kuznick 2013: 93). In reality, his administration was already pushing toward war, including by imposing an oil blockade on Japan and supplying Britain with much of its military needs, including artillery, tanks, machine guns and thousands of planes.

Roosevelt defied and sought to manipulate public opinion, as well as congressional attempts, such as the Neutrality Act of 1939, to restrain him. As will be examined in more detail in Chapter 11, Democratic Representative Louis Ludlow's motion for a constitutional amendment to require a national referendum to declare war was narrowly defeated in Congress after Roosevelt and members of his administration lobbied aggressively against it. Presciently, Ludlow warned:

> It is always possible, as matters now stand, for a president to maneuver Congress into declaring war. Members of that body would have to be men of steel and iron if they could stand up and vote for what they believe is right after a president has set the stage for war.
>
> (Zeisberg 2013: 61)

Zeisberg (2013: 61–65) provided a summary of some of the ways in which Roosevelt used executive powers to advance intervention, skirting around congressional restrictions, even as he affirmed the value of neutrality for US security interests.

- Roosevelt pushed war supplies out to the democracies, beginning with planes. In early 1938, he developed a scheme to build aircraft in Canada, using US parts, and to ship them to France, suggesting that '[i]f London could avoid an actual declaration of war, he might be able to ignore the Neutrality Act and continue arms sales, as he was doing with China'. In May and June of 1940, he committed vital military equipment to the Allies. Such transfers would have been (had they happened) illegal until the Lend-Lease Act of 1941. The promises were not illegal, but they did undermine Congress's neutrality policy.
- Roosevelt requested that the British trade use of its Caribbean bases in return for US action to patrol the waters of the western hemisphere, and he strategically timed that request in 1939, before war broke out, to avoid 'awkward questions about unneutral conduct'. The British Foreign Office complied. In June 1939, Roosevelt also approved a series of secret conversations between top US and British naval officials to discuss a coordinated naval defence strategy. None of these behaviours were prohibited, but none were consistent with the legislature's emphatic vision of a neutral foreign policy.
- Roosevelt coordinated fleet movements with those of the British in the Far East and began patrols of the Atlantic for U-boats in 1939. In the summer of 1941, when Admiral Stark, chief of naval operations, asked for clarification about the proper response to German U-boat presence in the Atlantic, Roosevelt replied: 'Don't ask me that.' The fleet commander 'simply ordered the fleet to go after any German submarine or raider close by or at "reasonably longer distances".'

- The September 1940 destroyers-for-bases agreement gave 50 destroyers to the British in exchange for leases on territory in the Caribbean. Some claim that the deal was simply illegal. The 1917 Espionage Act criminalised exporting vessels of war to belligerent nations. This bar was reinforced by the Walsh Amendment to a naval bill, which barred the transfer of military material from the United States unless it could be certified as surplus and obsolete. Executive branch lawyers issued a series of convoluted statutory interpretations that pressed the grammar of the Espionage Act and Walsh Amendment to its absolute limit. Ultimately, the critical legal resource was a claim made on the president's war authority. Roosevelt, supported by Robert Jackson, argued that the president's status as commander-in-chief gave him authority to execute the trade. Jackson's legal opinion argued that the Walsh Amendment itself was 'of questionable constitutionality'.
- The imposition of embargos on Japan of iron, steel and aviation gasoline in December 1940 was a response to Japanese aggression in China and Indochina.
- Secret meetings between US and British military staffs took place between 29 January and 27 March 1941, establishing key elements of US grand military strategy, eventually leading to the ABC-1 staff agreements prioritising battle in Europe and the Atlantic, extending American neutrality patrols farther out in the Atlantic, and an agreement that the US Navy would assume convoy as soon as it was ready (forbidden by the Neutrality Act of 1939).
- Roosevelt imposed sanctions on Japan and gave notice of the United States' intention to terminate a 1911 commercial treaty. These led to a de facto oil embargo, leaving the Japanese the choice between de-escalating in China or going to war with the United States before running out of oil.

In mid-November 1941, Congress removed all remaining restrictions of the Neutrality Acts at Roosevelt's request, permitting US ships to carry supplies right across the Atlantic. In late November, Roosevelt and his War Council met, and Secretary of War Henry Stimson noted that '[t]he question was how we should maneuver them [the Japanese] into the position of firing the first shot without allowing too much danger to ourselves' (Zeisberg 2013: 64).

The Roosevelt administration's actions against Japan led Congress to investigate whether the president had actually incited the Pearl Harbor attack. The minority report of the congressional investigating committee blamed Pearl Harbor on Roosevelt and core members of his administration.

Several authors, including journalist Robert Stinnett (1999) and former US Rear Admiral Robert Alfred Theobald (1954), have argued that various parties high in the US and British governments knew of the attack in advance, and that they may have let it happen or even encouraged it to force the United States into war.

Various historians have contested this view (Prange and Holland 1991). There is no doubt, however, that Roosevelt sought to provoke Japan into war.

Rear Admiral Frank Beatty (1954: 48), who was, at the time of the Pearl Harbor attack, an aide to Navy Secretary Frank Knox and very close to Roosevelt's inner circle, later recalled:

> Prior to December 7, it was evident even to me . . . that we were pushing Japan into a corner. I believed that it was the desire of President Roosevelt, and Prime Minister Churchill that we get into the war, as they felt the Allies could not win without us and all our efforts to cause the Germans to declare war on us failed; the conditions we imposed upon Japan—to get out of China, for example—were so severe that we knew that nation could not accept them. We were forcing her so severely that we could have known that she would react toward the United States. All her preparations in a military way—and we knew their over-all import—pointed that way.

There is also no doubt that Roosevelt repeatedly used his powers in a pro-war direction, contrary to public opinion and congressional measures. On more than one occasion, as a result, Roosevelt expressed worry about impeachment (Zeisberg 2013: 64–65).

War was again accompanied by political repression. During 1940, even before the United States entered the war, Congress re-enacted the Espionage Act of 1917, making its provisions applicable in peacetime for the first time. It then went further, passing the Alien Registration Act of 1940 (the Smith Act), which required all resident non-citizens to register with the government, streamlined deportation procedures and forbade any person 'knowingly or wilfully' to 'advocate, abet, advise, or teach the duty, necessity, desirability, or propriety of overthrowing or destroying any government in the United States by force or violence'. Roosevelt declined to veto the Act, claiming that its advocacy provisions 'hardly . . . constitute an improper encroachment on civil liberties in the light of present world conditions' (Stone 2004: 252).

The first prosecution under the Smith Act came just before the December 1941 Japanese attack on Pearl Harbor that provided the pretext for Roosevelt administration to enter the war. The accused were 29 leaders of the Socialist Workers Party (SWP), the Trotskyist party that opposed World War II as an inter-imperialist conflict waged in the interests of the business elites. The SWP had been involved in several major work stoppages that affected the military industry in Minneapolis. Before instigating the prosecution, Attorney General Francis Biddle advised Roosevelt that bringing some prosecutions might have a 'salutary effect' (Stone 2004: 255). Eighteen of the defendants were convicted and jailed for conspiring to advocate the forceful overthrow of the government, and the Supreme Court denied review. (For a detailed examination of this case, see Head 2011: 77–81.)

During World War II, almost 5 million non-citizens were registered under the Smith Act, some 900,000 Japanese, German and Italian nationals were classified as 'enemy aliens', and more than 9,000 were detained. Another 120,000 people of Japanese descent, two-thirds of whom were US citizens, were ordered to leave their West Coast homes to live in detention camps, even though there was not one documented act of espionage, sabotage or treason committed by anyone of Japanese descent residing on the West Coast (Stone 2004: 283–303). The Supreme Court sanctioned these internments in *Korematsu v. United States* 323 US 214 (1944), commenting that 'hardships are part of war' (Stone 2004: 300).

The Korean War

From 1789 to 1950, presidents who engaged in military actions against other nations generally came to Congress either for statutory authority or a declaration of war. From President Truman's instigation of the 1950–53 Korean War onward, however, these constitutional strictures have increasingly been abrogated.

On 26 June 1950, Truman announced to the American public that the UN Security Council had ordered North Korea to withdraw its forces from South Korea. At that point, he made no commitment of US military forces. On the following day, he said that North Korea had failed to cease hostilities, and that he had ordered US air and sea forces to give South Korea cover and support. With the Soviet Union absent, the Security Council voted 9–0 to call upon North Korea to withdraw its forces from South Korea. Secretary of State Dean Acheson claimed that Truman acted in conformity with the resolutions of the Security Council of 25 and 27 June, giving air and sea support to the troops of the Korean government. But Truman never requested nor did he receive authority from Congress. Instead, he denied that a war existed.

At a news conference on 29 June, a reporter asked Truman if the country was at war. He responded: 'We are not at war.' Asked whether it would be more correct to call the conflict 'a police action under the United Nations', he agreed: 'That is exactly what it amounts to.' During Senate hearings in June 1951, Acheson conceded the obvious by admitting 'in the usual sense of the word there is a war' (Fisher 2013: 269).

Truman's precedent of circumventing Congress and seeking 'authority' from the UN Security Council was later followed by President Clinton in Haiti and Bosnia. When Clinton could not obtain UN authority for military action in Kosovo, he reached out to NATO allies for support. At no time did he seek authority from Congress for those actions. In 2011, in preparing to use military force in Libya, President Obama sought authority not from Congress, but from the Security Council. One constitutional scholar commented: 'Whether relying on the UN or NATO, treaties may not shift constitutional authority from Congress to outside bodies' (Fisher 2013: 270).

The Vietnam War and the 1973 War Powers Resolution

As the Pentagon Papers documented (see Chapter 2), successive administrations entered and escalated the war in Vietnam behind the backs of the American people, on the basis of subterfuge, fabrications and lies. Since the 1950s, the United States had been providing covert military assistance and support, first to the French colonial forces, then to the government of South Vietnam, provoking conflict with the government of North Vietnam.

The violence perpetrated by the United States in Vietnam was of a genocidal character. Eight million tons of bombs were dropped on North and South Vietnam alone—far more than in all theatres of World War II combined. In addition, US warplanes dropped 370,000 tons of napalm and sprayed 21 million gallons of toxic defoliant chemicals such as Agent Orange. Approximately 58,000 Americans died in the war, compared to more than 3 million Vietnamese and many Cambodians and Laotians (Obermeyer, Murray and Gakidou 2008).

The go-ahead for direct, large-scale military involvement in Vietnam was provided to the White House by the 1964 congressional Gulf of Tonkin Resolution. On 2 August 1964, a US destroyer, the *USS Maddox*, was allegedly attacked by North Vietnamese torpedo boats while off the coast of North Vietnam, in the Gulf of Tonkin. Two days later, further attacks by North Vietnamese vessels against US destroyers were reported. President Lyndon Johnson immediately, on the same day, sent US military aircraft to bomb 'gunboats and certain supporting facilities' in North Vietnam that had allegedly been used in the actions against US naval vessels. After meeting with congressional leaders, on 5 August 1964 Johnson formally requested a congressional resolution that would 'express the support of the Congress for all necessary action to protect our armed forces and to assist nations covered by the SEATO [Southeast Asia Treaty Organization] Treaty' (Elsea and Weed 2014: 9–10).

Congress responded to Johnson's request by passing a joint resolution to 'promote the maintenance of international peace and security in southeast Asia'. This legislation has come to be popularly known as the Gulf of Tonkin Resolution. This Joint Resolution, enacted on 10 August 1964, stated that 'the Congress approves and supports the determination of the President, as Commander-in-Chief, to take all necessary measures to repel any armed attack against the forces of the United States and to prevent further aggression'. The Joint Resolution further stated that:

> Consonant with the Constitution of the United States and the Charter of the United Nations and in accordance with its obligations under the Southeast Asia Collective Defense Treaty, the United States is, therefore, prepared, as the President determines, to take all necessary steps, including the use of armed force, to assist any member or protocol state of the Southeast Asia Collective Defense Treaty requesting assistance in defense of its freedom.

The Joint Resolution stated that it would expire whenever the President determined that the 'peace and security of the area is reasonably assured', or earlier if Congress chose to terminate it by concurrent resolution (Elsea and Weed 2014: 9–10).

Congress repealed the Gulf of Tonkin Resolution only in 1971, by which time it had been used to send hundreds of thousands of troops to Vietnam, and to conduct carpet-bombing campaigns the length and breadth of the small country.

Despite the repeal, the Nixon administration continued the war anyway, openly defying Congress (Elsea and Weed 2014: 9–10).

Congress passed the 1973 War Powers Resolution during the deep military and political crisis (including the Watergate scandal) that arose because the Vietnam War became a debacle and, ultimately, a humiliating defeat. The Resolution still provides presidents with immense scope to initiate wars without formally declaring them.

On paper, as previously outlined, the Resolution requires that the president report to Congress within 48 hours of authorising military action. It also requires that the president request congressional approval within 60 days of launching hostilities. If congressional approval is not obtained, the president must cease the war within 90 days. President Nixon vetoed the Act, but Congress overrode the veto with a two-thirds majority.

Section 2(a) of the Resolution states that its purpose is 'to fulfill the intent of the framers of the Constitution of the United States and insure . . . the collective judgment' of both the legislative and executive branches of government when US forces are introduced into hostilities. For the period of 60–90 days, however, a president has carte blanche. Under section 3, the president is to consult with Congress only 'in every possible instance', leaving full discretion to the president.

After introducing forces into hostilities, the president is required to report to Congress within 48 hours. Section 2(c) attempts to define the president's constitutional power to introduce US forces into combat. Troops may be ordered into hostilities only pursuant to (1) a declaration of war, (2) specific statutory authorisation, or (3) a national emergency created by attack upon the United States, its territories or its armed forces.

The language in section 4 governing reports to Congress is broader. It speaks of hostilities or 'situations where imminent involvement in hostilities is clearly indicated by the circumstances'. Other language in section 4 appears to sanction presidential use of military force in situations wholly unrelated to attacks against US territory and troops.

There is also uncertainty about what starts the 60–90 day clock ticking. It does not begin unless the president reports under a very specific subsection: section 4(a)(1). Presidents may decide to report more vaguely. For example, when President Reagan reported to Congress on his air strikes against Libya in 1986, he reported simply, 'consistent with the War Powers Resolution', so the clock never started. Military interventions in Grenada by Reagan and in Panama by President George H. Bush were conducted as though the 60-day limit applied. Since then, increasingly, the limit has been disregarded. Clinton's military operations in Kosovo lasted 78 days—the first time the 60-day clock was exceeded. Obama's military actions in Libya went beyond 90 days (Fisher 2017: 272–73).

Clinton and Yugoslavia 1999

President Bill Clinton utilised US armed forces in various operations, such as air strikes and the deployment of 'peacekeeping forces', in the former Yugoslavia—especially Bosnia and Kosovo. Some of these operations were pursuant to UN

Security Council resolutions; others were conducted without UN approval, in conjunction with other member states of NATO. Clinton made a number of reports to Congress 'consistent with the War Powers Resolution', but never cited section 4(a)(1) of the Act and thus did not trigger the 60-day time limit.

The decision by the United States to go to war against Serbia in 1999—taken with the full backing of Britain—was based on definite geo-political calculations. The claim to be fighting ethnic cleansing was used to justify a war drive to cripple Serbia, considered by the US government to be an obstacle to American economic and political interests in the strategically vital Balkan peninsula and the oil-rich Caucasus and Caspian regions to the east (Bacevich and Cohen 2001).

The war was deliberately provoked by the United States, using as a pretext exaggerated claims of Serbian human rights violations against Kosovar Albanians. By 1998, the United States had shifted from denouncing the separatist Kosovo Liberation Army (KLA) as terrorists to a policy of arming it, while imposing sanctions on Serbia and bolstering NATO's military capabilities in both Albania and Macedonia. By mid-July, the United States and NATO had completed contingency plans for a military intervention in Kosovo, including air strikes and the deployment of ground troops (Bacevich and Cohen 2001).

On 15 January 1999, the report of a Serbian massacre at the village of Racak, the veracity of which massacre is still disputed, provided the pretext for NATO's assault on Serbia. At the Rambouillet talks in February, the Milosevic government in Yugoslavia was presented with an ultimatum it could not accept, which included the stationing of a large, long-term NATO force within Kosovo and free access of NATO military forces to all parts of Yugoslavia. On 24 March, the first NATO bombs were dropped.

Once the bombing began and the Serbs countered with their offensive in Kosovo, the United States escalated the war. From March to June, US and NATO bombs rained down on Belgrade and other cities and towns, hitting factories, hospitals, schools, churches, bridges, oil refineries, water and electricity supply installations, and even television stations. The NATO bombing campaign remained controversial, because it did not gain the approval of the UN Security Council and because it caused at least 488 Yugoslav civilian deaths, including among them Kosovar refugees (Bacevich and Cohen 2001).

In Congress, various measures regarding the use of these forces were defeated without becoming law. Representative Tom Campbell and other members of the House of Representatives filed a suit in the Federal District Court for the District of Columbia against the president, charging that he had violated the War Powers Resolution—especially since 60 days had elapsed since the start of military operations in Kosovo. Clinton noted that he considered the War Powers Resolution constitutionally defective. The Court ruled in favour of the president, holding that the members lacked legal standing to bring the suit. This decision was affirmed by the US Court of Appeals for the District of Columbia and the Supreme Court refused to hear an appeal, in effect letting the ruling stand (*Campbell v. Clinton* 203 F.3d 19 (DC Cir. 2000)).

George W. Bush, the 'war on terror', and the 2001 and 2003
Authorizations for the Use of Military Force

Over the past several decades, and accelerating during the course of the 'war on terror', even the nominal constraints of the War Powers Resolution have been abrogated in practice. Successive administrations have adopted more hostile attitudes to the Resolution, reflecting the growing assertiveness of presidential and executive power. This process has featured pseudo-legal justifications that rest on ever-wider and more extravagant interpretations of the sweeping war resolutions adopted by Congress in 2001 and 2003.

As discussed at the outset of this chapter, both houses of the US Congress enthusiastically and overwhelmingly passed AUMFs in 2001 and 2003 to endorse the George W. Bush administration's invasions of Afghanistan and Iraq, respectively.

In September 2001, Congress gave the president virtually open-ended permission to use 'necessary and appropriate force' against anyone he determined had 'planned, authorized, committed, or aided' the 9/11 attacks, or 'to deter and preempt any future acts of terrorism or aggression against the United States'. This sweeping language was matched in October 2002, during the lead-up to the Iraq invasion, when Congress endorsed a second AUMF allowing Bush to use the armed forces 'as he determines to be necessary and appropriate' to 'defend the national security of the United States against the continuing threat posed by Iraq; and enforce all relevant United Nations Security Council Resolutions regarding Iraq'.

Both resolutions were based on false assertions. Afghanistan was to be invaded solely because it was allegedly responsible for harbouring Al Qaeda, not because of its strategic importance in the resource-rich Middle East and Central Asia. Iraq was said to be 'continuing to possess and develop a significant chemical and biological weapons capability' and 'actively seeking a nuclear weapons capability'. Both of these charges of 'weapons of mass destruction' (WMDs) were later exposed as contrived, as discussed in Chapter 2.

Obama and Libya 2011

In his first speech to the American public on what was then a nine-day-old war against Libya, on 28 March 2011 President Barack Obama made a case for a US president's right to carry out military aggression anywhere in the world where US 'interests and values' were deemed to be at stake (Obama 2011).

Obama's speech failed to enunciate in any comprehensible form what these 'interests and values' are nor did it explain to the American people why and how he had arrogated to himself the right to launch a war without first explaining its causes and aims, much less seeking a vote of authorisation from the US Congress.

Obama put forward a narrative of the events leading up to the Libyan intervention that was misleading from start to finish. 'For more than four decades,' he said, 'the Libyan people have been ruled by a tyrant—Muammar Gaddafi.' In the previous month, he said, 'Libyans took to the streets to claim their basic rights', but Gaddafi began 'attacking his own people'. Gaddafi had lost 'the legitimacy to lead', prompting the US government to go the UN Security Council to obtain a resolution authorising 'all necessary measures to protect the Libyan people'. In the face of what Obama asserted was an imminent massacre in the eastern Libyan city of Benghazi, he found himself compelled to authorise military force because 'it was not in our national interest to let that happen' (Obama 2011).

First of all, this potted history failed to explain why, over the previous decade, successive US administrations had established ever-closer—and more lucrative— relations with this Libyan 'tyrant'. In the wake of 9/11, Gaddafi's secret service had been one of the most important regional allies of the US Central Intelligence Agency (CIA) in the 'global war on terror'. Bush's national security adviser, Condoleezza Rice, had flown to Tripoli to cement the US–Libyan alliance.

Under Obama, relations became even more cordial. In April 2009, Secretary of State Hillary Clinton welcomed Gaddafi's son—and national security minister—to the State Department, proclaiming the administration's desire to 'deepen and broaden our cooperation' and 'build on this relationship' (Isikoff 2015). Presumably, American 'values' were placed on hold during the decade in which Clinton and her predecessors concentrated on currying favour—and signing oil deals—with Gaddafi.

The claim that the regime was on the verge of launching a massacre of near-genocidal proportions in the city of Benghazi was presented as fact, even though there was no evidence that killing on any such scale had taken place in other cities that had been retaken by forces loyal to Gaddafi. Obama claimed that the US military action had been carried out 'to stop the killing'; in reality, Washington intervened in a civil war that it had played no small role in fomenting. The US Air Force, along with smaller numbers of warplanes provided by Washington's NATO allies, functioned as the air force of the anti-Gaddafi rebels, obliterating the air troops loyal to the government in Tripoli, thereby clearing the way for the US-backed forces on the ground.

Having presented a false justification for the action, Obama went on to suggest that the United States' role was largely over, with his administration acting to 'transfer responsibilities to our allies and partners'—namely, NATO. The patent aim of the speech was to present the Libyan intervention as something other than a US war. This was a deception. Placing military operations in Libya under formal NATO command no more removed the United States from playing the decisive role than had the formal command of NATO in Afghanistan made the war there any less of a US operation. NATO was dominated by the US military and the US supplied some 75 per cent of its funding.

While the US government had sought and, to a large extent, secured a profitable relationship with the Gaddafi regime, it had always viewed the Libyan leader—by dint of his anti-imperialist posturing and historical association with the struggle against colonialism—as an unreliable ally. Moreover, the US ruling elite viewed with increasing alarm the signs that both Russia and China were establishing connections with Libya, in the form of oil deals, infrastructure projects and arms contracts, which threatened US interests in the Mediterranean and North Africa.

The launching of a war by the United States, in alliance with the former colonial powers in North Africa—Britain, France, Italy and Spain—also reaffirmed their hegemony in conditions under which popular uprisings had broken out in neighbouring Egypt and Tunisia (sometimes referred to as the Arab Spring).

In concluding his speech, Obama drew attention to 'what this action says about the use of America's military power, and America's broader leadership in the world, under my presidency', noting that he would 'never hesitate to use our military swiftly, decisively and unilaterally when necessary to defend our people, our homeland, our allies and our core interests' (Obama 2011).

But, he added, military force was also justified in situations in which 'our safety is not directly threatened, but our interests and values are'. In circumstances ranging from 'genocide' to 'keeping the peace, ensuring regional security, and maintaining the flow of commerce', said Obama, the United States 'should not be afraid to act' (Obama 2011).

This represented a more expansive assertion of the right to wage war than had been made even under the Bush administration, which had claimed, while based upon lies, that its wars in Afghanistan and Iraq were necessitated by an imminent threat from terrorism and WMDs. Obama insisted that no such threat was needed; merely a challenge to US 'interests and values'. Obama was arguing for a rationale for US military aggression anywhere in the world to further the interests of America's ruling capitalist class.

On 15 April 2011, in an open letter issued and printed simultaneously in the *International Herald Tribune*, London's *The Times* and *Le Figaro* in France, Obama, together with the heads of government in France and Britain, openly acknowledged that the purpose of the NATO bombing of Libya was regime change—that is, the forcible expulsion of Libyan leader Muammar Gaddafi from power.

The three leaders, Obama, French President Nicolas Sarkozy and British Prime Minister David Cameron, wrote that the world would have committed an 'unconscionable betrayal' if it were to leave the Libyan leader in government. If Gaddafi remained in place, they continued, Libya risked becoming a failed state (Obama, Cameron and Sarkozy 2011).

The letter also indicated that the United States and its allies in the Libyan campaign were digging in for a prolonged war. The letter declared:

> So long as Gaddafi is in power, NATO and its coalition partners must maintain their operations so that civilians remain protected and the pressure on the regime builds. Britain, France and the United States will not rest until the UN Security Council resolutions have been implemented and the Libyan people can choose their own future.
>
> (Obama et al. 2011)

On 19 June 2011, the US-backed NATO war against Libya became illegal under the 1973 War Powers Act, which mandated that any presidential dispatch of US military forces into 'hostilities' in any other country must receive congressional approval within 60 days. If the president were to fail to gain such approval, he had an additional 30 days to carry out the safe withdrawal of all US forces.

The Obama administration had sent US forces into combat against Libya on 20 March 2011, with the bombing of Libyan anti-aircraft installations and radar sites. The 60-day deadline had passed on 20 May, without any effort by the administration to gain congressional approval. The 30-day period for withdrawal of US forces elapsed on 19 June, but the war continued.

Just before the 90-day deadline expired, the White House issued a document supporting its claim that the War Powers Act did not apply to the Libyan conflict because the US forces were not engaged in 'hostilities', as defined by the law:

> US operations do not involve sustained fighting or active exchanges of fire with hostile forces, nor do they involve the presence of US ground troops, US casualties or a serious threat thereof, or any significant chance of escalation into a conflict characterized by those factors.
>
> (White House 2011)

The one-sided character of a war, however, does not exempt it from the War Powers Act.

The White House also argued that the transfer of direct command of the attack on Libya from the United States to NATO allowed US military forces to step back into a 'support' role—another sophistry. Aside from the fact that US forces continued to participate in occasional air strikes, as well as by employing Predator drones and other weapons of war, NATO was a largely American operation.

Obama received legal advice from both Pentagon counsel and the Justice Department's Office of Legal Counsel—the agency that traditionally provides rulings on the legal obligations of the government—that the War Powers Act required congressional approval for the war in Libya. Obama chose to ignore these opinions, relying instead on advice from the office of White House counsel and State Department counsel—the direct legal subordinates of Obama himself and Hillary Clinton—that Congress could be bypassed.

From the standpoint of waging war in flagrant defiance of the law, Obama went a step beyond even the Bush administration. The wars that Bush launched in Afghanistan and Iraq were exercises in imperialist plunder, aimed at securing territory that was strategically critical for the domination of the oil and gas resources of the Persian Gulf and Central Asia. But the Bush administration did go through the formality of seeking congressional approval in advance of each act of aggression, using first the pretext of 9/11 and then a bogus campaign against alleged Iraqi WMDs to obtain resolutions authorising military action.

Leading congressional Democrats, including Senate Majority Leader Harry Reid and House Minority Leader Nancy Pelosi, endorsed Obama's defiance of the War Powers Act. House Republicans passed a resolution criticising Obama's disregard of the law, but had already voted to increase the Pentagon budget by more than the total cost of the war in Libya (Hendrikson 2013).

Likewise, the *New York Times*, in an editorial headlined 'Libya and the War Powers Act', bemoaned the White House's failure to gain congressional support. But the starting point of the commentary was support for the war, with the newspaper declaring: 'It would be hugely costly—for this country's credibility, for the future of NATO and for the people of Libya—if Congress were to force President Obama to abandon military operations over Libya' (*New York Times* 2011).

When Obama had reported to Congress on 21 March 2011, he had stated that US forces operating under the UN Resolution had begun a series of strikes against Libyan air defence systems and military airfields, 'for the purposes of preparing a no-fly zone'. He had said that the strikes would 'be limited in their nature, duration, and scope' (Fisher 2012: 177). Not only was this a deceptive minimisation of what inevitably became a full-scale operation to oust Gaddafi, but also the use of military force against another country that has not threatened the United States is an act of war.

According to Obama, military initiatives were taken 'pursuant to my constitutional authority to conduct U.S. foreign relations and as Commander in Chief and Chief Executive'. A memo released by the Office of Legal Counsel (OLC) on 1 April concluded that the military actions against Libya did not constitute 'war' because of the limited 'nature, scope, and duration' of the planned military operations. In a statement made on 21 March 2011, Obama had claimed that the United States anticipated that operations would conclude 'in a matter of days and not a matter of weeks' (Fisher 2012: 177). In reality, the military operations ultimately lasted seven months, exceeding the 60–90 day limit of the War Powers Resolution.

Having received the OLC's memo that 'war' did not exist, Obama then wanted a legal judgment that 'hostilities' did not exist. The OLC declined to produce that memo. Jeh Johnson, General Counsel in the Department of Defense, also refused Obama's request. He could not deny the existence of hostilities in the form of Tomahawk missiles, armed drones and NATO aircraft bombings. Eventually, White House Counsel Robert Bauer and State Department Legal Advisor Harold Koh agreed to affirm that no hostilities existed in Libya. The Obama administration made many efforts to deny the existence of hostilities in Libya (Fisher 2013: 271).

Before he was elected president, Obama had stated that a '[p]resident does not have the power under the Constitution to unilaterally authorise a military attack in a situation that does not involve stopping an actual or imminent threat to the nation'—and yet, in office, he did exactly that, and Congress and lawyers assisted him (Fisher 2012: 177).

In the OLC's 1 April opinion, Principal Deputy Assistant Attorney General Caroline Krass provided Obama with an expansive interpretation of presidential power, despite falling short of what Obama subsequently sought—an open mandate to go to war. Krass stated that the president possessed 'independent authority' to take military action when he could 'reasonably determine that such use of force [is] in the national interest', at least when 'Congress has not specifically restricted [such authority]'. Obama had reasonably determined that 'at least two national interests' were involved: the US interest in 'security and stability in the Middle East'; and 'the longstanding US commitment to maintaining the credibility of the United Nations Security Council and the effectiveness of its actions to promote international peace and security' (Krass 2011).

Such invocations of 'national interest' are calculated to produce an almost unlimited presidential war power, based on the bald assertion of US global primacy. Moreover, they clearly violate the 1973 War Powers Resolution, which explicitly limited the power—without a formal war declaration or a specifically congressional authorisation—to 'a national emergency created by attack upon the United States, its territories or possessions, or its armed forces'. None of these prerequisites were even remotely present in Libya in 2011.

As media reports documented later, the US intervention sought to overthrow a government based on mercenary calculations of enhancing the power of the United States and the profits of its corporations—particularly in the oil industry. In 2016, the *New York Times* published a two-part series entitled 'The Libya Gamble' in its 28 and 29 February editions detailing the leading role played by Secretary of State Clinton in fomenting the Libyan war.

Within the Obama administration, the newspaper reported, Clinton pressed for direct US military intervention on the grounds that the British and French governments would go ahead without the United States, and Washington would be 'left behind' and 'be less capable of shaping' the scramble for control of Libya and its oil wealth. The pretext, that Libyan government forces were on the verge of a 'genocidal massacre' of 'protesters' in the eastern city of Benghazi, was subsequently refuted by international human rights groups (House of Commons Foreign Affairs Select Committee 2016).

The Obama administration's regime-change goal was realised in October 2011 with the vicious lynch-mob murder of Gaddafi by the US-backed Islamist 'rebels'. After watching a video on an aide's BlackBerry of the Libyan leader being beaten and sodomised with a bayonet before he was killed, Clinton exclaimed, 'Wow!' She then infamously turned to her television interviewer, exclaimed 'We came, we saw, he died!' and laughed in delight (Van Auken 2016).

The Libyan operation highlighted again the complicity of Congress and the courts. On 21 March 2011, President Obama had reported the intervention to Congress, supposedly 'consistent with the War Powers Resolution'. When US military operations continued past the time horizons of the Resolution, still without legislative authorisation, some members of Congress challenged the president's conduct. By early June, the House of Representatives had resolved that the Libyan mission had not been legislatively authorised, but this did not translate into a willingness to shut down operations. Some members of the House sued the president, but the US District Court threw the case out, noting its 'frustration' at being asked to hear the case, given long-standing precedent (*Dennis Kucinich et al. v. Barack Obama* (2011), Civil Action No. 11–1096 (RBW) 7, fn 4).

Obama and Syria 2013

There was one apparent exception to the increasingly untrammelled exercise of executive war powers. In a speech nationally televised on September 2013, President Obama made an awkward and embarrassing tactical retreat on his announced plans to carry out military strikes against Syria. Obama announced that he had asked Congress to put off any vote authorising the use of military force, while saying he had 'ordered our military to maintain their current posture to keep the pressure on [Syrian President Bashar al-]Assad, and to be in position if diplomacy fails' (Obama 2013). In other words, he reserved the right to launch an attack at any time, with or without congressional approval.

US plans were well advanced and the moment for launching them had arrived. Obama had decreed a 'red line' in Syria and all it took was an incident or a provocation to provide the pretext for implementing his threat. That was forthcoming on 21 August in a chemical weapons attack in Ghouta, near Damascus, which was, in all likelihood, staged by the so-called rebels in collusion with US and Saudi intelligence to provide the *casus belli* sought by Washington.

But a major spanner was thrown into the works by the unanticipated virulent hostility to war among the American people and populations around the world. This opposition had only increased in the teeth of a barrage of propaganda and lies delivered by the US political establishment and the media, which were screaming for war. The popular opposition found its first reflection in a British House of Commons vote against a resolution supporting military action, as will be discussed in Chapter 4. This resulted in the British government, which was the United States' principal ally in Syria, ruling out participation in the planned attack.

Given its international isolation, the Obama administration concluded it needed a vote in Congress, which it had previously had no intention of seeking, to provide a fig leaf of legality and a false veneer of popular support. Both the Democratic and Republican leaderships in the House and Senate lined up behind war and promised to seek an AUMF. But the popular hostility to another war of aggression in the Middle East again made itself felt in a way that members of Congress could not easily ignore. Growing numbers of constituents contacted their representatives and senators about the impending attack, with nine out of ten members of the public declaring their angry opposition to the war plans. It became increasingly apparent that Congress would not vote in favour of the resolution under these conditions (Gerson 2013).

In December 2013, the release of a UN chemical weapons inspectors' report pointing toward multiple sarin gas attacks carried out by 'rebel' forces cast further doubt on the Obama administration's claims of Syrian government responsibility for the 21 August chemical shelling of the Ghouta area (UN Secretary-General 2013).

The 82-page UN chemical weapons report was based on extensive on-the-ground investigations of multiple sites where allegations of chemical weapons use had been raised by either the Syrian government or the American, British and French governments. The inspectors analysed soil and other environmental samples, examined hair, urine, tissue and blood samples for trace chemicals, interviewed survivors, witnesses and medical personnel, and documented munitions allegedly used to deliver the sarin in each incident (UN Secretary-General 2013).

They concluded that, in addition to the Ghouta incident, there had been at least four 'probable' sarin attacks. In three of these attacks, Syrian army soldiers were the victims of the deadly gas; in the fourth, civilians were affected. Not a single one of the confirmed chemical attacks were against 'rebel' militia fighters. The inspectors were not asked to determine who was responsible for the sarin attacks that they confirmed, so the report was silent on this issue. The report, moreover, was couched in cautious language, restricting itself to relaying scientific findings. Nevertheless, the only conclusion that could be drawn was that the US-backed, Islamist-dominated militias were responsible for multiple war crimes in the form of chemical attacks against both Syrian soldiers and civilians (UN Secretary-General 2013).

The appearance of the UN report followed the publication of a detailed article by Pulitzer-Prize-winning investigative journalist Seymour Hersh in the *London Review of Books* revealing that the Obama administration deliberately manipulated intelligence to falsely assert it had proof of Syrian government and military responsibility for the Ghouta attack (Hersh 2013: 9–12).

Hersh cited current and former US military and intelligence officials on the falsification of intelligence regarding the 21 August attack, as well as the Obama administration's concealment of the existence of intelligence reports warning that the Al-Qaeda-affiliated Al Nusra Front militia had the capacity to manufacture and weaponise the nerve gas sarin used in the Ghouta attack.

Obama, Syria and Iraq 2016

It was not long before the Obama administration did launch military action in Syria, albeit under the pretext of fighting a war against the so-called Islamic State in Syria and Iraq (ISIS). Legal challenges have proven ineffective to halt the expansion of presidential war-making powers, with lawsuits stymied by a combination of White House and Pentagon obstruction and judicial complicity in the process.

In May 2016, US Army Captain Nathan Michael Smith filed a lawsuit alleging that the Obama administration's unilateral decision to launch a war against ISIS in Syria and Iraq violated the US Constitution and the 1973 War Powers Resolution, since only Congress has the power to declare war.

The lawsuit shed light on the assertion of unlimited presidential powers to launch and wage wars. In 2014, Obama announced that he was ordering the US military to begin hostilities in a 'war against ISIS', which included Syria and Iraq. This occurred after the Obama administration had declared a formal end to hostilities in Iraq.

On 23 September 2014, President Obama reported to Congress on the deployment of forces to Iraq and Syria. He identified this legal authority:

I have directed these actions, which are in the national security and foreign policy interests of the United States, pursuant to my constitutional and statutory authority as Commander in Chief (including the authority to carry out Public Law 107–40 and Public Law 107–243 [the AUMFs of 2001 and 2002]) and as Chief Executive, as well as my constitutional and statutory authority to conduct the foreign relations of the United States.

Under that interpretation, presidents would be authorised to take military action for decades (Fisher 2017: 276).

In unilaterally declaring war and sending soldiers into combat, Obama, a former constitutional scholar, simply ignored the US Constitution and the War Powers Resolution. Yale Law Professor Bruce Ackerman, who represented Smith in his lawsuit, wrote in a *New York Times* article in September 2014 that Obama's actions constituted 'a decisive break in the American constitutional tradition'. He continued: 'Nothing attempted by his predecessor, George W. Bush, remotely compares in imperial hubris' (Ackerman 2014).

In December 2015, Obama went further. After promising at least 16 times on camera not to put American 'boots in the ground' in Syria, he revealed the deployment of 50 Special Forces soldiers to Syria. In April 2016, the number of US soldiers in Iraq rose to almost 5,000 (Thompson 2016).

The nominal political and legal justification for the ongoing US military aggression throughout the Middle East remained the 2001 and 2002 AUMFs. However, this pretext for unlimited war had worn increasingly threadbare and absurd. In 2001 and 2002, ISIS did not exist; it came to prominence during the US- and Saudi-supported efforts to overthrow the Syrian government of Bashar al-Assad, beginning in 2011.

Smith's lawsuit alleged a total of five counts of illegal conduct by the Obama administration: violation of the War Powers Resolution; violation of the president's constitutional duty to 'take care that the laws be faithfully executed'; violation of the 2001 AUMF; violation of the 2002 AUMF; and violation of limits on the president's powers as commander-in-chief. Smith's lawsuit requested a declaration 'that the war against ISIS in Syria and Iraq violates the War Powers Resolution because the Congress has not declared war or given the president specific statutory authorization to fight the war', and that 'the War Powers Resolution will require the disengagement, within thirty days, of all United States armed forces from the war against ISIS in Iraq and Syria' (Fisher 2017: 273).

On 11 July 2016, the Justice Department filed a brief asking the district court to dismiss Smith's case. Four broad reasons were offered: his claims raised non-justiciable political questions; he lacked legal standing to assert his claims; there was no waiver of sovereign immunity that permitted his claims to proceed; and he could not obtain equitable relief against President Obama (Fisher 2017: 273–74).

With regard to the first point, the Justice Department noted that, following the enactment of the War Powers Resolution, 'nearly every President has committed US armed forces into combat operations overseas'. That was quite true, although those operations generally ceased within 60 days. The Obama administration's military intervention in Libya lasted seven months. With regard to air strikes against ISIS, they began in August 2014 and executive officials predicted that military operations would continue well beyond the Obama administration, possibly lasting up to ten years or more (Fisher 2017: 273–74).

The government's brief in the *Smith* case pointed out that previous deployments had prompted lawsuits seeking judicial determination of the division of war powers between Congress and the president, and '[n]ot one of these suits has prevailed', with 'virtually all of them' dismissed on jurisdictional grounds. According to the Justice Department, the political question doctrine barred judicial review of Smith's claims because the Constitution 'leaves it to the political branches to decide, generally through the give and take of the process, under what circumstances the President can use military force overseas' (Fisher 2017: 273–74).

Judicial review would be 'inappropriate absent a clear conflict between the political branches over the President's authority to act'. The government's brief said that no such conflict existed because Congress had appropriated 'billions of dollars in support of the military operation'. Moreover, the issue was one in which 'courts are particularly ill-equipped to venture' and lack 'relevant expertise or access to the type of information necessary to render an informed decision' (Fisher 2017: 273–74).

As for standing, the government claimed that courts 'repeatedly have rejected the proposition that swearing an oath to support and defend the Constitution can transform such a generalized interest into a concrete form'. The government cited *Crane v. Johnson* 783 F.3d 244 (2015), in which the court had rejected a challenge by an immigration agent who objected that the administration's decision to protect undocumented aliens from deportation conflicted with the duty of enforcement officers to carry out statutory policy (Fisher 2013: 273–74).

A main argument in the brief concerned 'an unbroken stream of appropriations' passed by Congress supporting military actions against ISIS. This funding support was 'by itself sufficient to foreclose any conceivable role for the courts' in a challenge to the administration's use of military force against the group. The reliance on appropriations was not disturbed by section 8(a) of the War Powers Resolution, which purports to bar Congress from authorizing military operations through an appropriations measure unless that measure 'states that it is intended to constitute specific statutory authorization within the meaning of this chapter'. This argument echoed those of the Johnson administration, which insisted that Congress authorised the escalation of the Vietnam War by appropriating funds (Fisher 2017: 273–74).

On 18 August 2016, Smith's attorneys filed a response to the government's motion to dismiss. Their brief argued that the district court had jurisdiction to hear the case, that Smith had standing and that it was his duty as a military officer to disobey orders that were beyond the president's authority as commander-in-chief. Regarding the harm that Smith faced, the brief explained that if he disobeyed an order he regarded as illegal, he faced the prospect of a court martial and lengthy imprisonment, as well as a dishonourable discharge. As to the government's claim that the case represented a political question unfit for the courts, Smith's attorneys responded, 'This is a garden-variety statutory construction case', pointing to language in section 8(a)(1) of the War Powers Resolution. Similarly, they asked the court to determine whether President Obama could rely for legal support on two other congressional resolutions, the 2001 and 2002 AUMFs (Fisher 2017: 275–76).

Attorneys for Smith argued that the 1973 Resolution required Obama to withdraw US forces involved in hostilities with ISIS within 60 days unless Congress had declared war or given the president 'specific statutory authority' to continue. No such legislation was enacted to support the war against ISIS. The filing disputed the government's central claim that the 'specific authorization' required by section 5(b) of the 1973 Resolution can be established by appropriations bills that have funded military actions against ISIS. Smith's lawyers said that section 8(a)(1) of the Resolution requires an appropriations bill to specifically authorise the introduction of US armed forces into hostilities. Yet the government did not argue that military operations against ISIS were authorized by appropriations bills; rather, it pointed toward the 2001 and 2002 AUMFs (Fisher 2017: 276–77).

On 21 November 2016, US District Judge Colleen Kollar-Kotelly granted the government's motion to dismiss Smith's complaint, clearing the way for the conflict to continue under President Donald Trump. She concluded that Smith had not alleged an injury sufficiently concrete or particularised to establish legal standing. On page 11 of her Opinion, she stated that Smith 'has no qualms about participating in a fight against ISIL' (*Smith v. Obama*, USDC Col. Civil Action No. 16-843, Memorandum Opinion of District Judge Kollar-Kotelly, 21 November 2016). While it is true that Smith supported military action against ISIS, he certainly had legal and constitutional reservations that led him to file his lawsuit (Fisher 2017: 277–78).

In her 34-page Opinion, the judge insisted that Smith's desire to have a court clarify the legal issues was not a sufficient injury to give him a right to bring the case. While there were Vietnam-era precedents in which courts had ruled that soldiers did have a right to challenge the legality of their orders to deploy, she said that those cases involved plaintiffs who did not support that war effort.

Moreover, she held that Smith's claims presented non-justiciable political questions unsuitable for a court. Whether the war had been properly authorised was a question for the two elected branches of government, not a court, to decide:

> This case raises questions that are committed to the political branches of government. The court is not well equipped to resolve these questions, and the political branches who are so equipped do not appear to be in dispute as to their answers.
>
> (*Smith v. Obama*, USDC Col. Civil Action No. 16–843, Memorandum Opinion of District Judge Kollar-Kotelly, 21 November 2016, at 33–34).

In response to the decision of the district court, on 3 April 2017Smith's attorneys filed a brief with the US Court of Appeals for the DC Circuit, stating that Smith had standing to bring the suit. As to the political question doctrine, Smith's brief said the district court 'ignored' the *Youngstown v. Sawyer* 343 US 579 (1952) (known as *The Steel Seizure Case*) and was that the decision in this case was 'flatly inconsistent' with the Supreme Court's decision in that case. The brief noted that '[n]o controversial fact finding is needed to establish that the AUMFs enacted by Congress in 2001 and 2002 cannot serve as the "specific authorizations" required by the WPR for the President's decision to initiate "hostilities" against ISIL in 2014', adding that 'Congress's rules prohibit the use of appropriations as vehicles for substantive legislation' (Fisher 2017: 277–78).

When Smith's appeal was heard in October 2017, the US Justice Department declared that courts should have no say over how the administration stretches the post-9/11 war authorisations to justify new wars. According to a media report, Judge Thomas Griffith, one of three members on the Court of Appeals, expressed concern about accepting the government's argument that courts could not rule on the matter. 'What if the president were to initiate hostilities with a nation or organisation that wasn't plausibly within these AUMFs, would that be subject to review?' Griffith asked. Justice Department Attorney Thomas Byron answered: 'No, I think, is the short answer. No' (Nelson 2017).

Griffith, exploring potential consequences, asked: 'Under what circumstances would the judiciary be entitled to limit the president's exercise of his war powers? Help me understand that. It sounds to me like you're saying none.'

Byron responded: 'I think what I'm saying is we haven't seen it yet.'

The judge, pressing further, asked whether AUMFs actually placed any constraints on the president: 'Is there any example where the president initiates hostilities that are beyond the scope of the AUMF and a plaintiff with standing comes here to challenge it, do we have authority to enforce the AUMF against the president?'

Byron replied: 'I think probably not, and there are many reasons as we discussed today.'

Later, Byron added, 'It can be enforced but not in court'—arguing that the proper remedy for illegal wars is congressional action (Nelson 2017).

Another judge on the panel, Raymond Randolph, recalled an 8–1 US Supreme Court ruling in 1973 (*Schlesinger v. Holtzman* 414 US 1321 (1973)), which struck down an injunction to halt President Richard Nixon's congressionally unauthorised three-year secret bombing of Cambodia during the Vietnam War. He noted that Congress had stepped in, reaching a deal with Nixon to eventually end the bombing. The revelation of the secret bombing of Cambodia, which had triggered a widespread public outcry, had been a factor prompting Congress to pass the 1973 War Powers Resolution.

Attorneys for Smith said that it would be troubling if judges were to find that presidential war-making is off limits. In closing remarks, Yale Law Professor Bruce Ackerman warned that the stakes were high:

If the court fails to act in this case, it will have established a precedent that permits future presidents of the United States with a mere assertion [to declare] that one or another terrorist group, without any provision of evidence to anybody, is an object of war. Forever.

(Nelson 2017)

The government sought the dismissal of the lawsuit on several grounds. It argued that Smith did not suffer an injury that would require legal remedy, that the court cannot pass a ruling over a political question like this and that a declaratory judgment is not possible against a US president. It also said Congress had given an implicit authorisation of the war against ISIS by funding it, reprising the argument President Bill Clinton used to explain why he never sought congressional approval for the bombings of Serbia in 1999, which passed the War Powers Resolution's 60-day deadline (*Smith v. Trump*, USCA Case No. 16-5377, Brief for Appellee, 9 June 2017).

Obama, Trump and Niger

Unauthorised military operations were unearthed in Niger during 2017, when four US soldiers were killed on 4 October of that year. This could be seen as a case study in the ongoing expansion of US militarism without legal restraint. Any attempt to assess the extent of presidential war powers is misleading unless it takes into account the record of deception practised by successive presidents, including Obama, to drag the country into war after war.

In February 2013, the Obama White House announced that 100 US troops were being sent into Niger. Hundreds more were to follow. At the time, it was revealed that Washington had signed an agreement with the Niger government allowing the US military to set up a drone base in the country's territory, creating the conditions for spreading the Obama administration's remote-control assassination programme throughout the region. That base was constructed in the city of Agadez, containing facilities to house and launch MQ-9 hunter-killer drones.

According to AFRICOM, the US military command based in Stuttgart, Germany, the US Special Forces deployed to Niger were tasked with providing training, logistics and intelligence to assist the Nigerien military in fighting militants affiliated with Al Qaeda in Mali and Boko Haram in neighbouring Nigeria. AFRICOM officially stated that its forces interact with the Nigerien army in a 'non-combat advisory' capacity.

On 20 October 2017, however, the *Washington Post* reported that the Pentagon was instituting a 'status-based targeting' system in Niger, allowing its troops to hunt down and employ lethal force against any suspected member of an Islamist insurgent group 'even if that person does not pose an immediate threat'. The employment of such assassination squads, along with drone killings and similar methods, serves only to intensify civil war conditions throughout the region, providing the pretext for even greater US intervention (Attiah 2017).

Indeed, the principal source of the Niger conflict lay in the 2011 US-NATO war to topple Gaddafi in Libya, which shattered the tenuous equilibrium that Gaddafi had maintained among the Tuareg and other tribal groups in Niger and elsewhere in the Sahel. The rise of Islamist groups was directly tied to the utilisation of Al Qaeda elements by Washington and its allies as proxy ground forces in the war for regime change that ended with Gaddafi's lynching and the decimation of Libyan society. In the aftermath of the Libyan government's fall, its arms stockpiles found their way into the hands of Islamist groups throughout the region.

According to the Congressional Research Service:

> Congress has shaped US engagement with Niger and the US military footprint in the country through its authorization and appropriation of funding for US security cooperation and assistance programs, and through its authorization of funding for US military construction.
>
> (Arieff et al. 2017: 1)

Many in Congress, including Senator Lindsey Graham (R-South Carolina) and Senate Minority Leader Chuck Schumer (D-New York), claimed not to be aware that US troops were stationed in Niger. However, Senator Bob Corker (R-Tennessee), chair of the Senate Foreign Relations Committee, stated at a hearing that Congress had been notified of troop deployments around the world, including the build-up in Niger, and had responded by funding the Department of Defense (Corker 2017).

Corker cited President Trump's 27 June 2017 notice to Congress identifying 19 countries in which US military personnel were deployed and equipped for combat, comprising Afghanistan, Iraq, Syria, Yemen, Somalia, Libya, Kenya, Cameroon, Uganda, South Sudan, Democratic Republic of Congo, Central African Republic, Djibouti, Jordan, Turkey, Egypt, Cuba, Kosovo and Niger (Corker 2017). The list indicates the extent to which the Obama administration's expansion of US interventions laid the foundation for further escalation under Trump.

In the midst of the controversy over the troop deaths in Niger and President Trump's response, some Democratic Party politicians and media commentators took up the call for Congress to debate the ongoing US military interventions and to pass a new AUMF. On 24 October 2017, *Washington Post* columnist Eugene Robinson wrote: 'Congress needs to do more than investigate the deaths. It needs to authorise this conflict—or shut it down.'

Robinson (2017) described the generals and ex-generals in the Trump administration—White House Chief of Staff John Kelly, Defense Secretary James Mattis and National Security Advisor H. R. McMaster—as 'the last line of defense between our great nation and the abyss'. At the same time, however, he suggested that this military presence in the administration made it all the more important for Congress to 'reclaim its war-making powers' by passing a new AUMF.

Such columns reflected increasing nervousness within ruling circles that the controversy over Niger had lifted the lid on both the ever-expanding global military operations of the Pentagon and the increasingly open turn toward military control of the government at home. Any new AUMF passed by Congress, which long ago gave up even the pretence of defending its constitutional powers, would provide only a legislative fig leaf to facilitate this process. As discussed in the Introduction to this volume, other international proposals have been made for a congressional or parliamentary role in mobilising public support for a war.

Donald Trump: expanding Obama's precedents in Syria and beyond

The Trump administration has exploited the precedents set by the Obama and George W. Bush administrations, with the complicity of Congress, to go even further in asserting executive war-making powers, starting with Syria. With regard to Syria itself, the White House asserted the right to expand the US military operations indefinitely, long past the defeat of ISIS, the ostensible purpose for the intervention.

This position was laid out in letters to former Democratic Party vice-presidential candidate Senator Tim Kaine, from the Pentagon and the State Department, on 29 January 2018 and 12 February 2018, respectively. The letters asserted inherent executive power to wage war not only in Syria, but also by implication all over the world (Kaine, Tillerson and Mattis 2018).

Kaine had called publicly for the passage of a new AUMF to provide a legal facade for war in Syria, directed at bringing down the government of Syrian President Bashar al-Assad. The senator had accused Trump of 'acting like a king by unilaterally starting a war'.

In letters to the Pentagon and State Department dated 19 December 2017, Kaine merely asked the Trump administration to explain its understanding of its authority to stay on in Syria. According to the Pentagon letter in response, ongoing operations in Syria still fell within the framework of the supposed campaign to defeat ISIS, even though all cities and towns controlled by ISIS had been retaken. The Trump administration, as with the Obama administration before it, absurdly claimed that the 'war against ISIS' was justified by the 2001 AUMF against Al Qaeda, adopted more than 16 years ago, providing congressional sanction for the invasion of Afghanistan.

Deputy Undersecretary of Defense for Policy David Trachtenberg wrote: 'Just as when we previously removed U.S. forces prematurely, the group will look to exploit any abatement in pressure to regenerate capabilities and reestablish local control of territory.' The letter asserted that '[t]he campaign to defeat ISIS is transitioning to a new phase in Iraq and Syria'; The US military, 'optimizing and adapting our military presence to maintain counterterrorism pressure on the enemy, while facilitating stabilization and political reconciliation efforts needed to ensure the enduring defeat of ISIS'.

The State Department sent Kaine a similar letter, which also argued that international law provided a basis for US forces to remain in Syria—despite the lack of consent from the Syrian government—to protect Iraq and the United States from terrorists.

Both letters also said that American troops may strike at Syrian government or Iranian forces deemed to threaten Americans or Syrian rebel groups that are assisting the United States in fighting ISIS.

Mary K. Waters, Assistant Secretary of State for Legislative Affairs, wrote:

> The United States does not seek to fight the government of Syria or Iran or Iranian-supported groups in Iraq or Syria. However, the United States will not hesitate to use necessary and proportionate force to defend U.S., coalition, or partner forces engaged in operations to defeat ISIS and degrade Al Qaeda.

These assertions are so sweeping—and subject to such arbitrary and subjective interpretation—as to justify an indefinite US military occupation of Syria and a wider war against Iran.

The Pentagon and State Department letters conceded that neither Syrian government forces nor their allies, such as Hezbollah and Iran, could be considered 'associated forces' of ISIS or Al Qaeda, as required under the 2001 War Powers Resolution. Instead, US attacks on Syrian government forces and their allies were characterised as acts of 'self-defense' by American military forces, even though the US forces entered Syria in violation of its sovereignty and without the consent of its government.

Further, the Pentagon letter revealed that more troops were operating in Syria, secretly, than its official statistics indicated. It asserted the president's unilateral right to boost troop numbers and conduct secret operations, noting that some classified details are provided to congressional committees in closed sessions:

> As part of our effort to accelerate the campaign against ISIS, [the US Department of Defense] revised how it publicly reports force levels in Iraq and Syria. As a result, [it] now publicly reports that it has approximately 2,000 forces in Syria. These numbers do not reflect an increase in the number of personnel on the ground; rather, they represent a change in how these numbers are publicly reported. Under previous reporting practices, certain forces in Syria on a temporary duty status were not publicly reported, but they are now included in the 2,000 force total. For operational security reasons, US forces conducting sensitive missions are not included in the publicly reported numbers. As you know, [the US Department of Defense] provides these classified details to its congressional oversight committees in closed sessions. We anticipate these numbers will decrease as the nature of our operations change in Iraq and Syria, but we do not have a timeline-based approach to our presence in either Iraq or Syria.
>
> (Kaine et al. 2018)

Thus, behind the backs of the American people, congressional leaders have agreed to unknown numbers of troop expansions and 'sensitive missions', with no 'timeline' for ending the operations. This further highlights Congress's complicity in the further expansion of presidential war powers.

Even more sweeping was the legal justification advanced for the missile strike that Trump ordered against a Syrian airbase in April 2017, after a US-led media campaign claiming that the Syrian government had used nerve gas on a town in Idlib province held by anti-Assad forces. According to the Pentagon letter, 'the President authorized that strike pursuant to his power under Article II of the Constitution as Commander in Chief and Chief Executive to use this sort of military force overseas to defend important US national interests' (Kaine et al. 2018).

This language is entirely open-ended, making a mockery of the US constitutional structure under which the power to declare war is reserved to Congress, while the president serves as commander-in-chief to direct the military operations authorised by the legislature.

When Trump announced the April 2017 air strike, the president said: 'It is in this vital national security interest of the United States to prevent and deter the spread and use of deadly chemical weapons.' He also invoked the Syrian refugee crisis and continuing regional instability (Goldsmith 2017).

Jack Goldsmith, a Harvard law professor who led the Office of Legal Counsel at the Justice Department during the George W. Bush administration, wrote that this criteria for what is sufficient to constitute a national interest was even thinner than previous precedents and would seemingly justify almost any unilateral use of force:

> The interests invoked—protecting regional security and in upholding or enforcing important treaty norms—will always be present when the president is considering military intervention . . . Taken alone—and they are all we have here—these interests provide no practical limitation on presidential power.
>
> (Goldsmith 2017)

The White House made similar open-ended assertions after conducting even bigger missile strikes against Syria in April 2018. In an address to the nation announcing the bombings, President Trump said: 'Today, the nations of Britain, France, and the United States of America have marshaled their righteous power against barbarism and brutality' (White House 2018).

Trump made no attempt to justify the attack in terms of self-defence, for purposes of international law, nor did he bother explaining why, and by what power, he acted without congressional approval. Instead, he invoked a catch-all conception of 'national security interest', and foreshadowed further military and other aggression:

> The purpose of our actions tonight is to establish a strong deterrent against the production, spread and use of chemical weapons. Establishing this deterrent is a vital national security interest of the United States. The combined American, British and French response to these atrocities will integrate all

instruments of our national power: military, economic and diplomatic. We are prepared to sustain this response until the Syrian regime stops its use of prohibited chemical agents.

(White House 2018)

Conclusion

Unrestrained war powers are today being asserted and exercised by US administrations, with serious and ominous implications both globally and domestically. With the complicity of Congress, the judiciary, the corporate media and academic commentators, the world's greatest military power is seeking to prevent its identified rivals, starting with Russia and China, from developing the ability to obstruct or challenge the supremacy that the United States established as a result of World War II. The threat of a third world war—which would be a nuclear one—is being accompanied by preparations for internal repression to prevent any opposition, as will be seen in Chapters 7 and 8.

References

Ackerman, B. 2014. 'Obama's betrayal of the Constitution', *New York Times*, 11 September, www.nytimes.com/2014/09/12/opinion/obamas-betrayal-of-the-constitution.html (accessed 20 June 2016).

Arieff, A., Blanchard, L., Feickert, A., McInnis, K., Rollins, J., and Weed, M. 2017. *Niger: Frequently Asked Questions about the October 2017 Attack on U.S. Soldiers*, 27 October, Washington, DC: Congressional Research Service.

Attiah, K. 2017. 'After Niger, ramping up U.S. "aggression" in Africa is a really, really bad idea', *Washington Post*, 23 October, www.washingtonpost.com/news/global-opinions/wp/2017/10/23/after-niger-ramping-up-u-s-aggression-in-africa-is-a-really-really-bad-idea/?noredirect=on&utm_term=.a6215cda6fd7 (accessed 25 January 2018).

Bacevich, A., and Cohen, E. 2001. *War over Kosovo: Politics and Strategy in a Global Age*. New York: Columbia University Press.

Barnes, M. 2010. *The Spanish-American War and Philippine Insurrection, 1898–1902*. London: Routledge.

Beatty, F. 1954. 'Another version of what started the war with Japan', *U. S. News and World Report*, 28 May.

Beede, B. 2013. *The War of 1898 and U.S. Interventions, 1898 to 1934: An Encyclopedia*. London: Taylor & Francis.

Bloomberg. 2018. 'President Trump wants $686 billion for the military. here's how he plans to spend it', *Fortune*, 12 February, http://fortune.com/2018/02/12/trump-military-budget/ (accessed 6 May 2018).

Commager, H. 1974. *The Defeat of America*. New York: Simon & Schuster.

Corker, R. 2017. *Corker Statement at Hearing on Authorizations for the Use of Military Force*, 30 October, US Senate Committee on Foreign Relations, www.foreign.senate.gov/press/chair/release/corker-statement-at-hearing-on-authorizations-for-the-use-of-military-force (accessed 21 January 2018).

Corwin, E. 1951. 'The president's power', *New Republic*, 29 January.

Editorial Board. 2017. 'America's forever wars', *New York Times*, 22 October, www.nytimes. com/2017/10/22/opinion/americas-forever-wars.html (accessed 12 November 2017).

Elsea, J., and Weed, M. 2014. *Declarations of War and Authorizations for the Use of Military Force: Historical Background and Legal Implications*, 18 April, Washington, DC: Congressional Research Service.

Emerson, J. 1975. 'The War Powers Resolution tested: the president's independent defense power', *Notre Dame Law Review*, 51(2): 187–216.

Fisher, L. 2012. 'Military operations in Libya: no war? No hostilities?', *Presidential Studies Quarterly*, 42(1): 176–89.

Fisher, L. 2013. 'Foreword'. In C. Edelson, *Emergency Presidential Power: From the Drafting of the Constitution to the War on Terror*. Madison, WI: University of Wisconsin Press.

Fisher, L. 2017. 'A challenge to presidential wars: *Smith v. Obama*', *Congress & the Presidency*, 44(2): 272–73.

Foner, P. 1972. *The Spanish-Cuban-American War and the Birth of American Imperialism*. New York: Monthly Review Press.

Friedman, T. 1984. 'America's failure in Lebanon', *New York Times Magazine*, 8 April, www.nytimes.com/1984/04/08/magazine/america-s-failure-in-lebanon.html (accessed 25 May 2018).

Friedman, T. 1999. 'A manifesto for the fast world', *New York Times*, 28 March.

Friedman, T. 2000. *The Lexus and the Olive Tree: Understanding Globalization*. New York: Anchor.

Gerson, M. 2013. 'Obama's missteps on Syria lead to retreat', *Washington Post*, 11 September, www.washingtonpost.com/opinions/michael-gerson-obamas-missteps-on-syria-lead-to-retreat/2013/09/11/e6fec8de-1b1d-11e3-a628-7e6dde8f889d_story. html?utm_term=.e9fc8290c9d6 (accessed 11 June 2017).

Glennon, M. 1991. 'The Gulf War and the Constitution', *Foreign Affairs*, Spring, www. foreignaffairs.com/articles/iraq/1991-03-01/gulf-war-and-constitution (accessed 11 June 2017).

Goldsmith, J. 2017. 'The constitutionality of the Syria strike through the eyes of OLC (and the Obama administration)', *Lawfare*, 7 April, www.lawfareblog.com/constitutionality-syria-strike-through-eyes-olc-and-obama-administration (accessed 21 February 2018).

Head, M. 2011. *Crimes against the State*. London: Ashgate.

Head, M. 2016. *Emergency Powers in Theory and Practice: The Long Shadow of Carl Schmitt*. London: Ashgate.

Hendrikson, R. 2013. 'Libya and American war powers: war-making decisions in the United States', *Global Change, Peace & Security*, 25(2): 175–89.

Hersh, S. 2013. 'Whose sarin?', *London Review of Books*, 35(24): 9–12.

House of Commons Foreign Affairs Select Committee. 2016. *Libya: Examination of Intervention and Collapse and the UK's Future Policy Options*, https://publications. parliament.uk/pa/cm201617/cmselect/cmfaff/119/11902.htm (accessed 13 November 2017).

Isikoff, M. 2015. 'What Clinton left out about her history with Gadhafi', *Yahoo!*, 14 October, www.yahoo.com/news/what-clinton-left-out-about-her-history-with-180109258.html (accessed 20 June 2016).

Kaine, T., Tillerson, R., and Mattis, J. 2017–18. 'Kaine letter to Mattis/Tillerson; DOD letter to Kaine; State Dept letter to Kaine', 19 December, 29 January, 12 February, www.documentcloud.org/documents/4383185-Kaine-Trump-ISIS-war-power-letters.html (accessed 22 February 2018).

Krass, C. 2011. *Authority to Use Military Force in Libya: Memorandum Opinion for the Attorney General*, 1 April, https://fas.org/irp/agency/doj/olc/libya.pdf (accessed 17 June 2017).

McGinnis, J. 1996. 'The spontaneous order of war powers', *Case Western Reserve Law Review*, 47(4):1317–29.

Nelson, S. 2017. 'Trump Justice Department: wars are off limits to court review', *Washington Examiner*, 27 October.

New York Times. 2011. 'Libya and the War Powers Act', 16 June, www.nytimes.com/2011/06/17/opinion/17fri1.html (accessed 11 June 2016).

Obama, B. 2011. 'Remarks by the President in Address to the Nation on Libya', 28 March, https://obamawhitehouse.archives.gov/the-press-office/2011/03/28/remarks-president-address-nation-libya (accessed 20 June 2016).

Obama, B. 2013. 'Transcript of Obama's Syria speech', *Chicago Tribune*, 10 September, http://articles.chicagotribune.com/2013-09-10/news/chi-transcript-of-obama-syria-speech-20130910_1_chemical-weapons-sarin-gas-assad (accessed 15 June 2016).

Obama, B., Cameron, D., and Sarkozy, N. 2011. 'Libya letter by Obama, Cameron and Sarkozy: Full text', *BBC News*, 15 April, www.bbc.com/news/world-africa-13090646 (accessed 20 January 2018).

Obermeyer, Z., Murray, C., and Gakidou, E. 2008. 'Fifty years of violent war deaths from Vietnam to Bosnia: analysis of data from the World Health Survey Programme', *British Medical Journal*, 336(7659): 1482–86.

Peter G. Peterson Foundation. 2018. *U.S. Defense Spending Compared to Other Countries*, 7 May, www.pgpf.org/chart-archive/0053_defense-comparison (accessed 23 September 2018).

Prange, G., and Holland, D. 1991. *Pearl Harbor: The Verdict of History*. New York: Penguin Books.

Robinson, E. 2017. 'Congress needs to reclaim war-making powers from Trump, generals', *The Mercury News*, 24 October, www.mercurynews.com/2017/10/24/robinson-congress-needs-to-reclaim-war-making-powers-from-trump-generals/ (accessed 22 January 2018).

Rostow, E. 1972. 'Great cases make bad law: the War Powers Act', *Texas Law Review*, 50(5): 833–900.

Smith v. Obama, USDC Columbia Civil Action No. 16–843, Memorandum Opinion of District Judge Kollar-Kotelly, 21 November 2016, www.documentcloud.org/documents/3223769-Smith-Opinion-Dismissing-Case.html (accessed 21 October 2017).

Smith v. Trump, USCA Case No. 16–5377, Brief for Appellee, 9 June 2017, https://assets.documentcloud.org/documents/4113473/Smith-v-Trump-DC-Circuit-DOJ-Appellee-Brief-6-09.pdf (accessed 15 December 2017).

Stinnett, R. 1999. *Day of Deceit: The Truth about FDR and Pearl Harbor*. New York: Simon & Schuster.

Stone, G. 2004. *Perilous Times: Free Speech in Wartime*. New York: Norton.

Stone, O., and Kuznick, P. 2013. *The Untold History of the United States*. London: Ebury Press.

Theobald, R. 1954. *Final Secret of Pearl Harbor*. New York: Devin-Adair.

Thompson, M. 2016. 'Number of U.S. troops in Iraq keeps creeping upward', *Time*, 18 April, http://time.com/4298318/iraq-us-troops-barack-obama-mosul-isis/ (accessed 21 June 2016).

Turner, R. 1994. 'War and the forgotten executive power clause of the Constitution: a review essay of John Hart Ely's *War and Responsibility*', *Virginia Journal of International Law*, 34(4): 903–79.

Tushnet, M. 2007. 'The political constitution of emergency powers: some lessons from Hamdan', *Minnesota Law Review*, 91(5): 1451–72.

UN Secretary-General. 2013. *Report of the United Nations Mission to Investigate Allegations of the Use of Chemical Weapons in the Syrian Arab Republic on the Alleged Use of Chemical Weapons in the Ghouta Area of Damascus on 21 August*, 13 September, http://repository.un.org/handle/11176/24321 (accessed 20 June 2017).

Uchitelle, L. 2017. 'The U.S. still leans on the military-industrial complex', *New York Times*, 22 September, www.nytimes.com/2017/09/22/business/economy/military-industrial-complex.html (accessed 2 February 2018).

US Department of Defense. 2018. *Summary of the 2018 National Defense Strategy of the United States*, www.defense.gov/Portals/1/Documents/pubs/2018-National-Defense-Strategy-Summary.pdf (accessed 3 March 2018).

Van Auken, B. 2016. '*New York Times* on Clinton and Libya: portrait of a war criminal', *World Socialist Web Site*, 1 March, www.wsws.org/en/articles/2016/03/01/clin-m01.html (accessed 18 May 2017).

White House. 2011. 'United States activities in Libya', 15 June, https://assets.document cloud.org/documents/204673/united-states-activities-in-libya-6-15-11.pdf (accessed 20 November 2017).

White House. 2018. *'Joined by allies, President Trump takes action to end Syria's chemical weapons attacks'*, 14 April, www.whitehouse.gov/articles/joined-allies-president-trump-takes-action-end-syrias-chemical-weapons-attacks/ (accessed 20 May 2018).

Wormuth, F., and Firmage, E. 1989. *To Chain the Dog of War: The War Power of Congress in History and Law*. Chicago, IL: University of Illinois Press.

Yoo, J. 2005. *The Powers of War and Peace: The Constitution and Foreign Affairs after 9/11*. Chicago, IL: University of Chicago Press.

Zeisberg, M. 2013. *War Powers: The Politics of Constitutional Authority*. Princeton, NJ: Princeton University Press.

4 Britain's royal war prerogative reasserted and reinforced

In Britain, as in the United States, successive governments have increasingly resorted to, and expanded, executive war-making powers, although in the seemingly peculiar and anachronistic form of a 'prerogative' inherited from Britain's pre-17th-century absolute monarchy. This royal mandate, once said to be derived from the 'divine right of kings', has morphed into an authoritarian power, said to be held in the personal hands of a prime minister, possibly in consultation with a formal council, or an informal cabal, of ministers and military and intelligence chiefs.

Limited attempts to constrain the 'war prerogative' following the exposure of the lies told to justify the invasion of Iraq in 2003 have ultimately come to nothing. Instead, the ancient and legally unchallengeable royal prerogative to go to war has been reasserted.

Since the exposure of the lies about 'weapons of mass destruction' (WMDs) and the threat of nuclear attack exploited by Prime Minister Tony Blair's Labour government to justify Britain joining the US-led invasion of Iraq in 2003, a plethora of government and parliamentary reports have sought to pacify popular outrage by devising ways of pretending that the House of Commons is able to vote on any decision to enter a war.

Each proposal to legislate in the form of a US-style 'War Powers Act', however, has ultimately been killed off, leaving the war prerogative intact. In 2007, shortly after replacing Blair, Prime Minister Gordon Brown promised to limit the royal prerogative under which the prime minister can unilaterally declare war. Parliament, Brown proposed, would be guaranteed the right to approve 'significant, non-routine' deployments of the armed forces to 'the greatest extent possible'—but the Labour government later abandoned any such proposal.

Nonetheless, claims were made, both official and academic, that Blair's decision to secure parliamentary approval of the Iraq operation established a 'convention' that a prime minister must allow the House of Commons to debate and vote on the deployment of forces. This convention supposedly obviated the need for legislation to ensure parliamentary consent.

Events since 2011, in which British military forces, including special forces, have conducted overt and covert operations in Libya, Syria, Mali and Yemen without any preceding parliamentary vote, have shattered these claims.

In the case of the major Libyan intervention in 2011, which culminated in the violent overthrow of the Libyan government, Parliament approved it only retrospectively. Prime Minister Cameron brushed aside the supposed convention. The government had stated only a few months earlier that such a convention existed, while reserving to itself the power to ignore the convention in what it judged to be 'an emergency'. But there was no debate until three days after the deployment began. Cameron claimed that there was no time for consultation before military action because of the urgency of avoiding the 'slaughter of civilians' (Joseph 2013: 106). That humanitarian pretext was just as false as those offered for the Iraq invasion just eight years earlier, as demonstrated by the overthrow and murder of Gaddafi and the subsequent descent of Libya into brutal internal wars in which thousands of civilians were indeed slaughtered.

For the 2013 intervention in Mali, involving some 400 military personnel to support French forces, no debate or vote was held. The government justified this by saying it was in response to an emergency request, in support of a UN Security Council resolution, and that British forces were not deployed in a combat role. Other deployments of special forces, such as in Yemen, were kept secret.

With one exception, governments effectively disregarded the supposed convention. In 2013, facing widespread public opposition to a war with Syria, Prime Minister Cameron moved a House of Commons resolution to authorise and politically legitimise military operations in Syria. But he suffered an embarrassing defeat. So no such vote was permitted five years later, in April 2018, when Prime Minister Theresa May and her cabinet ordered British forces to join a missile attack on Syria without a parliamentary vote, despite opinion polls showing even greater public opposition than in 2013. Acting in concert, the United States, France and Britain fired more than 100 cruise missiles into Syrian military bases and other buildings.

May insisted that her decision was legal, under both domestic and international law. She claimed that it was justified by unsubstantiated reports that the Syrian government had used unspecified chemical weapons against civilians in the Syrian town of Douma. Under Article 51 of the UN Charter, however, self-defence is the only justification for military aggression; otherwise, it is a war crime. Yet there was no assertion of acting in self-defence—even 'pre-emptive' self-defence, as Blair and US President George W. Bush had claimed in 2003. There was no suggestion whatsoever that Syria had attacked, or threatened to attack, Britain or its US and French allies, who participated in the missile strikes.

Syria 2018: executive war powers reinforced

Prime Minister May's government refused to convene Parliament before joining the Syrian attack and refused to allow the House of Commons to vote on the operation even after the event.

The pretext for the missile attack was unproven allegations that Syrian President Bashar al-Assad's military forces used banned chemical weapons against US-backed rebel militias in the city of Douma. Both Syria and Russia, which had significant military contingents in Syria to support Assad's government in its seven-year civil war against predominantly Islamist-based militias, categorically rejected these claims. They accused British intelligence of pressuring Syrian rebel organisations to manufacture a video that purported to show victims of a chemical weapons attack. A team from the Organisation for the Prohibition of Chemical Weapons (OPCW) was scheduled to arrive in Douma to carry out an inspection of the alleged site, but the missile strikes pre-empted that.

In a series of media statements and speeches immediately after the missile strikes, May claimed only that it was 'highly likely' that Syria had carried out a chemical weapons attack (Prime Minister's Office, 10 Downing Street and May 2018a).

May's decision also flew in the face of public opinion. A YouGov poll showed that Britons were overwhelmingly opposed, by two to one, to military strikes on Syria. Of 1,600 people surveyed, only 22 per cent supported air strikes—less than the 25 per cent that backed Prime Minister David Cameron's desired intervention in 2013 (Curtis 2018).

Seeking to bolster its position, a day after the missile strikes, the government released a 'policy paper' on its 'legal position'. Without providing any evidence, legal opinion or judicial precedents for its claims, the document asserted that:

> The Syrian regime has been killing its own people for seven years. Its use of chemical weapons, which has exacerbated the human suffering, is a serious crime of international concern, as a breach of the customary international law prohibition on the use of chemical weapons, and amounts to a war crime and a crime against humanity. The UK is permitted under international law, on an exceptional basis, to take measures in order to alleviate overwhelming humanitarian suffering.
>
> (Prime Minister's Office and
> 10 Downing Street 2018)

Without citing any authority, the paper said the intervention was legal because it met three conditions:

(i) there is convincing evidence, generally accepted by the international community as a whole, of extreme humanitarian distress on a large scale, requiring immediate and urgent relief;

(ii) it must be objectively clear that there is no practicable alternative to the use of force if lives are to be saved; and

(iii) the proposed use of force must be necessary and proportionate to the aim of relief of humanitarian suffering and must be strictly limited in time and in scope to this aim (i.e. the minimum necessary to achieve that end and for no other purpose).

> (Prime Minister's Office and 10 Downing Street 2018)

Delivering a statement in the House of Commons on 16 April, three days after the strikes, May further revealed the flimsy character of the allegations against

Syria, while insisting that only she, not Parliament, could authorise such military operations and that the missile strikes were legal under international law, regardless of the lack of a UN mandate. May said that the government had relied on unverified videos and other questionable sources involved in the Syrian civil war. She told the House:

> On Saturday 7th April, up to 75 people, including young children, were killed in an horrific attack in Douma, with as many as 500 further casualties. All indications are that this was a chemical weapons attack. UK medical and scientific experts have analysed open-source reports, images and video footage from the incident and concluded that the victims were exposed to a toxic chemical. This is corroborated by first-hand accounts from NGOs and aid workers.
>
> (Prime Minister's Office, 10 Downing Street, and May 2018b)

Despite the exposure of the lies produced by the intelligence agencies as the pretext for the 2003 invasion of Iraq, May asked Parliament and the public to rely on such sources, plus unspecified 'open source' information. She stated:

> A significant body of information—including intelligence—indicates the Syrian Regime is responsible for this latest attack. Open source accounts state that barrel bombs were used to deliver the chemicals. Barrel bombs are usually delivered by helicopters . . . The Opposition does not operate helicopters or use barrel bombs.
>
> (Prime Minister's Office et al. 2018b)

In other words, the government's 'information' was derived from social media posts by the Islamist opposition.

May also asserted Britain's unilateral right to launch military attacks without any UN authorisation, even in defiance of UN Security Council votes not to authorise such aggression. She denounced Labour Party leader Jeremy Corbyn for pointing toward the need for such authority under the UN Charter. May said: 'The Leader of the Opposition has said that he can "only countenance involvement in Syria if there is UN authority behind it". The House should be clear that would mean a Russian veto on our foreign policy' (Prime Minister's Office et al. 2018b).

This was an extraordinary assertion, repudiating the UN system put in place after World War II to prevent and outlaw military attacks, except in self-defence or with a UN mandate. Labour's stance was based on legal advice it had sought from Dapo Akande, a professor of public international law and co-director of the Oxford Institute for Ethics, Law and Armed Conflict. He advised that, contrary to government claims, neither the UN Charter nor international law permitted military action on the basis of humanitarian intervention. He also suggested that accepting Britain's position on the use of force would undermine the supremacy of the UN Charter. He concluded that the UK government's position could set a precedent for individual states making their own assessments of when force was necessary to achieve humanitarian ends in future, with the risk of abuse (Akande 2018).

Akande stated that even if a doctrine of humanitarian intervention did exist under international law, the strikes against Syria would not meet the three tests set out by the government, because they did not bring 'immediate and urgent relief' from the evils it sought to prevent and were taken before international chemical weapons inspectors were able to reach eastern Ghouta (Akande 2018).

May further argued that the intervention was lawful because it did not seek to overturn the Syrian government and was based on previous precedents established in Iraq. 'This was not about intervening in a civil war. And it was not about regime change', she stated:

> Our intervention in 1991 with the US and France—and in 1992 with the US—to create safe havens and enforce the no fly zones in Iraq following the Gulf War were also justified on the basis of humanitarian intervention.
> (Prime Minister's Office et al. 2018b)

Citing this precedent undercut May's own case. The 1991–92 interventions effectively carved out a northern Kurdish enclave in Iraq and helped to lay the basis for the next phase of the operation: the 2003 invasion to oust the Iraqi government and install a US-friendly regime.

Finally, May answered the question: '[W]hy did we not recall Parliament?' Without actually referring to the royal prerogative, she laid out a doctrine that essentially ruled out Parliament's right to be consulted, let alone vote or even scrutinise any evidence, before a prime minister initiated military action:

> Mr Speaker, the speed with which we acted was essential in co-operating with our partners to alleviate further humanitarian suffering and to maintain the vital security of our operations. This was a limited, targeted strike on a legal basis that has been used before. And it was a decision which required the evaluation of intelligence and information much of which was of a nature that could not be shared with Parliament. We have always been clear that the government has the right to act quickly in the national interest. I am absolutely clear, Mr Speaker, that it is Parliament's responsibility to hold me to account for such decisions—and Parliament will do so. But it is my responsibility as Prime Minister to make these decisions. And I will make them.
> (Prime Minister's Office et al. 2018b)

This statement was the very negation of democracy. If members of Parliament (MPs) have no right to a say on war because they are not privy to state secrets, then neither is the electorate to be allowed to intrude on actions with the gravest consequences supposedly taken in their name and in their interests.

After May's Commons statement, there was a limited three-hour debate on the Syrian action. The government refused to put the attacks to a vote; instead, the debate ended in a wholly symbolic vote called by the Scottish Nationalist Party (SNP) on a motion that the House 'has considered the current situation in Syria and the UK government approach', which the government won 314–36. The vote indicated that the government would have won a majority for its missile strikes, but deliberately chose not to do so, so that it could set a new precedent for bypassing Parliament and give itself a free hand for further attacks on Syria.

Parliament's role brushed aside

Three days after the April 2018 missile strikes on Syria, Prime Minister May went further, indicating that Britain's Parliament would never again be allowed to prevent a planned military intervention, as it had done when voting against an attack on Syria in 2013.

May's defence in Parliament of her refusal to recall Parliament before the 14 April missile strikes was framed to exclude any future vote prior to military action. Parliament met to debate a motion proposed by Labour Party leader Jeremy Corbyn for Parliament to 'take back control' of military matters by passing a Military Powers Act requiring the government to seek MPs' approval before launching action overseas.

Corbyn referred to the *Cabinet Manual*, drawn up by the previous Conservative–Liberal Democrat coalition government, which stated that military interventions should have prior parliamentary approval 'except when there [is] an emergency and such action would not be appropriate' (HC Deb, 17 April 2018, vol. 639, col. 196).

May replied that the 'exception' covered the action against Syria and would do so in all conceivable cases, except a premeditated formal declaration of war. Corbyn's proposed War Powers Act would make 'small-scale' military interventions unviable, primarily because any debate would endanger British and allied troops and aid the enemy. 'Uncertainty' was 'a critical part' of an operation's success, said May—despite US President Donald Trump having announced his intention to attack Syria to the world in advance on Twitter.

May stated:

> Making it unlawful for Her Majesty's Government to undertake any such military intervention without a vote would seriously compromise our national security, our national interests, and the lives of British citizens at home and abroad. And for as long as I'm prime minister, that will never be allowed to happen.
>
> (HC Deb, 17 April 2018, vol. 639, col. 209)

May alluded to her broader concern that a debate that might throw up awkward questions regarding the spurious basis for the strikes against Syria. Referring obliquely to the lies of the Blair government and the Bush administration in 2003 regarding WMDs, she said: 'In the post-Iraq era, it is natural for people to ask questions about intelligence' (HC Deb, 17 April 2018, vol. 639, col. 206).

However, May insisted that the government had an obligation to protect its supposed intelligence sources—a reference to Islamist terrorist groups in Syria. Parliament could never be allowed access to such intelligence, she said: 'This is not a question of whether we take Parliament into our confidence. It is a question of whether we take our adversaries into our confidence . . .' (HC Deb, 17 April 2018, vol. 639, col. 207).

In her speech, May acknowledged the support she had on the Labour Party benches—speaking of 'a tradition of support for military intervention on humanitarian grounds' in both parties. More directly still, she concluded her closing remarks by stating that the 'mood of the House' was unquestionable: '[W]e have the support of the House . . . A clear majority of the House believes we did the right thing' (HC Deb, 17 April 2018, vol. 639, col. 209).

The vote proved her estimation to be correct, pointing not only to the pro-war character of the Labour Party, but also to the historic collusion of Parliament in war-making. The government won the Syria debate by 317–256—that is, by a majority of 61. This meant that 54 Labour MPs—a fifth of the total—did not back Corbyn in his demand for a parliamentary vote, let alone in opposing military action (HC Deb, 17 April 2018, vol. 639, cols 242–46).

During the debate, the prime minister brushed aside the previously stated parliamentary convention, essentially rendering it redundant. She said that there was 'a fundamental difference between the policy and the perception of it that is conveyed in today's motion', and she quoted the *Cabinet Manual*:

> In 2011, the Government acknowledged that a convention had developed in Parliament that before troops were committed the House of Commons should have an opportunity to debate the matter and said that it proposed to observe that convention except where there was an emergency and such action would not be appropriate.
>
> (HC Deb, 17 April 2018, vol. 639, col. 200)

May said that more detail on the government's position had been set out in 2016 in a written ministerial statement from then Defence Secretary Michael Fallon, who wrote:

> The exception to the convention is important to ensure that this and future Governments can use their judgment about how best to protect the security and interests of the UK. In observing the convention, we must ensure that the ability of our armed forces to act quickly and decisively, and to maintain the security of their operations, is not compromised . . . If we were to attempt to clarify more precisely circumstances in which we would consult Parliament before taking military action, we would constrain the operational flexibility of the armed forces and prejudice the capability, effectiveness or security of those forces.
>
> (HC Deb, 17 April 2018, vol. 639, col. 200)

Exactly who holds the war powers?

Thus, in Britain, behind the appearance of parliamentary democracy, governments formally exercise the war powers via the seemingly anachronistic powers of the monarchy. Unlike the United States, where the American War of Independence swept away Britain's absolute monarchy and military colonial rule, the English Civil War and Revolution of the 17th century left the royal powers in place, preserved for use by the ruling political and military establishment.

Today, the official view, embraced by the parliamentary elite, as well as the executive and judicial authorities, is that sweeping prerogative powers govern war-making and military decisions. According to the final report in 2009 of a British government review of the royal prerogative powers: 'The domestic legal position on the deployment of force is relatively straightforward: Her Majesty's armed forces are deployed under the royal prerogative, exercised in practice by the Prime Minister and the Cabinet' (Ministry of Justice 2009: para. 46).

That report said that the prerogative extended over a broad range of military matters:

The Royal prerogative is the legal mechanism which allows the State to appoint people to carry arms in its service. Thus, the prerogative provides the authority for the Crown to:

- recruit members of the Armed Forces;
- appoint commanders and grant commissions to officers;
- establish the Defence Council; and
- make agreements with foreign states about stationing troops on their soil.
  (Ministry of Justice 2009: para. 46)

In its former guise as the House of Lords, Britain's highest court has reiterated the continued existence of such extensive powers. In *Chandler v Director of Public Prosecutions* [1964] AC 763, at 800, Lord Hodson stated: 'The Crown has, and this is not disputed, the right as head of State to decide in peace and war the disposition of its armed forces.' In *Burmah Oil Co. Ltd v Lord Advocate* [1965] AC 75, at 100, Lord Reid said:

There is no doubt that control of the armed forces has been left to the prerogative . . . subject to the power of Parliament to withhold supply and refuse to continue legislation essential for the maintenance of a standing army.

A shroud of secrecy surrounds who exactly exercises these powers, whom they consult, and what role is played by the military and intelligence chiefs, the royal palace and the governments of the US and other allied powers, in deciding to launch military operations. The Chilcot Inquiry into the disastrous outcome of the 2003 Iraq invasion criticised what it called the informal approach taken by Labour Prime Minister Tony Blair's cabal. The Chilcot report stated:

Most decisions on Iraq pre-conflict were taken either bilaterally between Mr Blair and the relevant Secretary of State or in meetings between Mr Blair, Mr Straw [then Foreign Secretary] and Mr Hoon [then Defence Secretary], with No.10 officials and, as appropriate, Mr John Scarlett (Chairman of the JIC [Joint Intelligence Committee]), Sir Richard Dearlove [head of the British Secret Intelligence Service] and Admiral Boyce [Chief of the Defence Staff]. Some of those meetings were minuted; some were not.

(Chilcot 2016: executive summary, para. 399)

To head off such criticism, Prime Minister David Cameron established the National Security Council (NSC) in May 2010. He announced that the NSC would be chaired by the prime minister. Its permanent members would be the deputy prime minister, the chancellor of the exchequer, the secretary of state for foreign and Commonwealth affairs, the home secretary, the secretary of state for defence, the secretary of state for international development and the security minister. Other cabinet ministers, including the secretary of state for energy and climate change, would attend as required. The chief of the defence staff, heads of intelligence agencies and other senior officials would also attend as required (Prime Minister's Office 2010).

That seems to remain the practice. According to its website, the NSC is chaired by the prime minister, with other cabinet members attending as required, along with the national security adviser and 'Chief of the Defence Staff and Heads of Intelligence Agencies' (gov.uk 2018).

However, no legislation authorises this institution. Legally, the power remains in the hands of the prime minister, supposedly to exercise personally. Despite Cameron's attempt to cloak the power in some formality, for political purposes, the situation is still as stated in a 2006 House of Lords select committee report titled *Waging War: Parliament's Role and Responsibility*:

It is commonly accepted that the prerogative's deployment power is actually vested in the Prime Minister, who has personal discretion in its exercise and is not statutorily bound to consult others, although it is inconceivable that he would not do so in practice.

(House of Lords Select Committee on the Constitution 2006: para. 12)

Exactly whom the prime minister would consult was not specified. Certainly, it is not the population. This concentration of power in the realm of a shadowy and undefined ruling class circle is totally anti-democratic.

According to a 2005 House of Commons Library report, the legal authority to go to war resides in Letters Patent Constituting the Defence Council, most recently issued in the name of Queen Elizabeth II, set out in Queens Regulations in 1975. After listing the prerogative powers, ending with 'the legal prerogatives of the Crown and the prerogative executive powers', that report states:

It is under this latter category of powers that are exercisable by Ministers on behalf of the Crown that the legal authority for conducting defence of the realm rests. The Letters Patent Constituting the Defence Council set down this relationship. However, in the event of a declaration of war or committing British forces to military action, constitutional convention requires that authorisation is given by the Prime Minister on behalf of the Crown. The Defence Council, through the Secretary of State for Defence, would advise the Cabinet of its requests and recommendations.

(House of Commons Library 2005: 8)

Vast royal prerogative powers protected

A significant episode in 1999 shed further light on the retention of the monarchical war powers for contemporary anti-democratic purposes. An attempt was made, via a private member's Bill, to require prior parliamentary approval before any air strikes could be conducted against Iraq. However, Queen Elizabeth II, formally acting on the advice of the Blair Labour government, refused to grant her consent to allow the Military Action against Iraq (Parliamentary Approval) Bill to be debated in Parliament and so it was dropped. Significantly, the government said that the Queen's consent was needed before debate could take place because the Bill affected the royal prerogative (HC Deb, 23 July 1999, vol. 335, col. 1546).

In 2013, internal Whitehall documents released by court order, under freedom of information laws, confirmed that the Queen had vetoed the Bill. A Buckingham Palace spokesperson said:

It is a long established convention that the Queen is asked by parliament to provide consent to those bills which parliament has decided would affect crown interests. The sovereign has not refused to consent to any bill affecting crown interests unless advised to do so by ministers.

(Quoted in Booth 2013)

Some three centuries after the struggle for parliamentary and civilian supremacy over the British monarchy—and within a political system that professes to be democratic—the power of the government to declare war, to call out the military domestically and to impose draconian emergency measures still rests on vestiges of regal authority. Such power is incompatible with genuine democracy.

The royal prerogative powers extend well beyond war; they are said to cover any situation not otherwise dealt with by statute. Moreover, as will be discussed in this chapter, these prerogative powers—especially those directly related to war—are largely unreviewable by the courts (*Burmah Oil Co. Ltd v Lord Advocate* [1965] AC 101).

Successive British governments have deliberately left open recourse to prerogative powers. Prime Minister Gordon Brown's government initially professed enthusiasm for constitutional reform to limit the royal prerogative powers. It was under intense public pressure to do so—particularly with regard to the powers to declare war or commit troops overseas—after the exposure of the lies and fabrications of WMDs used by the US administration, the Blair government and other allied governments to justify the 2003 invasion of Iraq. However, ultimately, no abolition, or even formal restriction, of the prerogative powers took place (Head 2016: 172).

A Brown government discussion paper on *The Governance of Britain* noted that the executive had, for hundreds of years, 'been able to exercise authority in the name of the Monarch without the people and their elected representatives in their Parliament being consulted' (Ministry of Justice 2009: 1). It concluded that such an arrangement was 'no longer appropriate in a modern democracy'. The paper proposed a review to consider whether the royal prerogative as a whole should be 'codified or brought under statutory control'. Yet it specifically ruled out changes to the status of the 'legal prerogatives of the Crown or the Monarch's constitutional or personal prerogatives' (Head 2016: 173).

The only conclusion that can be drawn is that the ruling establishment in Britain is determined to retain unfettered powers to instigate or to join wars and to deal with serious political, economic and social upheavals. For all of the references to 'rule of law' and 'democracy', great care has been taken to preserve the royal prerogative powers, described by Dicey (one of the traditional authorities on the 'rule of law' and the British constitution), as 'the residue of discretionary or arbitrary authority, which at any given time is legally left in the hands of the Crown' (quoted in Head 2016: 173).

No definitive, let alone legally binding, list of prerogative powers exists. No comprehensive account is even provided in constitutional law texts. As part of the Brown government's review, the Ministry of Justice produced something approaching an official outline, comprising four categories.

- *Ministerial prerogative powers* included the deployment of the armed forces and confiscation of private property (in times of 'grave national emergency').
- *Constitutional/personal prerogatives* featured dismissals of governments and an emergency right to 'require the personal services of subjects in case of imminent danger'.
- *Powers exercised by the Attorney General* and *archaic prerogative powers* covered such things as imposition of service in the Royal Navy and wartime internment of 'enemy aliens' (Head 2016: 173).

Another review of prerogative powers related to the military found that many, while depicted as disused and 'obsolete', have not in fact been abolished. They include the right to conscript subjects into the armed forces, to billet members of the armed forces in people's homes and to impose martial law (Head 2016: 173–74).

The refusal of governments and parliaments to abolish or circumscribe these powers points toward the fact that they are consciously retaining a free hand for these anti-democratic powers to be utilised in new wars and to stifle the accompanying domestic dissent and social tensions.

A contrary view?

In her 2013 treatise, *The War Prerogative*, Joseph argued that an examination of 'the war prerogative in practice' over the past four centuries demonstrates that the House of Commons has played 'an active and influential role', despite the 'orthodox view' of an exclusive executive power (Joseph 2013: 107). As noted in the Introduction, Joseph (2013: 105) reached her conclusion despite admitting that the effectiveness of Parliament's involvement in the decision-making process leading up to the 2003 invasion of Iraq was 'questionable'. As she recounted, the case that the British governments presented to Parliament for deployment was not only 'selective and misleading' in relation to false claims of supportive legal advice, but also based on an intelligence 'dossier' that was subsequently discredited (Joseph 2013: 105). Moreover, the timing of the Commons' debate, after 40,000 British troops had already been mobilised into the region, made it a 'rubber stamp of a fait accompli' (Joseph 2013: 105).

Joseph (2013: 184) proposed to retain the royal prerogative, but introduce legislation to define types of military deployment for which a government must obtain prior approval from the House of Commons. Such post-2003 proposals for legislation to provide for parliamentary control over war-making have offered no genuine alternative. As discussed in the Introduction, they seek to legitimise decisions to go to war by providing a fig leaf in the form of a parliamentary mandate. Even where the proposals have specified requirements for parliamentary votes on the deployments of armed forces, they have invariably provided exceptions for 'urgency', the need for secrecy to protect 'security' and the dispatch of special forces. These provisos, examined later in this chapter, make such legislation meaningless. As history shows, governments have long records of provoking or fabricating incidents to trigger their own military interventions.

The monarchical powers, their evolutiom and shifting justifications

Before the English Civil War and revolution of the 17th century overturned the absolute monarchy and established the primacy of the rising capitalist class via Parliament, the supreme 'kingly powers' of war-making, treaty-forging and foreign policy were regarded as axiomatic, said to be established by custom and practice and the 'ancient constitution'.

Sir Walter Raleigh, a courtier during the reigns of Elizabeth I and James I, stated: 'The second mark of majesty is authority to make war, and conclude peace, at his pleasure.' In 1641, before he lost his crown and was later executed, Charles I described his power to deploy and command the militia as 'the just power prerogative which God and the laws of this kingdom have placed in him for the defence of his people'. The courts enforced this view: *Calvin's Case* (1608) 7 Co

Rep 25ba proclaimed that '*bellim indicere* [the power to declare war] belongth only and wholly to the king' (quoted in Joseph 2013: 16).

With the restoration in 1660, the monarch's untrammelled powers over war, peace, treaties and foreign policy were again asserted. This remained the official orthodoxy after the 'Glorious Revolution' of 1688–89, which effected a compromise settlement that left the monarchy in place, albeit on Parliament's terms. In effect, Parliament's victory meant that the royal powers were increasingly shifted into the hands of the executive, in the name of the Crown. Robert Walpole, who was generally regarded as Britain's first prime minister, and is credited with establishing working relations between the monarchy and the parliamentary leadership, said 'our constitution has trusted intirely to the Crown, the power of making peace and war' (quoted in Joseph 2013: 17).

Writing later in the 18th century, William Blackstone, the author of much-cited volumes on the laws of England, identified the powers over 'intercourse with foreign states' as direct prerogatives of the king. Direct prerogatives were those that are 'such positive substantial parts of the royal character and authority, as are rooted in and spring from the king's political person' (quoted in Joseph 2013: 18–19). These powers of intercourse with foreign states included sending and receiving ambassadors, making treaties and alliances, making war and peace, and admitting foreigners. In the exercise of these powers, Blackstone declared, the king was the delegate and sovereign representative of his people; in the exercise of his war prerogative, the king was the 'generalissimo, or the first in military command, within the kingdom'. His position as 'general of the kingdom' accorded the king 'the sole power of raising and regulating fleets and armies'. Blackstone declared that military command 'ever was and is the undoubted right of his majesty, and his royal predecessors . . . and that both or either house of parliament cannot, nor ought to, pretend to the same' (Joseph 2013: 18–19).

By the 19th century, as the Industrial Revolution created a new rising class, the working class, the portrayal of the English constitution shifted to one of representative government, but the executive's exclusive powers over war and foreign policy were reinforced and extended to the British Empire. Chitty's oft-cited monograph on prerogative power, written in 1820, declared that '[a]s representative of his people, and executive magistrate, the King possesses . . . the exclusive right to make war or peace, either within or out of his dominions' (quoted in Joseph 2013: 19).

Even as wider layers of the population demanded, and were eventually granted, the right to vote, this power was increasingly consolidated in the hands of the executive, which was said to be directing the use of the prerogative powers. Although the formal legal distribution of powers attributed to the monarch powers of government, including powers over war, peace and foreign policy, in practice the monarch exercised those powers on the advice of ministers. Writing on the nature of parliamentary government in 1858, former colonial high official Earl Grey observed:

It is the distinguishing characteristic of Parliamentary Government, that it requires the powers belonging to the Crown to be exercised through Ministers, who are held responsible for the manner in which they are used, who are expected to be members of the two Houses of Parliament, the proceedings of which they must be able to generally guide, and who are considered entitled to hold their offices only while they possess the confidence of Parliament, and more especially of the Houses of Commons.

(Quoted in Joseph 2013: 19–20)

Likewise, in 1864, Benjamin Disraeli, a future prime minister, said, in a House of Commons debate:

If there be a prerogative of the Crown, which no one has ever challenged, it is the prerogative of the Crown to declare peace or war without the interference of Parliament, by her Majesty alone, under the advice of her responsible Ministers.

(Joseph 2013: 20)

By the end of the 19th century, constitutional theorists insisted that the war-making powers had been concentrated in the hands of the prime minister and cabinet, to the exclusion of Parliament, which, by this time, was elected by a wider suffrage. Referring to Blackstone's praise of the placement of the powers in the hands of the king, Albert Dicey wrote:

It has but one fault; the statements it contains are the direct opposite of the truth. The executive of England is in fact placed in the hands of a committee called the Cabinet. If there be any one person in whose single hand the power of the State is placed, that one person is not the king but the chairman of the committee, known as the Prime Minister.

(Quoted in Joseph 2013: 20)

This insistence on the anti-democratic exercise of the war powers by an executive committee, not Parliament, intensified during the 20th century, which was marked by two horrific world wars in which Britain played a central role. In a constitutional test published in 1939, the year in which World War II was declared, O. Hood Phillips wrote that the war prerogatives were '*legally* vested in the King, though this is a matter of form. By custom and convention prerogative powers must be exercised through and on the advice of other persons' (quoted in Joseph 2013: 21).

Today, in a new period of deepening great power conflicts, this aggregation of war powers in tight hands is being reasserted. While the media and official sources may loosely refer to the powers over war and foreign policy as being held by 'the government', these powers are those of the royal prerogative, exercised by a prime ministers, a small group of other ministers, and top military and intelligence chiefs.

In *The War Prerogative*, Joseph (2013) identified a shifting array of justificatory arguments for the asserted exclusive powers over war and foreign policy. Some of these conceptions competed and coexisted, but evolved remarkably during the four centuries (1600–2012) that she examined. The theory of the 'divine right of kings', which insisted that monarchs held their thrones and powers by God's will alone, not the will of the population, held sway until it was dealt a 'mortal blow' by the execution of Charles I in 1649 and laid to rest by the 1688–89 'Glorious Revolution' (Joseph 2013: 25). Then followed theories of paradigm 'kingly' powers essential to monarchical government, of the king's responsibility for the welfare of his subjects, of the existence of an 'ancient constitution', and of 'mixed government, 'social contract', 'Whig parliamentary government', 'democratic justifications' and 'institutional arguments' (Joseph 2013: 22–41).

Joseph's book was premised on a notion of a 'lawyer's legal history' or 'internal legal history', the sources of which are predominantly statutes, decided cases and 'lawyers' literature' (Joseph 2013: 8). This approach substantially divorces the law of war from the economic, geo-strategic and class interests that shape it. This means that Joseph presented these evolving justifications largely outside of the impact of the emergence of capitalism, the growth of the British colonial empire, the rise of the working class, the demand for democratic representation, and the eruption of inter-imperialist antagonisms in the 20th and 21st centuries. She therefore drew only limited conclusions from the evolution and trajectory of the arguments mounted to justify the executive war powers.

Nevertheless, Joseph observed that claims based on democratic mandates or responsibility are 'not prominent' today; rather, the key justifications were based on 'institutional competence'—featuring assertions of the necessity for flexibility, speed and secrecy, with firm and decisive leadership guided by experienced experts. She gave the example of Prime Minister Blair: in a written answer in the House of Commons in 2005, he said that a formal requirement to consult Parliament before deploying the armed forces 'could prejudice the Government's ability to take swiftly action to defend our national security where circumstances so require' (quoted in Joseph 2013: 41).

What Joseph failed to mention is that this belligerent defence of executive war-making power came from a man whose lies about the need for swift action in Iraq, based on concocted intelligence reports, led to Britain participating in an illegal war that killed more than 100,000 people, forced millions to flee and devastated an entire country.

The 20th-century record

World War I

Britain's entry into World War I was accompanied by systematic lies by the government to the Parliament and the population about the secret agreements that had been struck with France and Russia for British backing in return for post-war spoils at the expense of Germany and Turkey. Between 1911 and 1914, government ministers made misleading statements to the House of Commons denying any such secret pacts (Joseph 2013: 70).

Socialist and anti-war organisations vehemently opposed the war. Their objections found a limited expression in the House of Commons, where a small, but vocal, number of MPs criticised the government's conduct of 'secret diplomacy' (Joseph 2013: 70, 101–02).

On 3 August 1914, Foreign Secretary Edward Grey told the Commons that the government had decided to support France, but claimed that the House was free to give or withhold its support for the policy. Despite Grey's assurances, the government's consultation with the Commons was a pretence: the government had already, on the previous day, pledged to guarantee the protection of the French coast and shipping. Deployment was also already under way. The Royal Navy and Army had been mobilised.

Members of Parliament contributing to the debate observed that the government had essentially placed a *fait accompli* before them. One noted that, although the foreign secretary claimed that they were free to decide whether to support the plans for military action, he also informed them that the country was under obligations on which it could not turn back (Joseph 2013: 102).

Further, as was subsequently revealed after the October 1917 Bolshevik-led Revolution in Russia, Grey did not disclose that the government had entered secret arrangements with France and Russia, creating ties that were specifically denied in the Commons. Far from the official and media claims of a war being fought for liberty, the true interests were mercenary and imperialist. In early September 1914, a meeting of the French and British ambassadors with the Russian foreign minister led to a secret statement of war aims that included the Russian Tsarist Empire's annexation of parts of the Austro-Hungarian Empire, as well as the division of Germany's colonies between England, France and Japan.

In 1916, the Sykes–Picot Agreement was reached between London and Paris for the carve-up of the Ottoman Empire, behind the backs of the populations of the warring countries—and behind the backs of the populations of the territories in question. According to this agreement, Russia would gain control over what would later become eastern Turkey, while France would control what would later be southern Turkey, Lebanon, Syria and northern Iraq. Britain, notwithstanding its fraudulent promises to local leaders, would receive territory in what would later be Egypt, Jordan, Iraq and Kuwait. The secret pact contradicted London's promise in 1915 to Hashemite Sherif Hussein of Mecca, in what later became known as the McMahon–Hussein correspondence, of independence for the territories now known as Syria, Lebanon, Israel/Palestine, Jordan, Iraq and Saudi Arabia, in return for organising the Arab Revolt against the Turks (Cooke and Stickney 1931: 418–19).

These deals remained secret until the Bolsheviks came to power in Russia in November 1917 and began publishing them to expose the true war aims of the capitalist powers, and to call upon the working class of each country to end the war by overthrowing the governments responsible for the carnage. The first and most damning of the agreements published was the Anglo-Franco-Russian exchange of telegrams in March 1915, by means of which Tsarist Russia had first received the promise of Constantinople. Another agreement dated February 1917 had assured France of Russian support for its territorial demands in Western Europe (Carr 1953: 10–15).

The publication of the first series of treaties in *Izvestiya* was preceded by a note by Leon Trotsky, the People's Commissar of Foreign Affairs, which concluded:

> We desire the speediest overthrow of the domination of capital. Laying bare to the whole world the work of the ruling classes as expressed in the secret documents of diplomacy, we turn to the toilers with the challenge which constitutes the unchallengeable basis of our foreign policy: 'Workers of all countries, unite!.
>
> (Quoted in Carr 1953: 14)

World War II

In the case of World War II, the British government declared war without a prior vote in Parliament; it simply informed the Commons, two days before formally declaring war, of the preparations being made, which included complete mobilisation of the Royal Navy, Army and Air Force, while refusing to supply any details (Joseph 2013: 102). When the government declared war against Germany, it was reported to the Commons in a 'Prime Minister's Announcement'. Despite votes on related legislation, there was never a vote for the onset of hostilities (House of Commons Library 2005: 9).

This second world war was presented to the population, and to Parliament, as a 'war against fascism', but it was just as much an imperialist war for territories and hegemony as the first. It arose out of the same fundamental unresolved contradictions of capitalism that had erupted in World War I: the conflict between the increasingly globalised world economy, and its division between rival and antagonistic nation states, and between socialised production in large economic networks and the private ownership of the means of production in the hands of competing ruling classes.

The Hitler regime instigated the war in Europe. But the Nazi Reich was only the most extreme expression of the destructive and predatory nature of imperialism. The ruling classes of all the imperialist powers, including Britain and the United States, were involved in a struggle to redivide the world and increase their control of raw materials, markets and sources of cheap labour at the expense of their rivals.

The Versailles Peace Conference of 1919, and the treaty that resulted, resolved none of the conflicts that had given rise to World War I. In fact, the reparations and territories demanded from the defeated powers—especially Germany— exacerbated them. National antagonisms and conflicts remained, and economic conflicts among the major powers were intensified. France insisted that Germany pay crippling reparations payments, with the aim of trying to prevent its economic resurgence. Britain was owed money by Italy and France. But Britain, in turn, owed money to the United States, which insisted that it be repaid (Ferguson 2012: 309).

In the lead-up to both world wars, Britain was no less ruthless in pursuit of its interests than Germany—the crucial difference being that Britain's global economic and military power rested upon an already-acquired vast empire. Britain's position was summed up by First Sea Lord Sir Ernle Chatfield in 1934:

> We are in the remarkable position of not wanting to quarrel with anybody because we have got most of the world already, or the best parts of it, and we only want to keep what we have got and prevent others from taking it away from us.
>
> (Quoted in Callinicos 2009: 168)

There have been no declarations of war since World War II, although British forces have taken part in numerous armed conflicts.

Korean War 1950–53

As discussed in the previous chapter, the US-led Korean War was also based on misleading information. Prime Minister Clement Attlee did not ask the House of Commons to vote to join the United States in the Korean War in 1950. Winston Churchill, who supported the war as leader of the Opposition, argued that the prime minister should have conducted a Commons vote only to put on a display of unity. On 28 June 1950, Attlee informed the Commons that 'we [Her Majesty's Government] have decided to support the United States action in Korea'. No further information was given and no debate occurred until 5 July, when Attlee moved a resolution in support of the government's action, saying 'the only question before the House today is as to whether or not the government are right in the action which they have taken in the circumstances which have arisen in Korea'. The motion was passed, after a six-hour debate, with all but one or two MPs speaking in favour of the government's action (Joseph 2013: 103). The resolution asserted falsely that the military action sought to 'resist the unprovoked aggression against the Republic of Korea' (House of Commons Library 2005: 9).

Suez War 1956

Prime Minister Anthony Eden did not put the controversial and disastrous Suez war to a vote. On 2 August 1956, Eden announced that the government had thought it necessary to take military action as a precautionary step in response to President Gamal Abdul Nasser's nationalisation of the Suez Canal. Colonel Nasser had led the coup that overthrew Egypt's pro-British monarchy in 1952. The military intervention was not debated in the Commons until 12 September;

on 13 September, the government moved a resolution to adjourn the sitting of the House. Some MPs spoke vehemently against the proposed adjournment. One said that it was a 'negation of democracy, for the House to adjourn at a time like this'; another noted that '[i]f the House is not in session when great issues of foreign policy are occupying the attention of the country and the world, there is no democratic life within Britain' (Joseph 2013: 103).

Neither the Commons nor the British people were told that the joint British-French invasion of Egypt in 1956 was carried out in collusion with Israel. The invasion sought to overthrow the nationalist regime of Nasser and reclaim control of the nationalised Suez Canal. Nasser was widely denounced in the British press as a 'mad dog'. The Anglo-French invasion failed however, because the United States, which had its own plans to dominate the Middle East, would not tolerate the attempt by the European imperialists to restore their colonial empires. President Dwight D. Eisenhower compelled the French, British and Israelis to beat a humiliating retreat. He threatened serious damage to the British financial system by selling the US government's pound sterling bonds. Historians concluded that the crisis 'signified the end of Great Britain's role as one of the world's major powers' (Ellis 2009: 212).

Falklands (Malvinas) War 1982

Margaret Thatcher did not ask for a vote before dispatching the task force to retake the British colony of the Falklands (Malvinas) Islands. On 2 April 1982, she informed the Commons that the Falklands had been invaded by Argentine forces the previous morning and that her government was taking action in response. The next day, the House was recalled and a debate was held on a motion to adjourn (House of Commons Library 2005: 10) Later, she asserted the government's 'inherent jurisdiction' to make such decisions, on which the House of Commons could later 'pass judgment' (Joseph 2013: 104). In any case, the Labour Party opposition backed the operation, with only 33 of its MPs dissenting.

Some 900 people—255 British servicemen, 649 Argentineans and 3 islanders (killed during the naval bombardment of Port Stanley)—died during the 74-day war. Like Britain's other 20th-century wars, it was fought to defend long-standing imperialist interests. Britain had twice unsuccessfully attempted to invade Argentina itself, in 1806–07. During the wars that finally led to successful Argentine independence (1816–53), Britain occupied the islands in 1833. Renaming them the Falklands, it began settling the islands with British citizens, and has used them to stake claims to oil and mineral resources in southern polar waters ever since (Caviedes 1994).

Thatcher repeatedly insisted that the sovereignty of the Falklands was an issue of principle. But there were major domestic political calculations behind her determination to go to war. In 1982, the Tory government was widely reviled. Official unemployment figures stood at 3.6 million. Its policies were meeting opposition manifesting in a number of industrial disputes and strikes across the major industries. Government plans to close 23 coal mines had to be shelved in

1981 because of the threat of strike action. Thatcher's government was headed for electoral defeat—and the Labour Party's support for the Falklands war played a key role in rescuing it (Joseph 2013: 175–76; Dalyell 1983).

Gulf War 1991

Prime Minister John Major did not have a vote on the Gulf War in 1991, although 57 MPs—including the Labour Party's later leader Jeremy Corbyn—recorded their opposition by the procedural device of voting against a motion to adjourn. Major announced the military intervention on 17 January, but no debate was held until 21 January, when a motion was passed to express 'full support' for the 'British forces in the Gulf' on the grounds that they were helping to enforce UN resolutions (House of Commons Library 2005: 10).

On 16 January, a US-led coalition of the major powers had begun a devastating aerial bombardment of Iraq and its people. The US government claimed that its actions were justified by Iraq's invasion of Kuwait on 2 August 1990 and the need to uphold the 'right to self-determination' of this oil-rich sheikdom.

In reality, the United States had cynically encouraged Iraq's incursion into Kuwait to establish a pretext on the basis of which the United States could implement long-standing plans to seize control of the Persian Gulf and its vast oil reserves. Utilising its military and technological superiority, the United States sought to demonstrate its pre-eminent role in the 'new world order' to be established in the wake of the dissolution of the Soviet Union.

Over the course of 43 days, warplanes dropped 80,000 cluster bombs containing 16 million anti-personnel 'bomblets'. US forces fired an estimated 944,000 rounds of radioactive depleted uranium (DU) ammunition on Iraq and Kuwait. Iraq's schools, hospitals, industry and infrastructure were severely damaged, tens of thousands of innocent civilians were terrorised and killed, and air and water supplies were polluted (Workers League 1991: 32–35; Finlan 2003: 25–26).

Kosovo–Yugoslavia 1999

The crisis and subsequent three-month North Atlantic Treaty Organization (NATO) military intervention in Yugoslavia were the subject of statements and debates in the Commons during early 1999. Once again, however, Britain's military involvement was launched without any parliamentary vote. On 11 February, the secretary of state for defence informed the House of Commons that the government had decided to prepare the British forces for immediate deployment should a NATO force be sent to Kosovo. When one MP asked whether Parliament would be given an opportunity to give its judgement before British forces were committed, the minister fudged the response, saying: 'I have already made it clear that I will expect to keep Parliament informed of any decision that is taken about using the troops.' The government also repeatedly refused to address directly questions about the legal basis for intervention, which was far from clear. On 24 March, then Deputy Prime Minister John Prescott announced that, earlier that evening, British aircraft had attacked targets in Yugoslavia (House of Commons Library 2005: 11).

As explained in Chapter 3, the decision by the United States and Britain to go to war against Serbia was based on definite 'great power' geo-political calculations and it was never authorised by the UN Security Council.

Afghanistan 2001–

As for the Afghanistan war, which became the longest for centuries, the House of Commons was again informed, after the fact, that military action had been taken. Parliament was recalled from summer adjournment after the terrorist attacks on New York and Washington, DC, of 11 September 2001 (that is, 9/11). There were updates and debates on the attacks and subsequent events, but only after Britain's participation in the US-led invasion and occupation of Afghanistan was already well under way (Joseph 2013: 104).

Prime Minister Tony Blair had told the Commons that he would place information in the House Library setting out the reasons for concluding that Osama bin Laden and Al Qaeda were in close alliance with the Taliban-led government in Afghanistan. But he insisted that much of the supposed intelligence evidence had to be kept secret from Parliament and the people, claiming: 'It is not possible without compromising people or security to release precise details and fresh information that is daily coming in' (Joseph 2013: 72). In reality, as discussed earlier, the United States and its allies invaded Afghanistan and overturned its government because of the country's strategic importance in the resource-rich Middle East and Central Asia.

Iraq 2003–

Prime Minister Tony Blair's Labour government claimed that the decision-making processes leading up to the British invasion of Iraq in 2003 were unprecedented in terms of the extent of parliamentary involvement—but that involvement was cosmetic and based on fabricated claims.

First, the government provided Parliament with only selective and misleading information, as confirmed by the Chilcot Inquiry, discussed in Chapter 2. For example, on 17 March 2003, then Foreign Secretary Jack Straw circulated several documents to MPs, including: a copy of the Attorney-General's response to a written question in the House of Lords setting out the legal basis for the use of force against Iraq; a briefing paper summarising the legal background; a note summarising Iraq's record of non-compliance with UN Security Council Resolution 1441; and a compilation of recent UN documents. The legal briefing paper was subsequently shown to be a selective and misleading summary of the Attorney-General's full opinion. The intelligence 'dossier' alleging Iraqi possession of WMDs has since been discredited.

Secondly, the timing of the Commons' debate and vote on a substantive motion of support for the deployment reduced Parliament's input to a rubber stamp: by that time, 40,000 British troops already had been mobilised into the region (Joseph 2013: 105).

Libya 2011

The NATO intervention in Libya was also based on false pretences. On another 'humanitarian' pretext, the United States and its allies overthrew a government based on mercenary calculations of enhancing their power and the profits of their corporations—especially in the oil industry. Far from rescuing the Libyan people from a supposed looming massacre, the intervention devastated the country, as a subsequent House of Commons report confirmed (House of Commons Foreign Affairs Select Committee 2016).

From March to October 2011, an estimated 20,000 people were killed in the war, which plunged the Libyan people into a humanitarian catastrophe. After the toppling of the Gaddafi regime, the fighting between hundreds of militias for control of Libya's rich resources led to the flight of 2 million people—a third of the pre-war population—to Tunisia, Egypt and elsewhere, and the internal displacement of hundreds of thousands (House of Commons Foreign Affairs Select Committee 2016).

British participation in the operation to enforce the no-fly zone over Libya was announced on 18 March 2011; at the same time, the Prime Minister indicated that a substantive motion seeking retrospective approval for the deployment of forces would be tabled. On 21 March, the Commons approved a motion to support 'Her Majesty's Government . . . in the taking of all necessary measures . . . to enforce the No Fly Zone, including the use of UK armed forces and military assets'. During that debate, seeking to placate public opposition to the intervention, then Foreign Secretary William Hague promised: 'We will . . . enshrine in law for the future the necessity of consulting Parliament on military action' (House of Lords Constitution Committee 2013: para. 7).

There were no further public developments on that promise until November 2012, when Lord Wallace of Saltaire, the government's spokesperson in the House of Lords for the Cabinet Office, offered an essentially meaningless pledge. In a written answer, he stated:

> Since United Kingdom military intervention in Iraq in 2003, a convention has developed in the House of Commons that before troops are committed, the House of Commons should have an opportunity to debate the matter. The Government propose to observe that convention except when there is an emergency and such action would not be appropriate.
> (House of Lords Constitution Committee 2013: para. 7)

In 2016, following a year of deliberations, the House of Commons Foreign Affairs Select Committee published its report on Britain's military assault, alongside France and the United States, on Libya in 2011. It broadly followed the line of the Chilcot report, published a few months earlier, into the Iraq War (Chilcot 2016). David Cameron, who headed the Conservative–Liberal

Democrat coalition government at the time of the invasion, refused to give evidence. He announced that he was resigning his parliamentary seat just two days before the report was published.

In its conclusions and recommendations, the report made damning criticisms of the Cameron government for:

- falsely claiming, without any evidence, that Colonel Muammar Gaddafi was about to carry out a massacre of genocidal proportions against protesters in Benghazi;
- rushing into a military intervention without first pursuing other options, including sanctions, an arms embargo, diplomacy or leveraging Tony Blair's close links with the Gaddafi regime;
- failing to understand how Libya's system of government and society worked;
- pursuing 'an opportunistic policy of regime change', despite telling Parliament in March 2011 that the objective of the intervention was not such (even though, one month later, Cameron signed a joint letter with the French and US presidents that set out their aim to pursue 'a future without Gaddafi');
- supporting rebels among whom Islamist groups were known to be embedded; and
- failing to develop 'a strategy to support and shape post-Gaddafi Libya' (House of Commons Foreign Affairs Select Committee 2016: 39–42).

The report also criticised Britain's ongoing role in Libya for its apparent contradictions. Without parliamentary approval, the May government was deploying Special Air Service (SAS) troops to support a government of national accord and to battle the so-called Islamic State (ISIS) in the northwestern city of Misrata. At the same time, the Royal Air Force (RAF) was supporting rival forces led by General Khalifa Haftar, a US Central Intelligence Agency (CIA) asset airlifted by the Americans back into Benghazi during the 2011 war. His forces had seized control of 14 oilfields from the forces of Ibrahim Jadhran and the Petroleum Facilities' Guards (PFG), which sought autonomy for the east and attempted to sell oil independently of the government in Tripoli. In addition, the Royal Navy was patrolling the Libyan coast to combat weapons shipments.

In its summary, the Select Committee concluded:

In March 2011, the United Kingdom and France, with the support of the United States, led the international community to support an intervention in Libya to protect civilians from attacks by forces loyal to Muammar Gaddafi. This policy was not informed by accurate intelligence. In particular, the Government failed to identify that the threat to civilians was overstated and that the rebels included a significant Islamist element. By the summer of 2011, the limited intervention to protect civilians had drifted into an opportunist policy of regime change. That policy was not underpinned by a strategy to support and shape post-Gaddafi Libya. The result was political and economic collapse, inter-militia and inter-tribal warfare, humanitarian and migrant crises, widespread human rights violations, the spread of Gaddafi regime weapons across the region and the growth of ISIL in North Africa. Through his decision making in the National Security Council, former Prime Minister David Cameron was ultimately responsible for the failure to develop a coherent Libya strategy.

(House of Commons Foreign Affairs
Select Committee 2016: 3)

The Committee also noted that the National Security Council (NSC) mechanism created by Cameron to make war decisions after the exposure of the Iraq lies had not prevented the disastrous actions in Libya: 'Libya was the first test of the new NSC mechanism, which replaced the relatively informal process used during Tony Blair's premiership' (House of Commons Foreign Affairs Select Committee 2016: para. 59).

While blaming Cameron, the Committee made no suggestion that he or his government should be held culpable. To do so would have been to expose the support his war policy had in the political and financial establishment—with only 13 MPs voting against the war—as well as the media. To that end, the report concealed the broader geo-political objectives of the war, in which rival imperialist powers sought to stake their claim to domination of oil-rich North Africa and the Middle East, as discussed in the Introduction.

US diplomatic cables released by WikiLeaks dating from 2007 showed that the United States, like Britain under Prime Minister Blair, had pursued a policy of normalisation with the Gaddafi regime in a bid to secure access to Libya's resources. But Washington had become increasingly frustrated at what it called 'Libyan resource nationalism' and had warned Gaddafi in 2009 that 'putting pressure on US companies "crossed a red line" '. The United States began discussing regime change in Libya as early as 2008 (WikiLeaks 2010).

Syria 2013

Claims of an effective parliamentary role in war-making were boosted in 2013. Prime Minister Cameron moved a House of Commons resolution to authorise and politically legitimise military operations in Syria, only to suffer an embarrassing defeat. Commons MPs rejected the principle of British military action against President Bashar al-Assad's government by 285–272 and Cameron was forced to accept that he could not use the royal prerogative to join US-led strikes. As discussed in Chapter 3, that setback then compelled the Obama administration to retreat from a planned US-led attack.

As explained earlier in this chapter, however, the 2013 precedent was later overturned. Cameron's successor, Theresa May, did not make the same mistake. She ruled out any such vote over the missile attack on Syria in 2018. Moreover, as discussed in the next section, in 2016 Cameron's government had already moved to end any suggestion of a legal requirement for parliamentary approval by repudiating a 2011 promise to introduce a War Powers Act.

It must be noted, too, that the Cameron government's 2013 defeat came in a certain context: above all, deep public opposition to intervention in Syria following the disasters in Afghanistan, Iraq and Libya. This opposition had found a pale parliamentary expression earlier in that year. On 11 July 2013, the House of Commons agreed, by 114–1, a motion put forward by the Backbench Business Committee that 'this House believes no lethal support should be provided to anti-government forces in Syria without the explicit prior consent of Parliament'. As a House of Lords report noted after the vote:

> The Government's intentions as to the role Parliament should play as the civil war in Syria has escalated have been unclear. It took some time for the Government to give a commitment that the House of Commons should vote before any arms are supplied to the Syrian opposition, and it is unclear how they intend to involve Parliament should Her Majesty's armed forces become further engaged in the conflict.
>
> (House of Lords Constitution Committee 2013: 9)

As was to be made clear within months of that report, the government sought to defy that resolution, but could not get the numbers on the floor of the House of Commons. On the day of the vote, the chair of the Joint Intelligence Committee (JIC) issued a letter to the prime minister identifying the Assad regime as responsible for a chemical attack on Ghouta, yet could present no evidence. Instead, the JIC wrote of 'a limited but growing body of intelligence which supports the judgement that the regime was responsible for the attacks' and asserted a lack of a 'plausible alternative scenarios to regime responsibility' (Joint Intelligence Organisation 2013).

In fact, there was substantial evidence that Syrian opposition militias had access to chemical weapons and were behind the attack, aiming to create a pretext for Western military intervention. In the parliamentary debate, Prime Minister Cameron was forced to admit that there was 'no 100 per cent certainty about who is responsible' and that it was a 'matter of judgement' (quoted in Erlanger and Castle 2013).

The glaring holes in the government's case for war were especially damaging given the scale of public opposition. The overwhelming opinion in the country—especially after the 2003 invasion of Iraq—was that nothing said by the government could be trusted and that nothing justified another bloody military adventure. In addition, ruling circles were divided over the wisdom of military action against Syria, which some feared would further destabilise the Middle East and damage Britain's strategic interests (Erlanger and Castle 2013).

War Powers Act proposal abandoned 2016

In 2016, the British government abandoned plans to introduce a War Powers Act that would enshrine into law a commitment, however limited and qualified, to seek parliamentary approval before deploying British troops in combat.

Calls for war powers legislation had grown after the widely opposed and cata-strophic military interventions in Iraq, Afghanistan and Libya. But then Defence Secretary Michael Fallon told the House of Commons: 'I should . . . emphasise that the prime minister and I have to take decisions about the deployment of ships and planes and troops.' He said that they did not want to be 'artificially constrained in action to keep this country safe' (Norton-Taylor 2016).

Fallon, who first announced the decision in a written answer to a Commons question, told MPs later that ministers would 'keep parliament informed and we will of course seek its approval before deploying British forces in combat roles into a conflict situation'. The government argued that any statute would restrict its freedom of action, subject ministers to possible legal actionm and embroil them in arguments about the definition of training and combat missions. In his written statement, Fallon said:

> We cannot predict the situations that the UK and its armed forces may face in future. If we were to attempt to clarify more precisely circumstances in which we would consult parliament before taking military action, we would constrain the operational flexibility of the armed forces and prejudice the capability, effectiveness or security of those forces, or be accused of acting in bad faith if unexpected developments were to require us to act differently.
>
> (Quoted in Norton-Taylor 2016)

To support his claim that the government would seek parliamentary approval before sending troops into combat, Fallon referred to the *Cabinet Manual*, which stated:

> In 2011 the government acknowledged that a convention had developed in parliament that before troops were committed, the House of Commons should have an opportunity to debate the matter, and said that it proposed to observe that convention except where there was an emergency and such action would not be appropriate.
>
> (Cabinet Office 2011: para. 5.38)

Fallon said that the prime minister had made such a commitment in relation to Libya in March that year. But, he added, the convention did not apply to British military personnel embedded in the armed forces of other nations, which proviso would cover a wide range of deployments in which British personnel were inte-grated into other militaries—particularly those of the United States and NATO. Combined with the amorphous 'emergency' exception, plus the unstated excep-tion for the secret dispatch of special forces, this made the convention virtually meaningless.

In February 2010, Prime Minister Gordon Brown had announced a pro-ject 'to consolidate the existing unwritten, piecemeal conventions that govern much of the way central government operates under our existing constitution into a single written document'. That document became the *Cabinet Manual*.

Yet it was specifically stated to have no legal import. Sir Gus O'Donnell, in his preface to the first edition of the *Manual*, said it was 'not intended to be legally binding'—that it 'records rules and practices, but is not intended to be the source of any rule' (Cabinet Office 2011: iv). O'Donnell said that it was similar to the New Zealand *Cabinet Manual*, on which it was said to be based.

The revealing failure of 'reform' proposals

Following the exposure of the lies, fabrications and distortions that the Blair Labour government relied upon for Britain's barbaric and disastrous military intervention in Iraq in 2003, there was a litany of government, parliamentary and reviews of the war prerogative powers and proposals for reform.

The Labour government published a series of Consultation Papers and White Papers. The House of Lords Select Committee on the Constitution conducted an investigation into the war powers. The Public Administration Select Committee reported on the place of the prerogative in a supposed modern democracy. The Joint Committee on the Draft Constitutional Renewal Bill considered some issues concerning the war prerogative. In addition, individual MPs attempted to introduce private members' Bills to oblige governments to seek parliamentary approval of Parliament before deploying the armed forces. Various campaign groups and think tanks campaigned for greater parliamentary involvement in the exercise of the war prerogative (Joseph 2013: 181–82).

Further House of Commons and House of Lords reports were published in 2013. These reviews and proposals generally sought to formalise an enhanced role for the House of Commons—via either legislation, a parliamentary resolution or a convention—in deploying the armed forces. In the end, regardless of how limited or qualified the recommendations were, these projects all came to 'naught' (Joseph 2013: 184).

In 2006, the House of Lords Select Committee on the Constitution had published its inquiry findings, *Waging War: Parliament's Role and Responsibility*. As might be expected of the Lords, it rejected any suggestion of a statutory requirement for parliamentary involvement, claiming that it presented practical difficulties and uncertainties. Among these were the possibility of judicial review of war-making decisions, or of criminal prosecutions, and the need for 'emergency' exceptions. Instead, the report recommended the creation of a constitutional convention (Joseph 2013: 182–83).

The Labour government similarly rejected the use of statute. Its recommendations, set out in the Ministry of Justice White Paper, *The Governance of Britain: Constitutional Renewal*, advocated a House of Commons resolution that would require a majority Commons vote to support a proposed deployment, except in emergency situations, or for secret or special forces operations. The report described the government's power to exercise the war prerogative without formal parliamentary agreement as an outdated state of affairs in a modern democracy. The White Paper also acknowledged that a statutory requirement of parliamentary approval would provide certainty and avoid the proposed mechanism being ignored or circumvented. Nevertheless, it claimed that any mechanism would have to permit a high degree of flexibility and allow for emergency exceptions.

Such flexibility was, the White Paper declared, 'vital to ensure that our national security, our ability to conduct effective operations and the safety of the UK Forces are not compromised by the implementation of the new mechanism'. In its proposal, parliamentary approval would not be required if the deployment was necessary to deal with an emergency and there was insufficient time to seek approval, or if public disclosure about the decision could prejudice the effectiveness of military operations, or the security or safety of members of the armed forces. Operations involving members of the special forces would also be exempt (Joseph 2013: 183–84).

Joseph (2013: 185)—a proponent of giving Parliament a greater role, primarily for the purpose of politically legitimising a decision to go to war—said that these proposals were particularly deficient for three reasons:

> (1) the recommendation that the Prime Minister should determine the scope and nature of any information provided to Parliament; (2) the absence of any special arrangements for the recall of Parliament if deployment were deemed necessary when Parliament was adjourned or dissolved; and (3) the acceptance that the Prime Minister should have total discretion as to the timing of when the government would seek parliamentary approval.

Despite these and other loopholes, no such parliamentary resolution has ever been introduced (Joseph 2013: 184–85).

The voice of the political and military establishment

A further House of Lords report in 2013, titled *Constitutional Arrangements for the Use of Armed Force,* alluded to some of the anti-democratic conceptions behind the political and military establishment's rejection of any formal parliamentary role in waging war. It regarded Parliament's function as being to confer 'substantive and perceived legitimacy' on a decision to go to war (House of Lords Constitution Committee 2013: paras 14–15). But, relying heavily on the testimony of ex-military chiefs who were sitting in the House of Lords, the report declared that there too many risks associated with formalising that role. Referring to the 'convention' that Prime Minister May later threw overboard in 2018, the House of Lords Constitution Committee recommended that:

> [T]he existing convention—that, save in exceptional circumstances, the House of Commons is given the opportunity to debate and vote on the deployment of armed force overseas—is the best means by which the House of Commons can exercise political control over, and confer legitimacy upon, decisions to use force.
>
> (House of Lords Constitution
> Committee 2013: para. 4)

In one revealing passage, the report cited Jack Straw, who was the foreign secretary responsible for the 2003 invasion of Iraq. He told the Committee:

[O]ne of the many advantages of having conflict decisions made by the House of Commons is that it is a way of securing their legitimacy. I dread to think what the situation would have been in the country and in the armed forces if we had not put the decision to go to war in Iraq to the House of Commons with a very explicit resolution.

(Quoted in House of Lords Constitution
Committee 2013: paras 14–15)

That vote defied mass public opposition to the Iraq War, reflected in a march of hundreds of thousands of people through London, as part of the largest ever worldwide anti-war demonstrations. Millions of people had already rejected the false claims being made to justify the war. The parliamentary unity between the Labour government and the Conservative opposition enabled Britain's participation in the invasion, but the exposure of the lies around the WMDs ultimately discredited the parliamentary elite.

The report also argued that 'Parliament's approval may help improve the morale of service personnel, particularly if Parliament expresses its view by a large majority' (House of Lords Constitution Committee 2013: para. 15). Lord Guthrie of Craigiebank, a former British armed forces chief, told the Committee:

There were huge advantages if Parliament could be involved. When you visit people in the field on operations—for instance, when I went to Iraq—the questions you were asked were, 'is the country behind us? Is Parliament, the Government, behind us?'

(House of Lords Constitution
Committee 2013: para. 15)

Sir Mike Jackson, another former armed forces chief, added: 'If demonstrably Parliament has taken the decision to support an executive decision to use force in this or that circumstance, that gives considerable succour to the service man or woman on the ground' (House of Lords Constitution Committee 2013: para. 15).

Just as significantly, the House of Lords report insisted that governments must have the flexibility and leeway to initiate disputes and conflicts that are calculated, or at least likely, to evolve into larger wars. One of the dangers that the Committee identified with formalising any parliamentary role was:

[T]he speed with which situations can escalate, and the corresponding military (and political and diplomatic) flexibility required to respond to such escalations, must be taken into account when devising an appropriate parliamentary approval mechanism. Allied to that is the fact that the scope of an intervention may not be clear at the outset. Lord Guthrie of Craigiebank told us: 'you slide into a lot of . . . wars or operations. They start in a small way and may have unforeseen consequences. Before you know where you are, you are up to your neck in it.'

(House of Lords Constitution
Committee 2013: paras 16–17)

In addition to highlighting this candid and aggressive testimony from one of the country's top retired generals, the report declared that governments must have the capacity to dispatch the military to a widening range of 'situations' and 'grey areas':

One of the main obstacles to formalization is that of definition: formalization (either through legislation or resolution) would mean specifying the kind of action which would engage parliamentary involvement. As set out above, however, the range of situations in which the UK's armed forces might be deployed is very wide and getting wider. There are large grey areas between military and diplomatic engagements.

(House of Lords Constitution
Committee 2013: para. 18)

Another feature of the report was to insist that war-launching decisions must be kept immune from legal challenge or any form of legal accountability. As well as essentially advocating lawlessness, this line of argument involved a glaring contradiction. It claimed that Parliament was the appropriate institution to scrutinise and control military deployment decisions, yet rejected suggestions that Parliament have any legal authority to do so:

Another objection to formalisation is the risk of rendering deployment decisions justiciable, particularly through applications for judicial review. There was consensus amongst our witnesses that the appropriate forum for controlling and scrutinising deployment decisions is Parliament, not the courts. Specifying the parliamentary approval process in primary legislation may create a risk of the domestic courts being invited to rule on the lawfulness of a deployment decision.

(House of Lords Constitution
Committee 2013: para. 18)

Another reason the Committee offered for preventing any judicial review of war-related decisions was the assertion that whenever courts (particularly coroners' courts) scrutinised operational decision-making by service personnel, this had a deleterious effect on the morale of the armed forces and led officers to become more risk-averse. Lord Stirrup, yet another ex-chief of the armed forces, told the Committee:

Applying what can seem to be common sense [legal] principles in ordinary life to extraordinary situations can be extremely dangerous. There is no doubt that people in all three environments of the military are becoming more and more concerned about their personal legal positions in operations.

(House of Lords Constitution
Committee 2013: paras 18–19)

The Committee also cited former Foreign Secretary Jack Straw again, as an authority for the proposition that, to ensure 'flexibility', a prime minister must have 'a wide margin of discretion' over 'whether and when to bring a matter to parliament'. Straw informed the Committee:

The crucial thing . . . is that the triggers are entirely in the hands of the Prime Minister. The Prime Minister decides whether there is a conflict decision. If it is something rather trivial, he may decide that there is no conflict decision to be made, in which case he calls it something else and this resolution does not operate.

(House of Lords Constitution
Committee 2013: para. 19)

This from the man who, next to Prime Minister Blair, bore the most responsibility for the 2003 Iraq invasion.

Yet the Committee concluded that the current arrangements for 'allowing parliamentary approval' of deployment decisions seemed 'to be working well'. Moreover, the supposed constitutional convention had become 'politically binding' and 'it is inconceivable that the Prime Minister would either refuse to allow a Commons debate and vote on a deployment decision, or would refuse to follow the view of the Commons as expressed by a vote' (House of Lords Constitution Committee 2013: para. 21).

The worthlessness of that assertion was proven in 2018 by Prime Minister May's declaration of a government's right to attack another country without parliamentary approval.

A cosmetic proposal

In the wake of the collapse of the pretext for the Iraq invasion, numbers of private members' Bills were proposed to require parliamentary approval of involvement in military warfare. The primary political purpose of these Bills was to divert the ensuing public outcry with illusions that Parliament could or would exercise a democratic check on such calamitous decisions in the future.

Among the Bills drafted was one sponsored by former Secretary of State for International Development Clare Short, who had backed the Blair government's participation in the US-led assault on Iraq, but resigned from the cabinet two months later after the lies about the WMDs were exposed. The 2005–06 Armed Forces (Parliamentary Approval for Participation in Armed Conflict) Bill sought to establish a requirement that a government obtain the approval of both Houses of Parliament for the deployment of the armed forces in armed conflict and/or for a declaration of war (House of Commons Library 2005).

The Bill provided for two forms of parliamentary vote, as follows.

(1) *Prior approval* Clauses 1–3 set down the requirement for parliamentary approval to be sought prior to the deployment or involvement of British forces in any military action. The prime minister would lay a report before each House, setting out the reasons for proposed participation, the legal authority for doing so, and any information that the prime minister thought appropriate to make public on the geographical extent and expected duration of that participation, and which elements of the armed forces could expect to be deployed. A resolution of both Houses would be expressed in the form of approval of the report.

(2) *Retrospective approval* Under clause 4 of the Bill, retrospective parliamentary approval could be sought in the event that 'the Prime Minister has decided that participation by her Majesty's armed forces in an armed conflict is a matter of urgency', and consequently should begin before a report could be laid before both Houses and a subsequent resolution passed. The prime minister would be obliged to lay a report before each House 'as soon as is reasonably practicable after making the announcement'. Under clause 5, the prime minister, in the House of Commons, and a minister of the Crown, in the House of Lords, would then be obliged to make a motion for a resolution in each House 'as soon as is reasonably practicable'. Retrospective approval would be given in the same way as prior approval, with the adoption of a resolution approving the report.

Subsections 2–5 of clause 4 provided for the recall of Parliament in the event that either House was prorogued or adjourned within five days of the decision being made. Should retrospective approval be withheld by either House within ten days of the report being laid, clause 6 of the Bill stated that 'the continued participation of Her Majesty's armed forces in the armed conflict to which the report relates shall cease to be lawful after a period of thirty days'. However, there were two exceptions to this clause. Under clause 4(2), participation could continue for a period longer than 30 days where, 'in the opinion of the Prime Minister', it was considered necessary as a precursor to withdrawal. Under clause 4(3), the prime minister could lay a further report before each House within 20 days of the first report being laid. Each House would then be able to pass a resolution on that report.

Clause 7 stated that no declaration of war could be made by, or on behalf of, Britain unless that declaration was specifically contained in the reports laid before each House and subsequently approved by each House under the provisions set out in the previous clauses. Under clause 8, members of the armed forces were not prevented from taking action to defend themselves where that action obeyed a lawful command, was in accordance with lawful rules of engagement and was taken in 'the immediate defence of Her Majesty's armed forces (House of Commons Library 2005: 18–19).

The Bill left the door wide open for governments to initiate or provoke wars and then to use Parliament as a rubber stamp. In the first place, the requirement to provide only 'appropriate' information to Parliament and the public would do nothing to prevent the type of systemic fabrications presented before the 2003 Iraq invasion. And the phrases 'as soon as is reasonably practicable' and 'urgency' would have permitted a government to readily assert it had to act swiftly, without approval, and then delay any vote until such time as suited its military and political timetable.

Secondly, the Bill defined 'armed conflict' as 'any use of force which gives rise, or may give rise, to a situation of armed conflict to which the Geneva Conventions of 1949 or the Additional Protocols of 1977 apply'. This left doubt as to whether it would cover operational deployments that were labelled as 'peacekeeping' or 'peace enforcement' missions, or 'internal military callouts'. A House of Commons Library report on the Bill highlighted how far this loophole could be exploited.

In addition, all military operations carry the inherent risk that the dynamics of the security situation will change, therefore requiring a shift in the tempo and intensity of operations. A peacekeeping operation therefore has the potential to quickly shift into peace enforcement, as occurred in Somalia in 1993–94 (House of Commons Library 2005: 15).

The report cited the concept of 'mission creep', as outlined by Professor Ivan Shearer in his discussion of the *Rules of Conduct during Humanitarian Interventions*:

[There are] a number of actions that constitute (for the most part) non-forcible and thus uncontroversial forms of intervention. These . . . include disaster relief, humanitarian assistance [and] peace operations . . . the law applicable to such operations consists principally of the norms of human rights, as recognised in the major international Covenants and conventions, and established as general international law . . .

Some of these examples, may, of course, in the circumstances involve the use of armed force or grow through 'mission creep' to require the use of armed force . . . Lengthier presences, such as the operation in Somalia, may come to pose questions of the applicability of the laws of armed conflict as the situation escalates from a peaceable and unopposed intervention to armed conflict . . .

(House of Commons Library 2005: 15)

Thirdly, the Bill left considerable scope for governments to instigate military action, even secretly, then seek retrospective approval, effectively presenting Parliament with a *fait accompli*. Even if an operation were not retrospectively approved, the government would have 30 days in which to withdraw the armed forces (House of Commons Library 2005: 18).

Moreover, a prime minister could retain troops in an operation that had not received retrospective parliamentary approval where that prime minister deemed it necessary as a precursor to withdrawal (clause 6(2)). There was no time frame stated within the Bill for retaining troops in theatre under this exception and no definition of what constituted necessity. In addition, clause 4(1) allowed for retrospective approval of deployments that had already begun by the time the proposed legislation entered into force, permitting the ongoing deployment of troops in the Middle East (House of Commons Library 2005: 23–24).

Renewed calls for a War Powers Act

Following the 2018 missile strikes on Syria, there were renewed calls for some kind of War Powers Act. Labour Party leader Jeremy Corbyn proposed legislation akin to the 1973 US War Powers Resolution, which, as discussed in Chapter 3, is not only full of loopholes, but has failed to stem the escalation of executive war-making.

Earlier, in a 2016 interview, Corbyn said such an Act should be the absolute minimum to come out of the Chilcot Inquiry into the Iraq disaster (Hearst and Oborne 2016). He said that Prime Minister David Cameron had circumvented the supposed parliamentary convention requiring a Commons vote to send regular British forces to war by deploying the SAS instead, and that the loophole had been used to approve covert British military involvement or arms supply in Libya, Iraq, Syria and Saudi Arabia.

Corbyn compared missions by the SAS in Libya to when the United States sent military advisers to the South Vietnamese government in the 1960s, before Congress was invited to vote on whether or not the United States should be involved in the Vietnam War. 'I think the parallel is a very serious one', said Corbyn:

> Clearly, Britain is involved. Either through special forces in Libya or through arms supplies to Saudi Arabia to the war in Yemen. And indeed by the same process to the supply of anti-personnel equipment that is being used in Bahrain by Saudi Arabia. So I think we have to have a war powers act that is much more watertight on this.
>
> (Hearst and Oborne 2016)

'Non-justiciability' and other legal devices: the complicity of the courts

People challenging war decisions, or affected by them, have found it almost impossible to prosecute or obtain redress for such conduct. Courts have dismissed legal actions on various grounds, including non-justiciability (that is, that the action is beyond the jurisdiction of the courts), lack of legal standing by ordinary people to challenge war-related actions and potential damage to 'national security' or 'international relations'.

Thus, for example, in 2012, the High Court refused judicial review of a government decision to pass intelligence information from the Government Communications Headquarters (GCHQ) to aid drone assassinations, including of British citizens, by the United States in Pakistan's northwest region. The Court ruled that a legal challenge, accusing the government of conspiracy to murder, would compel the government to express a definitive view on the legal issues, 'complicating and damaging relations with our most important bilateral ally and, in consequence, damaging the United Kingdom's security' (*Khan v SSFCA* [2012] EWHC 3728 (Admin), at [17]).

Lord Justice Moses cited *Kuwait Airways Corpn v Iraqi Airways Co. (Nos 4 and 5)* [2002] 2 WLR 1353, 1362, as authority for 'the principle that the courts will not sit in judgment on the sovereign acts of a foreign state includes a prohibition against adjudication upon the "legality, validity or acceptability of such acts, either under domestic law or international law" ' (*Khan v SSFCA* [2012] EWHC 3728 (Admin), at [15]). Once again, this doctrine—regularly relied upon by governments and courts to block any legal examination of military or intelligence operations in support of the United States—was utilised to prevent any exposure of, or accountability for, conduct potentially involving the most serious crimes. (This case is reviewed at further length in Chapter 9.)

Such rulings are a chilling indication of the readiness of the courts to embrace and rubber-stamp war-related government activities, regardless of their apparent illegality, in the interests of 'national security' and military alliances. This has particular implications for decisions to join wars launched or triggered by allied powers, such as the United States.

When it comes to the war prerogative itself, the courts have been particularly anxious to rule out any legal challenge. Until *CCSU v Minister for the Civil Service* [1985] AC 374 (the *GCHQ* case), the courts would not entertain challenges to the manner of exercise of any prerogative powers, although they asserted a jurisdiction to determine the powers' existence and scope (see *Burmah Oil Co. Ltd v Lord Advocate* [1965] AC 75).

In relation to the war prerogative, the courts have limited any consideration even of its existence and scope, instead broadly asserting the Crown's exclusive prerogative, exercised by a government, to declare war and deploy the armed forces. They have not examined its precise existence or scope; rather, war-related powers have been treated as axiomatic and as matters that the courts should defer to the Crown.

In *GCHQ*, Lord Diplock said that national security—the defence of the realm against enemies—was the responsibility of the executive and not the courts of justice: 'It is par excellence a non-justiciable question' (*GCHQ* [1985] AC 374, at 412). Lord Roskill included the disposal of the armed forces among the prerogative powers that were not subject to judicial review (*GCHQ* [1985] AC 374, 418).

Over the years, courts have advanced varying justifications for this stance. In *China Navigation v AG* [1932] 2 KB 197, the Court of Appeal declared that the prerogative was the source of the government's powers over the government, command and disposition of the armed forces. The appellants had argued that the army had become a purely statutory body after 1689 and that the Crown's prerogative to raise and deploy an army no longer existed.

Significantly, in rejecting that argument, the Court cited the Preamble to a 1661 statute that declared that:

> [W]ithin all his Majesty's realms and dominions, the sole supreme government, command and disposition of the militia, and of all forces by sea and land, and of all forts and places of strength, is, and by the laws of England ever was, the undoubted rights of his majesty, and his Royal predecessors, Kings and Queens of England.
>
> (13 Car. II, st.1, c.6)

The judges regarded this Preamble as key evidence of the war prerogative, because the rest of the Act had been repealed in 1863, leaving only the Preamble in force. The Court acknowledged that, since the 1688 Bill of Rights, which asserted Parliament's power over the army, the military forces could be said to be a statutory and not a prerogative creation. However, Parliament had not expressly exercised or conferred upon the Crown any powers of disposing or using the army or administering its affairs. When Parliament consented to the raising and keeping of the army each year, it left the Crown to exercise its prerogative powers over the armed forces.

This stand was recited in *Chandler (Terence Norman) v DPP* [1964] AC 763, but the legal rationale sifted. The appellants were members of the 'Committee of 100' that sought to further anti-nuclear weapons demonstrations by the Campaign for Nuclear Disarmament (CND) by occupying part of an RAF base. In rejecting their appeals against criminal convictions for entering a 'prohibited place', the House of Lords cited *China Navigation* as affirming the existence of the war prerogative and its unsuitability for judicial consideration, despite the Preamble to the 1661 Act having been repealed in 1969.

The Law Lords spoke as if with one voice. Lord Reid said: 'It is in my opinion clear that the disposition and armament of the armed forces are and for centuries have been within the exclusive discretion of the Crown' (*Chandler (Terence Norman) v DPP* [1964] AC 763, at 791). Viscount Radcliffe stated: 'The disposition, armament and direction of the defence forces of the State are matters decided upon by the Crown and are within its jurisdiction as the executive power of the State' (*Chandler*, at 796). Lord Hodson asserted: 'The Crown has, and this is not disputed, the right as head of the State to decide in peace and war the disposition of its armed forces' (*Chandler*, at 800). And Lord Devlin insisted: 'It is by virtue of the prerogative that the Crown is the head of the armed forces and responsible for their operation' (*Chandler*, at 807).

Likewise, in *R v Secretary of State for Home Department, ex parte Northumbria Police Authority* [1989] QB 26, at 56, a decision dealing with the existence of a prerogative of keeping the peace within the realm, the Court of Appeal commented that '[t]he Crown's prerogative of making war and peace, the war prerogative, has never been doubted'.

Because of this ongoing judicial deference, Joseph (2013: 115) concluded that only 'a hazy outline of the scope of the war prerogative can be discerned' from judicial pronouncements. On the basis of the case law, she contended that the war prerogative extended, at least, to the powers to: declare war; deploy the armed forces; determine when to deploy the armed forces; determine the objectives of the deployment; determine the armament of the armed forces; and conduct the operations of war (Joseph 2013: 116).

This is a far-reaching scenario, which extends to effectively untrammelled legal power to override international law and deploy nuclear weapons. Several decisions suggest the sweeping scope of the war prerogative.

In *R (on the application of Campaign for Nuclear Disarmament) v Prime Minister* [2002] EWHC 2777 (Admin), a divisional court dismissed a challenge to the legality of the 2003 invasion of Iraq without UN Security Council approval.

The court said that the determination and evaluation of the purposes of military action was an aspect of the executive's war prerogative. It also indicated that the interpretation of Britain's obligations under international law fell under the war prerogative. The applicants sought a declaratory judgment that the invasion would be unlawful under international law; the court dismissed the application on the grounds that the questions raised were non-justiciable and, in any case, it lacked jurisdiction to interpret the relevant international resolution. The court said that it was for the government to determine the legal basis of its proposed military action—although the court did not explicitly identify this power as an aspect of the war prerogative or, alternatively, the prerogative to conduct foreign relations.

There was a similar result in *Gentle, Regina (on the Application of) & Anor v The Prime Minister & Anor* [2008] 1 AC 1356, in which the mothers of two servicemen who had died on active service in Iraq sought judicial review of the prime minister's decision to enter the war and a public inquiry. Lord Hope said that the issue of legality under international law was one of relations between states and a matter of political judgement (*Gentle*, at [24]). Baroness Hale said that the question could be decided only by the international institutions that policed the treaties on the law of war (*Gentle*, at [58]).

Several cases, including *Chandler*, ruled that the war prerogative extends to the deployment of nuclear weapons. In *Lord Advocate's Reference (No. 1 of 2000)* 2001 JC 143 (Scotland), at [60], the Court opined that 'the incorporation of Trident II in the United Kingdom's defence strategy, in pursuance of a strategic policy of global deterrence' should be regarded as non-justiciable, insisting that '*Chandler* remains binding authority in this court'.

In *Burmah Oil Co. Ltd v Lord Advocate* [1965] AC 75, at 115–16, 145 and 166, the House of Lords confirmed the existence of incidental war powers during times of war or imminent threat of invasion or attack, Lord Reid thinking that it 'certainly covers doing all those things in an emergency which are necessary for the conduct of war'. These powers depended on the existence of a state of war, but the courts generally have taken as conclusive the executive's position on the existence or not of a state of war, even if that issue has become more contested in recent decades (see *Amin v Brown* [2005] EWHC 1670 (Ch)).

Since 2002, claims have been made that some cases have indicated the courts' readiness to review exercises of prerogative powers over war and foreign policy, at least in an 'extreme case' in which the government refused to even consider a violation of fundamental human rights. Thus, in *Abbasi v Secretary of State* [2002] EWCA Civ 1598, the Court of Appeal was prepared to consider an application for relief by a British citizen detained in the US detention camp at Guantanamo Bay and denied diplomatic assistance by the British government. The judges said that the 'forbidden area' of foreign policy identified in the *GCHQ* case could be impinged upon where 'a clear breach of a fundamental human right' occurred (*Abbasi*, at [66] and [107]). However, the government was not ordered to seek Abbasi's release; the judges merely opined that if a government were to refuse to even consider to make representations on a detainee's behalf, it might be instructed to give 'appropriate consideration' to an applicant's case.

The Supreme Court took a similar approach in *Secretary of State for Foreign and Commonwealth Affairs v Rahmatullah* [2012] UKSC 48, in which a Pakistani national was detained by British forces, then transferred to US forces, who took him to Afghanistan to be detained. However, despite references to the importance of 'liberty' and *habeas corpus*, no order was issued for the government to seek Rahmatullah's release; instead, the British government was asked to test whether it had any control over his detention or to explain why that was not possible.

The underlying opposition to judicial testing of the war prerogative was indicated by Lord Bingham in *R v Jones (Margaret)* [2006] UKHL 16, at [30]:

[T]here are well established rules that the courts will be very slow to review the exercise of prerogative powers in relation to the conduct of foreign affairs and the deployment of the armed services, and are very slow to adjudicate upon rights arising out of transactions entered into by sovereign states on the plane of international law.

Similarly, in *R v Secretary of State for Foreign and Commonwealth Affairs, ex parte Bancoult (No. 2)* [2008] UKHL 61, the House of Lords decided 3–2 to uphold a 2004 Order in Council that barred the return to their homes of the people of the Chagos Islands. The residents of the Indian Ocean territory had been removed in 1971 so that the central island of Diego Garcia could be leased to the United States as a military base. The judges ruled that the Order was valid and, although judicial review actions could look at Orders in Council, the national security and foreign relations issues in the case barred them from doing so. The majority—Lords Hoffmann, Rodger and Carswell—held that the British Indian Ocean Territory was a 'conquered or ceded colony' and therefore was subject to the prerogative powers of the Crown.

Another hurdle for an applicant is to show that a war-related decision affected them in the sense necessary to establish legal standing. The test for standing in judicial review proceedings is that the applicant must show 'sufficient interest in the matter to which the application relates' (Supreme Court Act 1981, s 31(3)). Standing was refused to a foreign non-governmental organisation (NGO) in *R (on the application of Al-Haq) v Secretary of State for Foreign and Commonwealth Affairs* [2009] EWHC 1910 (Admin).

In *R (on the application of Evans) v Secretary of State for Defence* [2010] EWHC 1445 (Admin), standing was granted, on the ground that the claim was brought in the public interest, to a peace activist opposed to the presence of British and US military forces in Afghanistan. However, that application did not challenge the legality of the British military presence in Afghanistan, where 9,000 armed forces personnel remained at the time, nor did it contest the legality of the transfer of more than 400 detainees to the Afghan authorities. Instead, it objected to the implementation of the government's policy because of many instances of torture or serious mistreatment of prisoners at the hands of Afghanistan's National Directorate of Security (NDS).

A High Court bench dismissed the application for an order to halt the transfers, after noting that the case had important 'implications for security in Afghanistan and the effectiveness of UK operations there' (*Evans*, at [1]). The court asserted that the existing monitoring system was sufficient to guard against abuse. Its conclusion flew in the face of the evidence, which the judges admitted showed 'plainly a possibility of torture or serious mistreatment of UK transferees at those facilities' (*Evans*, at [323]). In a display of judicial deference to the military, the judges were prepared to accept the continued risk of illegal torture: 'Isolated examples of abuse may occur, but we are not satisfied that a consistent pattern of abuse is reasonably likely, such as to expose all UK transferees to a real risk of ill-treatment' (*Evans*, at [323]).

References

Akande, D. 2018. 'The legality of the UK's air strikes on the Assad government in Syria', 16 April, https://d3n8a8pro7vhmx.cloudfront.net/campaigncountdown/pages/2243/attachments/original/1523875290/Akande_Opinion_UK_Government's_Legal_Position_on_Syria_Strike_April_2018.pdf?1523875290 (accessed 21 May 2018).

Booth, R. 2013. 'Secret papers show extent of senior royals' veto over bills', *The Guardian*, 15 January, www.theguardian.com/uk/2013/jan/14/secret-papers-royals-veto-bills (accessed 22 May 2018).

Cabinet Office. 2011. *The Cabinet Manual*. London: HMSO, https://assets.publishing.service.gov.uk/government/uploads/system/uploads/attachment_data/file/60641/cabinet-manual.pdf (accessed 19 November 2017).

Callinicos, A. 2009. *Imperialism and Global Political Economy*. Cambridge: Polity.

Carr, E. 1953. *The Bolshevik Revolution, 1917–1923, Vol. 3*. London: Macmillan.

Caviedes, C. 1994. 'Conflict over the Falkland Islands: a never-ending story?', *Latin American Research Review*, 29(2): 172–87.

Chilcot, J. 2016. *The Report of the Iraq Inquiry*, HC264, 6 July, London: HMSO.

Cooke, W., and Stickney, E. (eds). 1931. *Readings in European International Relations since 1870*. New York: Harper.

Curtis, C. 2018. 'By two to one, the public oppose missile strikes on Syria', *YouGov*, 12 April, https://yougov.co.uk/news/2018/04/12/two-one-public-oppose-missile-strikes-syria/ (accessed 20 May 2018).

Dalyell, T. 1983. *Thatcher's Torpedo*. London: Cecil Woolf.

Ellis, S. 2009. *Historical Dictionary of Anglo-American Relations*. Lanham, MD: Scarecrow.

Erlanger, S., and Castle, S. 2013. 'Britain's rejection of Syrian response reflects fear of rushing to act', *The New York Times*, 30 August, www.nytimes.com/2013/08/30/world/middleeast/syria.html (accessed 18 November 2017).

Ferguson, N. 2012. *Civilization: The Six Killer Apps of Western Power*. London: Penguin Books.

Finlan, A. 2003. *The Gulf War 1991*. Oxford: Osprey.

gov.uk. 2018. '*National Security Council*', www.gov.uk/government/groups/national-security-council (accessed 11 February 2018).

Head, M. 2016. *Emergency Powers in Theory and Practice: The Long Shadow of Carl Schmitt*. London: Ashgate.

Hearst, D., and Oborne, P. 2016. '*Middle East Eye* meets Corbyn: the full interview', *Middle East Eye*, 29 July, www.middleeasteye.net/news/middle-east-eye-meets-corbyn-full-interview-742537858 (accessed 21 November 2017).

House of Commons Foreign Affairs Select Committee. 2016. *Libya: Examination of Intervention and Collapse and the UK's Future Policy Options*, https://publications. parliament.uk/pa/cm201617/cmselect/cmfaff/119/11902.htm (accessed 13 November 2017).

House of Commons Library. 2005. *Armed Forces (Parliamentary Approval for Participation in Armed Conflict) Bill*, Bill 16 of 2005–06, Research Paper No. 05/56, 8 August, researchbriefings.files.parliament.uk/documents/RP05-56/RP05-56.pdf (accessed 5 May 2018).

House of Lords Constitution Committee. 2013. *Second Report of Session 2013–14: Constitutional Arrangements for the Use of Armed Force—Report*, HL Paper 46, July, London: HMSO, https://publications.parliament.uk/pa/ld201314/ldselect/ldconst/46/46.pdf (accessed 12 November 2017).

House of Lords Select Committee on the Constitution. 2006. *Waging War: Parliament's Role and Responsibility*, Vol. 1, July, London: HMSO.

Joint Intelligence Organisation. 2013. 'Letter: Syria—reported chemical weapons use', 29 August, https://assets.publishing.service.gov.uk/government/uploads/system/uploads/attachment_data/file/235094/Jp_115_JD_PM_Syria_Reported_Chemical_Weapon_Use_with_annex.pdf (accessed 17 November 2017).

Joseph, R. 2013. *The War Prerogative: History Reform and Constitutional Design*. Oxford: Oxford University Press.

Ministry of Justice. 2009. *The Governance of Britain: Review of the Executive Royal Prerogative Powers—Final Report*, October, London: HMSO.

Norton-Taylor, R. 2016. 'Ministers drop plans for war powers law', *The Guardian*, 19 April, www.theguardian.com/politics/2016/apr/18/ministers-abandon-plan-war-powers-law-mps-troops (accessed 18 November 2017).

Prime Minister's Office. 2010. *'Establishment of a National Security Council'*, 12 May, http://webarchive.nationalarchives.gov.uk/20130102185915/http://www.number 10.gov.uk/news/establishment-of-a-national-security-council/ (accessed 4 April 2018).

Prime Minister's Office and 10 Downing Street. 2018. *Syria Action: UK Government Legal Position*, Policy paper, 14 April, www.gov.uk/government/publications/syria-action-uk-government-legal-position/syria-action-uk-government-legal-position (accessed 20 May 2018).

Prime Minister's Office, 10 Downing Street, and May, T. 2018a. 'Cabinet meeting: 12 April 2018', Press release, 12 April, www.gov.uk/government/news/cabinet-meeting-12-april-2018 (accessed 6 May 2018).

Prime Minister's Office, 10 Downing Street, and May, T. 2018b. 'PM statement on Syria: 16 April 2018', 16 April, Press release, www.gov.uk/government/speeches/pm-statement-on-syria-16-april-2018 (accessed 6 May 2018).

Wikileaks. 2010. 'Public Library of US Diplomacy', https://wikileaks.org/plusd/cables/07TRIPOLI967_a.html (accessed 9 May 2018).

Workers League. 1991. *Desert Slaughter: The Imperialist War against Iraq*. Detroit, MI: Labor.

5   From Whitehall to the White House
The war power in Australia— from legal subordination to political subservience

Introduction: idiosyncrasies of the Australian war power

In Australia, the executive exercise of the war power is completely unfettered by the Constitution. Additionally, the 'executive' that exercises the war power is very narrowly conceived, comprising only the prime minister and cabinet. The consequence is that, in Australia, a mere handful of people formally wield the war power. Since the Australian Federation was established in 1901, this unfettered legal power has 'developed' in a circle, from the royal war power prerogative of the British monarch to the executive war power prerogative of the Australian prime minister.

In comparison to the position in Britain and the United States, the exercise of the war power in Australia is the least constrained by law. No constitutional limit is provided in the Australian Constitution, such as a requirement that a vote be taken by the legislature, as is specified in the US Constitution. No convention has developed as is arguably the case in Britain, where, despite the absence of a constitutional requirement that Parliament vote on decisions to go to war, a vote was taken in 2013 and a planned attack on Syria was defeated in the House of Commons. That the convention faces executive resistance is clear: a vote was not taken in 2018, when Prime Minister May did not seek prior parliamentary approval for British air strikes in Syria.

The unconstrained character of the war power in Australia has been a key component in the participation of Australian troops in US military interventions since World War II despite considerable popular opposition to such participation.

In the 18th century, influential legal thinker William Blackstone ([1783] 2009: 250) reasoned that the 'same principle' that underpinned the Crown's prerogatives regarding foreign relations—entering into treaties, appointing and receiving ambassadors—supported his view that 'the king has also the sole prerogative of making war and peace'. Australia's historical transition from colony to independence has been one in which the British Crown's exercise of prerogative powers regarding foreign relations became, by virtue of section 61 of the Australian Constitution, exercisable by the Australian executive.

In this chapter, the historical development and exercise of the war power in Australia is traced from royal prerogative to executive prerogative. No discussion of the development and exercise of the war power in Australia would be complete without recognition of two crucial factors:

- the significance of Australia's colonial origins, which, although now legally transcended, played a pivotal role in the historical development and exercise of the war power in this country; and
- the crucial importance of Australia's close geo-strategic alliance with the United States, which now dominates the exercise of the Australian war power.

The Australian ruling establishment has always relied upon the military support of the predominant world power—a status once held by the British Empire, but achieved by the United States as a result of World War II.

Australian subordination to Britain

The development and exercise of the war power in Australia can be understood in terms of three phases. In the first phase—what we can call the 'colonial hangover' phase—the exercise of Australian war power between 1901 and 1941—despite the emerging status of Australia after the passage of the Constitution of Australia Act in 1901 as a self-governing 'dominion'—was in fact a subset of the exercise of British war power. Whenever Britain was at war, it was assumed by Australian governments that Australia would also be involved in the conflict. This automaticity is unsurprising, given that six British colonies had been established between 1788 and the mid-19th century and, in the decades leading up to Federation in 1901, Australian colonial forces had fought as part of British imperial forces in Sudan 1885, the Boxer Rebellion 1900 and the Second Boer War 1899–1902. Further, many Australians were born in Britain or were first-generation Anglo-Australians.

Australia suffered from what has been described as a prolonged civic adolescence (Belich 2009). The British patriotism that might have existed in the 19th century waned in the 20th century. Nonetheless, after Federation, 20th-century Australian nationalists 'saw their Australian-ness as lying in the fact that they were *really* "British", unlike the English who were too English to be British' (Horne 1966: 448). The two main Australian political parties and leading politicians were, when it came to matters of war, in lockstep with Britain: when the 'old country' was at war, so too was Australia. Similarly, Australian High Court judgments held that the war power was a royal prerogative, exercisable by the British monarch; it was the British sovereign who decided questions of war and peace for the British Empire as a whole, including Australia. Given the political, judicial and popular expectations of loyalty to Britain and the Empire, and the presence of Australian constitutional arrangements that were understood as reposing the war power in the British monarch, the reality was that Australia went to two world wars according to the dictates of the executive branch of a government of another nation. The decision to commit Australian blood and treasure to any conflict was made in Whitehall, not Canberra.

Brief independent exercise of the war power

The second, very brief, phase in the development of war power in Australia (1941–51) might be termed the 'imperceptibly independent vice-regal' phase. In 1941, the British king ceded the war power to the Australian governor-general, exercisable upon advice of the executive council. Accordingly, politicians and courts no longer regarded the war power as a royal prerogative exercisable by the British monarch; rather, it was now considered an executive prerogative that would be exercised by the Australian governor-general upon the advice of the Australian prime minister or the minister of defence on behalf of the Australian cabinet. Thus, at least in theory, the war power could now be legally exercised in a more independent manner. It is important to note, however, that this governor-general was acknowledged to be exercising the executive authority of the British Crown.

Formally, if not substantively, Australia's executive did in fact make independent decisions at this time. In 1941, the governor-general of Australia retrospectively declared war on Germany and Japan. In 1942, the governor-general declared war on Romania and Thailand. In 1951, the governor-general declared peace with Germany. However, this period of more or less independent vice-regal exercise of the war power was not to last and Australian reliance on a foreign power would soon reappear.

An important issue in this phase and even more so in the next was whether the Australian political community fully supported the idea of 'Australian independence'—to the extent that it contemplated complete legal and political severance from Britain—in the first place.

Detmold (1985: 89), for instance, argues that political legitimacy is necessary for 'legal independence' to exist. His position is that the emergence, in Australia, of a 'political people' had taken place by the time of Federation and that the Australian political community recognised the British Parliament in 1901 as the 'ultimate legal power in their legal order' (Detmold 1985: 91). As far as Detmold (1985: 89) is concerned, Australian independence is achieved as a gradual process: 'In Australia, the imperial power remained as an imperial power until, say, 1926. Then it began to drop out of the constitutional system . . .'

The irony, of course, is that the reluctance of the Australian political community to agree to the Statute of Westminster—it took 11 years for Australia to adopt it—suggests that the *legal* 'independence' arguably expressed by the Australian governor-general's exercise of the war power from 1941 to 1951 could not be said to have been 'politically legitimate' at the time. Not surprisingly, considerable debate among Australian jurists surrounds the issue of when Australian independence occurred and when it was legitimately exercised. Detmold (1985: 91) contrasts the view of two jurists: 'Murphy J. in a number of cases has held that the imperial Parliament ceased at the commencement of the federation to have any power at all in Australia', while Barwick CJ's judgment suggests that something other than 'law' is the source of Australian independence:

> The historical movement of Australia to the status of a fully independent nation has been both gradual and, to a degree, imperceptible. In that movement, the Statute of Westminster . . . and it adoption by the Parliament . . . played their very substantial part. Thus, though the precise day of the acquisition of national independence may not be identifiable, it certainly was not the date of the inauguration of the Commonwealth in 1901. The historical political and legal reality is that from 1901 until some period of time subsequent to the passage and adoption of the Statute of Westminster, the Commonwealth was no more than a self-governing colony though latterly having dominion status.
>
> (*China Ocean Shipping Co. v South Australia*
> (1979) 145 CLR 172, 183)

On Barwick's argument, then, the legitimacy of the constitutional exercise of the war power cannot depend on mere 'legality', as determined by judges of the High Court, but also—and centrally—depends on the support of the Australian political community. It is a matter of concern, then, whether and to what degree particular elites in Australia have come to dominate, manipulate or otherwise skew the formation of the political legitimacy required in a democratic polity regarding the vital issue of going to war.

The alliance between Australia and the United States, and the consequences for the Australian exercise of the war power

In the third, ongoing phase, which we might refer to as 'the executive unchained' (1951–), the executive prerogative escaped whatever minimal constraints were provided by the notion and reality of the 'advice' traditionally thought to be necessary regarding the exercise by the executive (in this period, the governor-general) of the war power. From 1951 onward, the prime minister and cabinet—that is, the elected, rather than appointed, members of the executive—exercised the war power without vice-regal input. In all of the major conflicts in which Australia has participated since 1945—Borneo, Malaya, Korea, Vietnam, Iraq (1991), Afghanistan, Iraq (2003), Iraq (2014) and Syria—the prime minister and cabinet have made the decision to commit troops. Given the reality that the prime minister and their cabinet ministerial colleagues will be members of the same political party, the possibility that a divergence of views might be present to provide a 'check' or a 'balance' to modulate the prime minister's decision is extremely unlikely. The legal subordination that was characteristic of the colonial hangover period has continued as political subservience in circumstances in which the United States has replaced Britain as the world's greatest superpower and Australia is still in the process of developing the robust political, economic and cultural institutions that can support true independence. Curran and Ward (2010: 256) provide a strong argument that Australia is not yet a post-imperial nation, arguing that it has not yet come up with 'credible alternatives to empire and Britishness', meaning that its 'passage out of Empire' is not yet complete.

In relation to the conflicts in Vietnam, Iraq and Afghanistan, as examined later in this chapter, the decision to send Australian forces to war was effectively made in the White House, not in Canberra. Rather than regarding the war power as a royal prerogative as it was in earlier times, today it seems appropriate to characterise it as a largely presidential prerogative. Rather than the British monarch deciding if and when Australia is at war, it can be argued that the US president now effectively makes that decision.

The loosening of what Stuart Ward (2001) calls the 'British embrace'—marked pointedly by the Macmillan government's attempts to join the European Economic Community (EEC) and the concomitant shock registered by many Australians—indicated a need for Australia to abandon sentiment and look to self-interest. By the 1960s, Manning Clark (1973: 194), surveying the crumbling of British civilisation, was asking: 'What will we put in its place?' Other scholars in this period shared a similar concern (Boyd 1967; Horne 1966; Conway 1971). In 1969, Arthur Koestler described Australia's search for identity as 'a real problem' and 'haunting' (quoted in Curran and Ward 2010: 19). Curran and Ward point toward the rise of a 'new nationalism' born of three factors: the unravelling of Britain, concomitant with decolonisation from the 1940s to the 1960s; the decline of Britain's economic, military, strategic and political capacity in the 1960s and 1970s; and her 'turn' toward Europe, combined with her ambivalent attitude toward South East Asian security issues both regarded by many Australians as 'double dealing' (Curran and Ward 2010: 143). The changing perspective of Australia's position internationally—particularly a desire to be seen to act, and in fact to act, independently—evolved as a means of resolving Australia's post-imperial uncertainties. Curran and Ward (2010: 23) cite Australian Prime Minister Gorton's 1968 description of Britain as a 'foreign country' and Labor Party candidate Whitlam's campaign in favour of a more 'independent' Australian voice in international contexts as crucial examples of Australia's moves toward a new Australian identity.

Australia's search for a new identity in the 1960s and 1970s also impacted on Australia's relations with the United States, which, according to Curran and Ward (2010: 143), had been crafted and understood hitherto in the 'dwindling light of the British Empire'. They state that the continuing influence of this imperial twilight could be seen:

> . . . among both US enthusiasts, who saw in the Americans a new guarantor of Australia's material well-being, and the detractors, who feared the presence of a new imperial master. Neither perspective was entirely sound, but it nonetheless demonstrates the power of the imperial legacy in simplifying complex new realities.
>
> (Curran and Ward 2010: 143)

As early as Australia's involvement in the Vietnam War, critics were concerned that the 'irresistible "logic of satellitism"—inherited from long experience with Britain—would prevail in Australian habit and thought' (Curran and Ward 2010: 144). Curran and Ward (2010: 144) quote both Geoffrey Serle's view that the 'transition from a British colony to an American province' was almost complete, with 'only a fleeting glimpse of independence on the way', and Humphrey McQueen's acid statement that Australia had transformed from 'British sycophant to American lickspittle'.

Since the end of World War II—and particularly since the Vietnam War, the first conflict in which Australia participated, but Britain did not—the United States has become Australia's main strategic ally. The alliance was spelled out initially in the Security Treaty between Australia, New Zealand and the United States of America 1951 (known as the ANZUS Treaty), but its significance extends far beyond the terms of the Treaty: the nature of the alliance is such that when the United States is at war, so too is Australia. Australia's increasingly close military alliance with the United States arguably renders Australian constitutional arrangements superfluous: decisions are made in the White House and the Australian executive in Canberra follows suit. At the very least, it can be argued that the current constitutional location of the Australian war power in the executive makes it much easier for Washington to garner Australia's agreement to, and participation in, its military actions across the globe.

In 2015, former Prime Minister Malcolm Fraser stated:

> The closeness of our relationship with the United States . . . means that we no longer have an independent capacity to stay out of America's wars under the policies that presently prevail in Australia. When those hard-hitting, three-service forces in Darwin are used to support a conflict in which America is involved, and when Pine Gap is used to target not only drones, but advanced American weapons systems, how can an Australian Prime Minister stand up in the Parliament and say Australia is going to pass this one by? The Prime Minister would not be believed. Australia could not stop America using those facilities. We have ceded Australian sovereignty, over matters of peace and war, to the United States. We have created a far more powerful linkage than ever existed in the days of Empire.
>
> These reasons emphasise the need for three things. Our relationship with the United States must be changed. We must recapture Australian sovereignty and sense of strategic independence. We must never again allow the circumstances to exist in which one man has the capacity to commit Australia to war . . . in many other democratic countries, including the United States, the basic authority to declare war or stay at peace rests with the Parliament. It is essential and urgent in Australia that the power to declare war or to stay at peace be transferred from the Prime Minister to the Australian Parliament.
>
> (Fraser 2015: 5)

So, for Fraser, one individual has the institutional capacity to commit Australia to war, and Australia's strategic relationship with the United States ensures that its foreign policy sovereignty is diminished—to such an extent that it is the United States that decides whether Australia is at war or at peace.

Richard Tanter (2015b: 57) argues that the so-called joint facilities, such as Pine Gap, Kojarena, North West Cape and Stirling, 'hardwire Australia into United States strategic objectives and military operations, pre-empting any consideration of sovereign responsibility for acts of war'. He continues:

> Under a pervasive doctrine of interoperability, substantial numbers of ADF [Australian Defence Force] personnel from major-generals down are embedded in US high-technology units from Qatar to Hawaii to Colorado, building careers based on strategic doctrines which assume Australian and US national interests always coincide.
>
> (Tanter 2015b: 56)

It is important to note that the problem is not confined to the embedding of Australian troops in the US military; additionally, a division of US marines has been on permanent rotation in Darwin since 2012. The combination of joint facilities, interoperability and the presence of US troops on Australian soil means that, for all intents and purposes, Australia is no longer in a position to exercise independent war powers. A further result of this 'hard wiring' into the imperatives of what Tanter (2018) describes as a 'networked alliance system' is that, arguably, Australia does not have the ability to conduct foreign affairs more generally, let alone the particularly important question of taking decisions to go to war, on an independent and democratic basis.

Given the current comprehensive nature of Australia's connection to the United States, it cannot be said that the war power can be exercised on a truly democratic basis; only a handful of people have the power to commit Australian troops to combat overseas. Any Australian government wishing to commit Australian troops to overseas action does not have to win the hearts and minds of the Australian public to achieve the political legitimacy that Detmold (1985) regards as vital. The decision to go to war, no matter how unpopular, is in the hands not of citizens, but of the executive arm of government—specifically, the prime minister and the cabinet. One product of the strategic dominance of this institutionalised anti-democratic element is the ease with which Australian foreign policy in general, and particularly the decision to go to war, has been 'captured' by the United States. To win Australian participation as an ally in any US-led war, such as the invasion of Iraq in 2003, the United States does not have to win the hearts and minds of the citizens of Australia either, but of only a handful of key people in the executive branch of government. The Iraq invasion in 2003 is, arguably, illustrative; more than 600,000 people marched against the imminent invasion just days before it was launched—but these people and those who agreed with them could safely be ignored because the war power is entirely in the hands of the executive.

A fundamental question for the nation, including—perhaps especially—any future republic, is: where *should* the war power lie? Is it appropriate for the war power to be in the hands of the executive branch of government? This fundamental question is all the more important given the presence today of not only continuing academic, party-political and popular concern regarding the obligations included in Australia's close relationship and formal alliance with the United States, but also ever-increasing geo-strategic tensions. We argue in this chapter that positioning the war power solely in the hands of the executive is undesirable.

The Australian Constitution, federal legislation and the war power

Before examining the development of the war power in Australia further, it is instructive to examine the constitutional basis for its exercise. The Australian Constitution does not explicitly set out which branch of government is charged with the exercise of the war power. As noted by George Williams (2004: 5), despite the central importance of such a power, the Australian Constitution 'says nothing about who can declare war for Australia or the circumstances in which we might go to war, including whether Australia can use military force in breach of international law as part of a unilateral or pre-emptive strike'.

Further, neither the Constitution nor the most pertinent piece of legislation—the Defence Act 1903 (Cth)—establishes a role for Parliament in declaring war and/or deploying Australian Defence Force (ADF) personnel overseas. Over time, the war power has developed from a royal prerogative exercised by the British monarch to an executive prerogative of the Australian government, so that today, as criticised by former Prime Minister Malcolm Fraser, the executive branch—that is, the prime minister—wields the war power. In essence, whether exercised by the British monarch or the Australian prime minister, the decision to exercise the war power is still inherently anti-democratic in nature. In the past, Australia's entry into war has been a topic of debate—but only subsequently, never prior, to war. This *post hoc* practice has been criticised by political parties, academics and non-governmental organisations (NGOs) alike.

What does the Australian Constitution say?

A number of sections in the Australian Constitution arguably provide some guidance as to who or what should exercise the war power.

On the 'defence power', section 51(vi) of the Australian Constitution sets out the 'defence power', providing that:

> The Parliament shall, subject to this Constitution, have power to make laws for the peace, order, and good government of the Commonwealth with respect to:

[...]

(vi) the naval and military defence of the Commonwealth and of the several States, and the control of the forces to execute and maintain the laws of the Commonwealth.

On the military powers of the governor-general as commander-in-chief, section 68 states:

The commander in chief of the naval and military forces of the Commonwealth is vested in the Governor-General as the Queen's representative.

Section 2 states:

A Governor-General appointed by the Queen shall be Her Majesty's representative in the Commonwealth, and shall have and may exercise in the Commonwealth during the Queen's pleasure, but subject to this Constitution, such powers and functions of the Queen as her Majesty may be pleased to assign to him.

On the executive power of the governor-general, section 61 states:

The executive power of the Commonwealth is vested in the Queen and is exercisable by the Governor-General as the Queen's representative, and extends to the execution and maintenance of this Constitution, and of the laws of the Commonwealth.

Relatively little academic commentary about this hugely important area of Australian law has been written to date. And, within this commentary, scholars disagree about which section of the Constitution contemplates who or what should exercise the war power. Professor George Williams (2004: 5) briefly discusses the sections set out above, but contents himself with saying that 'the Constitution does not expressly supply the answer'. McKeown and Jordan (2010), researching on behalf of Parliament, are equally cautious in their assessment. Like Williams, they briefly discuss sections 51, 61 and 62, but they make no mention of section 68. They seem to favour section 61 as the most appropriate. After observing that it vests the executive power of the Commonwealth in the Queen, exercisable by the governor-general, McKeown and Jordan (2010: 1–2) go on to say that '[f]ormer royal prerogatives—including the power to make war, deploy troops and declare peace—are now part of the executive power of the Commonwealth exercised by the Governor-General'. This view is shared by Geoffrey Lindell (2003: 46–47), who argues that:

[T]he Commonwealth constitution fails to refer explicitly to powers of the executive to declare war and peace . . . However, those powers are now taken to form part of the 'executive power of the Commonwealth' which is vested in the Governor-general as the Queen's representative under s 61 (and possibly also s 68) of the Constitution. The modern view is that the provisions of s 61 now include all the so-called 'prerogatives' of the Crown under the English common law.

The idea that the war power is covered by section 61 of the Constitution has further support. Sampford and Palmer (2009: 351), in their analysis of the war power in Australia, made note of a general discussion that Sampford had in February 2003 when he attended:

> . . . [a] conference that included every senior constitutional lawyer in the country, and asked his colleagues about the legal mechanism by which Australia would go to war. Everyone gave the standard answer, based upon a generally accepted interpretation of Australian constitutional law: as Australia had adopted the Statute of Westminster, the power to declare war . . . would be a matter for the prerogative of the Crown in right of Australia, which would be exercised by the Governor-General on the advice of the Prime Minister unless a statute permitted an alternative procedure.

Sampford and Palmer (2009) argue that this prerogative war power is located in section 61 as the most likely locus of the war power. They suggest that section 68 of the Constitution is:

> . . . best seen as the 'command and control' provision, operable once the decision to go to war has actually been made. Professor George Winterton has suggested that the Governor-General's exercise of the war power would be implemented under s 61 of the Constitution rather than s 68. The authors consider this interpretation to be the better view.
>
> (Sampford and Palmer 2009: 354)

The majority of academics who have discussed the constitutional location of the war power argue that, as wielder of the executive power of the Commonwealth and as commander-in-chief, and on advice and according to the Constitution, the governor-general should exercise the war power under section 61 of the Constitution. As we demonstrate next, the royal instrument of late 1941 by means of which the British monarch assigned the war-making power to the governor-general supports this view.

Does federal legislation establish clearly who should exercise the war power?

Although contested, the view that Parliament can legislate in an area of prerogative power such as the war power is dominant amongst constitutional scholars. Three key cases provide support for this view: *Attorney-General v De Keyser's Royal Hotel* [1920] AC 508; *Barton v Commonwealth* (1974) 3 ALR 70; and

Brown v West (1990) 169 CLR 195. Lindell (2003: 49, n 2), Williams (2004), McKeown and Jordan (2010), and Sampford and Palmer (2009) all take the view that section 51(vi) of the Constitution provides Parliament with the power to legislate in relation to war. The only relevant piece of legislation that might abrogate or regulate the prerogative war power and thus provide guidance as to the location of the war power is the Defence Act 1903 (Cth). The question is: has Parliament done so?

Section 63 of the 1903 Act provides:

> The Governor-General may:
>
> [. . .]
>
> (f) Subject to the provisions of this Act do all matters and things deemed by him to be necessary or desirable for the efficient defence and protection of the Commonwealth or of any State.

Sampford and Palmer (2009: 363) summarise the effect of this section thus:

> [T]he conferring of this broad power on the Governor-General rather than the minister would seem to confirm that, once the power to make war had passed to Australia in 1941, it would be exercised by the Governor-General on advice via the Executive Council.

Despite this assessment that the governor-general wields the war power, to complicate matters, the minister of defence is granted certain executive powers by virtue of section 8 of the Act:

> The Minister shall have the general control and administration of the Defence force and the powers vested in the Chief of the Defence Force, the Chief of Naval Staff, the Chief of the General Staff and the Chief of the Air Staff by virtue of section 9, and the powers vested jointly in the Secretary and the Chief of the Defence Force by virtue of section 9A, shall be exercised subject to and in accordance with any directions from the Minister.

Section 9(2) provides that: 'Subject to section 8, the Chief of the Defence Force shall command the Defence Force.'

Arguably, these sections could be construed as affording the defence minister the executive war power. Again, Sampford and Palmer's view is convincing. For them, sections 8 and 9 make:

> . . . significant inroads into the policy and operational aspects of the 'command in chief' role enjoyed by the Governor-General under section 68 of the Constitution . . . But, based on the government's intentions as outlined in the Tange Report and the second reading speech, the 1975 Amendments to section 8 do not appear to have had the intention of vesting the power

to go to war on the minister. Nor do the amendments on their ordinary meaning have this effect. The Act simply has nothing to say about how this power is to be exercised . . . the legislation, at most, regulates only that part of the executive power under s 68 of the Constitution which covers such operational matters.

(Sampford and Palmer 2009: 365)

So, for Sampford and Palmer, the only legislation that might displace the governor-general in relation to the exercise of the war power does not do so. The Defence Act 1903 (Cth) has not placed the war power in the hands of the minister of defence; at best, it has given the minister greater command-and-control or operational powers. Of course, it is well within Parliament's authority, in certain circumstances, to legislate to control a prerogative power such as the war power. For instance the Defence Act 1903 could clearly state that the decision to go to war requires the input of the minister of defence or that any decision to go to war requires a parliamentary vote prior to the commencement of hostilities. However, any such legislation must make it clear that it is controlling the prerogative power. The Defence Act 1903 does not do so.

At this point, it is important to repeat the argument made at the outset of the chapter: that, as Australia's relationship to Britain waned and a very close, multi-level alliance with the United States was consolidated, the constitutional role of the governor-general in respect of the war power was supplanted by that of the prime minister in exercising the war power.

The development and exercise of the war power in Australia: from last shillings and melancholy duty, to coalitions of the willing and beyond

This section examines the decisions of Australia when entering the major conflicts of the 20th and 21st centuries. 'The more things change, the more they stay the same' aptly describes the development of the war power in Australia. At Federation in 1901, the war power was the prerogative of the British monarch. As discussed earlier in the chapter, the exercise of Australian war powers can be divided into three phases. Although the phases are distinct, they share one common and disturbing characteristic: the exercise of the Australian war power may be described as subservient. Both in the past and now, the war power has been exercised in accordance with the interests of the strongest imperial power of the day.

World War I

In the first phase in the development of the war power in Australia, the colonial hangover, the Australian Parliament took no prior role in the entry of Australian forces into World War I. Indeed, it was not expected that Parliament would play such a role. As stated earlier, no such a role is required by the Constitution nor, at that time, was there any expectation that Australia would *not* enter into any war fought by Britain. The driving force behind Australia's entry into the war was popular and party-political loyalty to the 'old country'. Any Australian interests in participation were secondary to this overriding loyalty to the colonial power. Even after the creation of the Commonwealth of Australia in 1901 as a self-governing federation, Australia was not thought of, either domestically or internationally, as an independent nation, but rather as a semi-autonomous dominion of the British Empire. For most British-born and first-generation Anglo-Australians, Australia remained a part of the wider British Empire.

The 1926 Imperial Conference and the resulting Balfour Declaration of 1926 stated that the United Kingdom and the dominions were:

> . . . autonomous Communities within the British Empire, equal in status, in no way subordinate one to another in any aspect of their domestic or external affairs, though united by a common allegiance to the Crown, and freely associated as members of the British Commonwealth of Nations.
>
> (Inter-Imperial Relations Committee 1926: 3)

However, in this period, Australian elite political opinion did not seem to relish the allegedly increasing sense of national separateness (Marshall 2001: 541). Despite the 1930 Imperial Conference, which again emphasised dominion autonomy, and despite the codification (in the 1931 Statute of Westminster, which Australia resisted adopting until 1942) declaring that all Commonwealth dominions were legislatively independent from Britain, it was only after the fall of Singapore in February 1942 that many in Australia began to question the capacity of the former colonial power to protect Australia.

In terms of the exercise of the war power, this attitude of continuing deference to the 'old country' is demonstrated in Australia parliamentary speeches made at the onset of World War I and again before World War II, and in decisions of the Australian High Court that will be discussed shortly. The result of this colonial hangover was that, until 1941, Australia's war power was exercised by Britain. Australian political elites, including members of the executive branch of government, deferred to Britain. Any decision to go to war was made not in Canberra, but in Whitehall.

As the clouds of war gathered over Europe, the Australian Federal Parliament was dissolved on 30 July 1914. On 31 July, then Prime Minister Joseph Cook stated: 'If there is to be war, you and I shall be in it. If the old country is at war, so are we' (quoted in Bean c.1981: 17). Opposition Leader Andrew Fisher expressed similar sentiments: 'Should the worst happen, after everything has been done that honour will permit, Australians will stand beside the mother country to help and defend her to our last man and shilling' (quoted in Bean c.1981: 16).

On 3 August 1914, the cabinet met to discuss Australia's position regarding the war. On that day, a proclamation under the Defence Act 1903 (Cth) declared that there existed a time of war and called out the Citizen Forces of the British

Commonwealth (Commonwealth Government Gazette, 3 August 1914, p. 1335). At this point, Britain had yet to make a formal declaration of war against Germany and did so only on 4 September 1914.

On 5 September, a general election was held and the Australian Labor Party took up government. The new Parliament did not meet until 8 October 1914. On that day, there was no statement made to Parliament in relation to the war, but in his opening speech Governor-General Ferguson stated:

> You have been called together at the earliest moment after the return of the writs to deal with matters of great national importance, many of them arising out of the calamitous war in which the Empire has been compelled to engage . . . It has been necessary to anticipate Parliamentary approval of expenditure urgently required for war purposes. A Bill covering all such unauthorised expenditure will be submitted for your consideration at the earliest possible moment.
>
> (R. Ferguson, Senate, *Debates*,
> 8 October 1914, p. 7)

Senator David Watson, in the Address-in-Reply to the governor-general's speech, stated that '[o]ur duty to the British Empire must never be questioned—must never be forsaken in any degree' (D. Watson, Senate, *Debates*, 8 October 1914, p. 22). And, during the debate that followed, former Prime Minister and then Leader of the Opposition Joseph Cook expressed bipartisan support for the war cause:

> I wish to say to the Government that we shall be behind them most cordially with our best support—and not critical support—in prosecuting this war right to the end, and in financing it to the full in every legitimate and reasonable way.
>
> (J. Cook, House of Representatives,
> *Debates*, 14 October 1914, p. 174)

The unquestioning support of the major political parties for Britain's cause found judicial support in the Australian High Court. Early decisions clearly and unequivocally saw the war power as 'necessarily' lying with the British monarch. An important body of opinion regarded the war power as the quintessential royal prerogative. As the slaughter unfolded in Europe during one of the bloodiest years in human history, Isaacs J stated that '[t]he creation of a state of war and the establishment of peace necessarily reside in the Sovereign himself as the head of the Empire' (*Farey v Burvett* (1916) 21 CLR 433, 452) In the same year, Isaacs J clearly stated that the war power was vested in the British monarch: 'No doubt, the supreme power of creating a state of war or peace for the whole of the Empire resides in His Majesty in his right of his whole Empire' (*Welsbach Light Co. of Australasia Ltd v Commonwealth of Australia* (1916) 22 CLR 268, 278).

In a move away from Isaacs J's view of the Australian war power as purely a prerogative power of the British monarch, Higgins J took a more nuanced view in 1918:

> I certainly agree with the view that, if and so far as the royal prerogative as to war is exercisable by Australian authority, it has to be exercised, not by the State Ministers but by the Governor-General and his Federal ministers.
> (*Joseph v Colonial Treasurer* (1918) 25 CLR 32, 51)

Although, for Higgins J, the war power was to be understood as a royal prerogative (as it clearly was for Isaacs J), Higgins J takes a step further by suggesting that the prerogative was exercisable by the governor-general and federal ministers. This idea would find full expression more than 20 years later.

In summary, in 1914, at the outbreak of what was, until that time, the most calamitous conflict the world had ever seen, no legal or political capacity for an Australian exercise of the war power was recognised and no legal or political authority existed that contemplated a separate or independent Australian formal declaration of war. The sentiment, shared by politicians, popular opinion and the High Court, was that if the 'old country' was at war, so was Australia. It is clear from the sentiments expressed in Parliament and in the media that loyalty to Britain was the paramount inspiration for Australia to participate in the war. And, of course, there was no countervailing notion provided by the Constitution that the Australian Parliament should play any role in this decision. This deference to the British Empire continued until World War II (Birrell 1995).

World War II: a brief transition from colonial deference to an independent exercise of the war power

Once again, the Australian Federal Parliament had no prior role in the entry of Australia into World War II. Just as with entry into World War I, the war power was exercised entirely in accordance with Whitehall. Australian Prime Minister Menzies took the view that if the Empire was at war, then, as part of the British Empire, so too was Australia. The Australian Parliament had adjourned on 16 June 1939 and was not in session when British Prime Minister Neville Chamberlain announced that Britain was at war with Germany—an announcement received in Australia, via short-wave radio, at 8 pm on 3 September 1939. At 9.15 pm that night, Prime Minister Menzies publicly pronounced:

> It is my melancholy duty to inform you officially, that in consequence of persistence by Germany in her invasion of Poland, Great Britain has declared war upon her and that, as a result, Australia is also at war.
> (Australian War Memorial 2017)

That night, Prime Minister Menzies issued notice of the existence of war between Britain and Germany, and the governor-general proclaimed, under the Defence

Act 1903 (Cth), the existence of war in Australia (Commonwealth Government Gazette, 3 September 1939, p. 1849). Because the Australian Constitution does not contemplate a role for Parliament prior to entry into war, in 1939, as in 1914, the Australian prime minister's deference to Britain precluded any independent declarations of war.

However, in 1940, the High Court of Australia affirmed the more nuanced approach taken in 1918 by Higgins J in *Joseph v Colonial Treasurer* (1918) 25 CLR 32 to the question of the exercise of the war power. In *Federal Commissioner of Taxation v Official Liquidator of EO Farley Ltd* (1940) 63 CLR 278, at 320–21, Evatt J referred to the earlier *Joseph* decision, expressing the view that the war power is exercisable by the Australian representative of the British monarch:

> There [in *Joseph*] it was held that the royal prerogative as to war . . . is exercisable by the King's representative . . . There are many royal prerogatives by virtue of which the King or his representative is entitled to act, for example, to declare war, to make peace. Such prerogatives may be said to be . . . executive prerogatives.

Thus, by 1940, the High Court viewed the royal war power prerogative as an executive prerogative wielded by the Australian governor-general. This judicial notion found political expression in 1941 when Evatt, now holding the office of attorney-general, made the same argument in Parliament: that, given the equality of status among all members of the Commonwealth created by the Statute of Westminster, Australian authority included the power to declare war independently of Britain; and that such a declaration lay within the constitutional authority of the governor-general, upon advice.

The Japanese attack on the US naval base at Pearl Harbor took place on 7 December. The Australian war cabinet met on 8 December and, later that evening, Prime Minister John Curtin announced to the nation that Australia was at war with Japan. On 9 December, the government formally proclaimed 'the existence of a state of war with Japan as from 5 pm on 8 December' (Hasluck 1970: 5). The existence of a state of war with Finland, Hungary and Romania was also declared—again following the practice that Britain had declared war on these countries. Australian Prime Minister Curtin made a statement to Parliament on 16 December in which he asked Parliament to approve the action of the government in issuing the proclamations of the state of war with Japan, Finland, Hungary and Romania: 'Parliament is now asked to endorse the advice which led to the issue of the proclamation by the Governor-General of Australia on behalf of His Majesty the King' (J. Curtin, House of Representatives, *Debates*, 16 December 1941, p. 1068).

Also on 16 December, Attorney-General Evatt advised Parliament that:

> [I]t was important to avoid any legal controversy as to the power of the Governor-General to declare a state of war without specific authorization by His Majesty . . . Certainly the royal powers already exercisable under

the Constitution by the Governor-General as the King's representative are extremely wide. However, the matter was too important and too urgent to invite any legal controversy. We, therefore, decided to make it abundantly clear that there was an unbroken chain of prerogative authority extending from the King himself to the Governor-General. For that purpose we prepared a special instrument, the terms of which were graciously accepted by his Majesty . . . his Majesty assigned to His Excellency, the Governor-General, the power of declaring a state of war, first with Finland, Rumania and Hungary, and secondly, with Japan.

> (H. V. Evatt, House of Representatives, *Debates*,
> 16 December 1941, pp. 1088–89)

The key sections of the statutory instrument reads as follows:

Now therefore We acting by and with the advice of Our Federal Executive Council of Our Commonwealth of Australia and in exercise of all powers us thereunto enabling hereby assign to the Governor General of the commonwealth of Australia the power to declare and proclaim that as from a date and hour to be specified by the said Governor-General a state of war exists in the Commonwealth of Australia and its territories with the Japanese Empire . . .

> (Commonwealth Government Gazette,
> 7 April 1942, p. 859)

Sampford and Palmer (2009: 359) state that Australia's belated adoption of the Statute of Westminster on 9 October 1942 confirmed the transfer of the war prerogative to Australian authorities. They also argue that a more independent Australian foreign policy emerged. However, this second phase of the development of the war power in Australia, the imperceptibly independent vice-regal phase, was short-lived.

Despite Australia's newfound executive autonomy in exercising the war power during World War II, after 1951 Australian war power practice ignored the role of the governor-general, recognising instead the authority of the Australian political executive—that is, the prime minister and cabinet. This third, executive unchained, phase began immediately after the governor-general signed the peace with Germany on behalf of Australia in 1951. In Korea, Malaya, Vietnam, Afghanistan, Iraq I, II and III, and Syria, the governor-general did not play the role that was envisaged by Evatt in 1941. Instead, the role of the governor-general was ignored and a narrowly construed executive branch—that is, the prime minister and cabinet—effectively seized control of the war power. This arguably 'political' executive, loosed from the constraints of deference to Britain, eventually found a new 'colonial' protector in the United States. The dominant political and judicial view that the war power was vested in the executive, when combined with the subservience of the executive branch to the United States, has ensured that, as in earlier times, Australia does not practise an independent foreign policy when it comes to war. Where once decisions about war were made for Australia in Whitehall, now they are made in Washington.

Malaya 1948–60: continued subservience to Britain

In the aftermath of World War II, Britain regularised its former relationships in South East Asia with the rulers of Malay states—the Straits settlements (Penang, Singapore and Malacca) and protectorates (Sarawak, North Borneo and the Brunei Sultanate)—and the federation of Malaya was formed in 1948. The formidable Malayan Communist Party (MCP) developed among Chinese immigrant tin and rubber plantation workers. In 1948, the MCP adopted a position of armed revolt. The British declared an 'emergency' after three estate managers were killed in June 1948. Gyngell (2017: 29) argues that:

> The Chifley government had already agreed the month before to send shipments of weapons and radio equipment to assist the British in outlying areas, although it resisted the dispatch of personnel. Soon after Menzies took over, and partly driven by criticism from Keith Murdoch in the *Melbourne Herald* that Australia was taking too little notice of communist threats in Southeast Asia, RAAF [Royal Australian Air Force] aircraft and military personnel were also sent to help.

Prime Minister Robert Menzies, addressing Parliament on 30 May 1950, stated: 'The Government is giving careful consideration to the question of ways and means of assisting the United Kingdom Government in its Malayan problem' (R. Menzies, House of Representatives, *Debates*, 30 May 1950, pp. 3349–51). The next day, 31 May 1950, the Prime Minister related to the House that it had been decided that Australia would provide aid to the British government by providing aircraft, aircraft crews and support units. In June 1950, Australian air support units for the British Royal Air Force (RAF) were sent to Malaya.

Gyngell (2017: 29) links Australian involvement in Malaya to the outbreak of the Korean War:

> The outbreak of the Korean War in June 1950 deepened the sense that communism was on the march in Asia. Communist aggression, Menzies argued, linked what was happening in Korea to the insurgent movements in Indochina and Malaya. By sending bombers to Malaya, Australia would demonstrate to the communist movement internationally that there was 'no division among the British countries of the world'.

As the situation in Malaya deteriorated, consideration was given to the possibility of committing Australian infantry forces to the Malayan theatre of war. On 20 April 1955, in a ministerial statement, Prime Minister Menzies said:

I have already announced publicly that the Government proposes to contribute a comparatively small force to a strategic reserve in Malaya. I will, a
little later in this speech, indicate the acceptance of more extensive military
responsibilities in the event of war.

(R. Menzies, House of Representatives,
Debates, 20 April 1955, p. 49)

In response, Leader of the Opposition Herbert V. Evatt stated that 'the
Australian Labor Party is satisfied that the proposed use . . . of Australian armed
forces in Malaya at present will gravely injure our relations with Malaya and her
Asian neighbours' (H. V. Evatt, House of Representatives, *Debates*, 27 April
1955, p. 200).

The opposition moved an amendment that 'this House rejects the
Government's proposals to despatch Australian armed forces to Malaya as set out
in the paper read by the Prime Minister' (L. Haylen, House of Representatives,
Debates, 4 May 1955, p. 403). This amendment was defeated. This was the
first occasion in Australian history on which an opposition party had resisted a
government involvement in conflict. Such resistance was, and remains, purely
symbolic because there is no constitutional role for Parliament in relation to a
decision to engage in military action. However, in terms of Detmold's requirement of 'political legitimacy', the vote is significant.

As the emergency dragged on, Britain requested more assistance and,
although Parliament was in recess, the Australian Prime Minister announced
the commitment of additional Australian troops to the conflict after a meeting
of the cabinet on 15 June 1955. Again, no formal proclamation of war was
made; arguably, a declaration against such an ephemeral foe as a 'communist
insurgency' would have been not only risible, but also impossible to justify
in traditional political terms. However, following the practice adopted in the
Korean War, a declaration was made under section 4 of the Defence Act 1903
(Cth), relating ambiguously to 'active service' (Commonwealth Government
Gazette, 5 June 1952, p. 2712).

Formally, the emergency was declared over in July 1960. But its impact had
been far-reaching:

[T]he Emergency had generated a profound policy shift in Australia. Canberra
had agreed in 1955 to the stationing of Australian and New Zealand military
units in Malaya as part of a Commonwealth Strategic Reserve. This was the
first peacetime commitment of Australian ground forces outside Australian
territory, and it was to Asia, not the Middle East. It was both a way of rein-
forcing a British commitment to Asia and a signal to the United States that
Australia was prepared to carry some of the burden of its own defence. Labor
and Evatt, now its leader, were strongly opposed to the use of Australian
troops to 'bolster up imperialism in Southeast Asia'.

(Harper 1957: 191)

Nonetheless, the Australian role in this conflict can be seen broadly as supporting not only British formerly imperial economic interests in tin and rubber (Blakkarly 2015), but also a broader 'Western' interest in eradicating, or at least limiting, the spread of communism in the region. To these ends, the prime minister and cabinet had taken the decision to enter the conflict.

Korean War 1950–53: executive prerogative, the UN Charter, Britain and the United States

The outbreak of hostilities in the Korean War began on 25 June 1950. The Australian Parliament was recalled on 6 July 1950 and was addressed by Prime Minister Robert Menzies, who outlined the manner in which Australian troops became involved in the conflict. UN Security Council Resolution 83 of 27 June 1950 (Complaint of aggression upon the Republic of Korea) recommended that: 'Members of the United Nations furnish such assistance to the Republic of Korea as may be necessary to repel the armed attack and to restore international peace and security in the area.'

Sampford and Palmer (2009: 368, n74) analyse the announcement thus:

> Commitments to provide the services of the Australian Navy were made by Menzies by cable to British Prime Minister Attlee on 29 June; the decision to commit ground troops was made after tortuous negotiations among ministers while the Prime Minister was overseas and a statement to this effect was hurriedly drafted by the External Affairs Minister Percy Spender (in order to beat the announcement of a British commitment to the US effort) in the name of the acting Prime Minister Arthur Fadden and telephoned to the Australian Broadcasting Commission to be announced 'to Australia and the world' (p 76). Here the importance of the US alliance to Australia played a key role in the speed at which events moved. We do not know what role, if any, the Governor-General played in that process. However, it would be surprising if a traditional royalist and constitutionalist such as Menzies would not have kept him fully informed and sought his verbal assent using at least the kind of processes involved in the United Kingdom at that time.

On 29 June, Australia advised the United Nations that it would support the Security Council Resolution by 'placing an Australian naval force . . . at the disposal of the United States authorities on behalf of the Security Council for the purpose of furnishing assistance to the Republic of Korea' (McKeown and Jordan 2010: 14).

Additionally, on 30 June, the government announced that it 'had decided to place at the service of the United Nations, through the American authorities, the Royal Australian Air Force fighter squadron stationed in Japan' (R. Menzies, House of Representatives, *Debates*, 6 July 1950, p. 4837).

The motion proposed by the Prime Minister on 6 July 1950 stated that:

> [T]his House, having before it the Charter of the United Nations and the recent resolutions of the Security Council in relation to Korea, approves of the action taken by the Government in placing at the disposal of the United Nations the forces indicated in the statement of the Prime Minister.
>
> (R. Menzies, House of Representatives, *Debates*, 6 July 1950, pp. 4838–39)

Leader of the Opposition Ben Chifley informed the House that the opposition would support the motion. The motion was resolved in the affirmative and no formal vote was taken in either chamber—which illustrates that the Australian political executive, with no resistance from the opposition, exercised the war power by reference to the UN Charter to justify involvement in the conflict. As in the past, no parliamentary debate—as opposed to parliamentary endorsement or approval—took place in either the Australian House of Representatives or the Australian Senate and no opposition was expressed. Importantly, where previously the bonds of empire were mentioned as justification for unquestioning participation in war, on this occasion justification took the form of reference to the UN Charter and the relevant Security Council resolution. No proclamation was made that a state of war existed, although a declaration was made in relation to 'active service' in Korea under section 4 of the Defence Act 1903 (Cth) (Commonwealth Government Gazette, 5 June 1952, p. 2711).

In an interesting presage of ideas that found expression in the 1980s, Leader of the Opposition in the Senate William Ashley stated, during the Senate debate: 'Whilst it is not always opportune to call the Parliament together, and it is realized that certain matters must be dealt with urgently, I stress that any future Australian commitments should have the approval of Parliament' (W. Ashley, Senate, *Debates*, 6 July 1950, p. 4834).

This idea that Parliament should approve Australian military commitments is at the heart of calls for reform of the war power that have been made by political parties, NGOs and academics since the 1980s.

Crisis in Indonesia: Borneo 1963–66

Post-colonial problems with Britain's former South East Asian territories continued into the 1960s, again involving the commitment of Australian troops. At the end of 1962, Indonesia's Suharto regarded a projected new federation (of Malaya, Singapore, Sabah and Sarawak, and the Sultanate of Brunei) as a British 'neo-colonialist' plot, stating opposition as 'confrontation'. The confrontation involved 'hostile rhetoric, trade embargoes, political manoeuvring and, after April 1963, raids and military incursions' (Gyngell 2017: 34). Then External Affairs Minister Garfield Barwick sought to reconcile tensions; the United States had indicated a focus on ensuring that Indonesia remained stable and non-communist, but Britain's emphasis was on defending the new federation, Malaysia.

By the end of 1963, Australia had committed itself to assisting Britain to defend Malaysia against Indonesia, despite Washington's continuing neutrality. It saw its main interest as maintaining a forward military position in a British-influenced state, despite the risk of conflict—even war—with Indonesia. Australia consulted the United States about the support it could expect under the ANZUS Treaty if Australian troops were to come under Indonesian attack. The response Barwick received was cautious: any support from US ground forces, even in the case of direct Indonesian attack, was ruled out (Gyngell 2017: 35).

Indonesian troops landed in Malaysia on 17 August 1964 and paratroops, in September 1964. The danger of war was very real. Finally, on 27 January 1965, the foreign affairs and defence committee of the cabinet decided to commit three Royal Australian Regiment (RAR) and Special Air Service Regiment (SAS) troops to the conflict, and shifted its combat forces from the Malaya peninsula to Borneo. Acting Prime Minister John McEwen announced this on 3 February 1965. Parliament met on 16 March 1965, but it was not until 23 March 1965 that Minister for External Affairs Paul Hasluck made a ministerial statement, which he limited thus: 'I shall confine my remarks to a few of the more urgent topics. This is not intended . . . to limit the range of debate' (P. Hasluck, House of Representatives, *Debates*, 23 March 1965, p. 230). Surprisingly, the minister made no reference at all to the coalition government's decision to send troops to Borneo.

In reply, Leader of the Opposition Arthur Calwell stated:

> Aggression in all its forms must be resisted. We believe however, that the Australian Government has failed totally to take any diplomatic initiative either to end this dispute, or to reduce its temperature. I am optimistic enough to believe that war can be avoided; but if it is, it will be not because of any action taken by this Government.
>
> (A. Calwell, House of Representatives,
> *Debates*, 23 March 1965, p. 242)

As Gyngell (2017: 36) reports: 'Australia approved the possible use of Darwin and Fremantle in British plans to retaliate against selected military targets in Indonesia, and Australian and Indonesian forces engaged in sporadic hostilities on the Sarawak border.' According to his analysis, Australia managed the 'foreign policy test of Confrontation skilfully' (Gyngell 2017: 36). But whether Australia managed its war powers test as well is debatable. Again, the record shows that although the Labor Party opposition voiced its concerns, the executive branch was not required to gain parliamentary approval prior to war nor did it do so. The opposition's concerns fell on deaf ears.

Vietnam War 1965–75: the American embrace

The Australian Parliament adjourned on 17 May 1962 and did not meet again until 7 August 1962. In a press release dated 24 May 1962, Minister for Defence Athol Townley stated that, 'at the invitation of the government of the Republic of Vietnam, Australia was sending a group of military instructors to that country' (Frost 1987: 15). Cox and O'Connor (2012: 175) argue that the government took the decision on 15 May 1962.

Peter Edwards (1997b: 74), official historian of Australia and the Vietnam War, identified the broad context within which Australia committed combat troops to the South Vietnam conflict in late 1964 and early 1965: 'At this time Southeast Asia appeared full of actual and potential threats to the West and its allies.' Edwards cites the fact that, in late 1964, not only were Australian and Indonesian forces actually in combat in Borneo, but also Australia was concerned that Sukarno's announcement of a 'Jakarta–Peking axis' might prompt Indonesia to open another front on Australia's land border in eastern New Guinea. Additionally, he cites the instability that attended Singapore's secession from Malaysia in August 1965, communist insurgency in northeast Thailand, near the Laos border, continuing internal insecurity in the Philippines, and ongoing tension between India and Pakistan (which erupted into outright war in 1965).

Given such circumstances, it is not surprising that Australia sought to ensure that its 'great and powerful friends'—Britain and the United States—maintained their substantial military forces in South East Asia. As seen in relation to Borneo, earlier in the chapter, British and US emphases differed: Britain's focus was on Indonesia; that of the United States was on Vietnam. Edwards (1997b) points toward an additional issue for Australia: its characteristic reluctance to make major troop commitments. Australia's reliance on 'strong diplomatic and rhetorical support for its powerful allies, backed only by token military commitments' (Edwards 1997b: 75) led to increased pressure from Britain, and particularly the United States, in 1964.

Analysing the foreign policy context, Gyngell (2017) agrees with Edwards' emphasis that Australia's decision to commit troops was based on what many scholars have identified as the perceived strategic necessity of 'alliance maintenance' (Tanter 2015a):

> Australia was slow to give up the idea that it did not have to choose between Britain and United States. The ANZUS relationship developed cautiously on both sides. Major players in each country had reservations. Nevertheless, the dominance of America in the postwar world was clear from the beginning and, in Korea and then Vietnam, Australia became engaged in the first of a series of what might be called the 'Wars of American Engagement'. Conflicts, that is, whose rationale was less the places and circumstances in which they were fought, or their strategic purpose, than the desire to demonstrate allied support and solidarity: to pay the insurance premium.
>
> (Gyngell 2017: 86)

Edwards (1997b: 75) argues that:

> Given the combination of regional crises and Australia's dependence on its powerful allies, it was at least understandable that the Menzies Government felt it necessary to make some military commitment to support the American effort in Vietnam.

On 4 December 1964, the United States made a formal request for additional Australian troops. Australia offered to provide a battalion and, on 13 April 1965, US Secretary of State Dean Rusk accepted this offer. On 29 April 1965, Australian Prime Minister Robert Menzies made a ministerial statement to Parliament stating that:

> The Australian Government is now in receipt of a request from the Government of South Vietnam for further military assistance. We have decided . . . to provide an infantry battalion for Service in South Vietnam . . . I should say . . . that we decided in principle some time ago . . . that we would be willing to do this if we received the necessary request from the Government of South Vietnam and the necessary collaboration with the United States.
> (R. Menzies, House of Representatives, *Debates*, 29 April 1965, p. 1060)

Debate in Parliament in relation to the prime minister's statement occurred on 4 May 1965 and, by way of response, Leader of the Opposition Arthur Calwell said that, 'on behalf of all of my colleagues of Her Majesty's Opposition, I say that we oppose the Government's decision to send 800 men to fight in Vietnam. We oppose it firmly and completely' (A. Calwell, House of Representatives, *Debates*, 4 May 1965, p. 1102).

Arguably, however, the Labor Party opposition's concerns about Australia's military actions in Malaysia and in Vietnam were inconsequential, at least in terms of preventing conflict. After all, in the absence of a constitutional or other requirement that Parliament vote on the issue of war, any 'concerns' could not be translated into anything substantive.

Commitment to the war in Vietnam was deeply unpopular, with much of the opposition grounded less in the absence of a credible government justification than in hostility to conscription, even though the commitment at any one time was small—'never more than 8500 personnel from all three services' (O'Connor 1997; Maddox and Wright 1987). Edwards' (1997b) account states that even the army had doubts about conscription.

The research conducted by Cox and O'Connor (2012) reveals the existence of two schools of thought regarding the nature of Australia's relationship with the United States. On the one hand is the familiar position that Australia is a 'lapdog'—a 'pliant ally', who 'unthinkingly follows the US into foreign wars' (Cox and O'Connor 2012: 173); on the other are revisionist scholars, such as Bell (1988), Edwards (1997a), Edwards and Pemberton (1992), and Sexton (1981), who acknowledge Australian dependence on the United States without assuming sycophancy or the subordination of Australian interests to those of the United States. These latter scholars argue that Australia's alliance relationship has been dominated not by 'enthusiasm', but by strategic concerns to ensure continued US military involvement in and commitment to South East Asia. Cox and O'Connor then instance External Affairs Minister Barwick's speech to Parliament on 11 March 1964, rejecting French President Charles de Gaulle's advocacy in favour of a negotiated settlement for a neutral South Vietnam.

Barwick argued, on the basis of a consensus of opinion within the Department of External Affairs and the Department of Defence, that neutralisation, a non-military 'solution', should not be viewed as such. A briefing paper in early 1964, prepared for Barwick's meeting with the Southeast Asia Treaty Organization (SEATO) Council, argued that Australia 'must join in resisting pressure for a non-military solution', suggesting that the immediate objective was 'to continue to help the South Vietnamese Government to deal with and overcome Communist insurgency', and that this necessitated 'our full backing of the United States position' (Cox and O'Connor 2012: 177).

Cox and O'Connor (2012: 177) make the point succinctly: '[T]he Australia government enthusiastically endorsed and even demanded a military rather than a diplomatic solution in Vietnam.' Thus, they conclude, Australia was not 'press-ganged' into participation, but rather encouraged an escalation of US military action in Vietnam, while maintaining a modest commitment of Australian troops to secure continued US involvement.

What was to be gained?

The supposed benefits included improved security through lessening the:

> . . . threat of communist gains in Southeast Asia, closer engagement of the US in Australia's region, greater alliance intimacy with the US, and political advantage over the parliamentary opposition. Much of this would have a clear echo in the lead-up to the second Gulf War nearly 40 years later.
>
> (Cox and O'Connor 2012: 179)

With regard to the attack on Iraq in 1990–91, Cox and O'Connor (2012: 180) argue that, again, Australia's involvement could not be said to illustrate subservience or a forswearing of Australian interests, but rather, as argued in 2005 by Michael Thawley, Australia's ambassador to the United States, a calculated 'conscious, independent decision taken by an Australian government after much deliberation'. On this view, the strategic priority for Australia in the case of Iraq was—as it was in Vietnam—to uphold the strategic culture established in the second half of the 20th century that is committed to maintaining the US alliance despite the presence of short-term risks. For the revisionist view, the essential feature of this culture:

> . . . was, and is, cultivating the support of, and intimacy with, a great and powerful friend—not as an end in itself, but with the aim of increasing Australian security and attempting to ensure that friend's engagement in the Asian region.
>
> (Cox and O'Connor 2012: 185)

Given the capture of Australian war power sovereignty, the argument about sycophantic subservience to, or calculated compliance with, US interests is somewhat moot. The presence of a strategic culture, whether informed by sycophantic subservience or calculated compliance, and upheld so strongly by a comparatively small Australian military and political elite, arguably supports the exercise of the war power without reference to parliamentary or popular opinion.

As indicated earlier, former Prime Minister Malcolm Fraser regards the revisionist position as misconceived. He points toward a certain circularity in reasoning:

> Our leaders argue that we need to keep our alliance with the US strong in order to ensure our defence in the event of an aggressive foe. Yet the most likely reason Australia would need to confront an aggressive foe is our alliance with the US. It is not a sustainable policy.
>
> (Fraser 2014: 268)

Gulf War 1990–91: reliance on references to UN Security Council resolutions and the executive war power prerogative

On 2 August 1990, Iraqi forces invaded Kuwait. On 21 August 1990, Prime Minister Hawke's ministerial statement to the House of Representatives stated:

> I want to take this first opportunity available to me to inform the House of the view the Government has taken of the situation which has arisen in the Middle East over the past three weeks and of the measures we have adopted to meet that situation.
>
> (R. Hawke, House of Representatives, *Debates*,
> 21 August 1990, p. 1118)

Prime Minister Hawke condemned the invasion and called for the immediate withdrawal of Iraqi forces from Kuwait. His statement characterised the government's actions as implementing the sanctions imposed by the United Nations. In response, Leader of the Opposition John Hewson stated that '[t]he Opposition parties are pleased to support the motion that is before the House' (J. Hewson, House of Representatives, *Debates*, 21 August 1990, p. 1123).

On 4 December 1990, Prime Minister Hawke's ministerial statement to Parliament was that:

> [T]he Government unreservedly supports the United Nations Security Council resolution 678. Our support for the resolution imposes on us an obligation to respond to the request in its third paragraph for all nations to provide appropriate support for actions taken under the resolution. I emphasise that the resolution not only authorises all necessary means; it explicitly requests that member states provide support.
>
> (R. Hawke, House of Representatives,
> *Debates*, 4 December 1990, p. 4319)

Opposition Leader Hewson responded, 'We are committed as an Opposition to building a united national position on this issue' (J. Hewson, House of Representatives, *Debates*, 4 December 1990, p. 4325), despite criticising the government for not 'consulting' with the opposition prior to its original decision to deploy Australian defence forces to the Gulf. So, in this instance, the Liberal–National coalition opposition parties were sufficiently moved to express mild annoyance that they had not been consulted, but they were in no way disposed to formally resist the push for war in Parliament.

On 17 January 1991, US and allied forces began bombing Iraq. On that day, Prime Minister Hawke recalled Parliament and issued a statement in relation to the military operations taken by Australia's Naval Task Force in the Gulf. On 21 and 22 January 1991, Parliament debated the Gulf War. Four days after the bombing began, on 21 January 1991, the Prime Minister's statement to the House was that:

> The decision to commit Australian armed forces to combat is of course one that constitutionally is the prerogative of the Executive. It is fitting, however, that I place on parliamentary record the train of events behind the decision.
> (R. Hawke, House of Representatives,
> *Debates*, 21 January 1991, p. 2)

The motion proposed by the Prime Minister stated that the House of Representatives:

> . . . reaffirms its support for an ongoing role for the United Nations in promoting world peace and the self-determination of nations . . . affirms its support for Australia's positive response to the request made by the United Nations Security Council in Resolution 678 for support in implementing that Resolution; expresses its full confidence in and support for, Australian forces serving with the UN sanctioned multi-national forces in the Gulf; deplores Iraq's widening of the conflict by its unprovoked attack upon Israel.
> (R. Hawke, House of Representatives,
> *Debates*, 21 January 1991, p. 2)

Leader of the Opposition John Hewson stated that 'the Opposition parties strongly support this motion before the House' (J. Hewson, House of Representatives, *Debates*, 21 January 1991, p. 9).

On this occasion, Prime Minister Hawke explicitly characterised the exercise of the war power as an executive prerogative—an idea first expressed by Evatt J in 1940. Evatt's understanding of which branch of government was to exercise the war power seems not only to have constituted the undeclared authority for Australia's involvement in subsequent conflicts, but also is, seemingly, the basis for current practice by Australian governments. The executive branch sees itself as wielding the war power in the same vein as a British monarch: the war power is a remnant prerogative power of the English kings and is wielded as such by the executive branch of government. This exercise by the executive of the war power is extremely worrying given not only the dominance within the executive branch of a strategic culture emphasising the importance of maintaining close alliance relations with Washington, but also the capture, as argued by Tanter, of

Australian foreign policy emphases inherent in the contemporary multilevel, multisectoral nature of the alliance between Australia and the United States.

Afghanistan 2001: explicit invocation of the ANZUS Treaty and implied application of the executive prerogative doctrine

In a press release dated 14 September 2001, Prime Minister John Howard stated that the cabinet had met and decided that Article IV of the ANZUS Treaty applied to the terrorist attacks on the United States of 11 September 2001 (9/11). The relevant section of Article IV provides that:

> Each Party recognizes that an armed attack in the Pacific Area on any of the Parties would be dangerous to its own peace and safety and declares that it would act to meet the common danger in accordance with its constitutional processes.

On 4 October 2001, Prime Minister Howard announced at a press conference that Australian military forces would be participating in the newly formed coalition poised to attack Afghanistan. Again, the ANZUS Treaty was used by way of justification:

> An involvement of the type that I've outlined would be very much within Australia's defence capability and fully consistent of course with our obligations under the ANZUS Treaty which has been jointly invoked by Australia and the United States following the terrorist attack on the 11th of September.
> (Howard 2001)

No statement was formally read in Parliament. Because Parliament was dissolved on 8 October (a federal election was held on 10 November) and the new Parliament did not meet until 12 February 2002, there was no opportunity to hold an immediate parliamentary debate about Australia's participation in the broad military coalition led by the United States that began combat against Al Qaeda forces in Afghanistan on 7 October 2001. For Prime Minister Howard and his government, an explicit invocation of the ANZUS Treaty, supported by an underlying view that the exercise of the war power was an executive prerogative, sufficed to justify the prime minister and cabinet's decision to involve Australia militarily in Afghanistan.

Dobell (2014: 387) points out that:

> Afghanistan joins the two World Wars and Korea as a conflict that did not see Australia's political parties at war over the war. Afghanistan, indeed, saw broad unity in Canberra on how the war should be fought, as well as the agreement that it was a war worth fighting.

He questions the basis for such bipartisan unanimity—especially in the face of popular hostility: in 2013, 61 per cent of survey participants assessing the cost–benefit to Australia of the war said that it was 'not worth fighting' (Oliver 2013). Dobell's answer is that bipartisanship was able to continue over the 13 years of Australia's longest war not merely on the basis of a shared view of the central importance of the Australia–US alliance for Australian interests, but also because of the 'professionalism of Australia's all-volunteer Army', which convinced voters, despite their doubts about the war, to support not only Australian soldiers, but also the politicians who sent them to war (Dobell 2014: 389).

However, Dobell's analysis of post-Afghanistan rebalancing—for the first time since World War II, Australian and American strategic priorities converge—suggests 'a major new moment in the alliance' (Dobell 2014: 394). To the extent that the alliance envisages not only US forces training in Australia, but also the 'USA being based in and working from Australia', Australia's alliance management by political and military elites will necessarily go beyond 'loyalty' and the reliable provision of minimal forces. Heightened pressure on the Australian executive regarding going to war is inevitable. As Dobell (2014: 395) argues:

> The ultimate purpose of the alliance for Australia has always been about defending the home; now the alliance is coming to work from home. This will take Australia's alliance addiction to new levels and, ultimately, lead to some close-to-home questions about what Australia will and will not do for the sake of the alliance.

In such circumstances, it will be much more difficult for the elite to manage public opinion regarding the costs and benefits of the alliance, and it is conceivable that a role will emerge for the Australian Parliament in the exercise of the war power.

Iraq 2003: the 'coalition of the willing' and Senate resistance to war

After the 9/11 attacks and during the military actions against Afghanistan, it became increasingly clear that the United States intended to invade Iraq. In Australia, political groups became concerned about possible Australian involvement in such a conflict, given increasingly widespread awareness of the executive's propensity to engage in military activities—particularly those involving the United States and particularly without prior debate, much less approval, by Parliament. In August 2002, in an attempt to institute some kind of parliamentary oversight, the Australian Greens in the Senate proposed a motion to establish a select committee on the possible support by Australia of a US invasion of Iraq. The motion was rejected 2–45. It should be noted that, in the lead-up to the Iraq conflict, the opposition Labor Party did not support this attempt to establish an oversight role for Parliament, but that Labor members of the Senate did support a motion in the Senate decrying the war after the war had begun.

On 10 January 2003, Prime Minister Howard intimated at a press conference that there had been some 'forward deployment' of ADF personnel to the Persian Gulf. Interestingly, when asked if Parliament would be recalled to consider a forward deployment of troops before such a deployment took place, Prime Minister Howard responded as follows:

> I don't think a forward deployment requires the recall of Parliament. I think what would require the recall of Parliament would be if we took a decision to be involved in military conflict and that would certainly produce a recall of Parliament if Parliament is not already in session.
>
> (Parliament of Australia 2003a)

The idea that a forward deployment of Australian troops in preparation for possible military conflict does not and should not require discussion in Parliament indicates the pervasive acknowledgement of the executive prerogative doctrine. Such a dismissal of either the necessity or utility of parliamentary consultation is even more questionable given the reality that, according to at least one account, these forward-deployed troops began fighting before the ultimatum provided to Saddam Hussein expired. Arguably, Australian forces were deployed secretly, without the knowledge of the Australian population, and at least one scholar asserts that they participated in battle contrary to the law of war (Kevin 2004).

On 22 January 2003, Defence Minister Robert Hill announced the government's decision to deploy to the Gulf HMAS *Kanimbla* and personnel comprising a special forces task group and an RAAF reconnaissance team. On 4 February 2003, Prime Minister Howard made a ministerial statement in the House of Representatives that it was the 'government's belief that the world community must deal decisively with Iraq' (J. Howard, House of Representatives, *Debates*, 4 February 2003, p. 10642). The motion was proposed that the House take note of the statement although, as indicated below, a vote was not taken until 20 March. The debate on Australia's involvement in the Iraq conflict continued throughout February in the Main Committee.

On 15 and 16 February 2003, huge peace rallies were held both in Australia and in many places around the world. On 24 February, the United States, Britain and Spain proposed a draft resolution declaring that Iraq had failed to take its final opportunity to disarm. On 4–6 of March, the coalition government repeatedly used its numbers in the House of Representatives to preclude opposition parties' motions in relation to Iraq and attempts to debate the Iraq situation.

On 17 March 2003, the prime minister held a press conference in which he stated that the federal cabinet would meet that evening to discuss Australia's military role in Iraq. During the press conference, in response to media questions about when he would inform Parliament about any decision to go to war, the Prime Minister answered:

> As soon as practicable . . . I have no desire at all to deny Parliament the full opportunity of debating this, we will handle the issue in accordance with the constitutional processes of the Government and that decision is taken by the Cabinet and once the Cabinet's taken the decision it's given effect

to immediately in an executive sense and I would seek as soon as practicable, and I mean that, to take the matter to the Parliament and allow the Parliament the opportunity of a full debate.

(Parliament of Australia 2003b)

For Prime Minister Howard, the steps in the 'constitutional processes' are revealing: the prime minister, in conjunction with cabinet, makes the decision to go to war; this decision is then taken to Parliament for 'debate', but no vote is envisaged. In Prime Minister Howard's view, the executive prerogative doctrine accords entirely with the 'constitutional processes' he identifies, despite that the alleged 'processes' are not set out or even mentioned in the Constitution, have not been established by legislation and contradict the 1941 statutory instrument ceding the war power to the Australian governor-general.

On 18 March 2003, the prime minister proposed a motion regarding the situation in Iraq that:

> . . . this House condemns Iraq's refusal, over more than 12 years, to abide by 17 resolutions of the United Nations Security Council regarding the threat it poses to international peace and security . . . and endorses the government's decision to commit Australian Defence Force elements to the region.
>
> (J. Howard, House of Representatives, *Debates*,
> 18 March 2003, p. 12505)

In reply, Leader of the Opposition Simon Crean said: 'Labor opposes your commitment to war. We will argue against it and we will call for the troops to be returned' (S. Crean, House of Representatives, *Debates*, 8 March 2003, p. 12512). Debate continued in committee, preventing a vote on the motion on that date.

On 18 March 2003, President George W. Bush provided an ultimatum to Iraqi President Saddam Hussein and his sons to leave Iraq within 48 hours or war would begin. President Hussein refused to comply with the ultimatum and the so-called coalition of the willing, led by the United States, began bombing targets inside Iraq once the deadline had passed. On 20 March, Australian Prime Minister Howard, in his morning press conference, stated that ADF personnel 'have commenced combat and combat support operations' (Parliament of Australia 2003c).

On 20 March 2003, in the Australian House of Representatives, the motion initially put by the Prime Minister on 8 March was resolved in the affirmative, 80–63. In the Senate, the Labor Party, Australian Democrats, Australian Greens and an Independent senator supported an amended motion that opposed the attack on Iraq and called for ADF personnel to be brought back to Australia. This motion was resolved in the affirmative, 37–32. For the first time since Federation, the Senate, the 'House of review', had voted against Australian participation in a war. The votes recorded in both parliamentary Houses after the initiation of hostilities demonstrate that, had there been a constitutional requirement for approval by both chambers prior to war, such a requirement would have precluded Australian involvement. However, no such requirement exists in the Constitution or via legislation. In the current circumstances, then, the executive prerogative may be exercised by the government of the day against the wishes of the Senate—and indeed the wishes of millions of ordinary citizens.

Iraq and Syria 2014–15: bipartisan support for unfettered executive war power, the United States and mission creep

Australian military participation in what has been called the Third Iraq War (Tanter 2014) involved mission creep in three steps—from embassy security, to humanitarian assistance, and finally to military confrontation with so-called Islamic State in Iraq and Syria (ISIS).

This engagement encapsulates the history of the development of the war power in Australia, representing as it does the intertwined ills to be found in the executive war power prerogative in combination with acquiescence with the strategic imperatives of United States. Australian military commitment to the conflict began with announcements for a small deployment of troops to the Australian embassy in response to the crisis in Iraq precipitated by the rise and rise of ISIS, progressed to humanitarian operations to support those in Iraq threatened by ISIS and finally resulted in combat flights against ISIS. The executive war power prerogative is not questioned by either of the two major political parties in Parliament, and there was no real debate in Parliament and certainly no vote. The only parliamentary voice raised against the missions in Iraq, the Australian Greens, has no parliamentary support for its calls for prior parliamentary approval before ADF troops are committed to combat operations.

The first step on the path to direct engagement in combat in Iraq was taken on June 20 when the Australian government announced that, given the spectacular and worrying success of ISIS in recent months, a small detachment of ADF troops had been sent to guard the Australian embassy in Baghdad (ABC News 2014). The second step was taken less than two months later—again in response to ISIS victories and the siege of Mount Sinjar, where thousands of Yazidis were under threat from ISIS forces—Australian 'humanitarian assistance operations' in Iraq were announced in a press release on 14 August 2014 (Abbott 2014a).

In August 2014, the United States conducted a number of air strikes on ISIS in coordination with the Iraqi government. However, the larger international military coalition to conduct air raids against ISIS did not become operational until late September (Ruys and Verlinden 2015).

Numerous countries have since joined the coalition, also known as Operation Inherent Resolve, albeit that many states provide only logistical support or training. Apart from the United States and a range of Arab countries, several western states decided to actively participate in the offensive against ISIS by deploying aircraft—namely, Australia, Belgium, Canada, Denmark, France and the Netherlands. Contrary to the US–Arab coalition members, however, the latter countries initially limited their actions to Iraqi territory only. It was only in the course of 2015–16 that these countries gradually expanded their scope of operations to include Syrian territory (Ruys, Ferro and Haesebrouck 2017).

Australian humanitarian assistance operations in Iraq were announced in a prime ministerial press release on 14 August 2014. Parliament had risen on 17 July 2014 and, when it resumed on 26 August, Prime Minister Abbott made no statement to Parliament.

Australian Greens Adam Bandt MP asked a question without notice:

> My question is for the Prime Minister. Prime Minister, are you already engaged in mission creep with talks underway for Australian forces to fight in Iraq? If you cannot rule this out, will you at least bring the matter here for debate, and will you allow a vote on my bill to require parliamentary approval before troops are deployed?
>
> (A. Bandt, House of Representatives,
> *Debates*, 26 August 2014, p. 8556)

Prime Minister Tony Abbott replied:

> I assure the member that this government will not commit forces without the fullest possible consideration, without the consideration of cabinet, without consultation with the opposition. That is the way it always has been and that is the way it always will be.
>
> (T. Abbott, House of Representatives,
> *Debates*, 26 August 2014, p. 8556)

Here, the Prime Minister rejects, in terms of the question of committing forces, not only a parliamentary debate on current military operations, but also a parliamentary vote on the Greens' proposed Bill requiring prior parliamentary approval. Abbott argues, misleadingly and mistakenly, that cabinet and the opposition will be 'consulted'—and that that is the way it always has been. The Labor opposition made no statement in relation to this troop deployment.

On 31 August 2014, a prime ministerial press release informed the nation that:

> Australia will join international partners to help the anti-ISIL forces in Iraq. Following the successful international humanitarian relief effort air-dropping supplies to the thousands of people stranded on Mount Sinjar in northern Iraq, the Royal Australian Air Force will now conduct further humanitarian missions. The United States Government has requested that Australia help to transport stores of military equipment, including arms and munitions, as part of a multi-nation effort.
>
> (Abbott 2014b)

In Parliament on 1 September, Prime Minister Tony Abbott stated:

> So far, we have met requests for humanitarian relief and for logistical support. So far, there has been no request for military action itself. Should such a request come from the Obama administration, and be supported by the

government of Iraq, it would be considered against these criteria: Is there a clear and achievable overall objective? Is there a clear and proportionate role for Australian forces? Have all the risks been properly assessed? And is there an overall humanitarian objective in accordance with Australia's national interests?

(T. Abbott, House of Representatives, *Debates*, 1 September 2014, p. 9147)

In reply, Leader of the Opposition Bill Shorten said: 'Today all members and all parties have the opportunity to express their views . . . Labor has promised to take a constructive and cooperative approach to this most important question' (W. Shorten, House of Representatives, *Debates*, 1 September 2014, p. 9148).

The third and final step was made clear on 14 September 2014, when Chief of the Defence Force Air Chief Marshal Mark Binskin announced that some 600 ADF personnel were being deployed to the Middle East (Binskin 2014). This deployment is now known as Operation OKRA.

In Parliament on 22 September 2014, the prime minister stated:

Because protecting our people is the first duty of government, it is right that I should update the House on developing challenges to our national security . . . Last week, together, the Leader of the Opposition and I helped to farewell the Australian force that is ready to join the international coalition against ISIL. Later this week, I will be in New York for discussions at the United Nations which President Obama will chair. Subsequently, the cabinet will again consider the use of our forces to mount air strikes and to provide military advice in support of the Iraqi government.

(T. Abbott, House of Representatives, *Debates*, 22 September 2014, p. 9957)

In reply, Leader of the Opposition Bill Shorten stated:

Labor fully supports Australia's contribution to the international humanitarian mission to Iraq. We do not offer this lightly. Sending Australians into harm's way is the most serious of decisions. Our support for the government on this issue is not a matter of jingoism or nationalism; it is a calculation of conscience and national interest. There are four key principles that underpin Labor's approach: firstly, we have indicated that we do not support the deployment of ground combat units to directly engage in fighting ISIL; secondly, that Australian operations should be confined to the territory of Iraq; thirdly, our involvement should continue only until the Iraqi government is in a position to take full responsibility for the security of its nation and its people; and, fourthly, if the Iraqi government and its forces engage in unacceptable conduct or adopt unacceptable policies then we should withdraw our support. These four principles will guide our response to the evolving situation in Iraq. They represent the conditions that we have set for our support and the line that we have drawn for Australia's engagement in the region. Again, this is consistent with the government's approach.

> (W. Shorten, House of Representatives,
> *Debates*, 22 September 2014, p. 9960)

Australia's renewed military presence in Iraq would, in under a year, lead to Australian military involvement in Syria.

In the case of Syria during 2015, the exercise of the executive war power prerogative was justified by reference to the UN Charter, formal requests for help from the Iraqi and US governments, and the doctrine of collective self-defence.

Prime Minister Abbott made a short statement to Parliament on 9 September 2015:

> As members know, our armed forces have been engaged in military operations in Iraq for the best part of 12 months. In particular, the Royal Australian Air Force has been conducting air strikes against Daesh targets in Iraq. At the invitation and request of President Obama, the government has decided to extend our air strikes to include Daesh targets in Syria as well. We are doing this under section 51 of the UN Charter, which gives countries the right of collective self-defence. Iraq is threatened by Daesh forces based and supplied from Syria, and Syria is unable or unwilling to act against those forces. So, in conjunction with our coalition partners, Australia will act.
>
> (T. Abbott, House of Representatives,
> *Debates*, 9 September 2015, p. 9613)

Leader of the Opposition Bill Shorten replied:

> The ADF operations have to be constrained to the collective self-defence of Iraq because at the core of this action, this extension, is that we are acting at the request of the Iraq government and the self-defence of Iraq. Further, the use of force must be limited to what is necessary to halt these cross-border attacks and defend Australian personnel. We would also seek and have received assurances that effective combat search and rescue must be in place for our remarkable RAAF personnel, who may, heaven forbid, be downed in hostile territory before the operations commence. Further, the government should formally notify the United Nations Security Council of our decision, and the government, I believe, should agree to a parliamentary debate to explain the long-term strategy for Australia's role in Iraq.
>
> (W. Shorten, House of Representatives,
> *Debates*, 9 September 2015, p. 9614)

In a later statement made on the same day, Shorten reiterated:

> Fulfilling our responsibility to the Australian people and their parliament requires a detailed and considered explanation of our objectives in Iraq.

So I ask the Prime Minister to commit to a parliamentary debate where he can outline the government's long-term strategy regarding Australia's changing role in the defence of Iraq.

(W. Shorten, House of Representatives,
Debates, 9 September 2015, p. 9640)

So, here, the executive prerogative is essentially unquestioned. All that the Labor opposition calls for is a parliamentary debate that might consider the long-term strategy. Shorten does not question the merits of the decision nor does he question the exercise by the executive of the war-making prerogative.

However, O'Neill (2016: 4) challenges Prime Minister Abbott's reliance on the doctrine of collective defence:

> It is well settled international law that the collective self-defence provisions of Article 51 only apply when the State attacked is the one making the request for assistance. Abbott's idiosyncratic view has no foundation in international law. It is in any case academic because we now know that Abbott solicited an invitation from the Americans to join the Syrian campaign.

An attempt by the Greens in the Senate to discuss the matter of calling for a parliamentary debate was not supported (37–10), with the Greens and Independent Senator Jacqui Lambi voting against.

Ruys and colleagues (2017) discuss the Operation Resolve coalition, noting the phenomenal 'degree of involvement of national parliaments in the decision-making process pertaining to individual States' participation in this coalition'. Their discussion canvasses what they, agreeing with Damrosch (1996, 2015), note as a general trend, at least among Western democracies, 'towards parliamentary control over the decision to introduce troops into situations of actual or potential hostilities'.

It is worth noting that Damrosch, since the 1990s, has:

> . . . identified a striking pattern of parliamentary approvals for decisions to commit military support, including votes in the US Congress, the French *Assemblée Nationale*, and the Parliaments of Italy, Canada, Australia, the Netherlands, Greece, Turkey and Spain. When NATO launched Operation Allied Force against the then Federal Republic of Yugoslavia in 1999, intensive parliamentary deliberations similarly took place in all participating states.
> (Ruys et al. 2017: 9)

Damrosch's research has considered the role of national parliaments in the deployment of troops to the Gulf in 1991, Kosovo in 1999 and Iraq in 2003. She has discovered considerable variation among democratic nations, but, overall, a trend toward parliamentary involvement. Nonetheless, in respect of Operation Resolve, the US-led coalition launched against ISIS in 2014, Ruys and colleagues (2017) state:

Only in Australia, where there is neither domestic legislation nor any unwritten 'convention' providing for any (even modest) 'war powers' on the part of the legislative branch, was parliament completely kept out of the decision-making process: neither the initial Australian participation in 2014, nor the expansion of the scope of operations to Syrian territory in September 2015, led to any form of consultation by the government of the legislative branch (beyond a mere notification)—to the ostensible discontent of an independent MP, the Green party, and later (in 2015) also of the Labour [*sic*] opposition. In all, the Australia case strikes as the exception that proves the rule.

2017–18: Korea, Pine Gap and the Philippines

A series of events during 2017 and 2018 confirm two facts. One is that Australian governments increasingly commit the country to war without the slightest democratic consultation; the other is that, in reality, any decision to go to war has been determined in advance by the Canberra establishment's military alliance with the United States.

On 11 August 2017, Prime Minister Malcolm Turnbull pledged to join what would be a catastrophic war by the United States against North Korea. Without any public consultation, Turnbull vowed that his government would 'come to the aid of the United States' if it were attacked by North Korea. In a radio interview, he said that this pledge extended to a so-called North Korean attack on Guam, a heavily militarised US Pacific island territory (Head 2017a).

These comments followed US President Donald Trump's warnings that the United States would unleash 'fire and fury like the world has never seen' in response to further 'threats' by North Korea. Trump refused to rule out a 'pre-emptive strike' on North Korea in supposed 'self-defence'—the doctrine first enunciated by George W. Bush to invade and occupy Iraq.

Like Trump, Turnbull branded North Korea 'a reckless, provocative regime that seems determined to continue destabilising the region'. His remarks gave credence to Trump's insistence that the small, impoverished country with a relatively primitive weapons capacity is a dire threat to the United States, the world's largest nuclear power by far.

Turnbull's commitment has enormous implications. If the United States triggers a war against North Korea, Australia will be involved immediately in a conflagration that could rapidly draw in China, a major nuclear power.

Not only will the US–Australia Pine Gap satellite communications facility in central Australia be automatically engaged in coordinating the assault and targeting bombing sites, but also bases across northern Australia, from where US warplanes and marines operate, will become war staging posts. Beyond that, the United States is likely to request the deployment of Australian special forces troops, warships and planes—all of which are closely integrated into the US military. Prime Minister Turnbull made this very clear:

We stand shoulder-to-shoulder with the United States . . . The ANZUS Treaty means that if America is attacked we will come to their aid. If Australia is attacked, the Americans will come to our aid. We are joined at the hip. The American Alliance is the bedrock of our national security.

(Head 2017a)

This was only the second time an Australian government had cited the 1951 ANZUS Treaty on 'collective security' as requiring mobilisation of the Australian military behind a US-instigated war. Prime Minister John Howard invoked the Treaty to join the US-led invasions of Afghanistan and Iraq in 2001 and 2003, purportedly to 'defend' the United States from Islamic terrorists and, as it turned out, non-existent 'weapons of mass destruction'.

Yet this is a bipartisan commitment. Labor Party Opposition Leader Bill Shorten swiftly backed Turnbull's comments, affirming: 'I and the government share the same concerns and the same views, and Australians should be reassured that on this matter of North Korea and our national security, the politics of Labor and Liberal are working—absolutely together' (Head 2017a).

Later in August 2017, leaked US National Security Agency (NSA) documents confirmed that the US–Australian satellite surveillance base at Pine Gap in central Australia is pivotal to Washington's wars and war plans, particularly against China. The 38 radar dishes, many concealed beneath golf ball-like domes, provide 'real-time' targeting for the US military across Eurasia and Africa (Head 2017b).

The facility, near Alice Springs, is integral to US-led military operations globally. Any war or military attack by Washington—whether against North Korea, China or Russia, or in the Middle East—automatically involves Australia. Behind the backs of the Australian population, by defending the base, successive Liberal–National and Labor governments have committed the country to being on the frontline of a potential nuclear war.

Five 'top secret' documents were obtained by *The Intercept* from NSA whistleblower Edward Snowden and published in partnership with the Australian Broadcasting Corporation (ABC), although with various passages redacted. ABC said that the documents were 'submitted to the NSA for comment prior to publication' (Gallagher 2017).

Despite this vetting, the documents showed that the role of the Pine Gap complex—codenamed RAINFALL—has increasingly shifted since it was established in 1970, from spying on governments and people across the Asia-Pacific to providing critical data for military operations, including for targeting missile attacks and drone assassinations. According to a top secret NSA information paper dated April 2013, the so-called joint defense facility at Pine Gap 'plays a significant role in supporting both intelligence activities and military operations' (Gallagher 2017). These include battlefield operations in the Middle East, where hundreds of civilians, including US citizens, have been targeted and killed by US Central Intelligence Agency (CIA) drones directed by presidents Barack Obama and Donald Trump.

Since President Obama's 'pivot to Asia' to combat China's rising influence, however, the focus has been, above all, on China. The NSA paper stated:

China is changing the strategic balance in the Pacific by expanding its interests in the Asia-Pacific region and the Indian Ocean, modernizing its military, striking a more assertive strategic posture, and flaunting its power. Increased emphasis on China will not only help ensure the security of Australia, but also synergize with the US in its renewed emphasis on Asia and the Pacific.

(Gallagher 2017)

In 'specific divisions of effort', Australian Signals Directorate (ASD) officers are 'solely responsible for reporting on multiple targets in the Pacific area, including Indonesia, Malaysia and Singapore' (Gallagher 2017).

These arrangements mirror the underlying 'US–Australia alliance', with the Australian military and intelligence apparatus assigned parts of the Asia-Pacific where the Australian ruling class has sought to hold sway, while operating under the global umbrella of the United States.

Some 800 American and Australian operatives and other employees, including NSA, CIA and US military personnel, work at Pine Gap, which is located in a 'prohibited zone'. The presence of these US officials and their control by the US National Reconnaissance Office (NRO) is 'classified' information, not to be divulged to the American or Australian people.

The official NRO 'cover story', as outlined in the documents, is that the facility is intended to 'support the national security of both the US and Australia. The [facility] contributes to verifying arms control and disarmament agreements and monitoring military developments' (Gallagher 2017).

Behind this 'cover story', Pine Gap, together with the NSA's Menwith Hill base in Britain, has functioned as a command post for two missions that form part of Washington's aggressive military and surveillance activities directed at maintaining US hegemony worldwide. The first, named M7600, involved at least two satellites and was said, in a 2005 document, to provide 'continuous coverage of the majority of the Eurasian landmass and Africa'. This initiative was later upgraded as part of Mission 8300, which involved 'a four satellite constellation' and covered 'Former Soviet Union, China, South Asia, East Asia, Middle East, Eastern Europe, and the Atlantic landmasses' (Gallagher 2017).

A 2009 document listed 'NATO operations' as part of Pine Gap's mission, indicating that the base would be crucial to any US war against Russia, as well as China. The satellites monitor communications, such as those by mobile phone, radio and satellite uplink. They gather 'strategic and tactical military, scientific, political, and economic communications signals', according to the documents; they also monitor weapons tests in targeted countries, sweep up data from foreign military systems and provide surveillance support to US forces (Gallagher 2017).

One document explained:

> Mission 7600 was designed originally as a FISINT [Foreign Instrumentation Signals Intelligence] but now is primarily used as a COMINT [Communications Intelligence] collection system against targets of high intelligence value. Currently, about 85 per cent of Mission 7600 collection is against these COMINT targets.
>
> (Gallagher 2017)

Mission 8300 provided 'SIGINT [Signals Intelligence] to US military combat operations', as well as 'crisis monitoring' (Gallagher 2017).

One of the base's key functions is to gather geo-locational intelligence, which can be used to help to pinpoint airstrikes. An August 2012 NSA 'site profile' of Pine Gap said that it has a special section, known as the geopit, equipped with 'a number of tools available for performing geolocations' (*The Intercept* 2017).

The 'site profile' explained that the facility not only collects signals, but also analyses them: 'RAINFALL detects, collects, records, processes, analyses and reports on PROFORMA signals collected from tasked entities.' (PROFORMA signals are the communications data of radar and weapons systems, such as surface-to-surface missiles, anti-aircraft artillery and fighter aircraft.)

This evidence further supported earlier reports that Pine Gap played a key role in US drone strikes. These attacks—often taking place outside war zones, in places such as Afghanistan, Yemen, Somalia and Pakistan—have resulted in the deaths of thousands of people, including civilians, and therefore constitute war crimes.

Australia is also a member of the Five Eyes surveillance network, alongside the United States, Britain, Canada and New Zealand. The country's electronic eavesdropping agency, the ASD, maintains extremely close ties with its US counterparts at NSA. As Snowden's previous revelations proved, this includes conducting surveillance of the phone and online communications of tens of millions of people, with the collaboration of major corporations such as Microsoft, Apple, Google, YouTube and Facebook (Macaskill and Dance 2013).

For nearly 50 years, one Australian government after another has shielded Pine Gap's activities with official myths and protected the base from protests. Labor governments, in particular, have been prominent in defending the Pine Gap base. In 2009, the last Labor government made it a crime punishable by up to seven years' imprisonment to enter the facility's perimeters, to fly over it or to acquire 'a photograph, sketch, plan, model, article, note or other document of, or relating to' Pine Gap (Head 2009b).

As part of Obama's 'pivot', the Labor government also offered Darwin as the site for a US marine base, northern Australian airfields for more extensive use by US long-range bombers, and ports for expanded visits by US warships and submarines. These facilities, together with Pine Gap, thoroughly integrate Australia into US war plans.

On 29 August 2017, without any public consultation, the Turnbull government moved to place Australia on the front line of a US-led military intervention in Asia that could trigger a wider war. During a doorstop interview outside Parliament, Foreign Minister Julie Bishop let it be known that, at a recent meeting with Philippine President Rodrigo Duterte, she had made an offer to to send troops to the Philippines, supposedly on an 'advise and assist' mission (Head 2017c).

Pointedly, Bishop made the 'offer' public, despite conceding that Duterte had not yet accepted it. In most previous US and Australian interventions, the diplomatic pretence has been that the military forces were invited by the host country, which then announced the decision.

Bishop claimed that Australian troops could assist the fight against forces with alleged links to ISIS, in Marawi City on the southern island of Mindanao. In reality, Australian special forces would join US counterparts already on the ground in Mindanao as part of an intervention in collaboration with the Philippine military. The US Embassy in Manila and the Philippine military had revealed, on 9 June 2017, that US special forces have been involved in the Marawi battle since it was launched in May. Also in June 2017, the Turnbull government had announced the dispatch of air force surveillance planes to Mindanao (Head 2017c).

Bishop's declaration marked an escalation of Canberra's involvement in the Philippines, raising the prospect of ground troops being sent to Asia to join a US-led war for the first time since the disastrous Vietnam War. She drew a parallel with Australia's role in Iraq, where some 300 regular troops were training local forces, and about 80 special forces soldiers were 'advising and assisting' close to the front line—in other words, actively engaged in the fighting: 'We would be ready to support the Philippines in the same way we are supporting Iraq in advising, assisting and training' (Head 2017c).

Once again, the 'war on terror' was used as a cover for US militarism. Washington and the Philippines military seized upon the conflict in Marawi, which began as a battle between rival armed clans, to effectively discipline Duterte, who was shifting Manila's foreign policy away from the United States and toward China.

As part of a pitch for Chinese investment and financial assistance, Duterte previously vowed to eject US military personnel from the Philippines, a former US colony. Washington, which retained a large military presence under the Marcos dictatorship, had signed an agreement with Duterte's predecessor, Benigno Aquino, to secure virtually unlimited access to military bases in the country.

With its allies in the Philippines military, Washington is using the Marawi battle to reorient Manila's geo-political ties away from Beijing and Moscow, and firmly back into the camp of US imperialism.

Bishop's comments followed an extraordinary public call for Australian commandos to be dispatched to the Philippines, made by a visiting US marine general. Lieutenant General David Berger, in Australia for the biennial Talisman Sabre US-Australian military exercises, said on 29 June 2017 that he expected Australian forces could soon join US troops in that country.

He spoke of 'looking for stability' in the region to deter 'bad behaviour': 'Both of us have a long history of being an expeditionary force when needed, so we begin from a common point I think and we've operated alongside for 100 years' (quoted in Head 2017c).

Berger's remarks pointed toward concerns in Washington about the instability of the Duterte regime, which the United States and its partners had continued to shield from criticism, despite murderous, fascistic activities, mostly conducted under the cover of a 'war on drugs'. From the time that Duterte took office in July 2016 to mid-2017, government figures showed that police had killed close to 3,500 'drug personalities'. Thousands more had been murdered in unexplained circumstances in poor urban areas, even according to police data. Yet Duterte declared that he was 'happy to slaughter' millions of supposed addicts and dismissed the deaths of children as 'collateral damage' (Head 2017c).

Far from opposing Duterte's brutality, the United States and its allies have publicly appeased him as part of their intervention. Bishop's announcement came after a blatant display of support for Duterte by Director-General of the Australian Secret Intelligence Service (ASIS) Nick Warner, in Manila on 22 August 2017. The ASIS is Australia's equivalent of the US CIA. The presence anywhere of its chief, who was also involved in interventions in Iraq and Solomon Islands, and previously headed Australia's Defence Department, is a sign of intense Australian intelligence and military involvement.

Australia's top foreign spy chief, who rarely appears in public, met with Duterte and Philippine Defense Secretary Lorenzana at the Malacañang presidential palace. The president's office later released photos of Warner and Duterte not only smiling, but also using Duterte's signature closed-fist hand gesture—a symbol of his 2016 presidential campaign pledge to kill thousands of 'criminals' (Head 2017c).

The governor-general as a check on war-making power?

Legal scholars Sampford and Palmer (2009: 380) criticise what they regard as more than an 'irregularity'—and they are particularly scathing about the way in which, in 2003, the defence minister 'used his legal powers under the Defence Act to implement decisions taken by Cabinet and/or its Security Sub-Committee to give instructions to the service head(s) to take the actions which involved us in war'.

In their view, bypassing the governor-general's legal authority not only is *legally* wrong, but also ignores a useful *political* check and balance that the Constitution affords:

> It may be thought of little significance whether the Governor-General plays a role in the exercise of the war prerogative. After all, the decision to go to war is, as a matter of constitutional doctrine and political reality, taken by Cabinet. The Governor-General would not take such a decision on his or her own motion through reserve powers but on advice of the

responsible minister. However, the Queen's representative is entitled to ask questions about papers he or she is to sign. Asking pertinent questions is a legitimate function, particularly in the case of a power over which there is no parliamentary control. For better or for worse, Australia is still a constitutional monarchy. The Queen's role in the United Kingdom is to advise, warn and encourage ministers. Her representative in Australia plays a similar role—asking questions, especially as to the legalities of proposed action. The practice of circumventing vice-regal consideration of the exercise of the war power has evolved with little apparent consideration or public discussion, is of uncertain legal validity and has removed an important voice in the debate prior to military action actually being taken (and perhaps *the* only effective voice, other than public opinion).

(Sampford and Palmer 2009: 379)

Here, it must be said that Sampford and Palmer's assertion that a governor-general would not act 'through reserve powers', but 'on advice of the responsible minister', is somewhat problematic given that those powers are notoriously murky, controversial and ill-defined. Because the reserve powers of the governor-general are the vestiges of the royal prerogative, the development of the war power in Australia from what was the royal war prerogative of the British monarch means that their use in relation to Australian military matters would not be entirely surprising. Arguably, a future governor-general could do exactly what Sampford and Palmer suggest a governor-general would not do. Further, it is noteworthy that the Australian Constitution vests the governor-general's powers as commander-in-chief in 'the Governor-General' and not the 'Governor-General in Council'. Again, arguably, a degree of personal discretion attends the exercise of these powers (Stephen 1984).

The infamous dismissal of the Whitlam government by the governor-general in 1975 is surely a case in point. A less contentious example occurred in 1970 when Governor-General Paul Hasluck rejected Prime Minister John Gorton's request to authorise a Pacific Islands Regiment peacekeeping mission in the Territory of Papua and New Guinea, on the basis that the Australian cabinet had not been consulted. Gorton agreed to put the matter to his ministers. (In the event, the cabinet meeting agreed that troops should be called out only if requested by the Territory's administrator—Fraser and Simons 2011: 206.) Could the reverse also occur at some future point in time? Could a governor-general who strongly valued the US alliance, for instance, disrupt current settled practice in which the prime minister and cabinet exercise the war power by wielding the unregulated reserve powers, in combination or otherwise with their authority as commander-in-chief, to commit Australian military forces? Whether or not, given practice, such an action might precipitate a constitutional and/or political crisis, might the exercise of such a reserve war power nonetheless be 'legal'?

As Detmold (1985) points out, in a constitutional monarchy that is also a parliamentary democracy, the exercise of discretionary 'reserve powers'—whether by a monarch or their representative—will be highly controversial. While legal scholars may debate the existence of the power in whatever particular circumstance it is exercised, political scholars may focus instead on the 'rightness' of the decision, for the legal validity of the power's exercise is a different question from its capacity to be regarded as politically legitimate (Detmold 1985: 223–27).

Sampford and Palmer (2009) seem to suggest that the possibility of the discretionary exercise by the Australian governor-general of 'reserve' powers could operate as a political check on an authoritarian and/or war-minded Australian prime minister and cabinet. Note that, in the Canadian context, scholars argue that the 'decline' of monarchy has led to an increase in the governor-general's susceptibility to prime ministerial influence (Hicks 2010). In the Australian context, the certainty that a political check would operate is not only similarly arguable, but also certainly less 'democratic'. Indeed, Russell (2011: 19) argues that 'all' scholars agree that it is only in 'the most exceptional circumstances' that the governor-general may reject the prime minister's advice: 'That indeed is the constitutional convention that enabled a parliamentary system dominated by the Crown to evolve into a parliamentary democracy.' Additionally, a literal interpretation of section 68 of the Constitution, which establishes the governor general as the commander-in-chief of the armed forces might argue that an independent governor-general may act in unrealised ways in the event of extreme social breakdown or political crisis.

Summing up Australian war powers

This chapter tells a complex story. It demonstrates the implications for what many may regard as a 'constitutional nicety'—that is, who bears the constitutional responsibility to exercise the war power—and the myriad issues that attend Australia's political, economic and military development beyond its former colonial and dominion status in a 'British embrace'. Since the 1950s, the Australian constitutional monarchy finds itself presented with two intertwined issues: the necessity of not merely unravelling Australia's 'multilayered closeness' to Britain and negotiating new perceptions of itself and its interests, given a new 'multilayered closeness' to the US alliance, but also of continual vigilance regarding the possibilities and uncertainties inherent in its role as a regional power in a global world—a world increasingly beset by local conflicts and now a new era of more aggressive great power competition.

The first part of the chapter identified and discussed the particular problem posed for Australia in grappling with the many aspects of becoming increasingly independent, both legally and politically. The 'gradual', 'imperceptible' movement toward Australian independence observed by Chief Justice Barwick is complicated, to a considerable degree, by the formation of a strong, multilevel alliance with the United States. In the period 2001–05, Australia's reliance on the US alliance led to successive military commitments, which, although ostensibly responding to UN resolutions and/or the need to uphold international law (such as the commitment of Australian naval forces to liberate Kuwait from Iraq invasion, or the Australian contingent sent to Afghanistan to fight against the Taliban and al Qaeda), effectively deepened Australia's alliance ties in terms of troop interoperability, intelligence and hardware. The uncomfortable reality is that, today, not only does the Australian executive, narrowly defined, wield the war power, but also this very small group of people can commit Australian troops to war, whatever its dimensions. The presence of a 'democratic deficit' is obvious.

The chapter then focused on the gradual transfer of the authority to exercise the war power in three stages: first, its exercise by the British monarch from Federation in 1901 until 1941; second, its brief exercise by the Australian governor-general upon advice of the executive council, until 1951; and third, the emergence of the practice that the prime minister in cabinet exercises the power.

The subsequent discussion has canvassed the particular conflicts in which the war power has been exercised on behalf of or by Australia, indicating who wielded the war power and discussing the perceived legal and/or political authority justifying the commitment of military forces. The discussion here focused on the role taken by specific actors—the British monarch; the Australian governor-general and executive council; the Australian prime minister and cabinet—and the gradual movement away from the first two. Although many of the interventions in which Australia engaged might not appear to many to be 'real' or 'world' wars (for example Korea, Malaya and Vietnam), Sampford and Palmer (2009: 370) argue that:

> [T]he two Iraq wars and Afghanistan are clearly wars in any sense of the word, and Australia's participation in these commenced without the exercise of the war prerogative by the Governor-General or its delegation to the Prime Minister or other ministers. This would seem to involve a major shift in practice without any apparent debate or public consideration of its desirability, let alone constitutionality.

Our conclusion supports Sampford and Palmer's central point that:

> Australian practice suggests that no formal procedural steps have been taken to give the Prime Minister and/or Cabinet the power to, in effect, wage war by authorising the deployment of our troops overseas in a hostile action. If Australia's practice has legally altered the way in which the war power is exercised, this has been done without any public or parliamentary discussion. Unstated convention would be a poor instrument by which to change the way in which the decision to go to war is made. However, in view of Australia's written constitution and the stringent tests applied by the courts even in relation to displacement of important prerogatives by *statute*, it seems unlikely that the few instances of parliamentary practice concerning the exercise of the war prerogative could legally alter the means by which the power is exercised.
>
> (Sampford and Palmer 2009: 379)

Domestic implications of unfettered executive war power: a nascent police state and the potential for continual warfare

Finally, what are the domestic implications of the unconstitutional and unfettered war power wielded by a very narrowly defined political executive? In our view, there are, in particular, three profound and overwhelmingly negative implications. First, unfettered executive war power in combination with the other side of the coin—that is, the recently expanded power of the executive branch to call out troops domestically—gives a monopoly to the executive branch in relation to military actions (Head 2009a). These military call-out powers are discussed in Chapter 8. Moreover, positioning the war power and the domestic call-out power in executive hands in combination with 100-plus pieces of anti-terror legislation made since September 2001 is arguably laying the groundwork for the construction of a nascent police/military/authoritarian state.

This idea is not ours; long ago Madison, amongst others, warned against executive war power. In 1787, Madison stated that the executive branch of government should not possess the war power, because that particular constitutional power, in the hands of the executive, inevitably produces tyranny:

> In time of actual war, great discretionary powers are constantly given to the Executive Magistrate. Constant apprehension of War, has the same tendency to render the head too large for the body. A standing military force, with an overgrown Executive will not long be safe companions to liberty. The means of defence against foreign danger have been always the instruments of tyranny at home. Among the Romans it was a standing maxim to excite a war, whenever a revolt was apprehended. Throughout all Europe, the armies kept up under the pretext of defending, have enslaved the people.
>
> (Madison [1787] 1911: 465)

For Madison, the combination of the means—a standing military force—with a too-powerful executive branch offers great potential for tyranny. Madison ([1795] 1865: 491) further outlined the threat to liberty occasioned by war:

> Of all the enemies to public liberty war is, perhaps, the most to be dreaded, because it comprises and develops the germ of every other. War is the parent of armies; from these proceed debts and taxes; and armies, and debts, and taxes are the known instruments for bringing the many under the domination of the few. In war, too, the discretionary power of the Executive is extended; its influence in dealing out offices, honors, and emoluments is multiplied; and all the means of seducing the minds, are added to those of subduing the force, of the people. The same malignant aspect in republicanism may be traced in the inequality of fortunes, and the opportunities of fraud, growing out of a state of war, and in the degeneracy of manners and of morals engendered by both. No nation could preserve its freedom in the midst of continual warfare.

Second, the executive war power prerogative facilitates control of the war power by a foreign power—the United States.

Third, and inextricably linked with the second, the participation of Australian troops in US wars that are arguably not in the long-term interests of either Australia or the United States means that Australia is a poor 'ally', which does not, or is not able to, voice its objections strongly enough.

In a seven-nation comparison of the degree to which 'crises' or 'emergencies'— what Schmitt ([1922] 2005) would call 'exceptions'—transformed the relationship between the executive and the representative assembly branches of government, Owens and Pilizzo (2013) argue that no automatic strengthening of the executive or weakening of the legislature can be found. They argue, against Schmitt, that any such effects are *conditional*, and they develop a nuanced matrix through which to analyse the preservation or otherwise of the balance between executive and legislature. Their view, broadly, is that the seven cases they investigate demonstrate that 'the constitutional order and the constitutionally sanctioned balance of power between the executive and the assembly branch can be preserved *in spite of* critical events' (Owens and Pilizzo 2013: 322). Their conclusion—at least in respect of Australia's experience of entry into the Iraq War—is that the 'war on terror' provided the justification for the expansion of executive power, but did not lead to a weakening of the assembly (Parliament) at least while the government enjoyed majorities of seats in both chambers.

However intriguing and worthy of further consideration and research the Owens and Pilizzo thesis may be, the cases they analyse illustrate the executive's worrying disposition toward avoiding legislative scrutiny and tilting a perceived constitutional balance toward itself. After all, Larkin and Uhr (2009) point out that once the Howard government secured a Senate majority in 2005, the Senate's capacity to shape Australia's 'war on terror' diminished.

The issue, in terms of maintaining a constitutional balance between executive and legislature in an era dominated by 'war on terror' imperatives is that 'executive creep'—whether illustrated by a small political executive (that is, the prime minister and cabinet) committing Australian troops or by increased executive capacity to call out troops in a domestic context—is a constant temptation. And public attitudes that arguably might fear the creation of extraordinary executive authority may not provide much of a corrective. Denmark's analysis of Australian attitudes toward controversial police, surveillance and other security policies that expanded government authority after 9/11 found that Australians' confidence in government was so high that only when citizens considered governmental authorities to be corrupt were they 'more likely to oppose stop-and-search powers' (Larkin and Uhr 2009: 102).

Of course, it might be argued that public attitudes toward government overreach regarding police or surveillance powers is different from public attitudes toward going to war. And it also might be argued that, in many countries, it is academics, rather than members of the general public, who are concerned about whether the exercise of the war power meets either 'legal' or 'legitimacy' requirements. Nonetheless, in the 'world risk society' that Beck (2002) outlines, acute dilemmas concerning the exercise of all these powers in the face of transnational terrorist actions press for immediate action by political decision-makers. The research of Goldsmith (2008: 144) canvasses whether, in a *synoptic age*, marked by the capacity of the many to witness the actions of a few, as well as the uncertainty and incalculability of threats, any room remains for policymaking or for politics. His analysis of the enactment in Australia of anti-terrorism 'reform' legislation queries not only the dangers for civil liberties noted by many scholars (Hocking 2004; Head 2002), but also a chronology ruled by haste and alliance solidarity. Goldsmith (2008: 148) argues that risk assessments were conducted 'without reference to estimations of risks arising at the national i.e., domestic level' and were 'completed in a way to indicate solidarity with a shared view of the risks arising from recent terrorist events and even a substantial delegation of responsibility for such an assessment to one's allies in intelligence and defense matters'.

These indications, together with the lack of formal consultation with the state or territory governments constitutionally responsible for criminal law, suggest that the Australian federal legislature, along with the federal executive, is not capable of resisting alliance addiction—especially under circumstances in which a mentality of 'do something quickly in these exceptional circumstances' rules. Governance by fear is a danger to democracy.

References

Abbott, T. 2014a. 'Humanitarian assistance to Iraq', Press release, 14 August, http://parlinfo.aph.gov.au/parlInfo/search/display/display.w3p;query=Id%3A%22media%2Fpressrel%2F3335348%22 (accessed 12 May 2018).

Abbott, T. 2014b. 'International supply mission to Iraq', Press release, 31 August, http://parlinfo.aph.gov.au/parlInfo/download/media/pressrel/3368877/upload_binary/3368877.pdf;fileType=application/pdf#search=%22International%20Supply%20Mission%20to%20Iraq%22 (accessed 12 May 2018).

ABC News. 2014. 'Iraq crisis: Australian troops to be sent to guard embassy in Baghdad', 20 June, www.abc.net.au/news/2014-06-20/australia-to-send-troops-to-iraq-to-bolster-embassy-security/5539084 (accessed 12 May 2018).

Australian War Memorial. 2017. 'Prime Minister Robert G. Menzies: wartime broadcast', 24 October, www.awm.gov.au/articles/encyclopedia/prime_ministers/menzies (accessed 5 May 2018).

Bean, C. c. 1981. *The Story of Anzac: Official History of Australia in the War of 1914–1918*, St Lucia: University of Queensland Press, https://s3-ap-southeast-2.amazonaws.com/awm-media/collection/RCDIG1069874/document/5519348.PDF (accessed 4 May 2018).

Beck, U. 2002. 'The terrorist threat: world risk society revisited', *Theory, Culture and Society*, 19(4): 39–55.

Belich, J. 2009. *Replenishing the Earth: The Settler Revolution and the Rise of the Anglo-World 1783–1939*. Oxford: Oxford University Press.

Bell, C. 1988. *Dependent Ally: A Study in Australian Foreign Policy*. Melbourne: Oxford University Press.

Binskin, M. 2014. 'Chief of the Defence Force statement on Iraq', Press release, 14 September.

Birrell, R. 1995. *A Nation of Our Own: Citizenship and Nation-building in Federation Australia.* Melbourne: Longman.

Blackstone, W. [1783] 2009. *Commentaries on the Laws of England, Vol. 1.* Oxford: Oxford University Press.

Blakkarly, J. 2015. 'Behind the mask of an emergency: between Australia and the Malayan war', *Griffith Review*, 49: 83–96.

Boyd, R. 1967. *Artificial Australia* (1967 Boyer Lectures). Sydney: ABC.

Clark, M. 1973. 'The years of unleavened bread: December 1949–December 1972', *Meanjin Quarterly*, 32(3): 245–50.

Conway, R. 1971. *The Great Australian Stupor: An Interpretation of the Australian Way of Life.* Melbourne: Sun Books.

Cox, L., and O'Connor, B. 2012. 'Australia, the US and the Vietnam and Iraq Wars: "Hound Dog, not Lapdog" ', *Australian Journal of Political Science*, 47(2): 173–87.

Curran, J., and Ward, S. 2010. *The Unknown Nation: Australia after Empire.* Melbourne: Melbourne University Press.

Damrosch, L. 1996. 'Is there a general trend in constitutional democracies toward parliamentary control over war-and-peace decisions?', *Proceedings of the Annual Meeting of the American Society of International Law*, 90: 36–44.

Damrosch, L. 2015. 'Democratization of foreign policy and international law, 1914–2014', *ILSA Journal of International and Comparative Law*, 21(2): 281–92.

Detmold, M. 1985. *The Australian Commonwealth: A Fundamental Analysis of its Constitution.* North Ryde, NSW: Law Book.

Dobell, G. 2014. 'The alliance echoes and portents of Australia's longest war', *Australian Journal of International Affairs*, 68(4): 386–96.

Edwards, P. 1997a. *A Nation at War: Australian Politics, Society and Diplomacy during the Vietnam War.* Sydney: Allen & Unwin.

Edwards, P. 1997b. 'Australia and the Vietnam War 1965–1975', *The Sydney Papers*, 9(3): 72–80.

Edwards, P., and Pemberton, G. 1992. *Crises and Commitments: The Politics and Diplomacy of Australia's Involvement in Southeast Asian Conflicts 1948–1965.* North Sydney: Allen & Unwin.

Fraser, M. 2014. *Dangerous Allies.* Melbourne: Melbourne University Press.

Fraser, M. 2015. 'Preface'. In A. Broinowski (ed.), *How Does Australia Go to War? A Call for Accountability and Change.* Melbourne: Campaign for an Iraq War Inquiry.

Fraser, M., and Simons, M. 2011. *Malcolm Fraser: The Political Memoirs.* Carlton, Vic.: The Miegunyah Press.

Frost, F. 1987. *Australia's War in Vietnam.* Sydney: Allen & Unwin.

Gallagher, R. 2017. 'The U.S. spy hub in the heart of Australia', *The Intercept*, 20 August.

Goldsmith, A. 2008. 'The governance of terror: precautionary logic and counterterrorist law reform after September 11', *Law & Policy*, 30(2): 141–67.

Gyngell, A. 2017. *Fear of Abandonment: Australia in the World since 1942.* Melbourne: Schwartz.

Harper, N. 1957. 'Australia and the United States'. In G. Greenwood and N. Harper (eds), *Australia in World Affairs 1950–1955*, Melbourne: F.W. Cheshire.

Hasluck, P. 1970. 'War in the Far East, December 1941–January 1942'. In *Australia in the War of 1939–1945.* Canberra: Australian War Memorial, https://s3-ap-southeast-2.amazonaws.com/awm-media/collection/RCDIG1070621/document/5519904. PDF (accessed 11 May 2018).

Head, M. 2002. ' "Counter-terrorism" laws: a threat to political freedom, civil liberties and constitutional rights', *Melbourne University Law Review*, 26(3): 666–89.

Head, M. 2009a. *Calling out the Troops: The Australian Military and Civil Unrest.* Sydney Annandale, NSW: Federation Press.

Head, M. 2009b. 'Australia: Rudd government attacks right to protest at Pine Gap spy base', *World Socialist Web Site*, 20 March, www.wsws.org/en/articles/2009/03/pine-m20.html (accessed 21 May 2018).

Head, M. 2017a. 'Australian government commits to a US-led war on North Korea', *World Socialist Web Site*, 12 August, www.wsws.org/en/articles/2017/08/12/turn-a12.html (accessed 2 June 2018).

Head, M. 2017b. 'Pine Gap base automatically involves Australia in US wars', *World Socialist Web Site*, 24 August, www.wsws.org/en/articles/2017/08/24/pine-a24.html (accessed 21 May 2018).

Head, M. 2017c. 'Australian government offers to send troops to the Philippines', *World Socialist Web Site*, 30 August, www.wsws.org/en/articles/2017/08/30/turn-a30.html (accessed 28 May 2018).

Hicks, B. 2010. 'The Crown's "democratic" reserve powers', *Journal of Canadian Studies*, 44(2): 5–31.

Hocking, J. 2004. *Terror Laws: ASIO, Counter-Terrorism and the Threat to Democracy.* Sydney: UNSW Press.

Horne, D. 1966. 'Australia looks around', *Foreign Affairs*, 44(3): 446–57.

Howard, J. 2001. Press conference, 4 October, Canberra.

Inter-Imperial Relations Committee. 1926. *Imperial Conference: Report, Proceedings and Memoranda*, www.foundingdocs.gov.au/resources/transcripts/cth11_doc_1926.pdf (accessed 24 April 2018).

Kevin, T. 2004. 'Australia's secret pre-emptive war against Iraq, 18–20 March 2003', *Australian Journal of International Affairs*, 58(3): 318–36.

Larkin, P., and Uhr, P. 2009. 'Bipartisanship and bicameralism in Australia's "war on terror": forcing limits on the extension of executive power', *The Journal of Legislative Studies*, 15(2–3): 239–56.

Lindell, G. 2003. 'The constitutional authority to deploy Australian military forces in the Coalition War against Iraq', *Constitutional Law and Policy Review*, 5(3): 46–50.

Macaskill, E., and Dance, G. 2013. 'NSA files: decoded', *The Guardian*, 1 November, www.theguardian.com/world/interactive/2013/nov/01/snowden-nsa-files-surveillance-revelations-decoded#section/1 (accessed 2 May 2018).

Maddox, K., and Wright, B. (eds). 1987. 'Introduction'. In *War: Australia and Vietnam.* Sydney: Harper & Row.

Madison, J. [1787] 1911. 'Speech, constitutional convention (1787-06-29)'. In M. Farrand (ed.), *Records of the Federal Convention of 1787, Vol. 1.* New Haven, CT: Yale University Press.

Madison, J. [1795] 1865. 'Political observations (1795-04-20)'. In *Letters and Other Writings of James Madison, Vol. IV.* Philadelphia, PA: J.B. Lippincott & Co.

Marshall, P. 2001. 'The Balfour Formula and the evolution of the Commonwealth', *The Round Table*, 90(361): 541–53.

McKeown, D., and Jordan, R. 2010. *Parliamentary Involvement in Declaring War and Deploying Forces Overseas. Background Note.* Canberra: Parliamentary Library, Parliament of Australia.

O'Connor, M. 1997. 'Vietnam, conscription and all that', *Quadrant*, July–Aug: 111.

O'Neill, J. 2016. 'The US–Australia alliance: in Australia's interest?', *Australian Socialist*, 22(2): 2–5.

Oliver, A. 2013. *Lowy Institute Poll 2013*, http://lowyinstitute.org/publications/lowy-institute-poll-2013 (accessed 11 May 2018).

Owens, J., and Pilizzo, R. 2013. 'Rethinking crises and the accretion of executive power: the "war on terror" and conditionality evidence from seven political systems', *Asian Politics & Policy*, 5(3): 321–36.

Parliament of Australia. 2003a. 'Parliament House, Canberra: transcript of press conference— Iraq; North Korea; war against terror; Pat Rafter', Press release, 10 January, http://parlinfo.aph.gov.au/parlInfo/search/display/display.w3p;query=Id%3A%22media%2Fp ressrel%2FB3A86%22 (accessed 10 May 2018).

Parliament of Australia. 2003b. 'Transcript of press conference: 17 March 2003— Parliament House, Canberra: Iraq', Press release, 17 March, http://parlinfo.aph. gov.au/parlInfo/search/display/display.w3p;query=Id%3A%22media%2Fpressrel%2F U8T86%22 (accessed 10 May 2018).

Parliament of Australia. 2003c. 'Transcript of address to the nation', Press release, 20 March, http://parlinfo.aph.gov.au/parlInfo/search/display/display.w3p;query=Id %3A%22media%2Fpressrel%2FRZU86%22 (accessed 10 May 2018).

Russell, P. 2011. 'Discretion and the reserve powers of the Crown', *Canadian Parliamentary Review*, 34(2): 19–25.

Ruys, T., and Verlinden, N. 2015. 'Digest of state practice: 1 July 31 December 2014', *Journal on the Use of Force and International Law*, 2(1): 119–62.

Ruys, T., Ferro, L., and Haesebrouck, T. 2017. 'Parliamentary war powers and the role of international law in foreign troop deployment decisions: the US-led coalition against "Islamic State" in Iraq and Syria', *International Journal of Constitutional Law*, forthcoming.

Sampford, C., and Palmer, M. 2009. 'The constitutional power to make war: domestic legal issues raised by Australia's action in Iraq', *Griffith Law Review*, 18(2): 350–84.

Schmitt, C. [1922] 2005. *Political Theology: Four Chapters on the Concept of Sovereignty*. Chicago, IL: Chicago University Press.

Sexton, M. 1981. *War for the Asking: Australia's Vietnam Secret*. Ringwood, Vic.: Penguin Books.

Stephen, N. 1984. 'Address on the Occasion of Course No. 27–83 of the Joint Services Staff College, Canberra on Tuesday, 21 June 1983: the Governor-General as Commander-in-Chief', *Melbourne University Law Review*, 14(4): 563–71.

Tanter, R. 2014. 'Australia in America's third Iraq War', *The Asia-Pacific Journal/Japan Focus*, 12(51): 1–30.

Tanter, R. 2015a. 'Addiction to alliance war', *Arena*, 139: 30–34.

Tanter, R. 2015b. 'To war, like it or not: the "joint facilities", interoperability, and the erasure of independent war powers'. In A. Broinowski (ed.), *How Does Australia Go to War? A Call for Accountability and Change*. Melbourne: Citizens for an Iraq War Inquiry.

Tanter, R. 2018. 'Tightly bound: Australia's alliance-dependent militarization', *Global Asia*, 26 March.

The Intercept. 2017. 'Pine Gap site profile', 20 August, https://theintercept.com/document/2017/08/19/pine-gap-site-profile/ (accessed 21 May 2018).

Ward, S. 2001. *Australia and the British Embrace: The Demise of the Imperial Ideal*. Melbourne: Melbourne University Press.

Williams, G. 2004. 'The power to go to war: Australia in Iraq', *Public Law Review*, 15(1): 5–9.

6 The failure of reform proposals
An Australian case study

Australia, where proposals to curb or modify the executive war-making have been made for three decades, provides a telling example of the inadequacy and failure of such efforts.

None of these proposals has suggested a referendum or a plebiscite as a means of trying to establish popular democratic control over war powers. Instead, they have involved highly problematic suggestions of restoring the war declaration powers of the governor-general, inherited from the war prerogative of the British monarchy, or limited reviewing roles for one or both Houses of Parliament.

This chapter reviews various academic and party-political proposals for change through the lens of 'war power theory'.

War power theory consists of several competing traditions or schools. The first, the *autocratic* tradition, understands the exercise of the war power as the prerogative of the executive branch of government. The decision of one person—or, at most, a very few officials—is akin to the ancient war-making privilege exercised by monarchs. Historically, contingent subcategories exist within the autocratic tradition and early practical examples can be seen in the royal war prerogative of the past, where the king, raj, emperor, pharaoh, pope, lord, etc. made the decision to go to war and his followers obeyed. This type of war power was the dominant form for millennia.

With the rise of parliamentary authority within modern nation-states and the development of the doctrine of the separation of powers, monarchical war power was supplanted by executive branch war power, at first throughout the Anglo-Saxon diaspora and now across much of the globe. This type of war power exists in nation-states where no formal legal requirement exists that a vote be taken in a parliament to approve the executive's decision to go to war. Despite the change in title from king to prime minister or president and notwithstanding the power-sharing potential of parliaments in contemporary democracies, the war-making power of the modern executive in such nations is a direct descendant of the autocratic tradition, raising crucial questions in contemporary supposed democracies.

A second, competing, school sees the exercise of the war power as the responsibility of the legislative branch of government. This is the *representative* war power tradition. The representative tradition considers it to be preferable for the legislative branch of government to authorise any decision to go to war or to engage in military conflict abroad. Adherents contend that, under the wise guidance of a parliament or congress, the exercise of the war power can be constrained and directed, thus addressing a perceived 'democratic deficit'. Given today's global context, this idea appears naive. In a world in which war is endemic as great powers contend at many levels for dwindling resources, and in which the United States has been engaged in an open-ended 'war on terror' and is currently focused on strategic competition, the notion that representative branches of government can constrain the war power seems dangerously misplaced.

In particular, given Australia's dependence on a military alliance with the United States, set out elsewhere in this book, the notion that the legislative branch could or would provide an effective brake on the war power is questionable. This notion is further brought into question given the role played by what many analysts refer to as the 'deep state' or 'national security state' (Lofgren 2016; Smith 2015; McCoy 2014; Misra 2018). It is unlikely that the Australian national security state would allow the legislative branch of government to seize the war power.

A third, *globalist* tradition regards the exercise of the war power as the responsibility of the UN Security Council. Its earliest expression emerged in Kant's idea of perpetual peace. In 1795, Kant called for a halt to the internecine and barbaric wars that had plagued Europe for centuries, arguing in favour of a perpetual peace in Europe to be established via an early prototype of the United Nations. The idea found expression in 1945 in Chapters I and VII of the UN Charter. Except for acts of self-defence, the Charter holds that states are not to engage in military action against each other without the authorisation of the Security Council.

However, although at times the Labor Party and Greens have questioned Australian participation in war without Security Council authorisation, the notion that war power sovereignty ought to be transferred to the United Nations has garnered no support among Australian academics or political parties.

Australian reform proposals

To date, little has been written by Australian academics, lawyers or politicians in relation to the exercise of the war power. By comparison to the scholarship that has emerged over two centuries in the United States and more recently in Britain, Australian war power scholarship can only be described as 'nascent'. Which branch of government 'should'—as opposed to 'does'—exercise the war power has not been a focus of constitutional scholars until relatively recently and, even then, it has not yet been addressed by many (Lindell 2003; Williams 2004; Sampford and Palmer 2009; Barratt 2015; Brown 2016).

The three traditions identified at the start of the chapter can be found in the Australian debate.

- The autocratic tradition, in the form of adherence to the executive war power prerogative, has support from the two main political parties, the Liberal–National coalition and the Labor Party. It has also received qualified supported from commentators such as Brown (2016), and Sampford and Palmer (2009).

- The representative tradition, advocating some kind of role for Parliament, has had support from the Australian Greens (and the now defunct Australian Democrats), as well as academics such as Williams (2004), Lindell (2003) and Barratt (2015).
- The globalist tradition has no support, although at times the Labor Party has favoured requiring a UN resolution before Australian troops engage in armed conflict.

The autocratic tradition: the executive war power prerogative

Currently, the Australian prime minister does not take advice from the governor-general, the titular head of the Australian Defence Force (ADF). In 1991, Prime Minister Bob Hawke simply notified the governor-general of his decision to commit combat troops to Iraq. The governor-general was bypassed again for the 2003 Iraq invasion. Prime Minister John Howard at first sought to include the governor-general in the decision-making process, but quickly backtracked once Governor-General Hollingsworth asked the attorney-general some questions about the legality of the proposed deployment in the light of international law principles.

As discussed in Chapter 5, Sampford and Palmer (2009: 370) condemned the Australian practice of deploying troops:

> . . . without the exercise of the war prerogative by the Governor-General or its delegation to the Prime Minister or other ministers. This would seem to involve a major shift in practice without any apparent debate or public consideration of its desirability, let alone constitutionality.

They argued that the 'few instances' of recent Australian practice should not be regarded as altering, legally, the requirement that the prerogative powers be exercised by the governor-general, acting on advice.

In relation to the invasion of Iraq in 2003, the *political* basis of Australia's commitment of troops was a cabinet decision, supported not by a vote, but a limited debate in the House of Representatives. The cabinet has no legal powers and relies on either statutory or executive authority to implement its decisions. The House of Representatives resolution in support did not provide for implementation of the cabinet's decision to deploy troops. So the *legal* basis seems to have been the Defence Act 1903 (Cth) (Lindell 2003: 47), although Sampford and Palmer (2009: 380) doubt the constitutionality of this mechanism in the absence of express words that indicate that the statute was intended to regulate executive power to declare, wage and end wars. No writer accepts the possibility that UN Security Council resolutions declaring war (and, arguably, there were none in this case) could have domestic legal effect.

Sampford and Palmer decry what they refer to as the unconstitutional usurpation by various prime ministers of the role they say should be played by the governor-general. To them, the governor-general plays an important advisory or warning role and this role should be reinstituted. They state that although such gubernatorial scrutiny:

> . . . falls well short of the accountability provided by the potential of litigation before a court of competent jurisdiction, it can occur before rather than after Australia has gone to war. Following Australia's little-known and less-discussed decision to alter its acceptance of the compulsory jurisdiction of the International Court of Justice in March 2002 in a way that precluded Iraq from taking the matter to the most obvious and eminent court of competent jurisdiction, it may be the only independent scrutiny such decisions can receive.
>
> (Sampford and Palmer 2009: 380)

One possible advantage of this reform—a return to the vice-regal exercise of the war power—is that it would not require any constitutional amendment or legislation. It is, however, unlikely that the executive would choose to return to the embrace of the governor-general. Moreover, as discussed in Chapter 5, the assertion that a governor-general would not act 'through reserve powers', but rather 'on the advice of the responsible minister' is problematic. The governor-general's reserve powers are notoriously murky, controversial and ill-defined, and theoretically provide a range of presumptively constitutional actions unconstrained by ministerial advice, as vestiges of the royal prerogative.

There has been a hybrid proposal that purports to check the executive from the 'outside'. In 2016, James Brown, a former military officer, proposed prime ministerial exercise of the war power on the basis of: improved advice from a national security adviser; 'oversight' by a new parliamentary committee system; and a review role for Parliament after three months of military activities.

Notwithstanding his consultative suggestions, Brown's reforms can be characterised as belonging to the autocratic tradition. For him, in the end, the executive's exercise of the war power is effectively unconstrained by consultative window-dressing. Brown rejects the idea of prior parliamentary approval (that is, approval before deployment of troops); rather, his preferred role for Parliament is similar to Parliament's existing role with respect to treaties. Brown (2016: 105–06) explains thus:

> The need for full parliamentary approval before any substantial military action by the prime minister would inhibit an effective response to a crisis, and successive prime ministers have rightly resisted this. But there is a compelling case for parliament to review whether a military deployment is in the national interest within a period of, say, ninety days. Here we have a model in the way parliament deals with foreign treaties. Of course it is the role of the executive to sign treaties with other countries, and in the past it was

entirely up to the foreign minister to present these treaties to the parliament for domestic legislation. But in 2005 reforms were introduced which require a new joint committee on treaties to prepare a statement on whether a treaty is in the national interest or not, and table it before the parliament. A similar system could be applied to the decision to go to war.

As explained in Chapter 1, of great concern to Brown is re-establishing public trust in the exercise of the war power. To this end, he calls for parliamentary oversight through the monitoring activities of committees:

> To restore public trust in the decision to go to war, better democratic accountability is also essential. This is not just about giving parliament a vote on military deployments—after all, a prime minister will always command the approval of the lower house of parliament. Instead, democratic accountability means developing a system of exercising genuine oversight of the national security agencies and departments, particularly Defence. At the moment that oversight takes pace in a few ways: through overly adversarial and hasty questioning at Senate estimates, abridged discussion in the lower house when prime ministers and their cabinets deign to allow discussion of national security or defence issues, and in the committee system . . . The next parliament needs committees dedicated to assessing each of the ADF, the Department of Defence, national strategy and foreign affairs.
>
> (Brown 2016: 103)

Brown (2016: 102) also suggests that the quality of national security advice given to the prime minister must be improved:

> At present, the formulation of independent national security advice for the prime minister is a somewhat haphazard process—at the highest levels it lacks institutional rigour and continuity. No one is formulating long-term strategy for the government, or conducting the deep thinking necessary for a world in which competition between our friends and allies is the new normal. DFAT [the Department of Foreign Affairs and Trade] has largely vacated this role, and in its place the Department of Defence has all too often been solipsistically crafting its own strategic direction. This is not a role for Prime Minister and Cabinet, focused as it is on the prime minister's immediate needs and the day-to-day coordination of departments and agencies. Rather, what is needed is a new national security council headed by a national security adviser with a role and powers detailed in legislation . . .

As discussed in Chapter 1, Brown's proposals have many flaws, not least being that, once a war were under way, little prospect would exist that a parliamentary vote would be taken, by either House, to veto and withdraw from the conflict. Most revealing, however, is that Brown quite explicitly connects the quest for a parliamentary role in war decision-making to the needs to prepare public opinion for coming wars and to provide a veneer of democratic legitimacy to going to war. Arguably, he erects a facade of parliamentary consultation to help overcome considerable public opposition to war.

The representative tradition: proposals for parliamentary authorisation

The idea that the Parliament should approve Australian commitments to engage in military activities first found political expression during the conflict in Korea when Leader of the Opposition in the Senate William Ashley called for exactly this (W. Ashley, Senate, *Debates*, 6 July 1950, p. 4834). For more than 30 years, minor political parties have been attempting to reform the executive war power prerogative via amendment of the Defence Act 1903 (Cth).

In 1985, the Australian Democrats first proposed the Defence Amendment Bill 1985 (Cth)—a Bill that, similarly to the US War Powers Resolution of 1973, would require parliamentary approval before Australian troops could be committed to war overseas (C. Mason, Senate, *Debates*, 17 April 1985, p. 1186). The proposed legislation is a classic example of the representative tradition's view of the war power as the responsibility of the legislative branch of government. The autocratic lineage of the executive war power prerogative has been of some concern, at least to the Australian Democrats and the Australian Greens. Their proposed reforms of the Defence Act 1903 (Cth) constitute an attempt to partially wrest the war power from the executive—the direct inheritor of the 'divine right of kings'—and to situate the war power with the legislative branch.

The 1985 Bill proposed that an amended section 50 of the Defence Act 1903 require both the House of Representatives and the Senate to authorise any commitment of ADF personnel overseas. However, the proposal still allowed the government to initiate a military conflict, by means of the governor-general proclaiming an 'emergency'. This left open the possibility that the Parliament would, in effect, be reduced to the role of rubber-stamping, as a *fait accompli*, a war that had already been launched or provoked. The amendment provided as follows:

50C **Parliamentary approval of territorial limits of service of members of defence force**

(1) Members of the Defence Force may be required to serve within the territorial limits of Australia.

(2) Subject to subsection (3), members of the Defence Force may not be required to serve beyond the territorial limits of Australia except in accordance with a resolution agreed to by each House of the Parliament authorising the service.

(3) The Governor General may by proclamation declare that an emergency exists requiring the service beyond the territorial limits of Australia of members of the Defence Force, and such service may be required in accordance with such proclamation.

(4) If the Parliament is not in session when a proclamation under subsection (3) is made, it shall be summoned to meet within 2 days after the making of the proclamation.

(5) If the Parliament is in session when a proclamation under subsection (3) is made, but either House of the Parliament is adjourned for an indefinite period of time or for a period of time which will expire more than 2 days after the making of the proclamation, the Presiding Officer of that House within the meaning of the Parliamentary Presiding Officers Act 1965, or the person who is deemed to be the Presiding Officer of that House for the purpose of that Act, shall summon that House to meet within 2 days after the making of the proclamation, notwithstanding anything contained in the resolution of adjournment of that House.

(6) A proclamation made under subsection (3) shall cease to have effect on the day next succeeding the day on which the Parliament next meets after the making of the proclamation.

(7) For the purpose of this section, service beyond the territorial limits of Australia does not include service by members of the Defence Force:

(a) pursuant to their temporary attachment as provided by section 116B; or

(b) as part of an Australian diplomatic or consular mission; or

(c) on an Australian vessel or aircraft not engaged in hostilities or in operations during which hostilities are likely to occur; or

(d) for the purpose of their education or training; or

(e) for purposes related to the procurement of equipment or stores.

Although the Bill proceeded to second reading, the Labor government and Liberal–National coalition opposition parties opposed it, and it did not pass. An identical Bill, the Defence Amendment Bill 1988, was introduced and again defeated in 1988. From 1985 until 2007, the Australian Democrats periodically brought this Bill, or one substantially similar, to the Commonwealth Parliament; each time, it was defeated by the combined votes of the Australian Labor Party and the Liberal–National coalition.

In 2003, Australian Democrat Senators Andrew Bartlett and Natasha Stott-Despoja introduced a private senator's Bill—the Defence Amendment (Parliamentary Approval for Australian Involvement in Overseas Conflicts) Bill 2003—which again sought repeal of section 50C of the Defence Act 1903 (Cth) allowing ADF personnel to be deployed overseas. As with the Democrat amendments from the 1980s, an amended section 50 would require both the House of Representatives and the Senate to approve any commitment of ADF personnel overseas. This Bill also did not pass as a result of the resistance of the Liberal–National coalition government and the Labor opposition.

In February 2008, Australian Democrats Senator Andrew Bartlett introduced the Defence Amendment (Parliamentary Approval of Overseas Service) Bill 2008. Once more, the Liberal–National coalition government and the

Labor opposition resisted the Bill, and it did not pass. Following the political demise of the Australian Democrats, the Australian Greens took over carriage of the Bill. This party introduced it again and again from 2008 until 2016, at that time encouraged by the findings of the Chilcot Inquiry in Britain, which criticised the process leading up to the invasion of Iraq in 2003, but again these proposals were each defeated.

In September 2008, Australian Greens Senator Scott Ludlam introduced the Defence Amendment (Parliamentary Approval of Overseas Service) Bill 2008 (No. 2). This Bill also sought to repeal section 50 of the Defence Act 1903 (Cth) and replace it with a section requiring parliamentary approval for deployment of ADF forces overseas. Almost one year later, in August 2009, the Bill was referred to the Senate Foreign Affairs, Defence and Trade Legislation Committee. That committee reported in February 2010 and recommended that the Bill not proceed. Its chair, Senator Mark Bishop, said that the committee was concerned about the practical operation of the Bill. In 2014 and 2015, the Australian Greens put forward the Defence Legislation Amendment (Parliamentary Approval of Overseas Service) Bill. This Bill, identical to the previous Bills in requiring approval of both Houses of Parliament, was defeated once more—with no support from either of the main political parties forthcoming.

In summary, there has not been any degree of mainstream political party support for parliamentary authorisation prior to war for more than 30 years. Since 1985, the Labor Party and the Liberal–National coalition parties have repeatedly resisted any move to broaden the exercise of the war power beyond a narrowly defined political executive.

Scholarly adherents of the representative tradition also have also recommended involving Parliament in providing more muscular control. Lindell (2003: 49), concerned by monopoly executive control of the exercise of the war power, explores the possibility, via legislation passed by Parliament, of making 'prior parliamentary approval a legal condition for a declaration of war or the deployment of armed forces in any military engagement'. Although he notes that there are competing views in relation to the constitutional capacity of Parliament to constrain executive branch prerogative powers, he states that the 'better view' is that:

> . . . legislation can be enacted to strengthen parliamentary control of the executive branch of government in the exercise of its prerogative powers. This is supported by the statement by the High Court in *Brown v West* [[1990] HCA 7] that: 'Whatever the scope of the executive power of the Commonwealth might otherwise be, it is susceptible of control by statute'.
>
> (Lindell 2003: 49)

Lindell (2003: 49) further argues that, 'consistently with the traditional understanding of the British system of government, legislation can be enacted to strengthen parliamentary control of the executive branch of government in the exercise of its prerogative powers'.

For Lindell (2003: 49):

> The system of prior approval need not necessarily make the decision making process in this area unacceptably cumbersome—as was illustrated by the relative ease with which the US President obtained constitutional authority in relation to the 2003 war with Iraq. A different outcome might, however, have resulted in Australia if the decision to deploy military forces was proposed by a Government that lacked a majority in the Senate at a time when the community was opposed to such action.

Like the legislation proposed by the Australian Democrats and the Australian Greens, Lindell's recommendation appears to support authorisation from each House of Parliament prior to war. His discussion raises one interesting point: the impact of mass popular anti-war opposition.

Another adherent of the representative tradition, George Williams, advocates a more limited form of legislative authorisation. He criticises the proposed amendment of section 50C of the Defence Act 1903 (Cth), tabled by the Australian Democrats and Australian Greens since 1985, saying that it would not achieve 'the right balance. It is not appropriate to require the support of the Senate for such a decision given the difficulties of doing so and the nature of the decision' (Williams 2004: 7). Instead, the decision to go to war should be approved by a joint sitting of both Houses of Parliament:

> This would emphasise the importance of the decision and would involve all members. However, it would also generally allow the government, with its greater majority in the lower house offsetting its deficit in the Senate, to gain the outcome it wishes so long as it can maintain party discipline. This would involve an appropriate measure of symbolism and deliberation. It would not, however, remove the capacity of the executive in most cases to determine the course for which it will ultimately have to answer at the ballot box.
>
> (Williams 2004: 8)

Williams' minimalist contribution is beset with difficulties. It should be noted that Williams wrote before the 2010–13 hung Parliament, in which a declaration of war may have had real difficulty making it through a joint sitting, not to mention a separate sitting, of each House. Additionally, as Williams admits, a political executive enjoying the benefits of party discipline would retain its current position as the sole arbiter in questions of declarations of war or deployment of troops. His claim that a political executive, exercising the war power, is somehow checked by ultimately having to face the wrath of an angry electorate arguably reflects an ahistorical reading of the Australian electorate. The 2003 commitment of troops to invade Iraq, for example, was clearly unpopular, yet the Liberal–National coalition won the 2004 election. The presence of many policies at elections makes it difficult to identify whether voters are 'sending the government a message' about any one of them. And in circumstances in which both major political parties support military action, no opportunity exists for voters use the ballot box to 'send a message'.

Plebiscite?

Explicitly rejected by Williams, and not discussed by Sampford and Palmer or Lindell, is there any justification for holding a plebiscite prior to a declaration of war? Williams (2004: 7) makes the following argument:

> I believe that such a decision is generally not one for the people. A plebiscite is too unwieldy an exercise on such an issue, and for the same reasons that citizen-initiated referenda are not consistent with Australia's system of representative government, a popular vote on whether to go to war should be rejected.

Surely, however, such fundamental decisions as going to war, which have so many ramifications in terms of blood and treasure and civic harmony, are ones that citizens—rather than their representatives—*ought* to take? This issue is taken up in Chapter 11.

References

Barratt, P. 2015. 'The war powers in Australia: why reform is needed'. In A. Broinowski (ed.), *How Does Australia Go to War? A Call for Accountability and Change*. Melbourne: Campaign for an Iraq War Inquiry.

Brown, J. 2016. 'Firing line: Australia's path to war', *Quarterly Essay*, 62: 1–68.

Lindell, G. 2003. 'The constitutional authority to deploy Australian military forces in the Coalition War against Iraq', *Constitutional Law and Policy Review*, 5(3): 46–50.

Lofgren, M. 2016. *The Deep State: The Fall of the Constitution and the Rise of a Shadow Government*. New York: Viking/Penguin/Random House.

McCoy, T. 2014. 'How Australia just became a "national security state" ', *Washington Post*, 7 October.

Misra, A. 2018. 'Australia's counter-terrorism policies since September 11, 2001: harmonising national security, independent oversight and individual liberties', *Strategic Analysis*, 42(2): 103–18.

Sampford, C., and Palmer, M. 2009. 'The Constitutional power to make war: domestic legal issues raised by Australia's action in Iraq', *Griffith Law Review*, 18(2): 350–84.

Smith, D. 2015. 'From the military-industrial complex to the national security state', *Australian Journal of Political Science*, 50(3): 576–90.

Williams, G. 2004. 'The power to go to war: Australia in Iraq', *Public Law Review*, 15: 5–9.

7 War and dissent

Sweeping domestic powers

Wars, whether formally declared or not, have serious domestic consequences, including the loss of soldiers' and other victims' lives, the diversion of massive resources into the war effort, the channeling of funds from social spending into war expenditure and the development of anti-war opposition. Both world wars and every major US-led war since—Korea, Vietnam, Afghanistan and Iraq—have been accompanied by draconian internal measures to enforce the war mobilisation and suppress social unrest and dissent. Governments have invariably resorted to repressive provisions, including emergency powers, special legislation and regulations, detentions without trial, widespread surveillance and police harassment, particularly directed against opponents of the war.

Military conflicts—even one-sided invasions such as those in Afghanistan and Iraq—inevitably cause terrible casualties. Millions of people, including innocent civilians, have been killed in these wars, alongside the death of and serious injuries suffered by those personnel sent to wage them. In addition, wars require massive expenditure and resources, invariably at the cost of social programmes, and sometimes even the profits of some corporate interests.

A 2017 study of 16 years of war in Iraq, Afghanistan, Pakistan and Syria concluded that it had drained US$5.6 trillion from the US economy (Watson Institute 2017). This figure, cited in a *Costs of War* report published by the Watson Institute of International and Public Affairs at Brown University, was more than triple the estimate offered by the Pentagon itself. It factored in huge costs that the US military does not include when tallying up the bills for its wars, such as medical expenses for wounded and disabled veterans, war-related spending by the Department of Homeland Security and the increased cost of borrowing money to pay for military operations (Crawford 2017).

The report did not include spending on US military operations elsewhere in the world, including in Chad, Niger and throughout the African continent, US participation in the Saudi-led war against Yemen and special operations interventions around the globe. The cost of the wars dealt with in the report was over and above the annual Pentagon budget of nearly $700 billion. At the same time, there was a continuous refrain sung by the US government that there was not enough money to pay for health care, public education, infrastructure and social security.

The Watson Institute report acknowledged that the financial costs did not begin to account for the slaughter, destruction and human misery involved:

> Moreover, a full accounting of any war's burdens cannot be placed in columns on a ledger. From the civilians harmed and displaced by violence, to the soldiers killed and wounded, to the children who play years later on roads and fields sown with improvised explosive devices and cluster bombs, no set of numbers can convey the human toll of the wars in Iraq and Afghanistan, or how they have spilled into the neighboring states of Syria and Pakistan, and come home to the US and its allies in the form of wounded veterans.
>
> (Crawford 2017)

Larger-scale wars, involving conflicts between the United States and other major powers, would be even more devastating and costly. To impose such sacrifices on a population necessarily entails extraordinary legal and punitive measures, going far beyond 'peacetime' provisions in their impact on basic democratic rights, including freedom of political opinion.

Internal war-related powers in the United States

Early American jurisprudence drew a distinction between general, or perfect, war and limited, or imperfect, war, and understood a declaration of war under Article I, §8, of the US Constitution to commit the entire nation to a general war. In *Bas v. Tingby* 4 US (4 Dall.) 37, 40 (1800), Justice Washington described the distinction as follows:

> It may, I believe, be safely laid down, that every contention by force between two nations, in external matters, under the authority of their respective governments, is not only war, but public war. If it be declared in form, it is called solemn, and is of the perfect kind; because one whole nation is at war with another whole nation; and all the members of the nation declaring war are authorised to commit hostilities against all the members of the other, in every place, and under every circumstance. In such a war all the members act under a general authority, and all the rights and consequences of war attach to their condition.

Justice Chase, more simply, stated: 'Congress is empowered to declare a general war, or congress may wage a limited war; limited in place, in objects, and in time' (*Bas v. Tingby*, at 43). Thus, at least in the 18th and 19th centuries, authorisations for the use of force were understood to be included within Congress's power to declare war and to have narrower legal consequences than declarations of war. In the 21st century, authorisations have been broader and arguably equivalent in scope to a declaration of war.

Strictly speaking, the domestic legal consequences that flow from such authorisations may be more limited than those that would flow from a formal declaration of war. Nevertheless, they are far-reaching—and successive US administrations have sought to expand them.

A declaration of war automatically brings into effect a host of statutes that confer special powers on the president and the executive branch. A declaration, for instance, activates statutes that empower the president to interdict all trade with the enemy, to order manufacturing plants to produce armaments and to seize control of the plants if they refuse to do so, to control transportation systems to give the military priority use and to command communications systems to give priority to the military. A declaration triggers the Alien Enemy Act of 1798, which gives the US president substantial discretionary authority over nationals of an enemy state who are in the United States. Under the Foreign Intelligence Surveillance Act of 1977 (FISA), it activates the use by special authorities of electronic surveillance, without a court order, for the purposes of gathering foreign intelligence information. It automatically extends enlistments in the armed forces until the end of the war; it can make the US Coast Guard part of the US Navy; it gives the president substantial discretion over the appointment and reappointment of commanders; and it allows the military priority use of the natural resources on the public lands and the continental shelf (Elsea and Weed 2014: 23–25).

An authorisation for the use of military force (AUMF) does not automatically trigger these standby statutory authorities. Some of them can come into effect if a state of war does in fact come into being after an AUMF is enacted; the great majority of them, including many of the most sweeping ones, can also be activated if the president issues a proclamation of a national emergency.

Despite this distinction, the authorisation to use force in response to the terrorist attacks of 11 September 2001 (that is, 9/11) has been asserted as legal authority for comprehensive executive actions in the domestic context. The Bush administration asserted that the authorisation permits detention without trial of persons arrested in the United States on suspicion of terrorism related to Al Qaeda, which it regarded as bolstered by the Supreme Court's decision in *Hamdi et al. v. Rumsfield* 542 US 507, 531 (2004), in which the Court found the detention of enemy combatants captured in Afghanistan to be authorised as 'a fundamental incident of waging war'.

In previous wars, the Alien Enemy Act had provided the chief means of interning suspected enemies domestically. The Bush administration took the position that the authorisation to use force legalised detention powers without any of the few rules or restrictions specified in the Alien Enemy Act and hence authorised the detention of US citizens as an exception to the Non-Detention Act of 1971. Similarly, it argued that the authorisation to use force permitted electronic surveillance outside the strictures of FISA, even though that Act provides for only a two-week exception triggered by a declaration of war. According to this logic, any similarly broad authorisation to use force legalises any power characterised as 'a fundamental incident of waging war' under the circumstances (Elsea and Weed 2014: 23–25).

Other statutes triggered by a declaration of war give the president the authority to order plants to convert to the production of armaments and to seize control of those plants that refuse to do so, to take control of the Tennessee Valley Authority to manufacture explosives or for other military purposes, to assume control of transportation systems for military purposes, to condemn land for military uses, to have the right of first refusal over natural resources and to take control of communications facilities. They also give the president full power over agricultural exports. The full list of legislation triggered by a war declaration or a state of war is lengthy, including more than 50 statutes, ranging from measures against 'aliens' to electronic eavesdropping without court orders under FISA. Another host of statutory powers are activated by presidential declarations of national emergency (Elsea and Weed 2014: 44–75).

Internments and other violations of liberty

First enacted in 1798, the Alien Enemy Act broadly authorises the US president to deport, detain or otherwise condition the stay of alien enemies in the United States in cases of 'declared war' or 'any invasion or predatory incursion . . . perpetrated, attempted, or threatened against the territory of the United States by any foreign nation or government'. The president must publicly proclaim the event that gives rise to activation of the Act and make regulations regarding the treatment of those aliens. But, once a president does so, their power to 'apprehend, restrain, secure, and remove' enemy aliens extends to all 'natives, citizens, denizens, or subjects of the hostile nation or government, being of the age of fourteen years and upward, who shall be in the United States and not actually naturalized'. The president may intern or remove enemy aliens, or set lesser restraints on them, and may adopt any 'regulations which are found necessary in the premises and for the public safety'. Moreover, the US Supreme Court has ruled that '[e]xecutive power over enemy aliens, undelayed and unhampered by litigation, has been deemed, throughout our history, essential to war-time security' (quoted in Elsea and Weed 2014: 28–29).

During World War I, President Woodrow Wilson barred alien enemies from possessing firearms and explosives, from coming within a half a mile of a military facility or munitions factory, from residing in certain areas, from possessing certain communications equipment and from publishing certain types of material. President Franklin D. Roosevelt authorised similar restrictions during World War II and also set up more than 100 community hearing boards to make internment recommendations to the attorney general. The procedural rights of aliens who are subject to the Alien Enemy Act are drastically restricted compared with those that aliens otherwise enjoy, including hearing rights under the removal provisions of the Immigration and Nationality Act of 1965. The scope of judicial review is equally circumscribed. A very limited right to judicial review under a petition for a writ of *habeas corpus* is recognised. Generally, however, the power of the president to control alien enemies under the Act is sweeping (Elsea and Weed 2014: 28–29).

In both world wars, thousands of people were subjected to these powers, often detained or forcibly displaced by US governments in supposed prosecutions of the war efforts, overriding their most basic legal and democratic rights.

In World War II, President Roosevelt both worked with congressional authority and instigated actions on his own, justifying them as emergency responses to threats abroad. In part, he relied upon the Supreme Court's dicta in *United States v. Curtiss-Wright Export Corpn* 299 US 304 (1936), providing that the president had plenary and exclusive powers in the field of international relations and could take unilateral action without the congressional approval. In *Ex parte Quirin* 317 US 1 (1942), two groups of German saboteurs had been arrested and Roosevelt had ordered them to be tried by a military tribunal. The Supreme Court denied leave to file for *habeas corpus*.

By the end of the war, Roosevelt's executive orders had enabled the incarceration of more than 110,000 Japanese-Americans in camps (Daniels 1993: 104). This regime was effectively upheld by the Supreme Court in *Korematsu v. United States* 323 US 214 (1944).

Referring to Roosevelt's Executive Order 9066, which authorised the evacuation of people of Japanese ancestry from the West Coast, then Attorney-General Francis Biddle summed up the cynicism with which such issues are approached and the confidence that administrations have in the acquiescence of the judiciary: '[T]he Constitution has not greatly bothered any wartime President. That was a question of law, which ultimately the Supreme Court must decide. And meanwhile—probably a long meanwhile—we must get on with the war' (quoted in Gross and Aolain 2006: 95).

'Enemy combatants'

The George W. Bush administration deemed terrorist suspects to be neither prisoners of war nor enemy combatants, thus justifying their incarceration without trial. On 13 November 2001, President Bush signed a military order that denied suspects access to civilian courts, allowed the military to hold suspects indefinitely anywhere in the world and instituted military commissions that could impose the death penalty. The government chose to hold suspects in a naval base in Guantanamo Bay, believing that it would be a legal quagmire because it is not US territory (Thompson 2010).

Two Supreme Court cases eventually ruled that prisoners could file petitions for *habeas corpus*, but neither decision resulted in the release of a prisoner. In *Hamdi et al. v. Rumsfield* 542 US 507, 531 (2004), it was stated:

> We reaffirm today the fundamental nature of a citizen's right to be free from involuntary confinement by his own government without due process of law, and we weigh the opposing governmental interests against the curtailment of liberty that such confinement entails . . .
>
> We therefore hold that a citizen-detainee seeking to challenge his classification as an enemy combatant must receive notice of the factual basis for his classification, and a fair opportunity to rebut the Government's factual assertions before a neutral decision-maker . . . These essential constitutional promises may not be eroded.

The US Department of Defense established combatant status review tribunals (CSRTs) in the wake of this decision and expanded the definition of 'enemy combatant' to anyone who 'directly supported hostilities in aid of enemy forces'. Congress then lent support by passing the Detainee Treatment Act of 2005, which allowed for only very limited review of CSRT decisions.

In 2006, the Supreme Court found that the military tribunals violated both US military law and the Geneva Conventions. In *Hamdan v. Rumsfield* 548 US 557 (2006), the Court said that the president did not possess unlimited power to decide how to try detainees and that congressional support was necessary. Congress then passed the Military Commissions Act of 2006, which overcame the *Hamdan* ruling. The Act allowed the president to interpret the meaning and application of the Geneva Convention, and allowed evidence to be hidden from detainees on national security grounds. The Act was challenged, but the Supreme Court found only section 7, denying prisoners the right of *habeas corpus* to federal courts, to be unconstitutional (*Boumediene v. Bush* 553 US 723 (2008)).

In the past, the courts have been reluctant to recognise the authority of military tribunals over civilians. This view was upheld, albeit in a limited manner, in the Guantanamo Bay *habeas corpus* cases that challenged the constitutionality of the military commissions established to try 'enemy combatants'. In 2004, the Supreme Court, by a 6–3 majority, ruled that Guantanamo Bay detainees could seek writs of *habeas corpus* in US courts. The majority judgment, delivered by Stevens J, suggested that democratic conceptions were at stake that dated back nearly 800 years to Magna Carta (*Rasul v. Bush; Al Odah v. United States* 542 US 466 (2004)).

Four years later, in *Boumediene v. Bush* 553 US 723 (2008), the Supreme Court ruled 5–4 that Guantanamo detainees could immediately file *habeas corpus* petitions in US district courts challenging the legality of their confinement. Most had been held at the US naval base under brutal conditions, often enduring solitary confinement, water-boarding and other coercive techniques or torture, for more than six years, without having the merits of their cases reviewed by a court of law. However, the ruling did not question the executive branch's ability to declare someone an 'enemy combatant'—a power that the Supreme Court had upheld four years earlier in *Hamdi v. Rumsfeld* 542 US 507 (2004).

Later in 2008, a 5–4 decision by the US Court of Appeals for the Fourth Circuit backed the Bush administration's contention that the president has such power. In *Al-Marri v. Pucciarelli* (4th Cir. July 15, 2008), the court effectively overturned a decision reached by a three-judge panel of the same court in 2007 that had compared the assumption of such sweeping powers to military rule and the oppression of the American colonies by King George III. The appellate ruling denied *habeas corpus* to Al-Marri, a legal US resident before the White House declared him an enemy combatant in 2003 and ordered the military to detain him in a Navy brig in South Carolina. The government claimed that the AUMF passed by Congress in 2002 gave the president the power to carry out such detentions. In the alternative, it asserted that the commander-in-chief has unchallengeable authority to imprison anyone without charges for the duration of a global 'war on terror'.

While many had hoped that the Obama administration would rein in such actions (as a presidential candidate, Obama had in fact called for the closure of Guantanamo Bay), it allowed such detention systems to continue, justified by similar memoranda (Edelson 2013; Thompson 2010).

Detention of US citizens

The 2012 National Defense Authorization Act (NDAA) included provisions that appear to both codify and expand a power that the executive branch has claimed to possess—the power to hold individuals, including US citizens, in military detention, potentially indefinitely—based on the AUMF passed by Congress three days after the 9/11 attacks in New York and Washington, DC.

In theory, the NDAA's provisions apply only to someone involved with the 9/11 attacks or who 'substantially supported al-Qaeda, the Taliban, or associated forces', but similar language has proven elastic. The 2001 AUMF did not give explicitly give such sweeping detention powers to the executive branch, but the George W. Bush administration claimed that it did so implicitly. Section 2 of that document authorised the president to:

> . . . use all necessary and appropriate force against those nations, organizations, or persons he determines planned, authorized, committed, or aided the terrorist attacks that occurred on September 11, 2001, or harboured such organizations or persons, in order to prevent any future acts of international terrorism against the United States by such nations, organizations or persons.

The administration used this purported power after José Padilla, a US citizen born in Brooklyn, New York, was arrested at Chicago's O'Hare Airport in May 2002 when returning from the Middle East. Bush designated Padilla an 'enemy combatant', claiming that he was 'closely associated with Al Qaeda' and had 'engaged in conduct that constituted hostile and war-like acts'. On this basis, Bush placed him in a military prison without charges or a trial (Schwarz 2018).

The US Supreme Court never ruled on whether this was legitimate. The Bush administration moved Padilla to the civilian court system before the higher Court could do so. Before Padilla's transfer, however, a three-judge panel from the US Court of Appeals for the Fourth Circuit declared that the 2001 AUMF did, in fact, give the president 'the power to detain identified and committed enemies such as Padilla' (*Padilla v. Hanft* 423 F.3d 386, 397 (2005)). That result appears to have been legislated by section 1021 of the NDAA, which stated:

AFFIRMATION OF AUTHORITY OF THE ARMED FORCES OF THE UNITED STATES TO DETAIN COVERED PERSONS PURSUANT TO THE AUTHORIZATION FOR USE OF MILITARY FORCE.

(a) In General—Congress affirms that the authority of the President to use all necessary and appropriate force pursuant to the Authorization for Use of Military Force (Public Law 107–40; 50 U.S.C. 1541 note) includes the authority for the Armed Forces of the United States to detain covered persons (as defined in subsection (b)) pending disposition under the law of war.

(b) Covered Persons—A covered person under this section is any person as follows:

   (1) A person who planned, authorized, committed, or aided the terrorist attacks that occurred on September 11, 2001, or harbored those responsible for those attacks.

   (2) A person who was a part of or substantially supported al-Qaeda, the Taliban, or associated forces that are engaged in hostilities against the United States or its coalition partners, including any person who has committed a belligerent act or has directly supported such hostilities in aid of such enemy forces.

(c) Disposition Under Law of War—The disposition of a person under the law of war as described in subsection (a) may include the following:

   (1) Detention under the law of war without trial until the end of the hostilities authorized by the Authorization for Use of Military Force.

   (2) Trial under chapter 47A of title 10, United States Code (as amended by the Military Commissions Act of 2009 (title XVIII of Public Law 111–84)).

   (3) Transfer for trial by an alternative court or competent tribunal having lawful jurisdiction.

   (4) Transfer to the custody or control of the person's country of origin, any other foreign country, or any other foreign entity.

(d) Construction—Nothing in this section is intended to limit or expand the authority of the President or the scope of the Authorization for Use of Military Force.

(e) Authorities—Nothing in this section shall be construed to affect existing law or authorities relating to the detention of United States citizens, lawful resident aliens of the United States, or any other persons who are captured or arrested in the United States.

(f) Requirement for Briefings of Congress—The Secretary of Defense shall regularly brief Congress regarding the application of the authority described in this section, including the organizations, entities, and individuals considered to be 'covered persons' for purposes of subsection (b)(2).

This provided a congressional codification of the executive branch's power 'to detain covered persons' under the 2001 AUMF. It also expanded the power, however, giving a legislative imprimatur to previous broad executive and judicial interpretations of the AUMF. The AUMF purported to cover only anyone involved in the 9/11 attacks, in language that the NDAA reproduced in subsection (b)(1) above. Yet subsection (b)(2) defined 'covered persons' to also include:

> . . . a person who was a part of or substantially supported al-Qaeda, the Taliban, or associated forces that are engaged in hostilities against the United States or its coalition partners, including any person who has committed a belligerent act or has directly supported such hostilities in aid of such enemy forces.

The NDAA did not define 'associated forces', 'a belligerent act' or 'direct support'—terms that could mean many things, including opposing wars conducted by the US government. Moreover, the Act defined the 'disposition under the law of war' to include detention by the military without trial, or transfer to a foreign country, until the 2001 AUMF was repealed.

An amendment to state that this language did not apply to Americans was voted down. Subsection (e), which was inserted instead, had no such effect because the executive branch had already successfully claimed that the 2001 AUMF alone gave it the authority to detain Padilla and, by extension, other US citizens.

A group of journalists and human rights activists, including Chris Hedges, Daniel Ellsberg, Noam Chomsky and Alexa O'Brien, sued the government, claiming that the NDAA would chill their speech and put them at risk of arrest. Hedges, a Pulitzer Prize winner, stated that his extensive work overseas—particularly in the Middle East, covering terrorist (or suspected terrorist) organisations—could cause him to be categorised as a 'covered person' who, by way of such writings, interviews and/or communications, 'substantially supported' or 'directly supported' Al Qaeda, the Taliban or 'associated forces' that are engaged in hostilities against the United States or its coalition partners.

US District Judge Katherine Forrest found section 1021(b)(2) of the NDAA to be unconstitutional and issued an injunction preventing the government from relying on it, but the injunction was stayed by the US Court of Appeals for the Second Circuit, pending appeal by the Obama administration. In July 2013, the appellate court vacated the injunction on the basis that the plaintiffs lacked legal standing to challenge the detention powers of the NDAA (*Hedges v. Obama* 724 F.3d 170 (2d Cir. 2013)). The Supreme Court declined to hear the case on 28 April 2014, leaving the Second Circuit decision intact.

Other draconian powers

During the Korean War, President Truman tested the limits of emergency presidential power by committing US forces to Korea without congressional approval. When he made orders relating to the war that effected a domestic crisis, the Supreme Court placed limits on this emergency power, but the decision protected the property interests of big business, not democratic rights.

A labour dispute over pay resulted in a national strike in the steel industry, an important producer of military material for the troops in Korea. Truman issued an executive order for the steel mills to be seized and operated. He also informed Congress that he did not need its approval, to which Congress was silent (Edelson 2013: 102). In *Youngstown Sheet & Tube Co. v. Sawyer* 343 US 579, 587 (1952), Mr. Justice Black, delivering the opinion of the Court, held in favour of the steel companies:

> Even though 'theatre of war' be an expanding concept, we cannot with faithfulness to our constitutional system hold that the Commander in Chief of the Armed Forces has the ultimate power as such to take possession of private property in order to keep labor disputes from stopping production. This is a job for the Nation's lawmakers, not for its military authorities.

Mr. Justice Jackson continued:

> His command power is not such an absolute as might be implied from that office in a militaristic system, but is subject to limitations consistent with a constitutional Republic whose law and policymaking branch is a representative Congress. The purpose of lodging dual titles in one man was to insure that the civilian would control the military, not to enable the military to subordinate the presidential office.
>
> (*Youngstown*, at 645)

Despite such admonitions, the 1950s and 1960s continued to see an expansion in the use of presidential emergency power (Edelson 2013: 117). President Nixon stretched that power to use for espionage—wiretapping, opening mail, burglary, an 'enemies list'—and claimed the courts had no power over him. In *United States v. Nixon* 418 US 683, 706 (1974), Nixon refused to comply with a subpoena issued by the Court and the Court rejected his claim to privilege (but only because there was no proof of the need to protect official secrets):

> Absent a claim of need to protect military, diplomatic, or sensitive national security secrets, we find it difficult to accept the argument that even the very important interest in confidentiality of Presidential communications is significantly diminished by production of such material for *in camera* inspection with all the protection that a district court will be obliged to provide.

Authoritarian wartime powers in Britain

In the event of war, potentially authoritarian powers can be activated in Britain, as they were in World War I and World War II. The courts have held that the government can imprison and deport British subjects and aliens in the exercise of its prerogative.

World War I

During World War I, the executive relied mainly upon statutory powers, imposed via the Defence of the Realm Act 1914 (DORA), for executive imprisonment and internment. This legislation conferred vast powers on the executive to make regulations, including to suppress opposition to the war (Head 2016: 49–50).

Regulations made under the Act were utilised for broader purposes than the war effort—in particular, to suppress industrial action and political opposition. The measures were especially applied to socialist opponents of the 'Great War', who indicted the war as an essentially capitalist conflict over markets, trade, profits and colonial possessions, suggesting that workers should reject nationalism, fraternise and unite with their fellow workers in a common struggle against the nation-based wealthy elites.

By regulation 42, it became an offence to cause mutiny, sedition or disaffection among the civilian population. This provision was used to suppress political and industrial unrest on Clydeside. A particular victim was British Socialist Party leader John MacLean, who was jailed in 1916 and again in 1918 for anti-war speeches (Ewing and Gearty 2000: 57). Maclean was initially sentenced to three years' penal servitude for allegedly making inflammatory statements against conscription and encouraging the Clyde workers to strike. At one meeting, police reported that he said: 'Workers are being made slaves to suit the bloody British capitalists, which was pure Kaiserism and Prussianism' (quoted in Ewing and Gearty 2000: 77–78).

Maclean was released after 14 months, only to be arrested again in 1918, accused of 'making statements likely to prejudice recruiting and cause mutiny and sedition among the people'. The essence of his crime was to urge workers to follow the example of the October 1917 Russian Revolution by taking control of the Glasgow city chambers, the post office and the banks. Addressing the jury, the Lord Advocate said that there was nothing in the law, as then framed, to prevent people talking about socialism, 'however inappropriate it might be, but there came a time when such discussion of social questions became seditious' (quoted in Ewing and Gearty 2000: 79–80). Maclean was sentenced to five years' jail, but released several months later, then imprisoned again before his death in 1923 (Ewing and Gearty 2000: 80).

Taken as a whole, DORA gave the civilian and military authorities vast powers to restrict civil liberties. These included: freedom of assembly and association, either by banning meetings or authorising a police presence at them; freedom of the press, by censoring or suppressing newspapers; and personal liberty, by interning or deporting those who behaved 'in a manner prejudicial to the public safety or the defence of the Realm' (Ewing and Gearty 2000: 61–62). The courts proved to be reliable enforcers of the measures, regardless of the impact on those rights and liberties traditionally regarded as enjoying the protection of the common law. A study of the emergency measures adopted in Britain found that 'there is not a single case of significance in the Law Reports of legislation passed between 1914 and 1945 to restrict personal and political liberties being restrained in its scope by the judicial power of interpretation' (Ewing and Gearty 2000: 29).

World War II

World War II again saw resort to emergency powers. Provisions included 'corruption of public morale', intention to 'foment opposition' to the war and intention to 'cause alarm or despondency', as well as wide-ranging internment powers (Ewing and Gearty 2000: 401). The House of Lords' ruling in *Liversedge v Anderson* [1942] AC 206 demonstrated the judiciary's willingness to accept the wide-ranging use of war powers, including for mass detentions without trial.

The issue in *Liversedge* arose from the internment of people suspected of being of 'hostile origin or association' under regulation 1B of the Defence (General) Regulations 1939, made under the Emergency Powers (Defence) Act 1939. After parliamentary objections to the initial form of the regulation, it was redrafted to require a minister to have a 'reasonable cause to believe' certain facts before exercising the power. This formulation was thought to impose an objective test, but, after a series of legal challenges, the Home Office declined to file affidavits to justify internments. By a majority of 4–1, the House of Lords upheld this practice, effectively interpreting 'reasonable cause' as merely requiring a belief in such a cause.

Lord Atkin dissented on the basis that some evidence was essential if the proper, objective meaning was to be given to the regulation, commenting that, on the majority's interpretation, the minister enjoyed 'an absolute power which, so far as I know, has never been given before to the executive' (*Liversedge*, at 226). Atkin commented that, in the case, he had heard arguments that 'might have been addressed acceptably to the Court of King's Bench in the time of Charles I' and that his colleagues had responded in a manner that was 'more executive minded than the executive' (*Liversedge*, at 244). Atkin's dissent was a narrow one, however: all he sought was the filing of a pro forma Home Office affidavit, of the kind he had accepted in *Greene v Secretary of State for Home Affairs* [1942] AC 284.

For World War II, the Crown also relied on the prerogative to detain aliens. The courts said that this was a lawful exercise of the prerogative and beyond the purview of the courts. In *R v Bottrill, ex parte Keuchenmesiter* [1947] 1 KB 41, the court had upheld the executive detention of a German man who had lived in England for many years and had an English wife. The court declared that, by virtue of the prerogative, the Crown had the right to intern, expel or otherwise control an alien enemy according to its discretion and that right could not be questioned in the courts.

The prerogative was further relied on in Britain during the first Gulf War (1990–91) to detain 35 Iraqis who were classified as prisoners of war (Joseph 2013: 122).

Emergency powers framework

The Civil Contingencies Act 2004 was introduced to ostensibly cover the field of emergency preparations, declarations and powers. That Act provides what scholars have described as the 'most powerful and extensive' peacetime emergency powers ever enacted (Walker and Broderick 2006: 188). It can also be invoked during times of war or military conflict.

That Act, while itself containing vast powers, did not completely replace other far-reaching legislative provisions—notably, the Emergency Powers Act 1964. The 2004 Act also alludes to the continued application of royal prerogative powers. Section 22(3) stipulates that emergency regulations can make any provision that would be possible through an Act of Parliament or the royal prerogative.

In its 2009 review of the prerogative powers, the Ministry of Justice concluded—and the government of Prime Minister Gordon Brown readily agreed—that the possibility of using the prerogative powers should remain open. On the pretext that urgent emergency scenarios could make compliance with the Act's regulation-making procedures 'impractical', the review reached the conclusion that the Act, despite its sweeping provisions, would have to be cast aside. 'In practice, therefore,' the report stated, 'the Royal prerogative might need to be relied on in place of the Civil Contingencies Act in particularly extreme and urgent circumstances' (Ministry of Justice 2009: paras 70–72).

This declaration of the need to bypass the Civil Contingencies Act 2004 was part of a wider retention of the prerogative powers to deal with both major domestic emergencies and decisions to declare war or to conduct military interventions overseas.

Section 19 of the 2004 Act empowers 'Her Majesty', by an Order in Council (in ordinary times, this means senior cabinet ministers), to issue sweeping emergency regulations in any event that 'threatens serious damage to human welfare' or 'serious damage to the environment' or 'war or terrorism, which threatens serious damage to the security of the United Kingdom'.

Emergency powers can be triggered whenever the governing authorities, acting in the name of Her Majesty in Council, are 'satisfied' that an emergency has occurred, is occurring or is about to occur. That Order can suspend, modify or override any other Act of Parliament, with the sole exception of the Human Rights Act 1998 (Walker and Broderick 2006: 44–45). Even statutes regarded as essential to civil liberties and basic constitutional rights, such as Magna Carta 1297, the Bill of Rights 1688, the Parliament Acts 1911–49 and the Representation of the People Act 1983, can be swept aside (Walker and Broderick 2006: 192).

These can only be described as police-state provisions. Regulations can be promulgated that override basic legal and democratic rights. The authorities need only 'be satisfied' regarding the appropriateness, proportionality and geographical scope of the regulations. Such a test is extremely difficult to enforce via judicial review.

Regulations can last for up to 30 days and can be renewed. They must be laid before Parliament 'as soon as is reasonably practicable' and shall lapse after seven days unless both Houses of Parliament approve them, but in the meantime their effect is immediate. Moreover, even these limited provisions would mean little if Parliament could not or did not meet.

Although the Blair government presented the Act as one concerned primarily with responding to disasters, the 2003 Queen's Speech specifically referred to terrorism, and the proposal was also driven by concerns about civil unrest, including the eruption of fuel price protests and pickets outside oil refineries in 2000 (Walker and Broderick 2006: xiii, 47). The definitions of emergency are extensive—considerably wider than the previous provisions under the 1920 Act—and allow for politically 'interventionist stances' toward potential crises (Walker and Broderick 2006: 63–76). Possible threats to 'human welfare' extend to 'damage to property' and disruption to supplies, communications or transport. No criteria are provided for the key tests of 'serious damage to human welfare' and 'war or terrorism, which threatens serious damage to the security of the United Kingdom'. 'Serious' is not defined nor is 'security'. Ministers are given powers to specify that certain situations or events are emergencies.

Once an emergency has been declared, the authorities can assume 'almost boundless power' (Walker and Broderick 2006: 161). They can, among other things, prohibit assemblies, ban movement, create offences, deploy the armed forces and confer emergency powers on any individual. There are no specific powers of arrest or detention without trial, but the Act's sponsors refused to rule out such detention, which the courts have in the past been prepared to accept, even in peacetime 'civil emergencies' (see *Attorney-General of St Christopher, Nevis and Anguilla v Reynolds* [1980] AC 637). The scope of emergency regulations, spelt out in section 22 of the Act, is so sweeping that there are virtually no restrictions on the powers that a government can assume and then enforce via the armed forces. However, as section 23(3) confirms, emergency regulations cannot require a person to perform military service or prohibit any activity in connection with a strike or other industrial action (Head and Mann 2009: 85–88).

In a 2004 briefing on the legislation, Liberty (the National Council for Civil Liberties) called it 'the most powerful piece of peacetime legislation ever proposed in the UK' and warned that 'it seeks to grant the Government unprecedented powers to make emergency regulations which are unavailable under existing laws'. Liberty expressed concern that 'it is times of emergency that citizens' fundamental rights are at greatest risk' (Liberty 2004: para. 4).

Liberty also noted that the government had shown an increased willingness to declare an emergency, citing the declaration of a 'technical' emergency following the 9/11 attacks in the United States. This declaration enabled the government to derogate from Article 5 of the European Convention on Human Rights and Fundamental Freedoms (ECHR), thereby permitting indefinite detention without trial under the Anti-Terrorism Crime and Security Act 2001 (Liberty 2004: para. 5).

Martial law and indemnities

British law also combines other legacies of the monarchy and absolutism—notably, the doctrine of martial law—with traditional recourse to such extralegal measures as the granting of indemnities to retrospectively validate unlawful repression and the invocation of rules to block legal challenges to lawless government actions (Head 2016: 71–88).

Not only does martial law remain an option that has never been conclusively repudiated by legislation or judicial rulings, but also doubts exist about whether the ordinary courts have jurisdiction to decide whether a state of disorder warrants martial law. According to one authority, legal action could be brought against the military for manifestly unreasonable conduct and possibly for unnecessary use of force against people or property, but the law is unclear (de Smith 1981: 512). In any case, the legal uncertainty is academic, because indemnity legislation would almost certainly be passed to exonerate those who acted in supposed good faith to suppress an uprising (de Smith 1981: 514). Indeed, the British Parliament passed such an Act to cover the 1920 declaration of martial law in areas of Ireland (Rowe and Whelan 1985: 200).

Repressive wartime laws in Australia

Emergency powers were adopted in Australia during both world wars, and were used to suppress socialist and anti-war opinion. One study of the World War II national security legislation pointed out that it closely resembled its World War I equivalent, as well as the similar legislation in Canada, New Zealand and Britain (Douglas 2003). The legislation provided almost boundless regulation-making powers.

World War I

The punitive use of emergency regulations against opponents of the war and conscription provoked several political confrontations during World War I. In 1915, Tom Barker, a prominent leader of International Workers of the World (IWW), was convicted of publishing posters likely to prejudice recruiting. He was charged under New South Wales state war precautions regulations. A magistrate ruled that a poster with the words, 'Workers, follow your masters, stay at home', was prejudicial to recruitment and, in effect, the magistrate sentenced Barker to 12 months' jail. Amid protests, the conviction was quashed on appeal, with the court ruling that the state regulations were invalid in a field covered by federal law. The following year Barker was convicted again—this time, under federal regulations—and his appeal was dismissed. His jailing triggered threats of IWW retaliation, including acts of sabotage, which were then cited as evidence in the 1916 seditious conspiracy trial of the Sydney Twelve. In a bid to defuse discontent, the governor-general cut Barker's sentence by nine months and he was released after four (Turner 1969: 16–17, 37–38).

The Australian High Court lent direct support to the use of the regulations to suppress dissent in a 1918 case. Ernie Judd, a member of the New South Wales Labor Council, the state's primary trade union body, was convicted under the War Precautions Act 1914–15 (Cth) for successfully moving an amendment to a Labor Council resolution on the war effort. In the wake of the 1917 Russian Revolution, Judd's amendment set out the basis of socialist opposition to the war, as well as the union movement's grievances against the conduct of the war. His amendment concluded:

[We] refuse to take part in any recruiting campaign, and call upon workers of this and all other belligerent countries to urge their respective governments to immediately secure an armistice on all fronts, and initiate negotiations for peace.

(Turner 1969: 217–18)

On appeal, the High Court unanimously rejected Judd's objection that the War Precautions Act required prosecutions to be personally authorised by the attorney-general. Despite clear words in the Act forbidding indictments other than in the name of the attorney-general, the court delivered brief judgments simply declaring that the Act left the matter in the hands of the executive government. Only Justice Isaac Isaacs offered any explanation, saying that the legislation:

. . . allowed the Executive to take steps for the safety of the Commonwealth and of the Empire which might be of a very drastic character, and the enforcement of regulations made under that Act might involve a great deal of discretion on the part of the public authority.

(*R v Judd* [1919] HCA 9, (1919) 26 CLR 168, 172)

Judd was later convicted on two further counts under the Act, for making anti-war statements during public meetings in the Sydney Domain. On one occasion, he said that the fight of the Australian working class was not in France, but 'right on the job'; on another, he invoked Christ's command, 'Thou shalt not kill' (Turner 1969: 218).

In the meantime, an even more controversial case had occurred in 1916. In what became known as the trial of the Sydney Twelve, 12 members of the syndicalist IWW were accused of setting Sydney factories, warehouses and stores alight to force the federal Labor government to drop its plans to introduce conscription. They were arrested against a backdrop of emerging disquiet over the horrific losses of lives during World War I, widespread opposition to two ultimately defeated referenda on conscription and increasing working-class militancy, which was to culminate in 1917 in a virtual general strike in New South Wales (Turner 1969: 3, 20, 90–91).

The men were originally charged with 'treason felony' for endeavouring, among other things, to 'intimidate or overawe' Parliament (Turner 1969: 36). Before their trial began, however, that charge was replaced by three counts of conspiracy to commit arson, to defeat the ends of justice and to commit seditious conspiracy (Rushton 1973: 53–54). It was widely believed in the labour movement that the men were framed or railroaded for their anti-war views and opposition to conscription. That belief was reinforced by the fact that the charges were laid in the lead-up to a referendum on conscription called by Prime Minister Billy Hughes. Hughes sought to discredit the IWW, which agitated against conscription, and hence to undermine the 'no' campaign. While the 12 men were still awaiting trial, in highly prejudicial comments, he declared: 'The IWW not only preach but they practise sabotage . . . They are to a man anti-conscriptionist' (Turner 1969: 47–48).

In this political atmosphere, a jury found seven men guilty of all three counts, four guilty of conspiracy to commit arson and seditious conspiracy, and one guilty of seditious conspiracy.

On the other side of the country, in Western Australia, seditious conspiracy charges were laid against another 12 IWW members, with the federal government apparently instigating the prosecution and footing the bill (Turner 1969: 44). In that case, there was no allegation of arson, or other specific unlawful acts (except that one defendant was charged with threatening to destroy the property of a senator); rather, the indictment accused these 12 syndicalists of conspiring to 'carry into execution an enterprise having for its object to raise discontent and disaffection amongst the subjects of our Lord the King' and to 'promote feelings of ill-will and enmity between different classes of the subjects of our said Lord the King' (Turner 1969: 45). In essence, the Crown case alleged that the IWW itself was a seditious conspiracy. The prosecution contended that the IWW advocated sedition, sabotage and other 'lawless acts'. Even more so than in the Sydney case, it was the organisation rather than the individuals that was on trial.

Ultimately, after a legal appeal and two judicial inquiries, the Sydney convictions unravelled, but not before two of the men had served five years in custody and the IWW had been effectively dismantled. After an active public campaign for the release of the Sydney Twelve, a Royal Commission was convened in 1920, which concluded that six of the men were not 'justly or rightly' convicted of any offence, while the others had been excessively punished. Ten men were released in August 1920 and two late in 1921, but they were never compensated (Turner 1969: 247–50).

The framing of the IWW had also provided the pretext for further extraordinary legislation. After the conviction and jailing of the IWW members, the *Sydney Morning Herald* called for the IWW itself to be outlawed. The issue, the newspaper declared, was not of the right to free speech of 'visionaries intent upon bring in the millennium', but of incitement to anarchy and destruction. The newspaper said that the demands of war made the task even more urgent, because IWW sedition was undermining the national solidarity needed to confront the enemy (Turner 1969: 69). Prime Minister Hughes introduced an Unlawful Associations Bill, which provided that the IWW or any other association that incited the taking of life or the destruction of property was unlawful. Hughes declared that many IWW members were foreigners, including Germans, and that the organisation was holding 'a dagger at the heart of society'. The Bill was passed within five days, creating a summary offence, punishable by six months' imprisonment, to belong to such an association (Turner 1969: 70).

A year later—after IWW members had continued their activities under different organisational names—the Unlawful Associations Act 1916 (Cth) was amended to authorise the government to declare illegal any organisation whose purposes were proscribed by the Act. Six-month sentences were added for distributing an association's propaganda or raising or contributing funds (Turner 1969: 86). Within weeks, some 80 people had been jailed, substantially destroying the IWW. According to newspaper reports, the trials were conducted with 'indecent haste', with no opportunity for the accused to deny the allegations against them. In some cases, disdaining to conceal their membership, IWW members demanded the full six months' penalty (Turner 1969: 86–89).

World War II

During World War II, wide-ranging powers were again conferred upon the executive by the National Security Act 1939–40. Section 5 authorised the governor general to make regulations for securing the public safety and the defence of the Commonwealth, and for prescribing all matters necessary or convenient for the more effectual prosecution of the war. The Australian High Court upheld the validity of section 5 in *Wishart v Fraser* [1941] HCA 8, (1941) 64 CLR 470, in which Justice Dixon emphasised the open-ended breadth of the judiciary's interpretation of wartime powers. He and fellow judges unanimously dismissed an argument that section 5 was unconstitutional because the subject matter handed over to the executive was so wide or uncertain that the legislation was not a law with respect to the defence power or any other head of legislative power in the Constitution. Justice Dixon stated:

> The defence of a country is peculiarly the concern of the Executive, and in war the exigencies are so many, so varied and so urgent that width and generality are a characteristic of the powers which it must exercise.
>
> (*Wishart v Fraser* (1941) 64 CLR 470, 484–85).

Under the National Security (General) Regulations 1939, the federal government banned communist publications, outlawed the Communist Party of Australia (CPA) and the Trotskyist Communist League of Australia, and authorised police raids of offices and homes to enforce those proscriptions by seizing documents and arresting party members. Three members of the Trotskyist movement—Jack Wishart, Gil Roper and Allan Thistlewayte—were imprisoned for up to eight months for possessing or circulating dissenting material (Greenland 1998: 96–104).

The verdict in *Wishart v Fraser* (1941) 64 CLR 470, in which Wishart challenged his conviction in the High Court, demonstrated the extent to which these powers were employed to silence and punish socialist opponents of the war. In essence, the judges unanimously upheld the imprisonment of Wishart for propagating the analysis of international Trotskyist movement Fourth International that the war was an imperialist one—that is, a war fought between the major world powers for economic and strategic supremacy—and for advocating the election of soldiers' committees to establish democratic control over the armed forces.

In another case, *Francis v Rowan* [1941] HCA 6, (1941) 64 CLR 196, the High Court unanimously overturned a magistrate's acquittal of Rowan on a charge, under the same National Security (General) Regulations, of endeavouring orally to influence public opinion in a manner likely to be prejudicial to the efficient prosecution of the war. Without a single dissent, the judges reversed the verdict of the magistrate at first instance, who had interpreted the word 'endeavour' in the Regulations as requiring a conscious intention on the part of the accused to influence public opinion in the manner that the Regulations prohibited. In other words, the magistrate had insisted on the normal criminal law requirement that the necessary intent, or *mens rea*, be proven.

Rowan's offence had been to address an anti-conscription public meeting and express a definite political opinion: that the war was being fought in the interests of the ruling capitalist elite. According to Acting Chief Justice Rich, the speech attacked 'the government, [Prime Minister Robert] Menzies and his followers'. The Acting Chief Justice quoted sections of Rowan's speech at some length, including the following excerpts:

> The men in control of this country form a minority government which is controlled by the big combines and industries and monopolies in this country, who by reason of their smoothness of tongue and suave manners have tricked the people of this country and have lulled them into a sense of false security. Also because I know that the people of this country have been tricked and robbed and forced into things by false statements and promises which have never been carried out. I consider it my duty to speak to you tonight to oppose conscription which Menzies and his followers wish to introduce into this country . . . men like Essington Lewis and other leaders of the big combines are preying upon the working class the same as the people in France and in every country in the world; the same little clique praying upon the masses.
>
> (*Francis v Rowan* (1941) 64 CLR 196, 200)

The first-instance magistrate ruled that Rowan had not endeavoured to influence public opinion in a manner prejudicial to the efficient prosecution of the war, but the High Court judges insisted that such an intent was not necessary for guilt. In the words of Williams J: 'The offence would be committed if the statements he [Rowan] made were capable of influencing public opinion in the forbidden direction irrespective of any mens rea on his part' (*Francis v Rowan*, at 204).

It was a highly political ruling. Not only did *Francis v Rowan* effectively outlaw expressions of opposition to the Menzies government, but also it prohibited reference to the economic class interests involved in the war. The judgments revealed concern that articulating anti-government and anti-capitalist sentiment could undermine public support for the war. Justice Williams found it objectionable that:

> [T]he defendant was making a number of statements calculated to create mistrust in the minds of his hearers as to the bona fides of the Government, suggesting that it was a minority government acting in the interests of one class of the community to the detriment of the general public, that it had fascist tendencies and that the army under its control would be more of a menace than an asset to the country.
>
> (*Francis v Rowan* (1941) 64 CLR 196, 205)

At the same time, Justice Williams asserted that war made necessary a different approach to civil liberties: 'In time of war the necessity to protect the safety of the realm is paramount and must take priority over individual rights' (*Francis v Rowan*, at 204). This proposition suggests that courts should allow almost unlimited power to the executive to override traditional legal principles in periods of war or other alleged emergency.

A study of the use of the World War II legislation noted that some of the behaviours covered by the offences created by the National Security (General) Regulations 1939 would also have constituted sedition (Douglas 2003). Seditious purposes under the then Crimes Act 1914 (Cth), sections 24A–24E, included exciting disaffection against British, Dominion and Australian governments. However, the emergency Regulations had several advantages for prosecutors.

- Defendants in sedition cases had a right to opt for trial by jury—a basic legal right enshrined in the Australian Constitution for indictable offences—and juries might be sympathetic to anti-war sentiment. By contrast, defendants charged under the wartime regulations were tried summarily.
- There was no need to prove that statements were actually likely to arouse disaffection; only that they were calculated to do so.
- There was no 'good faith criticism' defence under the Regulations.
- Finally, as illustrated by *Francis v Rowan*, there was no need to prove any intention to cause disaffection.

Douglas (2003) estimated that, during World War II, governments approved the prosecution of at least 69 people, primarily communists, with some pacifists, fascists and a lone Jehovah's Witness. Of these, 61 were tried and 28 were jailed. However, a wider number of arrests were made, accompanied by 'massive' police raids and the seizure of literature. The Communist Party and the Trotskyist organisations were forced to dismantle and secret their printing presses away.

Despite the severity of these measures, Douglas (2003) argued that wartime political repression was limited, with a degree of official tolerance toward anti-war opinion. However, he noted that enforcement was constrained by political considerations—most importantly, governments' need to secure the support of the labour and trade union movement. Another major factor was the Communist Party's backflip to fervently support the war effort after the Nazi invasion of the Soviet Union in June 1941, from which point onward, prosecutions were rare. Douglas (2003: 113, footnotes omitted) summarised the political sensitivities related to the trade unions as follows:

> Unions were willing to work with the government, but the price of coopera-tion was recognition of union sensitivities. Thus, union papers were treated more favourably than communist papers, notwithstanding that they some-times published very similar articles. Communist union leaders could say certain things as union leaders, which they could not say as communists. Following the banning of the CPA, planning for raids proceeded on the basis that no prominent union officials were to be targeted.

These political considerations are revealing. Far from offering any guarantee of official tolerance, they point toward the politically calculating and discriminatory character of the application of such emergency powers.

World War II wartime powers were invoked to ban communist organisations. They were banned under the National Security (Subversive Associations) Regulations 1940, relying on the defence power in the Australian Constitution. A further move to ban the Communist Party was made in 1950. In 1951, however, in what is commonly known as the *Communist Party Case*, the High Court held the Menzies government's attempt to use the defence power to justify its domestic peacetime use to ban the Party to be constitutionally invalid (*Australian Communist Party v The Commonwealth* [1951] HCA 51, (1951) 83 CLR 1).

However, in 2007, in *Thomas v Mowbray* [2007] HCA 33, the High Court, by a 5–2 majority, sanctioned the substantial use of the defence power in peacetime and for domestic purposes. The language of the majority judgments was sweeping—in relation to both the potential breadth of the defence power and the lawful capacity of the Commonwealth government to effectively define for itself the limits of the power. In a joint judgment, Gummow and Crennan JJ spoke of the defence power covering 'the defence of the realm against threats posed internally as well as by invasion from abroad by force of arms' (*Thomas v Mowbray*, at [140]).

The judges also effectively expanded the doctrine of 'judicial notice' to accept the many untested assertions about the 'war on terror' made by the federal and state governments and their security agencies, such as the Australian Security Intelligence Organisation (ASIO). Callinan J declared it to be 'blindingly obvious' that 'groups of zealots forming part of, or associated with Al Qa'ida' were 'making common cause of hatred against communities posing no threat to them' and 'planned to undertake violent, literally suicidal attacks upon even the institutions and persons of those communities' (*Thomas v Mowbray*, at [543]–[553]).

The immediate effect of the decision was to uphold the constitutionality of the 'control order' imposed on Jack Thomas, an acquitted terrorism suspect, under the provisions of the Anti-Terrorism Act (No. 2) 2005 (Cth). By implication, the ruling constitutionally validated most, if not all, of the federal anti-terrorism legislation introduced since 2002. Significantly, it also seemed to interpret the defence power widely enough to permit the internal deployment of troops, whether or not under the military call-out legislation, to pursue the 'war on terror' or deal with any other 'threats posed internally'.

By leaving the government and its agencies broad scope to define for themselves the nature of alleged terrorist threats, the decision eroded the 50-year-old principle adopted by the High Court in the 1951 *Communist Party Case* that the defence power cannot be defined or expanded unilaterally by the executive for domestic political purposes.

References

Crawford, N. 2017. 'United States budgetary costs of post-9/11 wars through FY2018: a summary of the $5.6 trillion in costs for the US wars in Iraq, Syria, Afghanistan and Pakistan, and post-9/11 Veterans Care and Homeland Security', November, http://watson.brown.edu/costsofwar/files/cow/imce/news/Costs%20of%20 U.S.%20Post-9_11%20NC%20Crawford%20FINAL%20.pdf (accessed 10 December 2017).

Daniels, R. 1993. *Prisoners without Trial: Japanese Americans in World War II.* New York: Hill & Wang.

De Smith, S. 1981. *Constitutional and Administrative Law.* 4th edn, London: Penguin/ Longmans.

Douglas, R. 2003. 'Law, war and liberty: the World War II subversion prosecutions' *Melbourne University Law Review,* 27(3): 65–115.

Edelson, C. 2013. *Emergency Presidential Power: From the Drafting of the Constitution to the War on Terror.* Madison, WI: University of Wisconsin Press.

Elsea, J., and Weed, M. 2014. *Declarations of War and Authorizations for the Use of Military Force: Historical Background and Legal Implications,* 18 April, Washington, DC: Congressional Research Service.

Ewing, K., and Gearty, C. 2000. *The Struggle for Civil Liberties: Political Freedom and the Rule of Law in Britain 1914–1945.* Oxford: Oxford University Press.

Greenland, H. 1998. *Red Hot: The Life and Times of Nick Origlass.* Sydney: Wellington Lane Press.

Gross, O., and Aolain, F. 2006. *Law in Times of Crisis: Emergency Powers in Theory and Practice.* Cambridge: Cambridge University Press.

Head, M. 2016. *Emergency Powers in Theory and Practice: The Long Shadow of Carl Schmitt.* London: Ashgate.

Head, M., and Mann, S. 2009. *Domestic Deployment of the Armed Forces: Military Powers, Law and Human Rights.* London: Ashgate.

Joseph, R. 2013. *The War Prerogative: History Reform and Constitutional Design.* Oxford: Oxford University Press.

Liberty. 2004. *Liberty's Second Reading Briefing on the Civil Contingencies Bill in the House of Lords.* London: Liberty.

Ministry of Justice. 2009. *The Governance of Britain: Review of the Executive Royal Prerogative Powers—Final Report.* London: HMSO.

Rowe, P., and Whelan, C. (eds). 1985. *Military Intervention in Democratic Societies.* London: Croom Helm.

Rushton, P. 1973. 'The trial of the Sydney Twelve: the original charge', *Labour History,* 25: 53–57.

Schwarz, J. 2018. 'New bipartisan bill could give any president the power to imprison any U.S. citizens in military detention forever', *The Intercept,* 2 May, https://theintercept. com/2018/05/01/ndaa-2018-aumf-detention/ (accessed 15 May 2018).

Thompson, G. 2010. 'Guantanamo and the struggle for due process of law', *Rutgers Law Review,* 63: 1195–213.

Turner, I. 1969. *Sydney's Burning: An Australian Political Conspiracy.* Melbourne: Heinemann.

Walker, C., and Broderick, J. 2006. *The Civil Contingencies Act 2004: Risk, Resilience and the Law in the United Kingdom.* Oxford: Oxford University Press.

Watson Institute. 2017. 'The Costs of War Project', https://watson.brown.edu/cost sofwar/files/cow/imce/papers/2017/Costs%20of%20War%2C%20Brown%20 University%20%281%29.pdf (accessed 15 September 2018).

8 Contemporary preparations for wartime measures

In each of the three countries reviewed in this book, plans and blueprints have been prepared for future major wars. These include proposals based on imposing the 'law of war', for both international and domestic use, and expanding powers to deploy military forces domestically to deal with anticipated civil disorder. It is not possible, in this volume, to research and probe the full scope of such preparations. Undoubtedly, classified and other secret plans exist. However, the following review of some of the published documents provides an idea of the scale and impact of the preparations being made.

The Pentagon's *Law of War Manual*

The US Department of Defense's *Law of War Manual*, released in June 2015 and periodically updated since, insists that the law of war overrides other international and domestic law, as well as the US Constitution.

The *Manual* notes: 'Promulgating a DoD-wide manual on the law of war has been a long-standing goal of DoD lawyers' (US Department of Defense 2015: v). The document, which 'reflects many years of labor and expertise', applies to the entire US Department of Defense (DoD). This covers the US Army, Navy, Air Force, Marine Corps, four national intelligence agencies, including the National Security Agency (NSA), and numerous other departments and agencies, totalling 2.13 million personnel on active duty and 1.1 million in reserve. The *Manual* supersedes various policy documents that had accumulated piecemeal within different sections of the military and intelligence agencies.

The *Manual* was prepared, at very senior levels, by a 'Law of War Working Group', which is:

> . . . chaired by a representative of the DoD General Counsel and includes representatives of the Judge Advocates General of the Army, Navy, and Air Force; the Staff Judge Advocate to the Commandant of the Marine Corps; the offices of the General Counsels of the Military Departments; and the Legal Counsel to the Chairman of the Joint Chiefs of Staff.
> (US Department of Defense 2015: v–vi)

The *Law of War Manual* apparently reflects the views of the military authorities in Britain, Australia and other US allies. It states that it 'benefited from the participation of officers from the United Kingdom's Royal Air Force and the Australian Royal Air Force on exchange assignments with the US Air Force', continuing: 'In addition, military lawyers from Canada, the United Kingdom, New Zealand, and Australia reviewed and commented on a draft of the manual in 2009 as part of a review that also included comments from distinguished scholars' (US Department of Defense 2015: v).

The *Manual* states: '[T]he authority to take actions under the law of war would be viewed as emanating from the State's rights as a sovereign entity rather than from any particular instrument of international law' (US Department of Defense 2015: 14). In other words, the United States can brush aside treaties and conventions and other 'instruments of international law'—such as the Geneva Convention of 1949—while still claiming to adhere to its own version of international law.

This defies the opening statement at the post-war Nuremberg trials of the Nazis, in which US Chief Prosecutor Robert Jackson characterised the Nazi regime as a monstrous criminal enterprise—a giant illegal conspiracy that invoked 'law' in only the most tendentious, cynical and self-serving manner. The defendants, Jackson declared:

> . . . are surprised that there is any such thing as law. These defendants did not rely on any law at all. Their program ignored and defied all law . . . International Law, natural law, German law, any law at all, was to these men simply a propaganda device to be invoked when it helped and to be ignored when it would condemn what they wanted to do.
>
> (IMT, Nuremberg 1947: 98–102)

These words apply equally to the Pentagon's *Manual.* It explicitly gives the Pentagon a green light to repudiate, at any future time, the principles it ostensibly lays down. Its authors write that it does not 'preclude the Department from subsequently changing its interpretation of the law' (US Department of Defense 2015: 1).

Quoting a 1920 legal treatise, originally authored by US Army Colonel William Winthrop and entitled *Military Law and Precedents*, the *Manual* states that the law of war can supersede the US Constitution:

> By the term LAW OF WAR is intended that branch of International Law which prescribes the rights and obligations of belligerents, or—more broadly—those principles and usages which, in time of war, define the status and relations not only of enemies—whether or not in arms—but also of persons under military government or martial law and persons simply resident or being upon the theatre of war, and which authorizes their trial and punishment when offenders. Unlike Military Law Proper, the Law of War in this country is not a formal written code, but consists mainly of general rules derived from International Law, supplemented by acts and orders of the military power and a few legislative provisions. In general it is quite independent of the ordinary law. 'On the actual theatre of military operations,' as

is remarked by a learned judge, 'the ordinary laws of the land are superseded by the laws of war. The jurisdiction of the civil magistrate is there suspended, and military authority and force are substituted.' Finding indeed its original authority in the war powers of Congress and the Executive, and thus constitutional in its source, the Law of War may, in its exercise, *substantially supersede for the time even the Constitution itself*—as will be hereinafter indicated.

(US Department of Defense 2015: 10, emphasis added)

Within this pseudo-legal framework, the 'law of war' is an independent source of legal authority that overrides key democratic rights and sanctions arbitrary rule by the military. The *Manual* states: 'Although the law of war is generally viewed as "prohibitive law," in some respects, especially in the context of domestic law, the law of war may be viewed as permissive or even as a source of authority' (US Department of Defense 2015: 14). According to the Pentagon, the law of war is the exception to the general 'law of peacetime':

> An issue that often confronts law of war practitioners is the relationship of the law of war to other bodies of law, especially when rules in those bodies of law may appear to conflict with rules reflected in the law of war. These apparent conflicts are often resolved by considering the principle that the law of war is the *lex specialis* governing armed conflict [and], as such, is the controlling body of law with regard to the conduct of hostilities and the protection of war victims.
>
> (US Department of Defense 2015: 8–9)

Echoes of Nazi theories

This doctrine resembles that of German Weimar Republic theorist and Nazi 'crown jurist' Carl Schmitt. Under Schmitt's infamous 'state of exception' doctrine, in conditions of a national emergency, the executive is permitted to override democratic protections and disregard the rule of law. Under this doctrine, democratic rights are not formally abrogated; they are simply suspended indefinitely.

Schmitt's *Political Theology*, published in 1922, asserted in its opening statement: 'Sovereign is he who decides on the exception' (Schmitt 1985: 5). He insisted: 'It is precisely the exception that makes relevant the subject of sovereignty, that is, the whole question of sovereignty (Schmitt 1985: 6). In effect, Schmitt's theory of exception embraced a sovereign dictatorship: 'What characterises an exception is principally unlimited authority, which means the suspension of the entire existing order' (Schmitt 1985: 12).

More than that, the sovereign dictator could overturn and transform the legal order, in whole or part. The norm became subservient to the exception, reversing the relationship between the two. The exception 'cannot be circumscribed factually and made to conform to a preformed law' (Schmitt 1985: 6). Indeed, Schmitt (1985: 15) eliminated the notion of the normal and replaces it with the exception: 'The rule proves nothing; the exception proves everything: It confirms not only the rule but also its existence, which derives only from the exception.'

Schmitt argued that every legal norm presupposed a normal and ordinary state of affairs, and could be applied only as long as that normalcy continued. He insisted that '[t]his effective normal situation is not a mere "superficial presupposition" that a jurist can ignore; that situation belongs precisely to [the norm's] immanent validity', and that, '[f]or a legal order to make sense, a normal situation must exist' (Schmitt 1985: 12–13). Crises undermine this factual basis and undermine the foundations needed for ordinary norms: 'There exists no norm that is applicable to chaos' (Schmitt 1985: 13).

In practice, the sovereign dictator had unfettered discretion about both whether an exception existed and what countermeasures ought to be taken in response. These unlimited and indivisible powers were exercisable only in exceptional cases, but the logical outcome of Schmitt's model was that the dictator's powers were never turned off. Schmitt (1985: 6) regarded contemporary politics as a permanent state of crisis: at any time, without warning, there could be a 'danger to the existence of the state' (see also Head 2016: 122–23).

Under fascism, the political logic of the conceptions advanced by Schmitt, a virulent anti-communist, became clearer. Having asserted that rapid changes in the political situation rendered any legal system built on fixed legal codes unstable, he justified permanently in-built emergency powers. Schmitt supported Hitler's continual suspension of the legal constitutional order during the Third Reich, first with the decree of 28 February 1933 on the Reichstag fire, which was falsely attributed to communists, then with the suspension being renewed every four years.

The Nazi-controlled Reichstag passed 'enabling' legislation declaring that the executive had the power to make laws. The Act, referred to as 'The Act to Relieve the Distress of the People and the Reich', cemented dictatorial power in Germany under Hitler. In line with his previously expressed legal opinions, Schmitt defended the enabling legislation in the *Deutsche Juristen Zeitung*, maintaining that the executive prerogative was unlimited at a time of national crisis (Neumann 1942).

Schmitt's doctrine also supported Hitler's claim of supreme personal authority, which was a logical extension of his assertion in 1922 that the sovereign 'decides on the state of exception', and Schmitt (1985: 10) maintained that 'like every other order the legal order rests on a decision and not a norm'. Sovereignty itself was based on decision and not legality. There could be no 'normative' regulation of exceptional situations.

As the Nazis consolidated power, Schmitt propounded theories in support of the *Fuhrerprinzip*—the leader principle (Scheuerman 1997: 1753). He claimed that the Fuhrer was the highest judge in the nation, from whom there lay no appeal. The leader was the embodiment of the people's will and therefore, Schmitt claimed in 1934, 'law is the plan and the will of the leader' (quoted in Head 2016: 17).

The Pentagon *Manual* invokes Schmitt's 'state of exception' theory in all but name. Having claimed that the law of war is a 'special' discipline of law, as opposed to a 'general' discipline, it states that 'the special rule overrides the general law' (US Department of Defense 2015: 9).

The *Manual* continues: 'Underlying this approach is the fact that the law of war is firmly established in customary international law as a well-developed body of law that is separate from the principles of law generally applicable in peace' (US Department of Defense 2015: 10). The implication is that, during wartime, the United States' vast military establishment is a 'separate', independent branch of government, subject to its own rules and accountable to no one.

Despite references to the war powers of Congress and the executive under the US Constitution, the Pentagon's conceptions are the opposite of the framework envisioned by the framers of the Constitution. The Declaration of Independence, in its list of grievances against the British monarch, charges that the king 'affected to render the Military independent of and superior to the Civil power'.

'Human rights treaties', according to the Pentagon, are 'primarily applicable to the relationship between a State and individuals in peacetime' (US Department of Defense 2015: 22). Therefore, in 'wartime'—including the 'war on terror' of indefinite scope and duration—human rights treaties no longer apply.

This formula would allow the Pentagon to override more than only human rights treaties. The authors of the *Manual* include the Bill of Rights and other guarantees of civil liberties in the category of laws that apply in 'peacetime' only. Their arguments justify suspending the Bill of Rights altogether as a 'peacetime' law that is superseded for the duration of the 'war on terror'.

Global implications

The Pentagon's *Manual* asserts powers to override international law in the conduct of war itself. For example, regarding the killing of civilians, the document states: 'Civilians may not be made the object of attack, unless they take direct part in hostilities' (US Department of Defense 2015: 128). But it then introduces a caveat:

> Civilians may be killed incidentally in military operations; however, the expected incidental harm to civilians may not be excessive in relation to the anticipated military advantage from an attack, and feasible precautions must be taken to reduce the risk of harm to civilians during military operations.
>
> (US Department of Defense 2015: 128)

In other words, it is acceptable to kill civilians if, on balance, the expected 'military advantage' outweighs the harm to civilians. This effectively makes the rule against killing civilians meaningless.

The *Manual* does not state that the killing of civilians is prohibited per se; rather, it indicates that 'feasible precautions' should be taken to 'avoid' civilian casualties, which should not be 'excessive' or 'unreasonable'. However, the *Manual* defines 'feasible precautions' as merely 'those that are practicable or practically possible, taking into account all circumstances ruling at the time, including humanitarian and military considerations' (US Department of Defense 2015: 190).

The document gives an example:

> [I]f a commander determines that taking a precaution would result in operational risk (i.e., a risk of failing to accomplish the mission) or an increased risk of harm to their own forces, then the precaution would not be feasible and would not be required.
>
> (US Department of Defense 2015: 191)

This provides wide scope for killing civilians if a military leader decides that failing to do so would be an 'operational risk'.

Similar assertions are found throughout the *Manual*. In a section setting forth the Pentagon's authority as an 'Occupying Power', it states:

> [F]or the purposes of security, an Occupying Power may establish regulation of any or all forms of media (e.g., press, radio, television) and entertainment (e.g., theater, movies), of correspondence, and of other means of communication. For example, an Occupying Power may prohibit entirely the publication of newspapers that pose a threat to security, or it may prescribe regulations for the publication or circulation of newspapers of other media for the purpose of fulfilling its obligations to restore public order.
>
> (US Department of Defense 2015: 759–60)

A footnote includes the caveat that 'this sub-section focuses solely on what is permitted under the law of war and does not address possible implications of censorship under the First Amendment of the Constitution'—but elsewhere, as discussed above, the *Manual* postulates that the law of war can supersede the Constitution.

Likewise, according to the *Manual*, 'Detaining Powers' may segregate detainees in prison camps based on racial and ethnic criteria: 'Detainees may be segregated into camps or camp compounds according to their nationality, language, and customs, and the Detaining Power may use other criteria to segregate detainees for administrative, security, intelligence, medical, or law enforcement purposes' (US Department of Defense 2015: 498).

US military authorities are empowered to carry out mass resettlement of populations for 'imperative military reasons'. Under the heading 'Displacement of the Civilian Population', the *Manual* states: 'The Occupying Power may undertake total or partial evacuation of a given area if required for the security of the population or for imperative military reasons' (US Department of Defense 2015: 778).

The protocols outlined in the *Manual* for enforcing the law of war and establishing the legality of military orders recall the doctrine asserted by the main defendants at the Nuremberg Tribunal: that they were 'just following orders'. In contradiction to the principles upheld at Nuremberg, the *Manual* instructs subordinates to 'presume' that commands are lawfully issued. US military personnel are instructed and trained to regard orders emanating from the command unit as legal by default:

Subordinates are not required to screen the orders of superiors for questionable points of legality, and may, absent specific knowledge to the contrary, presume that orders have been lawfully issued.

(US Department of Defense 2015: 1058)

Citing Winthrop's 1920 treatise *Military Law and Precedents*, a footnote declares:

Except in such instances of palpable illegality, which must be of rare occurrence, the inferior should presume that the order was lawful and authorized and obey it accordingly, and in obeying it can scarcely fail to be held justified by a military court . . .

(US Department of Defense 2015: 1058, fn)

Domestic implications

The *Manual* is chiefly concerned with asserting the US military's powers in war theatres and in countries occupied by the United States. It says little about the domestic application of its doctrines. However, it insists that the law of war can also override domestic law and it proposes that any breach of a law of war obligation by a member of the armed forces would be dealt with by military institutions, not civilian courts:

The specific legal force of a law of war rule under US domestic law may depend on whether that rule takes the form of a self-executing treaty, non-self-executing treaty, or customary international law. Longstanding DoD policy has been to require DoD personnel to comply with the law of war obligations of the United States. Even if a violation of a rule is not directly punishable under US law, a variety of tools in US domestic law may be used to enforce a law of war obligation of the United States. For example, a violation of a law of war obligation may be made punishable through implementation of the obligation in military instructions, regulations, and procedures.

(US Department of Defense 2015: 38)

Military callout powers

Since the opening years of the 21st century, governments in the United States, Britain and Australia have adopted new powers to deploy the military internally, overturning long-standing precedents against the domestic mobilisation of the armed forces. Although mostly introduced under the cover of combating terrorism, the provisions permit wider use of the military to put down unrest.

In the United States, the Bush administration of 2001–09 initiated reviews of the Posse Comitatus Act of 1878, which restricts domestic use of the military. The British Civil Contingencies Act 2004 empowered the British government to deploy the defence forces in broadly defined 'emergencies'. In Australia, the

Sydney Olympics Games in 2000 provided the initial rationale for legislation giving the federal government explicit and expanded powers to call out troops to deal with 'domestic violence'.

United States

The terrorist attacks of 11 September 2001 (9/11) provided the pretext for significant changes to the military–civil relationship in the United States. This included the establishment of the Northern Command (a Pentagon command dedicated solely to domestic security), the staging of internal war game exercises and the deployment of federal troops for major political events, such as Democratic and Republican national conventions and presidential inaugurations.

In 2006, President George W. Bush signed into law the Department of Defense Authorization Act for Fiscal Year 2007, which substantially eroded the Posse Comitatus Act of 1878—a long-standing congressional prohibition on the use of the military for domestic policing. The 2007 legislation amended the Insurrection Act of 1807 to permit the president to 'employ the armed forces . . . to restore public order and enforce the laws of the United States' in the event not only of 'insurrection, domestic violence, unlawful combination or conspiracy', but also of 'natural disaster, epidemic, or other serious public health emergency, terrorist attack or incident, or other condition', in which civilian authorities are 'incapable of maintaining public order' and such violence 'opposes or obstructs the execution of the laws of the United States' (10 USC §333). The latter phrase could cover many forms of political dissent or industrial disruption.

Following considerable opposition, the 2007 amendment was repealed by the National Defense Authorization Act for Fiscal Year 2008. However, the repeal was accompanied by measures to upgrade the status of the National Guard Bureau and to strengthen the relationship between it and the Northern Command (Leahy 2008). Another measure adopted in 2007, the National Security and Homeland Security Presidential Directive (NSPD 51/HSPD-20), permits the President to declare an emergency, which declaration would establish extraordinary powers for the president and vice-president, creating a non-constitutional form of government (Office of the Press Secretary 2007).

In 2005, the *Washington Post* reported that the Pentagon had developed its first ever war plans for operations within the continental United States, in which terrorist attacks would be used as the justification for imposing martial law on cities, regions or the entire country. A total of 15 potential crisis scenarios were outlined, starting with 'low-end', which the report described as 'relatively modest crowd-control missions', in which the military would deploy a quick-reaction force of as many as 3,000 troops. The *Post* said that military lawyers had studied the legal implications of such deployments, which risked coming into conflict with the Posse Comitatus Act (Staff and agencies 2005).

Constitutional presidential authority has been asserted to provide a broad basis for the deployment of the military under the banner of homeland security.

Particularly since 2001, the White House has asserted that the executive powers of a president and their position as commander-in-chief support wide-ranging exceptions to the Posse Comitatus Act.

Overall, the courts have failed to enunciate a wider constitutional principle against military intervention, even in the context of the Posse Comitatus Act, in which the judges have generally avoided any examination of its possible constitutional underpinnings (Doyle 2000: 13–14). Thus, in *United States v. Walden* 490 F.2d 372 (4th Cir. 1974), at 376, the court said 'we do not find it necessary to interpret relatively unexplored sections of the Constitution in order to determine whether there might be constitutional objection to the use of the military to enforce civilian laws'.

It therefore seems that military action must violate one of the explicit constitutional prohibitions or guarantees, such as *habeas corpus*, the right to jury trial, freedom of expression, and freedom from unreasonable searches and seizures, before courts will object. This means that a president has substantial leeway, both as chief executive, charged with seeing that laws are faithfully executed, and as commander-in-chief, to mobilise the armed forces.

The Supreme Court has made it clear that the president does not require express congressional or statutory authorisation to exercise such powers. If an emergency threatens the freedom of interstate commerce, transportations of the mails or some other federal government responsibility, the president may call upon 'the army of the Nation, and all its militia ... to brush away the obstructions' (*In re Debs* 158 US 564 (1895), 581).

Such rulings have left the way open for increasingly aggressive assertions of presidential, executive and prerogative powers to use military personnel and resources against civilians, flying in the face of the clear intent of the US Constitution. In effect, the role of commander-in-chief has been transformed from a guarantor of civilian supremacy over the military to an instrument for utilising the armed forces against civil unrest and political dissent.

US Department of Defense regulations assert another 'constitutional' exception to the Posse Comitatus Act, founded on the 'inherent right of the US government ... to ensure the preservation of public order and to carry out governmental operations ... by force, if necessary'. The Civil Disturbance Statutes (10 USC §§331–35) allow the president to call up the armed forces and the National Guard (state militia) to suppress challenges to the political order, including insurrections, 'domestic violence', unlawful obstructions, combinations or assemblages and 'rebellion against the authority of the United States'.

The DoD Directive 3025.12, 'Military Assistance for Civil Disturbances (MACDIS)', provides for far-ranging use of the military against civil unrest:

> The President is authorized by the Constitution and laws of the United States to employ the Armed Forces of the United States to suppress insurrections, rebellions, and domestic violence under various conditions and circumstances. Planning and preparedness by the Federal Government and the Department of Defense for civil disturbances are important due to the potential severity of

the consequences of such events for the Nation and the population . . . The President has additional powers and responsibilities under the Constitution of the United States to ensure that law and order are maintained.

(US Department of Defense 1994: 3).

Directive 3025.12 also states that: 'Under reference (r), the terms "major disaster" and "emergency" are defined substantially by action of the President in declaring that extant circumstances and risks justify Presidential implementation of the legal powers in those statutes.'

Even greater authoritarian provisions have been introduced. The National Security Presidential and Homeland Directive (NSPD 51/HSPD-20) was promulgated in 2007. In the event of a 'catastrophic emergency', which the president can declare without congressional approval, NSPD 51 would institute virtual martial law under the authority of the White House and the Department of Homeland Security. It would suspend constitutional government under the provisions of 'Continuity in Government', leaving extraordinary powers in the hands of the president and vice-president. 'Catastrophic emergency' is loosely defined as 'any incident, regardless of location, that results in extraordinary levels of mass casualties, damage, or disruption severely affecting the U.S. population, infrastructure, environment, economy, or government functions'; 'Continuity of Government' is defined as 'a coordinated effort within the Federal Government's executive branch to ensure that National Essential Functions continue to be performed during a Catastrophic Emergency'(Head 2016: 178–79).

Britain

During 2004, legislation was adopted that potentially expands the scope for domestic military intervention in the name of responding to emergencies. The Civil Contingencies Act 2004 partly replaced the emergency powers and civil defence legislation (Walker and Broderick 2006). It empowers 'Her Majesty', via an Order in Council, to issue sweeping emergency regulations in any event that 'threatens serious damage to human welfare' or 'war or terrorism, which threatens serious damage to the security of the United Kingdom'. These regulations can, among other things, 'enable the Defence Council to authorise the deployment of Her Majesty's armed forces'. The powers can be triggered whenever the governing authorities—namely, Her Majesty in Council—are 'satisfied' that an emergency has occurred, is occurring or is about to occur. Emergency regulations can even suspend, modify or override any other Act of Parliament, with the sole exception of the Human Rights Act 1998 (Walker and Broderick 2006: 63–80, 153–88).

During the debate on the Civil Contingencies Act 2004, the government rejected, without argument, proposals to clarify the military's role by means of statute. The government argued that a case-by-case approach was needed and that the government was already sufficiently accountable to Parliament (Walker and Broderick 2006: 44–45). The end result is that ill-defined and extensive prerogative and common-law powers to call out the armed forces continue to exist, augmented by the 2004 legislation.

Government and military policy assumes that considerable powers exist to mobilise armed troops internally to deal with a variety of threats to 'public safety' or 'order'. The 2005 Ministry of Defence document, *Operations in the UK: The Defence Contribution to Resilience*, set out policy guidelines for military aid to the civil power (MACP):

> Based under common law, MACP is the provision of military assistance (armed if appropriate) to the Civil Power in its maintenance of law, order and public safety, using specialist capabilities or equipment, in situations beyond the capability of the Civil Power.
>
> (Ministry of Defence 2005: 4–1)

According to the guidelines, the legal basis for instructing Armed Forces personnel to provide MACP in the UK can be one, or a combination, of the following.

- Section 2 of the Emergency Powers Act 1964 (plus the Emergency Powers (Amendment) Act (Northern Ireland) 1964) enables the Defence Council to issue instructions to undertake 'work of urgent national importance'.
- Part 2 of the Civil Contingencies Act 2004 empowers the Queen or a senior minister, in particular circumstances, to issue emergency regulations, which can in turn enable the Defence Council to deploy the armed forces.
- A common-law tenet indicates that citizens should provide reasonable support to the police if requested to do so. All members of the armed forces have a duty to provide the support normally expected of the ordinary citizen. The same common-law tenet enables a defence minister to direct the armed forces, on a case-by-case basis, to provide specialist support to the police.
- Queen's regulations place an additional duty on military commanders to act on their own responsibility without a request by a civil agency where, 'in very exceptional circumstances, a grave and sudden emergency has arisen, which in the opinion of the Commander demands his immediate intervention to protect life or property' (Ministry of Defence 2005: 4–3).

Thus the guidelines assume or assert that, alongside specific statutory provisions, there are potentially far-reaching common-law and prerogative or executive powers to justify armed interventions. These can be invoked to deal with 'a varying range of criminal and malicious activities'. The request procedures envisage MACP operations for criminal investigations and major events (Ministry of Defence 2005: 4–2, 4B-2).

Significantly, the document sets out a long list of authorities considered to be a 'civil power' that can ask for military aid. A 'civil power' is loosely defined as a 'civil authority that has constitutional or statutory responsibility for the maintenance of law and order'. The civil powers are said to include not only government ministers and police forces, but also the security and intelligence services, Government Communications Headquarters (GCHQ), the customs, coastguard and serious crimes agencies, and maritime, rail and air accident investigation branches.

The Ministry of Defence suggests that the Emergency Powers Act and the Civil Contingencies Act 'provide a stronger basis for' MACP activity than the common law. It insists that the common law imposes a duty on every citizen, including service personnel, to assist in the enforcement of law and order when requested, where it is reasonable to do so, and that this requirement forms the 'main basis for the MACP mechanism'. However, the guidelines state that this duty is 'difficult to formulate and cannot be relied upon in all circumstances to provide a legal basis for a response, especially if commanders use it without Defence Council authorisation' (Ministry of Defence 2005: 4–2).

Australia

In Australia, legislation was introduced in 2000, and extended in 2006, giving federal governments and the chief of the Australian Defence Force (ADF) explicit peacetime powers to call out the troops if 'domestic violence is occurring or is likely to occur' that 'would be likely to affect Commonwealth interests' or to require the protection of a state or territory (Defence Act 1903 (Cth), ss 51A–Y).

'Domestic violence' is a vague, anachronistic and seemingly incongruous term, which in contemporary parlance normally refers to violence in the home. Although the expression is taken from section 119 of the Australian Constitution, it is defined neither there nor in the Defence Act or its regulations. No judicial definition exists either. Likewise, there is nothing in the law about how grave or widespread 'domestic violence' must be before the ADF is mobilised. Enormous discretion has thus been placed in the hands of the government and the ADF itself to intervene against civil unrest (Head 2009: 9).

Calling out the military onto the streets overturns a centuries-old principle, derived from the overthrow of the absolute monarchy in Britain, that militates against the use of the armed forces against civilians domestically (Head 2009: 10–11).

The Australian population was last confronted by heavily armed soldiers on the streets in 1978. The Fraser government seized upon a still-unexplained Sydney Hotel bomb incident to place 1,500 armed troops, with armoured personnel carriers and helicopters, along a major highway on Sydney's outskirts and in the nearby town of Bowral (Head 2009: 49–55).

The original call-out legislation passed in 2000 limited deployments to where the government alleged that a danger of 'domestic violence' existed, which required the protection of 'Commonwealth interests' or the protection of a state or territory where the state or territory could not, or was unlikely to be able to, protect itself (Defence Act 1903 (Cth), ss 51A–C).

Whatever doubts remain about the scope of 'domestic violence', the further amendments to the Defence Act adopted in 2006 permit the Australian Air Force and Navy, as well as the Army, to be mobilised more broadly and to deal routinely with incidents, including any alleged act or danger of terrorism, and threats to physical property, judged by ministers to be 'critical infrastructure' (section 51CB(2)). According to the Explanatory Memorandum attached to the legislation, the amended Act would apply to 'mobile terrorist incidents', allowing for military mobilisations under the broad banner of combating terrorist acts (Head 2009: 18–21).

The counterterrorism legislation passed since 2001 defines terrorism widely. A 'terrorist act' includes anything done 'with the intention of advancing a political, religious or ideological cause' and with the intention of 'coercing, or influencing by intimidation' any government (including a foreign government) or 'intimidating the public or a section of the public', if the act causes death, 'serious harm' to a person, 'serious damage to property' or 'serious risk to the health or safety' of a section of the public, or 'seriously interferes with' an electronic, information, financial or transport system (Criminal Code 1995 (Cth), art. 100.1). This definition can cover many traditional forms of political protest, such as mass demonstrations, blockades and picket lines (Head 2002: 673). While the definition exempts 'advocacy, protest, dissent or industrial action', that exemption is substantially nullified by the proviso that the action must not be intended to cause physical harm to a person, or to 'create a serious risk to the health or safety of the public or a section of the public'.

The procedures for calling out the ADF have been expedited so that, if satisfied that a 'sudden and extraordinary emergency' exists, the prime minister or the two other 'authorising ministers' (the defence minister and the attorney-general) can give the order, which does not need to be in writing (Defence Act 1903, s 51CA). Alternatively, one authorising minister, together with the deputy prime minister, foreign affairs minister or treasurer, can make the order (s 51CA(2)). In addition, standing orders can be issued for the activation of the ADF whenever the chief of the armed forces deems it necessary (s 51AB). Alternatively, authorising ministers can ask the governor-general to make a written call-out order (s 51A) (Head 2009: 18–21, 100–21).

As a result, it is now possible for the ADF to be called out whenever a federal government considers that a danger of 'domestic violence' exists that requires the protection of 'Commonwealth interests' or 'critical infrastructure' or a state or territory. The prime minister or two other 'authorising ministers' can, in the event of a 'sudden and extraordinary emergency', call out the ADF by making a simple telephone call, without a written order. Alternatively, standing orders can be issued for the activation of the ADF whenever the chief of the defence force deems it necessary.

Once deployed, military personnel have extraordinary powers. They will be authorised, among other things, to shoot down aircraft, to sink ships, to use deadly force, to interrogate civilians, to issue orders, to enter and search premises, and to seize documents. Potentially lethal force can be used where an ADF member considers it necessary 'on reasonable grounds' to protect themselves or another person, or any infrastructure that the government designates as 'critical' (Defence Act 1903, s 51T(2A). These provisions raise the spectre of soldiers— who are, after all, specifically trained to shoot to kill—killing innocent civilians.

Citizens will have no right to refuse to answer questions or not to hand over material on the grounds of self-incrimination. In such circumstances, they can be jailed for non-compliance (s 51SO). Similar powers have been given to the intelligence and police agencies where people are detained without trial under the counterterrorism laws passed since 2002—such as under Australian Security Intelligence Organisation Act 1979 (Cth), s 34G—but their extension to the military raises even greater issues, given the lethal weaponry available to the armed forces, which may potentially be used to enforce compliance.

Under the 2006 amendments, all of the ADF powers are protected by a defence of 'superior orders', which exempt ADF members from criminal liability, except if the order they obeyed was 'manifestly unlawful' (Defence Act 1903, s 51WB). Furthermore, any criminal prosecutions will be handled by federal authorities under federal law, overriding state laws (s 51WA) (Head 2009: 100–21).

The turn toward the wider domestic engagement of the ADF began before 9/11 and the 'war on terror'. The Sydney Olympic Games in 2000 provided the initial rationale for call-out legislation. Both major parties cited the danger of a terrorist incident at the Games to justify the swift passage of the legislation, without any significant public or parliamentary debate. Six years later, the Melbourne Commonwealth Games became the pretext for the 2006 amendments. No specific terrorist threats were reported to either event and no terrorist acts occurred. Nonetheless, the new powers have remained, without any sunset clauses.

Since the 9/11 terrorist attacks, the declaration of a 'war on terror' and the wars in Afghanistan and Iraq, aspects of Australian society have been increasingly militarised. Thousands of soldiers have been mobilised, on alert, for major sporting events such as the Sydney 2000 Olympic Games, the Rugby World Cup 2003 and the Melbourne 2006 Commonwealth Games. Naval vessels have been dispatched to repel asylum seekers, with powers to fire on boats or to transport their passengers to remote islands. Frequent anti-terrorism exercises have been conducted in urban environments, involving heavily armed troops alongside police and intelligence officers. Deployments have been conducted against civilian populations in Afghanistan, Iraq, the Solomon Islands and East Timor (Head 2009: 77–94).

Domestically, the armed forces have been used in highly publicised shows of strength, including air force jets and helicopters flying overhead during major political events such as the 2002 Commonwealth Heads of Government Meeting at Coolum, Queensland, and US President Bush's visit to Australia in 2003. These operations have sought to condition public opinion to accept such military interventions, as well as to test out methods for combating eruptions of social and political discontent (Head 2009: 11–13).

In July 2017, the federal government announced a review of the military call-out powers, stating that they were no longer adequate. A joint media release by Prime Minister Malcolm Turnbull and Defence Minister Marise Payne proposed to remove a provision in the Defence Act that limited the call-out power. That provision required the government to assert that the supposed threat of 'domestic violence' is beyond the capacity of a state or territory government and its police and other security forces, and specified that a state or territory government must request the military call-out.

'Under extraordinary circumstances' the federal government would not need to wait for an invitation from a state or territory government to send in troops. According to the press release:

The Government will strengthen Part IIIAAA of the Defence Act to remove some constraints in the provisions to 'call out' the ADF to assist states and territories.

- This will include the removal of the provision that currently limits states and territories from asking for ADF support and specialist military skills until their capability or capacity has been exceeded.
- The Government will also make changes to the Act to make it easier for Defence to support the police response, such as the ability to prevent suspected terrorists from leaving the scene of an incident.

(Department of Defence Ministers 2017)

The two ministers said that Special Air Service (SAS) and other special forces commandos would provide 'specialised training' to state and territory law enforcement agencies, while ADF units also would be 'pre-positioned' to assist police forces (Department of Defence Ministers 2017).

Nearly a year later, in June 2018, the government tabled the Defence Amendment (Call out of the Australian Defence Force) Bill 2018, to further expand the military call-out provisions. The Bill proposed that federal government ministers should be able to swiftly call out SAS commandos and other military forces, as well as to grant them 'shoot to kill' powers, to put down riots and protests.

The government said the measures were mainly intended to deal with terrorist incidents—but the powers extend far beyond terrorism. Attorney-General Christian Porter told journalists that the military could, for example, be used to restore order in cases of 'widespread rioting' (Tillett 2018).

The legislation would hand almost limitless power to the prime minister or two other 'authorising ministers' to mobilise the armed forces for domestic purposes. The only requirement would be that they consider whether the military's deployment could 'enhance' the operations of state and federal police (Defence Amendment (Call Out of the Australian Defence Force) Bill 2018, proposed Division 2 in Defence Act 1903 (Cth)).

Previously, a state or territory government had to request military assistance to deal with 'domestic violence' beyond its means. Under the new laws, the federal government need not wait for such an invitation, to protect 'Commonwealth interests' or 'critical infrastructure'. Moreover, a state or territory government could request a military call-out even if their police forces have the capacity to respond themselves (Defence Amendment (Call Out of the Australian Defence Force) Bill 2018, proposed Division 2 in Defence Act 1903 (Cth)).

The new Bill would expand the military's powers, including by adding 'special powers' that could be authorised by the defence minister or exercised without ministerial authorisation in 'sudden and extraordinary emergencies'. Once deployed, the military would have greater powers to capture buildings, to shoot down planes, to sink vessels, to detain people, to search premises, to confiscate possessions and to free hostages. They would also have wider powers to issue commands to civilians, to interrogate them, to seize documents, to erect barriers and to commandeer vehicles (Defence Amendment (Call Out of the Australian Defence Force) Bill 2018, proposed Division 3 in Defence Act 1903 (Cth)).

References

Department of Defence Ministers. 2017. *'The Hon Malcolm Turnbull Prime Minister & Senator the Hon Marise Payne Minister for Defence joint media release: defence support to domestic counter-terrorism arrangements'*, 17 July, www.minister.defence.gov.au/minister/marise-payne/media-releases/hon-malcolm-turnbull-prime-minister-senator-hon-marise-payne (accessed 20 July 2017).

Doyle, C. 2000. *The Posse Comitatus Act and Related Matters: The Use of the Military to Execute Civilian Law.* Washington, DC: Congressional Research Service.

Head, M. 2002. 'Counter-terrorism laws: a threat to political freedom, civil liberties and constitutional rights', *Melbourne University Law Review*, 26(3): 666–89.

Head, M. 2009. *Calling out the Troops: The Australian Military and Civil Unrest.* Sydney: Federation Press.

Head, M. 2016. *Emergency Powers in Theory and Practice: The Long Shadow of Carl Schmitt.* London: Ashgate.

IMT (International Military Tribunal), Nuremberg. 1947. 'Second Day, Wednesday, 11/21/1945, Part 04'. In *Trial of the Major War Criminals before the International Military Tribunal, Vol. II.* Nuremberg: IMT.

Leahy, P. 2008. 'Bush signs bill enacting Leahy's National Guard empowerment reforms, and Leahy's repeal of the "Insurrection Act Rider"', Press release, 30 January, www.leahy.senate.gov/press/bush-signs-bill-enacting-leahys-national-guard-empowerment-reforms-and-leahys-repeal-of-the-insurrection-act-rider (accessed 8 August 2008).

Ministry of Defence. 2005. *Operations in the UK: The Defence Contribution to Resilience.* London: HMSO.

Neumann, F. 1942. *Behemoth: The Structure and Practice of National Socialism.* London: Victor Gollancz.

Office of the Press Secretary. 2007. 'National Security and Homeland Security Presidential Directive', Press release, 9 May, https://fas.org/irp/offdocs/nspd/nspd-51.htm (accessed 20 June 2008).

Scheuerman, W. 1997. 'After legal indeterminacy: Carl Schmitt and the National Socialist legal order, 1933–1936', *Cardozo Law Review*, 19(5): 1743–69.

Schmitt, C. 1985. *Political Theology: Four Chapters on the Concept of Sovereignty.* Cambridge, MA: MIT Press.

Staff and agencies. 2005. 'Pentagon prepares for homeland security role', *The Guardian*, 8 August, www.guardian.co.uk/usa/story/0,12271,1545109,00.html (accessed 12 January 2006).

Tillett, A. 2018. 'New laws extend military's powers to help state police', *The Australian Financial Review*, 28 June.

US Department of Defense. 1994. 'Military Assistance for Civil Disturbances [MACDIS]', Department of Defense Directive (DoDD) No. 3025.12. Washington, DC: Department of Defense.

US Department of Defense. 2015. *US Department of Defense Law of War Manual.* Washington, DC: Office of General Counsel, Department of Defense.

Walker, C., and Broderick, J. 2006. *The Civil Contingencies Act 2004: Risk, Resilience and the Law in the United Kingdom.* Oxford: Oxford University Press.

9 Martial law, official lawlessness and judicial complicity

In the event of war, in addition to whatever wartime or other emergency or extraordinary legislation is in place and regardless of any limits placed on governments by that legislation, the English-derived common law provides considerable scope for dictatorial measures to suppress anti-war dissent or other forms of social or political discontent.

First, the common law has been prepared to support recourse to the imposition of martial law, which is, in essence, the suspension of law altogether. Martial law declarations can pave the way for extensive military powers, including the right to summarily try and execute individuals, to put down civil unrest. It cannot be assumed that resort to martial law is no longer possible. Such declarations were made during the 20th century by British authorities in India, Egypt and Ireland.

Second, courts have recognised indemnities—immunities from prosecution and defences—such as self-defence and 'reasonable use of force' that protect governments from legal liability or accountability for the use of state violence against political opponents during times of war or strife.

Third, courts have protected governments from punishment for official lawlessness—acts of surveillance, harassment, violence or intimidation undertaken in the name of defending the state. Such lawsuits have been defeated, almost without exception, since the launching of the 'war on terror' in 2001, setting ominous precedents for future wars.

Finally, governments have succeeded, with the assistance of the judiciary, in using various legal devices to block attempts to challenge decisions to undertake military action or to engage in war-related activities, such as rendering prisoners to be tortured as part of the 'war on terror'.

Martial law

In Britain, after the final defeat of the absolute monarchy in 1688, martial law was regarded as an emergency suspension of the rule of law, strictly confined to cases of necessity in times of war, not in times of peace when ordinary courts were open (Capua 1977). Yet this view shifted during the 19th century.

At the beginning of that century, Blackstone conceded that the rules regarding the power to declare martial law were unclear and capricious. Writing in 1809, he said that martial law was 'built upon no settled principle, but is entirely arbitrary in its decisions'—that, indeed, it was 'in truth no law but something rather than allowed as law, a temporary excrescence bred out of the distemper of the state' (Blackstone 2001: 413).

Writing toward the end of the 19th century, however, Dicey (2005: 543–45) asserted that the right to invoke martial law is 'a right inherent in government'. Dicey—best known as a proponent of the concept of 'rule of law'—said that the term 'martial law' was most accurately 'employed as a name for the common law right of the Crown and its servants to repel force by force in the case of invasion, insurrection, riot, or generally of any violent resistance to the law' (Dicey 2005: 288). It was a 'right, or power' that was 'essential to the very existence of orderly government, and is most assuredly recognized in the most ample manner by the law of England' (Dicey 2005: 155, citing *R v Pinney* (1832) 5 Car & P 254).

To justify this view, Dicey drew a dubious distinction between two types of martial law. One, martial law 'in the proper sense of that term', meant the suspension of law and the government of a country or regions by military tribunals. This kind of martial law was 'unknown to the law of England' and that absence was 'an unmistakeable proof of the permanent supremacy of the law under our constitution (Dicey 2005: 182–83). Yet there was another meaning of martial law: the power of the government or citizens to 'maintain public order, at whatever cost of blood or property may be necessary' (Dicey 2005: 187).

Pollock (1902: 156) likewise stated: 'So-called "martial law", as distinct from military law, is an unlucky name for the justification by the common law of acts done by necessity for the defence of the Commonwealth when there is war within the realm.' Pollock's view of martial law was more expansive than Dicey's. Pollock insisted that necessity, as determined by government, would make nearly all actions taken under martial law legal and immune from any subsequent challenge in the courts.

Halsbury's Laws of England states that martial law applies 'when a state of actual war, or of insurrection, riot, or rebellion amounting to war, exists' (Hailsham 1973: vol. 8(2), para. 821). Other authorities contend that a modified form of martial law can be declared in cases of internal insurrection or disorder that is beyond the power of the civil authorities to quell, applying the same test of necessity as applies to 'military aid to the civil power' (Wade and Phillips 1970: 409; Dicey 2005: 543). It seems to have been accepted that martial law permits the creation of military tribunals to administer summary justice (Ewing and Gearty 2000: 362–63).

Doubt remains as to the legal basis of martial law. It is said to be either an example of a common-law right to employ force to repel force or, alternatively, a royal prerogative (Hailsham 1973: vol. 8(2), para. 821). Those contending that the royal prerogative has never been abolished can point to several 18th- and 19th-century Acts passed by Parliament to suppress opposition to British rule in Ireland. They stipulated that 'nothing in this act contained shall be construed to take away, abridge or diminish, the acknowledged prerogative of his Majesty, for the public safety, to resort to the exercise of martial law against open enemies or traitors' (Campbell 1994: 127–28).

Regardless of this fundamental uncertainty about the doctrinal basis for martial law, in the 1902 case *D. F. Marais v The General Officer Commanding the Lines of*

Communication and the Attorney-General of the Colony [1902] AC 109, on appeal from Britain's Cape Colony, the Privy Council extended the power to declare martial law to even where the ordinary civilian courts were still sitting. Their Lordships ruled that the Boer War was still under way and that this meant that the military authorities had unreviewable, and hence untrammelled, powers: '[Once let the fact of actual war be established, and there is an universal consensus of opinion that the civil Courts have no jurisdiction to call in question the propriety of the action of military authorities' (*Marais*, at 110–12).

The court specifically dismissed the 1628 Petition of Right forbidding the monarchy from invoking martial law, ruling that its 'framers . . . knew well what they meant when they made a condition of peace the ground of the illegality of unconstitutional procedure' (*Marais*, at 114). In other words, as long as the authorities insisted that there was no peace, military lawlessness could prevail.

Even more revealing was the massacre of anti-British colonial protesters in Amritsar, India, in 1919. Martial law was proclaimed and Brigadier-General Rex Dyer ordered his troops to open fire on 20,000 people who had gathered in defiance of regulations that prohibited meetings of more than four men (Simpson 2004: 64–66). The crowd was trapped within the walls of a meeting ground. Around 380 were killed and more than 15,000 wounded. Numerous *in camera* trials followed, at which 180 people were sentenced to death and 264 to transportation for life.

A committee of inquiry rejected Dyer's justification that the massacre was necessary to intimidate potential unrest elsewhere and he was condemned by the House of Commons, although not by the House of Lords (Simpson 2004: 64–66). Predictably, however, Dyer was never prosecuted, but only invalided out of the army (Ferguson 2004: 276–79). According to Simpson (2004: 66), the committee might have adopted a Diceyan theory, according to which Dyer and others were 'personally liable, and risked trial and indeed conviction for murder', but there was 'no real sense in which this was or could ever be done'. Simpson (2004: 62–71) cited other examples of martial law and military brutality in Palestine, Egypt and South Africa.

Despite the supposed nicety of the distinctions drawn by Dicey, the history of the use of martial law in Britain and throughout the British Empire is barbaric. Another example—from the period in which Dicey was writing—is the repeated imposition of martial law in Egypt, which was occupied by Britain from 1882.

Significantly, the first declaration of martial law, in 1914, was bound up with Britain's formal assertion of sovereignty over Egypt. The British government proclaimed Egypt a 'protectorate' that year, in the context of World War I and the British offensive against the Ottoman Empire, of which Egypt had been a province for four centuries (Reza 2007: 535). Thus British rule commenced with martial law, which was instrumental to the assertion of sovereignty itself.

During the war, the British poured masses of foreign troops into Egypt, conscripted more than 1.5 million Egyptians into the Labour Corps, and requisitioned buildings, crops and animals for the use of the army (Vatikiotis 1992: 246). A British governor was placed in command of the Egyptian military and its actions were removed from the jurisdiction of the courts (Reza 2007: 535).

That imposition cannot be dismissed simply as a wartime measure. Martial law continued after World War I, directed against the 1919 uprising of Egyptian nationalism, and ended only temporarily after Britain declared the country nominally independent in 1922 (Reza 2007: 535). By mid-1919, some 800 Egyptians had been killed by Allied (mainly Australian) troops and twice that number had been wounded (Jankowski 2000: 112).

No one was held to account for the killings. Instead, the British government sent a commission of inquiry, known as the Milner Mission, to Egypt in December 1919 to determine the causes of the uprising and to make a recommendation about the political future of the country. Lord Milner's report, published in February 1921, recommended that the protectorate status of Egypt be abandoned (Daly 1988: 249–50).

In effect, although the independence movement was crushed, ongoing popular resistance forced the British to grant a modicum of independence to Egypt in 1922. The British kept control over the strategic and lucrative Suez Canal, however, and continued to dictate Egyptian policy by means of a proxy ruler (Vatikiotis 1992: 264).

A 1936 Anglo-Egyptian treaty, which guaranteed the British a military presence in Egypt, permitted the British government to request declarations of martial law under the 1923 Egyptian Constitution, which was modelled on the Belgian Constitution. A 1939 declaration of martial law remained in place throughout World War II.

Another declaration, from 1948 to 1950, accompanied the outbreak of the first Arab-Israeli war. It was reimposed in 1952 after protests against the British control of the Suez Canal led to the killing of dozens of people by British troops and riots broke out in Cairo. This declaration lasted until 1956, until the consolidation of the victory of the 1952 Free Officers Revolution led by Army Colonel Gamal Abdel Nasser (Reza 2007: 535–36).

Martial law fell into disuse in Britain (but not its Irish colony) and most other 'advanced' countries during the 20th century, usually replaced by more statutory forms of emergency or repressive powers (Simpson 2004: 69–71). Nevertheless, it remains in reserve. Martial law is still loosely described as 'the right to use force against force within the realm in order to suppress civil disorder' (Heuston 1964: 152). This formulation could justify dictatorial measures.

According to de Smith (1981: 511)—a leading late-20th-century authority on English constitutional and administrative law—if martial law arises, it is generally thought that the officer commanding the armed forces will become all-powerful and their actions 'non-justiciable and, for the time being, absolute, subject only to consultation (if this is feasible) with the civil power'. 'Non-justiciable' means that the courts have no power to scrutinise the lawfulness of the actions taken.

In Australia, martial law was invoked several times during the 19th century against convicts, Aborigines and workers. In his 1984 work, *Emergency Powers*, Lee 'hazards a guess' that the power to resort to martial law continues in Australia as a creature of the common law. Lee considered that, while legislation was generally preferable, the doctrine of martial law should not be buried, 'for in the face of an extraordinary crisis it may come in useful . . . it may be better to rely on a "shadowy, uncertain, precarious something" than nothing at all' (Lee 1984: 224).

This argument would seem to justify dispensing with the rule of law. The words quoted by Lee were taken from a 19th-century English judgment in which Chief Justice Cockburn stated: 'Martial law when applied to the civilian is no law at all, but a shadowy, uncertain, precarious something, depending entirely on the conscience, or rather on the despotic and arbitrary will of those who administer it' (*R v Nelson and Brand* (1867) F Cockburn Sp Rep 85, 86).

Martial law in Ireland

How these propositions might apply during a large-scale war can be assessed from the experiences of British rule in Ireland, which provide a case study of the continuing operation of martial law during the 20th century (Campbell 1994).

The first instance was triggered by the Easter 1916 Rebellion, amidst World War I. The nationalist uprising was short-lived, lasting only five days in Dublin, while the insurrection never even got off the ground elsewhere. Officially, 124 Crown forces were killed and 388 injured in the five-day counterinsurgency operation, compared to 180 civilians killed and 614 wounded (Ewing and Gearty 2000: 338–39). Lord Lieutenant Lord Wimborne, a cousin of Winston Churchill, proclaimed an immediate state of martial law in Dublin city and county. Under this authority, the British army commander-in-chief in the region, General Friend, swiftly issued martial law regulations that imposed a curfew and declared that any civilian carrying arms was liable to be fired upon without warning.

A day later, martial law was extended across the whole of Ireland, with British Prime Minister Asquith informing Parliament that General Sir John Maxwell was being 'given plenary powers under martial law over the whole country'. Under War Office instructions, Maxwell was empowered to 'take all such measures as may in his opinion be necessary for the prompt suppression of insurrection in Ireland' (Ewing and Gearty 2000: 339, 339n). A further proclamation brought into operation an emergency regulation that contemplated two types of military justice, a general court martial and a field general court martial, to try anyone charged with offences against the Defence of the Realm Regulations then in force throughout Britain. These tribunals, which sat in secret, could impose the death penalty where the intention of the accused was to assist the enemy; in other cases, it could impose prison sentences up to life imprisonment (Ewing and Gearty 2000: 341). In the first few weeks of May 1916, 3,419 suspected Sinn Fein sympathisers were arrested by the military under internment and other emergency regulations, 188 civilians were tried by courts martial, 90 death sentences were passed and 15 people were executed (Ewing and Gearty 2000: 342).

No effort seems to have been made to challenge the legality of the executions, but one bid to challenge the closed-door conduct of the hearings was dismissed unanimously by a seven-member court of the King's Bench. Lord Chief Justice Viscount Reading considered that, having regard to the army commander-in-chief's opinion that it was necessary for public safety and the defence of the realm to exclude the public and the media, it was 'abundantly clear' that the *in camera* proceedings were lawful. The readiness of the judges to dispense with the legal principle of open courts was voiced most vehemently by Justice Darling. He declared that it would have been 'grotesque' to invite 'the public to come and hear witnesses give evidence against rebels with whom a great many of that same public sympathised (*R v Governor of Lewes Prison, ex parte Doyle* [1917] 2 KB 254, 272, 274). One month after its proclamation, martial law was extended indefinitely. It was never formally revoked by proclamation, but simply ceased to apply when not judged essential by the British government (Ewing and Gearty 2000: 339n).

Military tribunals re-emerged in Ireland in 1920, under the Restoration of Order in Ireland Act of that year, accompanied by an official policy of covertly authorised retaliation or reprisals. Entire towns were wrecked in revenge for the killing of army officers by the Irish Republican Army (IRA) and troops fired indiscriminately into a Dublin football crowd, killing 14 men, women and children in Ireland's first 'Bloody Sunday' (Ewing and Gearty 2000: 358–60). Three weeks later, martial law was proclaimed once more, covering the four southwestern counties. Two days after Lord French's declaration, Sir Nevil Macready, the military commander-in-chief, issued his first martial law proclamation. This made into capital offences, triable by the military, the unauthorised 'possession of arms, ammunition, or explosives', the wearing of military apparel and the harbouring or assisting of any rebels who were 'levying war' against the king. Within martial law areas, which soon included four further counties, a policy of 'official reprisals' was vigorously followed (Ewing and Gearty 2000: 360–61). Some confusion ensured, because the ordinary courts continued to function, alongside courts martial, operating under three distinct systems—martial law, the Defence of the Realm Consolidation Act 1914 and the Restoration of Order in Ireland Act 1920.

The willingness of the courts to legitimise martial law was demonstrated in three cases heard before the Irish divisional court of the King's Bench: *R v Allen* [1921] 2 IR 241; *R (Garde) v Strickland* [1921] 2 IR 317; and *R (Ronayne and Mulcahy) v Strickland* [1921] 2 IR 333. The first involved John Allen, who had been sentenced to death by a military tribunal for possessing a revolver, ammunition and an IRA publication, entitled 'Night Fighting'. Giving the unanimous decision of the court to uphold the sentence, even though it would not have been possible under the ordinary law or even the emergency legislation, Chief Justice Molony declared:

> It is the sacred duty of this Court to protect the lives and liberties of all His Majesty's subjects, and to see that no one suffers loss of life or liberty save under the laws of the country; but when subjects of the King rise in armed insurrection and the conflict is still raging, it is no less our duty not to interfere with the officers of the Crown in taking such steps as they deem necessary to quell the insurrection, and to restore peace and order and the authority of the law.
>
> (*R v Allen* [1921] 2 IR 241, 242)

In that case, there was no challenge to the government's proclamation of the existence of a state of war or to its claim that such a state of disorder existed when Allen was arrested. The court ruled that it was 'clear on the authorities that when martial law is imposed, and the necessity for it exists, or, in other words, while the war is still raging, this Court has no jurisdiction to question any acts done by the military authorities' (*Allen*, at 269). Relying upon the precedent set by the Privy Council in *D. F. Marais v The General Officer Commanding the Lines of Communication and the Attorney-General of the Colony* [1902] AC 109, the court in *Allen* held that the continued functioning of civilian courts in the martial law areas did not affect the legality of the military tribunals. And the lack of availability of the death penalty for these offences under the ordinary law was an objection 'rather for the consideration of Parliament than for this Court, which cannot, *durante bello* [during war], control the military authorities, or question any sentence imposed in the exercise of martial law' (*Allen*, at 272). Allen was executed four days later, together with five others (Ewing and Gearty 2000: 364).

In *R (Garde) v Strickland* [1921] 2 IR 317, death sentences imposed on seven men for levying war against His Majesty were challenged through writs of *habeas corpus* and *certiorari* on the basis that the military tribunal that had tried them had been improperly constituted. Chief Justice Molony asserted that the court had 'the power and the duty to decide whether a state of war exists which justifies the application of martial law' (*R (Garde) v Strickland*, at 329). But the court agreed with the military's assessment and therefore would not 'interfere to determine what is or what is not necessary' (*R (Garde) v Strickland*, at 332). On the same day, in *R (Ronayne and Mulcahy) v Strickland* [1921] 2 IR 333, the court rejected an objection that the power to declare martial law had been 'surrendered or released' by the Restoration of Order in Ireland Act 1920. In a one-page judgment, Chief Justice Molony and his fellow judges simply dismissed the submission as having 'no foundation in law' (*R (Ronayne and Mulcahy) v Strickland*, at 334).

Another judicial ruling, handed down in mid-1921, *did* call the continued application of martial law into question. *Egan v Macready* [1921] 1 IR 265 was a further challenge to a military court's death sentence, this time for possessing ammunition. Significantly, the case was heard following the partition of Ireland, after sweeping electoral victories in the south for Sinn Fein, and amid the announcement of a truce between the British forces and the IRA (Ewing and Gearty 2000: 365–66). Possibly influenced by the truce, Ireland's Master of the Rolls Charles O'Connor ruled that the power to declare martial law had been removed by the adoption of the Restoration of Order in Ireland Act—the very proposition rejected by Chief Justice Molony's Irish court of the King's Bench two months earlier. Master of the Rolls O'Connor insisted that the 'claim of the military authority to override legislation, specially made for a state of war, would seem . . . to call for a new Bill of Rights' (*Egan v Macready*, at 275). He cited the then very recent judgment in *Attorney-General v De Keyser's Royal Hotel* [1920] AC 508, in which the House of Lords had ruled that legislation could preclude the operation of prerogative powers by evincing an intention to cover the relevant field.

Master of the Rolls O'Connor's judgment led to an extraordinary confrontation with the military. General Macready refused to obey the *habeas corpus* order and another in a similar case decided by O'Connor on the same day. The judge issued writs of attachment against the general and his deputy, as well as the governor of the prison where the men were held, declaring that their obstruction amounted to a 'deliberate contempt of Court—a thing unprecedented in this Court and the whole history of British law' (*Egan v Macready* [1921] 1 IR 265, 280). The Crown argued that it had the right to hold the prisoners pending an appeal. General Macready threatened to 'arrest anyone, including the Master of the Rolls himself, who attempted to carry out the service of the writs'. A constitutional crisis was averted only when the government decided to release the men, telling Parliament that the decision was 'based solely upon the existing situation in Ireland' and 'not due to any decision given by a Civil Court in Ireland', since the courts had 'no power to over-rule the decisions of Military Courts in the martial law area' (Ewing and Gearty 2000: 367). It seems that the government was driven by concerns about not upsetting the truce negotiations, rather than by respect for the rule of law.

To say the least, the O'Connor affair left unresolved the claim for the primacy of martial law and, indeed, called into question the principle of civilian control of the military. Moreover, a prominent constitutional scholar cast doubt on O'Connor's ruling, saying that it had 'not met with approval' and appeared 'to depend upon the view that the right to use martial law is a prerogative right', rather than 'simply an extension of the ordinary common law power to meet force with force' (Heuston 1964: 159).

In summary, even if the ordinary courts have jurisdiction to decide whether the state of disorder warrants martial law, there is no precise and settled body of law for answering that question, which seems to depend on judging whether order could be restored only by handing over power to the military authorities. If the courts decide that martial law is warranted, then the military's actions will be unreviewable, at least until the courts decide that the disorder has been pacified. Legal action could be brought against the military for manifestly unreasonable conduct and possibly for unnecessary use of force against people or property, but the law is unclear (de Smith 1981: 512). In de Smith's opinion, the legal uncertainty is academic in any case, because indemnity legislation would almost certainly be passed to exonerate those who acted in good faith to suppress an uprising (de Smith 1981: 514). The British Parliament passed such an Act of Indemnity to cover the 1920 declaration of martial law in areas of Ireland (Rowe and Whelan 1985: 200).

Indemnities

Historically, governments and other authorities have been willing to exploit vague and elastic phrases such as 'emergency', 'essential' and 'security' to act without clear legal authorisation and, if necessary, to obtain retrospective indemnity.

Despite his 'rule of law' reputation, Dicey was a strong advocate of Acts of indemnity to 'make lawful acts which when they were committed were unlawful' (Dicey 2005: 142). For him:

> There are times of tumult or invasion when for the sake of legality itself the rules of law must be broken. The course which the government must then take is clear. The Ministry must break the law and trust for protection to an Act of Indemnity.
>
> (Dicey 2005: 272)

Dicey (2005: 144) observed, pointing backward at historical experience, that the expectation of executives that such Acts would be passed 'has not been disappointed'. Seven Indemnity Acts were passed in Ireland between 1796 and 1800 to protect the authorities against legal liability for their unlawful acts (Lee 1984: 222). Whelan traced this trend and gave some examples, one of which was the British government's press release during the 1926 General Strike:

> All ranks of the Armed Forces of the Crown are hereby notified that any action which they may find is necessary to take in an honest endeavour to aid the Civil Power will receive, both now and afterwards, the full support of His Majesty's Government.
>
> (Quoted in Whelan 1985: 289–90)

Another example was Attorney-General Sir Hartley Shawcross's advice during the 1949 docks strike about the doubtful legal enforceability of the emergency regulations:

> I do not think that matters . . . I have advised that this risk should be taken and that the Regulations should cover matters on which action is required without due regard to the niceties of the law. In an emergency the Government may have, in matters admitting of legal doubt, to act first and argue about the doubts later, if necessary obtaining an indemnification Act.
>
> (Quoted in Whelan 1985: 289–90)

Shawcross's phrase, 'without due regard for the niceties of the law', illustrates the propensity and capacity of governments to dispense with the finer points of the 'rule of law' when confronted by serious political, social or industrial challenges to the established order.

Although the 1974 Heathrow operation was officially justified as a precaution against terrorism, the legal authority of the government to use the army was not clear (Lee 1984: 211). The editor of the *Criminal Law Review* proposed that resort be had to the royal prerogative to address the legal vacuum:

> If on a future occasion the legal powers of police and soldier prove inadequate, reliance may, in the last resort, have to be placed on the Royal Prerogative governing emergencies. That power, with its requirements of compensation, may be an acceptable means of filling in gaps in statutory and common law powers.
>
> (Lee 1984: 211–12)

Official lawlessness

In the name of defending the state, governments or official security agencies may engage in unlawful surveillance, wars of aggression, military interventions, coups, assassinations, renditions and torture. Such practices have mushroomed in the 21st century. Considerable evidence has been produced of such crimes being committed from 2001 onward, both domestically and abroad. It is not possible to investigate or review these operations here—but it is important to note that those allegedly affected by these crimes have faced considerable difficulties in bringing lawsuits seeking to prosecute or obtain redress for such conduct.

Courts have dismissed legal actions on various grounds, including 'state secret' doctrines invoked by the government accused of being responsible. Two American cases decided in 2010 illustrate this development. One concerned the use of 'renditions' to secretly transport prisoners to locations in other countries where they could be tortured; the other involved the targeted assassination of people identified as terrorists.

In the first decision, the US Ninth Circuit Court of Appeals, in a 6–5 *en banc* ruling, dismissed a lawsuit by five victims of the Central Intelligence Agency (CIA) 'extraordinary rendition' programme against Jeppesen Dataplan, a unit of Boeing. The ruling relied upon the 'state secrets' doctrine advocated by the Obama administration. The American Civil Liberties Union (ACLU) brought the suit, charging that defence contractor Jeppesen Dataplan knowingly facilitated the renditions, also known as torture flights, by providing flight planning and logistical support to CIA personnel. The suit, *Mohamed v. Jeppesen Dataplan Inc.* 614 F.3d 1070 (9th Cir. 2010), sought to expose a web of connections between top executives of defence corporations, foreign intelligence agencies and the US government.

The Ninth Circuit's ruling argued that 'there is precious little Jeppesen could say about its relevant conduct and knowledge without revealing information about how the United States government does or does not conduct covert operations' (*Mohamed v. Jeppesen Dataplan*, at 1089). On this basis, the court dismissed the case. Earlier, a three-judge panel of the Ninth Circuit had ruled against the Obama administration. Writing for the panel, Judge Michael D. Hawkins wrote that the 'state secrets' doctrine advocated by the administration 'has no logical limit': 'As the Founders of this Nation knew well, arbitrary imprisonment and torture under any circumstance is a gross and notorious act of despotism' (*Mohamed v. Jeppesen Dataplan*, at 1101).

The Obama administration sought a review of Hawkins' decision, which was overturned by the entire Ninth Circuit in a judgment authored by Judge Raymond C. Fisher. While couching his opinion in the language of 'balancing' national security against individual liberties, Judge Fisher concluded that '[c]ourts must act in the interest of the country's national security to prevent disclosure of state secrets, even to the point of dismissing a case entirely' (quoted in Savage 2010).

In another 2010 decision, Federal District Judge John D. Bates dismissed a lawsuit that challenged the Obama administration's policy of targeted killings of individuals around the world, including US citizens. The administration had placed the name of US citizen Anwar Al-Aulaqi on a 'kill list', permitting any of the US government's military or intelligence agencies to carry out his assassination. Al-Aulaqi was reported to be in Yemen. The CIA had launched a cruise missile at a meeting Al-Aulaqi was attending there, but the intended victim survived.

In *Al-Aulaqi v. Obama* 727 F.Supp.2d 1 (D.D.C. 2010), the ACLU and the Center for Constitutional Rights (CCR) filed a lawsuit on behalf of Al-Aulaqi's father, Nasser Al-Aulaqi, challenging the targeted killing programme. The Obama administration argued that the president had the power to order the killing of a US citizen without a trial or judicial review, despite this being a clear violation of international law and the US Bill of Rights. The Fifth Amendment to the US Constitution states: 'No person shall be . . . deprived of life . . . without due process of law.' The administration further argued that the case should not be allowed to proceed because it threatened to reveal 'state secrets'.

In his ruling, Judge Bates acknowledged that the case raised 'stark' and 'perplexing' questions, asking: 'Can the Executive order the assassination of a U.S. citizen without first affording him any form of judicial process whatsoever, based on the mere assertion that he is a dangerous member of a terrorist organization?' (*Al-Aulaqi v. Obama*, at 9). However, Bates concluded that the case could not proceed because Anwar Al-Aulaqi's father, Nasser Al-Aulaqi, lacked legal standing to bring the case.

This ruling implies that, if the targeted killing programme is to be challenged, the persons marked for death must appear themselves in the courts of the country that is trying to assassinate them. Bates included in his opinion a passage suggesting that, in light of Anwar Al-Aulaqi's political and religious views, he should not be entitled to the protections of the US Constitution. The judge wrote that Al-Aulaqi had 'decried the US legal system and suggested that Muslims are not bound by Western law'; accordingly, Bates wrote, Al-Aulaqi would not 'likely want to sue to vindicate his US constitutional rights in US courts' (*Al-Aulaqi v. Obama*, at 21).

Judge Bates dismissed Al-Aulaqi's claims under international law because the doctrine of 'sovereign immunity' prevents the government from being the target of certain lawsuits without its express consent. Bates held that a judicial evaluation of the Obama administration's assassination programme would involve a 'political question' not subject to judicial review. Bates indicated that, in light of his other rulings dismissing the case, it was unnecessary to decide whether the 'state secrets' doctrine applied.

Another unsuccessful Al-Aulaqi case is examined in the next section.

Blocking judicial review: three case studies

Three cases decided during 2012 and 2013—one in the United States, one in Britain and one before the European Court of Human Rights (ECtHR)—provide a further revealing picture of the lengths to which the Obama administration, assisted by European governments, went to prevent any legal challenges to its assertion of far-reaching executive powers, such as to assassinate alleged enemies of the country, including US citizens, or to 'render' detainees to be tortured in other countries.

The three cases also demonstrate the readiness of the judicial authorities, and the judiciary itself, to facilitate these efforts. This is so even where judges themselves admit the Kafkaesque, or 'Alice in Wonderland', character of their rulings in favour of official legal claims that effectively make it impossible for citizens to challenge violations of basic legal and constitutional rights. The results essentially permit government lawlessness, exposing the sham of traditional claims that Western legal systems are governed by a rule of law.

In only one of the three cases, that argued before the European Court, did a victim of torture ultimately obtain some redress—albeit only against the government of the Republic of Macedonia, which had participated in the US torture programme, not against the US government itself. That limited victory also took ten years, during which time the victim was frustrated and blocked by the governments and courts in Germany, Macedonia and the United States.

Obama administration blocks information request on assassination of US citizens

In January 2013, as urged by lawyers for the Obama administration, US federal judge Colleen McMahon relied on an expansive 'national security' provision in freedom-of-information legislation to deny requests by the ACLU and the *New York Times* for government records related to the assassination of US citizens.

The case originated as separate and independent requests under the US Freedom of Information Act of 1966 (FOIA) by the ACLU and *New York Times* journalists for information related to targeted killings, particularly of US citizens, in the wake of the September 2011 assassination of Muslim cleric and US citizen Anwar Al-Aulaqi, in Yemen (discussed earlier in the chapter).

The ACLU requested several broad categories of documents, including records pertaining to the presumed legal basis for assassination of US citizens and to the process by which US citizens could be targeted, including who was authorised to make such decisions and what evidence was needed to support them. The ACLU also requested documents related to the killing of Anwar Al-Aulaqi's 16-year-old son, Abdulrahman Al-Aulaqi.

By the beginning of 2013, the US government's 'targeted killing' programme, initiated under the Bush administration and expanded under the Obama administration, had already resulted in the deaths of thousands of people far from any battlefield, including at least three US citizens. The victims, as well as many bystanders, had been murdered without being charged with any crime and without trial or judicial review of any kind.

As discussed earlier, the Obama administration's ongoing programme was in violation of a core historic concept of the US legal system, which is contained in the Fifth Amendment of 1791: 'No person shall . . . be deprived of life . . . without due process of law.' The issue before the court, however, was not the legality of this programme, but the ability of the American people simply to have access to the legal and political arguments from the Obama administration seeking to justify it.

Said Judge McMahon, US District Judge for the Southern District of New York:

> I can find no way around the thicket of laws and precedents that effectively allow the Executive Branch of our Government to proclaim as perfectly lawful certain actions that seem on their face incompatible with our Constitution and laws, while keeping the reasons for its conclusion a secret.

The judge acknowledged the 'Catch 22' and 'Alice-in-Wonderland nature' of her ruling, but she attributed the 'paradoxical' outcome to 'contradictory constraints and rules' outside her control.

At issue was whether the administration would be ordered under the FOIA to disclose to the public legal memos written by government lawyers defending the targeted killing overseas of US citizens who were suspected of involvement in terror operations. Said McMahon: 'This Court is constrained by law, and under the law, I can only conclude that the Government has not violated FOIA by refusing to turn over the documents sought in the FOIA requests.' Yet, despite this appeal to the rule of law, she concluded that the government could not be 'compelled by this court of law to explain in detail the reasons why its actions do not violate the Constitution and laws of the United States'.

By insisting on a constitutional separation of powers, the founders of the United States sought to avoid a government in which a single branch could wield the authority to act as judge, jury and executioner. Wrote McMahon:

> Presidential authorization does not and cannot legitimize covert action that violates the Constitution and laws of this nation. So there are indeed legitimate reasons, historical and legal, to question the legality of killings unilaterally authorized by the Executive that take place otherwise than on a 'hot' field of battle.

Nevertheless, the judge ultimately ruled that virtually all of the documents sought by the ACLU and the *New York Times* could be withheld from public disclosure under exemptions to freedom-of-information law.

McMahon's judgment cited extensively from documents and material from the period of the American Revolution, all of which confirmed that the framers of the US Constitution intended to forbid extrajudicial assassinations. Having reviewed these authorities, Judge McMahon quoted numerous public statements by Obama and senior administration officials that clearly indicated that the US government, with the direct involvement of Obama himself, was planning and carrying out such extrajudicial assassinations.

Citing 'national security' exceptions to the FOIA, government secrecy statutes and expansive executive privileges, the Obama administration not only failed to disclose the requested documents, but also refused to specify the documents that were being withheld, on the grounds that to acknowledge whether or not any of the requested documents existed would compromise national security.

In her judgment, McMahon referred to the sweeping powers that had been conferred on the presidency after the September 2001 terrorist attacks on the World Trade Center and the Pentagon (9/11). Congress had passed a resolution on the Authorization for the Use of Military Force (AUMF) that had empowered the president to:

> . . . use all necessary and appropriate force against those nations, organizations, or persons he determines planned, authorized, committed, or aided

the terrorist attacks that occurred on September 11, 2001, or harbored such organizations or persons, in order to prevent any future acts of international terrorism against the United States by such nations, organizations or persons.

That provision effectively gave the president carte blanche to take any action, without exception, that he deemed necessary to pursue the indefinite 'war on terror' that has ensued ever since. Both the Bush and Obama administrations interpreted that power as extending far beyond the supposed primary field of battle, in Afghanistan and neighbouring Pakistan. Judge McMahon noted that the 'war on terror' exercise had been pursued 'far from any 'hot' battlefield', including to Yemen, 'about 1500 miles from Afghanistan' and a country with which the United States was not at war.

The Obama administration openly argued that it was perfectly legal and constitutional for the president to order the assassination of anyone, including a US citizen. The judge referred to the administration's 'vociferous insistence' that a US citizen could be 'targeted by the Executive Branch and still be accorded due process'. She said the government had gone so far as to mount an 'extensive public relations campaign' to convince the public that its conclusions were correct. Judge McMahon observed that the government had good reason to feel somewhat defensive about this assertion: 'Some Americans question the power of the Executive to make a unilateral and unreviewable decision to kill an American citizen who is not actively engaged in armed combat against this country.'

The judge noted that the administration clung to its view notwithstanding the explicit language of the Fifth Amendment, as well as the Treason Clause of the US Constitution, in which the framers, 'as leery of accusations of treason as they were of concentrating power in the hands of a single person or institution', prohibited any conviction for treason unless on the testimony of two witnesses to an overt act or a confession in open court. Despite thus drawing some attention to the overturning or erosion of historic principles, the judge deferred to the administration's demand for the protection, under freedom-of-information exemptions, of classified secrets, intelligence-gathering methods and internal deliberative processes.

While the decision, on its narrowest basis, could be seen as resting only on the particular provisions of the FOIA, those sections of the Act and how courts interpret them are indicative of the wide-ranging and deferential approach of legislators and judges to executive secrecy claims based on 'national security'. Judge McMahon upheld, for example, the government's right to classify as secret, 'in the interest of national defense or foreign policy', the legal analysis that it asserts supports conduct such as targeted assassinations. As her judgment illustrates, such use of the 'classified documents' provisions enables governments to shield their operations, no matter how unlawful, from public scrutiny and challenge.

In a footnote in her decision, Judge McMahon indicated that she had sent a draft of her decision to the Federal Bureau of Investigations (FBI) before issuing it, 'to give the Government an opportunity to object to the disclosure of any classified information that may have inadvertently found its way into this document'. The judge also issued a secret 'appendix' to her ruling that was not made publicly available. She indicated in her decision that the secret appendix 'is being filed under seal and is not available to Plaintiffs' counsel'.

These practices indicate the readiness of even judges to seek government approval of their judgments before delivering them and to withhold basic information from plaintiffs, depriving them of information they may require to challenge such rulings by governments and courts. The ACLU and the *Times* intended to appeal the decision.

Judge McMahon's opinion in the consolidated cases *New York Times v. US Department of Justice* (11 Civ. 9336) and *ACLU v. US Department of Justice* (12 Civ. 794) can be viewed online at www.nysd.uscourts.gov/cases/show. php?db=special&id=251 (accessed 25 November 2013).

English High Court rejects inquiry into British role in Pakistan drone strikes

As mentioned in Chapter 4, in 2012 the High Court in London rejected a request for a judicial review of a decision by the Secretary of State for Foreign and Commonwealth Affairs to pass intelligence information from Government Communications Headquarters (GCHQ) to aid US drone strikes in Pakistan's northwest region. The case was brought by Noor Khan, a Pakistani man whose father was killed on 17 March 2011, along with 49 other people, by a US drone strike. Khan's father, Malik Daud Khan, was chairing a peaceful jirga (tribal assembly) meeting to discuss chromite mining rights in North Waziristan when he was killed by several missile strikes.

In his legal submission, Khan asked the court to look into whether British intelligence officials provided assistance in the killing of his father and whether they were liable for prosecution under British law. Those providing such information could be committing serious criminal offences, including conspiracy to commit murder (contrary to sections 1 or 1A of the Criminal Law Act 1977).

The ruling handed down by Lord Justice Moses and supported by Justice Simon was strongly in favour of the Foreign and Commonwealth Office (FCO). It provided a legal justification for ensuring that Britain's role in assisting the United States to carry out its drone assassinations would remain hidden from public exposure. Citing evidence from the FCO, the ruling stated:

> [I]f the Secretary of State were required to make a substantive response to the claim, the likely consequence would be serious harm to national security and international relations. The United Kingdom Government would be compelled to express a definitive view on legal issues, complicating and damaging relations with our most important bilateral ally and, in consequence, damaging the United Kingdom's security.
>
> (*Khan v SSFCA* [2012] EWHC 3728
> (Admin), [17])

The ruling dismissed Khan's claim, stating that:

> [T]he real aim and target of these proceedings is not to inform GCHQ employees that if they were prosecuted, no defence of combatant immunity would be available. The real aim is to persuade this court to make a public pronouncement designed to condemn the activities of the United States in North Waziristan, as a step in persuading them to halt such activity.
>
> (*Khan v SSFCA* [2012] EWHC 3728
> (Admin), [57])

The ruling took note of legal proceedings that Khan had undertaken in Pakistan to reiterate that under no conditions would the High Court make a ruling condemning the drone attacks or the GCHQ's alleged role in them. Referring to Khan's plea to the court in Peshawar, Lord Justice Moses wrote:

> [H]e contends that the Government of Pakistan, and various Ministries, are under a constitutional obligation to take all necessary action to stop 'illegal drone strikes' and 'safeguard its citizens from target killing by an external force'. He pleads that 'the act of killing of innocent people on March 17 2011 was extra-judicial killing, more generally referred to as murder' . . . .
>
> It is plain, from the nature of the claims, that the purpose of the proceedings in England and in Pakistan is to persuade a court to do what it can to stop further strikes by drones operated by the United States . . . .
>
> (*Khan v SSFCA* [2012] EWHC 3728
> (Admin), [12]–[13])

Lord Justice Moses dismissed the submission from Khan's legal team that clarification was required regarding the legal basis for the drone attacks carried out by the United States in North Waziristan, to establish whether British officials could be secondary parties to murder or guilty of war crimes if they were providing critical information to the United States. In its submission, Khan's team cited a *Sunday Times* article dated 25 July 2010. Written months before the attack that killed Khan's father and dozens of other innocent civilians, the information it contained, including quotes from a GCHQ official, confirmed that the GCHQ passed vital locational and other intelligence to the United States on the whereabouts of what were described as 'leading militants in Afghanistan and Pakistan'.

The ruling noted that the *Sunday Times* article was one of a 'number of reports' that alleged that the drone strikes were 'linked to agents of the US Government and to United Kingdom employees of GCHQ'. Lord Justice Moses, however, refused to permit Khan to pursue his suit to determine whether these reports had a 'firm factual foundation'. Moses observed that, 'through no fault of the claimant, his case rests on a respectable but unconfirmed report' (*Khan v SSFCA* [2012] EWHC 3728 (Admin), [11]).

The Secretary of State objected on the grounds that, first, the court would be required to adjudicate upon the acts of foreign sovereign states, second, the claimant was seeking a declaration as to whether future conduct was proscribed by domestic criminal law, third, the court should not be lured into giving an advisory opinion and, fourth, the case could not be tried at all in the absence of a statutory closed material procedure. In effect, after reviewing the claimant's arguments, the court accepted the first three objections and said it was not necessary to rule on the fourth.

Lord Justice Moses cited *Kuwait Airways Corpn v Iraqi Airways Co. (Nos 4 and 5)* [2002] 2 WLR 1353, 1362, as authority for 'the principle that the courts will not sit in judgment on the sovereign acts of a foreign state includes a prohibition against adjudication upon the "legality, validity or acceptability of such acts, either under domestic law or international law" ' (*Khan v SSFCA* [2012] EWHC 3728 (Admin), [15]). Once again, this doctrine, regularly relied upon by governments and courts to block any legal examination of military or intelligence operations in support of the United States, was utilised to prevent any exposure of, or accountability for, conduct potentially involving the most serious crimes.

The judgment in *Khan v SSFCA* [2012] EWHC 3728 (Admin) can be viewed online at www.judiciary.uk/judgments/khan-v-ssfca/ (accessed 22 November 2013).

European Court of Human Rights orders damages for CIA torture victim

Late in 2012, the ECtHR in Strasbourg awarded damages of €60,000 to Khaled El-Masri, a German citizen of Lebanese origin. The judges accepted that Macedonian security services had illegally seized El-Masri at the end of 2003, subjected him to abuse and finally handed him over to agents from the CIA. The CIA then transported El-Masri to a secret prison in Afghanistan, where he was tortured and mistreated for months. The Court said this was a serious violation of the European Convention on Human Rights and Fundamental Freedoms (ECHR), to which the Republic of Macedonia was a signatory.

Although only representatives of the Macedonian government were accused, the verdict had broader significance. It was the first time that the unlawful renditions conducted by the US government and its European accomplices had been condemned by an international court for breaching international laws.

Previously, El-Masri's attempts to seek redress in Macedonia, Germany and the United States had been systematically thwarted. Investigations, if they were conducted at all, were carried out reluctantly and half-heartedly; information was withheld by the investigating authorities, citing state secrecy. The ECtHR regarded all aspects of El-Masri's evidence as credible and supported by international investigations. His complaint that the measures taken against him, his handing over to CIA agents and the hindering of his attempts to seek legal remedies breached the core ECHR Articles was sustained in every point by the Court.

El-Masri had been arrested by security forces on his entry to Macedonia on 31 December 2003 and then taken to a hotel in Skopje, where he was held for 23 days without access to the outside world and under constant surveillance by secret service agents. Although he was not physically mistreated by the Macedonian secret service agents, they threatened to shoot him if he attempted to leave the hotel. On 23 January 2004, El-Masri was handcuffed and blindfolded, then taken to Skopje airport, where he was handed over to masked CIA agents and abused physically and sexually. He was then forcibly taken onto a plane, thrown to the floor, chained and sedated.

Since this happened in the presence of Macedonian security officials, the Strasbourg Court judged that the Macedonian authorities were jointly responsible for the torture that El-Masri suffered and guilty of breaching Article 3 of the Convention, which prohibits torture as inhuman and degrading treatment. Also, according to the judges, the Macedonian security forces were aware that the CIA plane would transport El-Masri to Afghanistan, since they had access to the flight plans. It must therefore have been clear to them that El-Masri would face further torture, said the judges.

In Afghanistan, El-Masri was taken to the infamous 'Saltpit' prison, where he was further mistreated and questioned for extended periods. In May 2004, after four months, he was transported to Albania and then to Germany. The CIA had finally come to the conclusion that El-Masri was completely innocent and had been falsely detained.

The Court in Strasbourg made the Macedonian government jointly responsible for the torture he suffered in Afghanistan. El-Masri was arrested on Macedonian territory, although there was neither an arrest warrant nor a valid extradition request from the US government. That El-Masri was detained in a hotel and his arrest was not logged was regarded by the Court as additional proof of the illegality of the actions of the Macedonian authorities.

The Court regarded El-Masri' illegal detention as a breach of the right to freedom and security of the person under Article 5 ECHR and—on the grounds of the illegitimacy of the measures taken against El-Masri—also as an illegal intervention into his right to private and family life under Article 8.

The judges in Strasbourg evaluated the fact that the charges against persons unknown within the Macedonian security services filed by El-Masri were not pursued and were eventually rejected as the hindering of a valid legal complaint—that is, as a breach of Article 13 and the right to an effective remedy.

The Macedonian government initially claimed that El-Masri's papers had merely been checked in Macedonia on the suspicion that they may be counterfeit. Later, he was said to have travelled to Kosovo. The Strasbourg Court possessed a written statement by then Macedonian Interior Minister Hari Kostov, who confirmed that El-Masri was arrested by the Macedonian security authorities, held in Skopje under the supervision of intelligence officials and disallowed contact with the outside world, and later handed over to a CIA team.

As well as El-Masri's evidence, the judges based their verdict on that statement and on inquiries conducted by European Council Special Investigator Dick Marty.

Marty had produced detailed reports in 2006 and 2007 showing the involvement of various European states in the crimes organised by the CIA under the guise of the 'war on terror'. El-Masri's case was characterised as a 'documented transfer' because his transportation was well researched. Nevertheless, El-Masri had been previously frustrated by all of the courts in which he sought justice.

In the United States, the courts rejected a suit filed by the ACLU against CIA Director George Tenet and other CIA agents in 2005. This rejection was then upheld by the Supreme Court in 2007, which ruled that the 'state interest in protecting state secrets' outweighed 'the individual claim for justice by El-Masri'. In 2008, the state prosecutor's office in Skopje rejected El-Masri's legal complaint against unknown Macedonian judicial officials.

In Germany, despite the involvement of the Munich state attorney's office in the case and a parliamentary committee of inquiry, as well as a mountain of evidence, no charges were filed. German Interior Minister Otto Schily, who was informed about the case by US Ambassador Dan Coats, remained silent. In 2005, Justice Minister Brigitte Zypries said that 'everything constitutionally possible was done to resolve the case'. Before that, Federal Prosecutor Kay Nehm had rejected that the case fell within the jurisdiction of the attorney general on the legally dubious grounds the El-Masri case was not one of 'political abduction'.

But even that was not enough and the Munich public prosecutor had since effectively branded El-Masri as a criminal, ordering his surveillance. The phones of El-Masri's lawyer, Manfred Gnjidic, were tapped for months, breaching the constitutionally enshrined lawyer–client privilege.

The Munich state attorney's office, which had received an official legal complaint from El-Masri in 2004, finally issued an arrest warrant against 13 CIA agents at the beginning of 2007. But this was never served, since the federal government refused to lodge an extradition request with the US authorities. Berlin wanted to avoid straining relations with Washington under all circumstances and therefore thwarted all of El-Masri's attempts to seek justice.

The diplomatic cables from the US embassy in Berlin in January and February 2007, published by WikiLeaks, demonstrate the compliance of the German authorities in covering up the crimes against El-Masri. For example, then Deputy US Ambassador John Koenig warned the German government that it should carefully weigh up the consequences to bilateral relations when issuing international arrest warrants.

In December 2010, a Cologne court finally dismissed El-Masri's lawsuit against the federal government that had sought to enforce the extradition warrants against the CIA agents. As far as the German judiciary was concerned, the case was now at an end.

El-Masri also met a wall of silence at the parliamentary committee of inquiry, which, until 2009, had been investigating the involvement of the German secret service in the Iraq War and German participation in the crimes of the US secret service.

Although the committee's final report came to the conclusion that El-Masri's presentation of the case was credible, it did not accept that there had been any

German involvement. In fact, the committee had been denied access to many files, on the grounds such access might damage 'state secrets'. Thus evidence of the involvement of German security forces in the mistreatment and transportation of El-Masri could not be pursued.

The judgment in *Case of El-Masri v The Former Yugoslav Republic of Macedonia* (Application no. 39630/09) [2012] ECHR 2067 can be viewed online at www. bailii.org/eu/cases/ECHR/2012/2067.html (accessed 21 November 2013).

References

Blackstone, W. 2001. *Commentaries on the Laws of England.* London: Routledge-Cavendish.

Campbell, C. 1994. *Emergency Law in Ireland, 1918–1925.* Oxford: Clarendon Press.

Capua, J. 1977. 'The early history of martial law in England from the fourteenth century to the Petition of Right', *Cambridge Law Journal,* 36(1): 152–73.

Daly, M. 1988. *The British Occupation, 1882–1922.* Cambridge: Cambridge University Press.

De Smith, S. 1981. *Constitutional and Administrative Law.* 4th edn. London: Penguin/ Longmans.

Dicey, A. 2005. *Introduction to the Study of the Law of the Constitution.* Boston, MA: Adamant.

Ewing, K., and Gearty, C. 2000. *The Struggle for Civil Liberties: Political Freedom and the Rule of Law in Britain 1914–1945.* Oxford: Oxford University Press.

Ferguson, N. 2004. *Empire: The Rise and Demise of the British World Order and the Lessons for Global Power.* New York: Basic Books.

Hailsham, L. 1973. *Halsbury's Laws of England.* 4th edn. London: LexisNexis Butterworths.

Heuston, R. 1964. *Essays in Constitutional Law.* 2nd edn. London: Stevens.

Jankowski, J. 2000. *Egypt: A Short History.* Oxford: Oneworld.

Lee, H. 1984. *Emergency Powers.* Sydney: Law Book Co.

Pollock, F. 1902. 'What is martial law?', *Law Quarterly Review,* 70: 152.

Reza, S. 2007. 'Endless emergency: the case of Egypt', *New Criminal Law Review,* 10(4): 532–53.

Rowe, P., and Whelan, C. (eds). 1985. *Military Intervention in Democratic Societies.* London: Croom Helm.

Savage, C. 2010. 'Court dismisses a case asserting torture by CIA', *New York Times,* 8 September.

Simpson, A. 2004. *Human Rights and the End of Empire: Britain and the Genesis of the European Convention.* Oxford: Oxford University Press.

Vatikiotis, P. 1992. *The History of Modern Egypt.* 4th edn. Baltimore, MD: Johns Hopkins University.

Wade, E., and Phillips, G. 1970. *Constitutional Law.* 8th edn. London: Longmans.

Whelan, C. 1985. 'Military intervention in democratic societies: the role of law'. In P. Rowe and C. Whelan (eds), *Military Intervention in Democratic Societies.* London: Croom Helm.

10 Can international law stop wars of aggression?

To what extent does the international law of war or international human rights law provide protection against illegal wars of aggression and associated human rights abuses? Despite the post-war Nuremberg principles outlawing wars of aggression, there seems little prospect of any major power being held to account, let alone the United States, which has refused to accept the jurisdiction of even the International Criminal Court (ICC).

These realities were underscored by the 2006 decision by the prosecutor of the ICC on the 2003 invasion of Iraq. As examined in this chapter, the prosecutor stated that the Court had a mandate to examine the conduct during the conflict, but not whether the decision to engage in armed conflict was legal or a crime of aggression.

Moreover, despite many documented complaints of war crimes committed by the invading allies, the ruling also declared that there was insufficient evidence of the targeting of civilians or clearly excessive attacks. And although there was sufficient evidence of wilful killing or inhuman treatment of civilians, the instances were not enough to argue that they were committed as part of a plan or policy or as part of a large-scale commission of such crimes; hence the cases were deemed to be outside the court's jurisdiction (Moreno-Ocampo 2006).

Domestically, international law reserves to the national state the power to override even the most basic legal and democratic rights amid war and alleged emergencies. In the Universal Declaration of Human Rights, the International Covenant on Civil and Political Rights and other related instruments, the listed civil and legal rights are mostly subject to far-reaching exemptions, such as 'national security', 'public safety' or 'public emergency which threatens the life of the nation'.

This chapter can only briefly survey the international law issues relating to the declaration or conduct of wars, formal or informal. Developments since 1990 have pointed toward a mounting disregard for international law by the United States and its partners.

Since the first Gulf War of 1990–91, the ever-greater assertion of US militarism by successive presidents—George H. Bush, Bill Clinton, George W. Bush, Barack Obama and Donald Trump—has brought humanity to the point at which the rules of war adopted after the massive casualties and horrors of the last world war are being openly flouted.

Over the quarter-century that followed the 1991 liquidation of the Soviet Union, the United States and other imperialist powers arrogated to themselves the so-called right to militarily attack, invade or overturn governments in other countries under the cover of 'humanitarian' interventions or 'pre-emptive self-defence'.

The advent of the Trump administration and its belligerent 'America First' doctrine took to a new level the drive by the US government to use its global military supremacy to claw back the hegemony that it had established in the wake of its victories over its main rivals—Germany and Japan—in World War II. In one strategic area of the globe after another, from the Middle East to the Balkans and the Indo-Pacific—US governments increasingly sidelined international law to resort to force.

The UN Charter

Article 2(4) of the UN Charter prohibits 'the threat or use of force against the territorial integrity or political independence of any state, or in any other manner inconsistent with the Purposes of the United Nations'. There is no provision for 'pre-emptive self-defence' or 'humanitarian intervention'. Article 51, in Chapter VII of the Charter, exempts only 'the inherent right of individual or collective self-defence if an armed attack occurs against a Member of the United Nations, until the Security Council has taken measures necessary to maintain international peace and security'.

In the first 1990–91 Gulf War assault on Iraq, the George H. Bush administration was able to obtain a fig leaf of authority for its invasion on the pretext of defending 'little Kuwait'. Assisted by Russia's complicity and China's abstention, Washington secured a UN Security Council resolution, invoking Chapter VII of the UN Charter, that empowered states to use 'all necessary means' to force Iraq out of Kuwait. This became a green light for a military assault and partial dismemberment of Iraq by a US-led coalition.

The UN Security Council, dominated by the major powers, proved itself to be a clearing house for war. Nevertheless, to free themselves from any—even formal—legal constraints, the United States and its allies later brought forward two doctrines to justify overturning the post-war prohibition of aggressive wars: 'humanitarian' interventions and 'pre-emptive self-defence'.

During the North Atlantic Treaty Organization (NATO) attacks in Kosovo and other parts of the former Yugoslavia in the 1990s, the Clinton administration operated outside the United Nations, but via the NATO alliances. Having helped to foment the break-up of Yugoslavia, the United States adopted a 'humanitarian' mask, claiming to be protecting minorities from Serbian aggression. Nevertheless, it was unable to push an authorising resolution through the UN Security Council.

In 2005, an attempt was then made to legalise such aggression, overriding Article 2(7) of the UN Charter banning domestic interventions. Article 2(7) stipulates that '[n]othing contained in the present Charter shall authorize the United Nations to intervene in matters which are essentially within the domestic jurisdiction of any state'. The United States and its allies—notably, Britain—pushed through a UN General Assembly a 'responsibility to protect' resolution, nominally to prevent governments committing 'genocide, war crimes, ethnic cleansing and crimes against humanity'.

However, the use of force for such purposes is still subject to approval by the UN Security Council. Paragraph 139 of the 2005 World Summit Outcome Document makes this clear:

> [W]e are prepared to take collective action, in a timely and decisive manner, through the Security Council, in accordance with the Charter, including Chapter VII, on a case-by-case basis and in cooperation with relevant regional organizations as appropriate, should peaceful means be inadequate and national authorities manifestly fail to protect their populations from genocide, war crimes, ethnic cleansing and crimes against humanity.

The illegal 2003 invasion of Iraq

None of those responsible for the 2003 invasion and occupation of Iraq—notably, US President George W. Bush, British Prime Minister Tony Blair and Australian Prime Minister John Howard—have been held to account in domestic or international courts. Despite overwhelming legal opinion that the war was illegal under international law, and clear evidence of immense human suffering, war crimes and abuse of detainees, none of these leaders has been placed on trial.

There is no precise count of how many Iraqis have died as a result of the criminal actions of the Bush administration and its allies. The US military deliberately kept no tally. A scientifically based estimate is, however, in the public domain. In October 2006, the *Lancet* medical journal published the results of a Johns Hopkins University survey into the number of deaths caused by the US invasion and occupation of Iraq. A total of 1,849 households—close to 12,000 people—were interviewed about fatalities in their families and the causes of death, during the period spanning 14 months prior to the invasion through to the time they were questioned. Death certificates were provided in the majority of cases and the sample spanned the whole of Iraq (Burnham et al. 2006).

The researchers concluded that the crude mortality rate in Iraq had soared from 5.5 per 1,000, before March 2003, to 7.5 per 1,000, then to 10.9 per 1,000, and to 19.8 per 1,000 between June 2005 and June 2006. Extrapolated to the entire population, the study estimated that 393,000–943,000 additional people had died as a result of the US occupation, with the median estimate being 655,000 deaths. The vast majority had died as a result of violence, including gunshots, car bombs and other explosive devices, and air strikes. Gunshot wounds caused 56 per cent of violent deaths and US or allied forces were directly involved in an estimated 31 per cent (Burnham et al. 2006).

The impact of the war has been far greater than the number of deaths indicated by the survey. The number of persons physically and psychologically injured has not yet been assessed. UN agencies conservatively estimate that close to 2 million

Iraqis have fled the country and a further 1.7 million are considered to be internally displaced persons. In other words, the invasion and brutal occupation of Iraq can credibly be held responsible for the death, injury or displacement of well over 20 per cent of the country's population (Burnham et al. 2006).

As discussed in Chapters 3–5, the governments of the United States, Britain and Australia insisted that the invasion was legal, despite their systematic deception and ultimate decision to proceed without the authority of a UN Security Council resolution. US and UK officials argued that existing UN Security Council resolutions related to the 1990–91 Gulf, the subsequent ceasefire (Resolutions 660, 678) and inspections of Iraqi weapons programmes (Resolution 1441) had already authorised the invasion.

But many international law experts rejected these assertions and established that an additional Security Council resolution, which the United States and Britain failed to obtain, would have been necessary to specifically authorise the invasion. These experts included the International Commission of Jurists, the US-based National Lawyers Guild, a group of 31 Canadian law professors and the US-based Lawyers Committee on Nuclear Policy (Miller 2013).

Then UN Secretary General Kofi Annan declared that the war was illegal. In September 2004, he stated: 'I have indicated it was not in conformity with the UN Charter. From our point of view and the UN Charter point of view, it [the war] was illegal' (quoted in MacAskill and Borger 2004).

After reviewing the arguments and evidence in some detail— particularly, the British government's decision to join the invasion—international lawyer Phillipe Sands drew the same fundamental conclusion (Sands 2005: 174–204). Sands (2005: 201–02) concluded that 'the legal arguments put forward by the US and British governments to justify the war are unsustainable . . . international law did not permit force to overthrow Saddam Hussein'.

According to a detailed legal investigation conducted by a Dutch government commission of inquiry, headed by former Netherlands Supreme Court President Willibrord Davids, the invasion did indeed violate international law (Hirsch 2010). The Dutch commission further concluded that the notion of 'regime change', as practised by the powers that invaded Iraq, had 'no basis in international law' and that UN Resolution 1441 'cannot reasonably be interpreted as authorising individual member states to use military force to compel Iraq to comply with the Security Council's resolutions' (Hirsch 2010).

As reviewed in Chapter 2, the British government's own Chilcot Inquiry concluded that the process of identifying the legal basis for the invasion of Iraq was unsatisfactory, and that the actions of the United States and Britain undermined the authority of the United Nations.

As outlined in Article 39 of the UN Charter, the UN Security Council has the ability to rule on the legality of the war, but no UN member nation has asked it to do so. The United States and Britain have veto power in the Security Council, so such action would be very unlikely even if the issue were raised. The UN General Assembly may ask the International Court of Justice (ICJ), 'the principal judicial organ of the United Nations' (Article 92), to give either an 'advisory opinion' or 'judgment' on the legality of the war, but no such vote has been taken either.

The United States and its partners were guilty of the primary crime for which leading Nazis were tried at the International Military Tribunal (IMT) at Nuremberg in 1946: conducting a war of aggression. Article 6(a) of the Charter of the International Military Tribunal, upon which the Nuremberg prosecution was based, defined as 'crimes against peace' the 'planning, preparation, initiation or waging of a war of aggression, or a war in violation of international treaties, agreements or assurances, or participation in a common plan or conspiracy for the accomplishment of any of the foregoing'. In its judgment, the Nuremberg Tribunal stated:

> War is essentially an evil thing. Its consequences are not confined to the belligerent states alone, but affect the whole world. To initiate a war of aggression, therefore, is not only an international crime; it is the supreme international crime differing only from other war crimes in that it contains within itself the accumulated evil of the whole.
>
> (Broomhall 2003: 46)

Benjamin Ferencz, a US prosecutor at the Nuremberg trials and a former law professor, concluded that President Bush should be tried for launching a war of aggression. In his Foreword to Michael Haas's 2008 book, *George W. Bush, War Criminal? The Bush Administration's Liability for 269 War Crimes*, Ferencz stated:

> [A] prima facie case can be made that the United States is guilty of the supreme crime against humanity, that being an illegal war of aggression against a sovereign nation . . . The United Nations charter has a provision which was agreed to by the United States, formulated by the United States, in fact, after World War II. It says that from now on, no nation can use armed force without the permission of the U.N. Security Council. They can use force in connection with self-defense, but a country can't use force in anticipation of self-defense. Regarding Iraq, the last Security Council resolution essentially said, 'Look, send the weapons inspectors out to Iraq, have them come back and tell us what they've found—then we'll figure out what we're going to do.' The U.S. was impatient, and decided to invade Iraq—which was all pre-arranged of course. So, the United States went to war, in violation of the charter.
>
> (Haas 2008: xii)

Ferencz quoted Elizabeth Wilmshurst, the British deputy legal adviser to the foreign ministry, who resigned before the Iraq War started, stating in her resignation letter:

> I regret that I cannot agree that it is lawful to use force against Iraq without a second Security Council resolution . . . [A]n unlawful use of force on such a scale amounts to the crime of aggression; nor can I agree with such action in circumstances that are so detrimental to the international order and the rule of law.
>
> (Quoted in Haas 2008: xii; see also
> Sands 2005: 189–90)

'Pre-emptive defence', from Bush to Trump

In an April 2017 US attack in Syria, the United States acted alone, without bothering to seek UN authorisation. While the 1999 NATO bombing of Kosovo for 'humanitarian' purposes violated the UN Charter, the Syrian airstrikes involved the United States acting alone and without exhausting the avenues for peaceful resolution of the issue (Kristof 2017).

The Trump administration's attacks also went beyond doctrine of 'pre-emptive' war, promulgated by the George W. Bush administration in 2002 and implemented in March 2003 with the invasion of Iraq, based on lies about 'weapons of mass destruction' (WMDs). The Bush White House had asserted the United States' right to take unilateral military action against another country before it could become a 'sufficient threat to our national security'. Under Trump, the United States did not claim that Syria's alleged use of chemical weapons or the presence of the so-called Islamic State terrorist group (ISIS) in Afghanistan constituted such a threat to the United States (Kristof 2017).

The Bush doctrine overturned the UN Charter's insistence that self-defence was confined to responding to an armed attack that had already occurred. The United States insisted it has the right to attack any state that it considers has the potential to pose a danger at some future point—placing virtually every country in the world on the list of possible targets.

The invasion of Iraq, which resulted in the deaths of countless thousands of innocent people and set in motion catastrophic processes that have engulfed the Middle East ever since, was conducted by the United States and its closest allies ('the coalition of the willing') in defiance of their inability to obtain a UN Security Council vote of authorisation. The war was launched despite the protests of millions of people, including hundreds of lawyers and legal academics who denounced it as an illegal war of aggression.

The bipartisan nature of the US war policy was demonstrated by President Obama's December 2009 speech—ironically accepting the Nobel Peace Prize—in which he embraced the Bush doctrine. Obama declared the United States' exclusive right to conduct 'preventative wars' against any identified 'threats' to Washington's interests. In effect, Obama sought to enunciate a wider principle to sanctify wars of aggression. He declared: 'Nations will continue to find the use of force not only necessary but morally justified.'

Elected as an anti-war candidate in 2008, Obama became the first US president to spend an entire two terms of office waging wars. In the case of the 2011 US-led NATO military intervention to oust the Gaddafi regime in Libya, the United States and the other powers first obtained a UN vote for a 'no-fly zone' over the country, ostensibly to end attacks against civilians that might constitute 'crimes against humanity'. They then exploited Libya's supposed breaches of that declaration to justify intensively bombing the country.

Trump's presidency represents both a continuation and a qualitative deepening of this process. Pretences of abiding by international law have been swept aside to assert the untrammelled right of the United States to use its military arsenal wherever and whenever it chooses. *New York Times* columnist Nicholas

Kristof (2017), a propagandist of 'humanitarian' war, summed up this doctrine when he wrote: 'President Trump's air strikes against Syria were of dubious legality . . . But most of all, they were right.'

With the breakdown of the post-war legal framework, the danger of another world war is growing. As Leon Trotsky forewarned in 1934, writing in the wake of the collapse of the UN's predecessor, the League of Nations, the irresolvable contradictions of the global capitalist nation-state system are again 'bringing humanity face to face with the volcanic eruption of American imperialism' (Trotsky 1934: para. 4).

Unlawful US attacks on Syria and Afghanistan in 2017

Arguably, the Trump administration's April 2017 cruise missile attack on Syria, followed closely by the dropping of the largest non-nuclear weapon in the US arsenal on the Afghanistan–Pakistan border, illustrated a new period of breakdown in international law.

First, unlike previous US governments, the Trump administration made no attempt to provide legal pretexts, however flimsy, for its bombardments. Second, the United States acted without any UN approval. Third, the dropping of the huge massive ordnance air blast (MOAB) bomb in Afghanistan marked the readiness of the United States to kill civilians indiscriminately, regardless of international sanctions against the disproportionate use of military force.

The UN Charter adopted in 1945, after the barbarism of two world wars, provides for only two justifications for the use of military force: authorisation by the UN Security Council or self-defence after an armed attack has occurred. There were no Security Council resolutions to sanction the US attacks and Washington did not even attempt to claim that they were necessary for self-defence.

At the UN Security Council meeting called to discuss the US attack, the Syrian government's denial of responsibility for the alleged use of chemical weapons was flatly dismissed by the United States and its allies, along with the fact that US-backed forces have used such weapons in Syria in the past and blamed it on the government, as in Ghouta in 2013.

The illegality of the US attack was also treated with disdain. Syria's ambassador to the United Nations called the missile strikes a 'flagrant act of aggression', in violation 'of the charter of the United Nations as well as all international norms and laws'. In response, US Ambassador to the United Nations Nikki Haley declared: 'When the international community consistently fails in its duty to act collectively, there are times when states are compelled to take their own action.' In other words, the United States insisted it has the right to wage war against any country it chooses.

As stated earlier, Article 2(4) of the UN Charter prohibits 'the threat or use of force against the territorial integrity or political independence of any state'. Article 51 provides for 'the inherent right of individual or collective self-defence', but only 'if an armed attack occurs against a Member of the United Nations' and 'until the Security Council has taken measures necessary to maintain international peace and security'.

Even then, as noted earlier, Article 2(7) specifies: 'Nothing contained in the present Charter shall authorise the United Nations to intervene in matters which are essentially within the domestic jurisdiction of any state.' That would include an internal gas attack by a government, even if proven.

Syria had not attacked the United States or any other country before Trump ordered the missile strike. Therefore Trump committed an illegal act of aggression against Syria.

Even if the Syrian government did carry out a chemical weapons attack on the town of Khan Sheikhun, in southern Idlib Province, on 4 April 2017—and no verified evidence of that has been produced—that would not legally justify the US missile strike. The use of chemical weapons within Syria is not an armed attack on the United States.

Article 8 of the 1998 Rome Statute of the International Criminal Court states:

1   For the purpose of this Statute, 'crime of aggression' means the planning, preparation, initiation or execution, by a person in a position effectively to exercise control over or to direct the political or military action of a State, of an act of aggression which, by its character, gravity and scale, constitutes a manifest violation of the Charter of the United Nations.

2   For the purpose of paragraph 1, 'act of aggression' means the use of armed force by a State against the sovereignty, territorial integrity or political independence of another State, or in any other manner inconsistent with the Charter of the United Nations. Any of the following acts, regardless of a declaration of war, shall, in accordance with United Nations General Assembly resolution 3314 (XXIX) of 14 December 1974, qualify as an act of aggression:

(a)   The invasion or attack by the armed forces of a State of the territory of another State, or any military occupation, however temporary, resulting from such invasion or attack, or any annexation by the use of force of the territory of another State or part thereof;

(b)   Bombardment by the armed forces of a State against the territory of another State or the use of any weapons by a State against the territory of another State;

(c)   The blockade of the ports or coasts of a State by the armed forces of another State;

(d)   An attack by the armed forces of a State on the land, sea or air forces, or marine and air fleets of another State;

(e)   The use of armed forces of one State which are within the territory of another State with the agreement of the receiving State, in contravention of the conditions provided for in the agreement or any extension of their presence in such territory beyond the termination of the agreement;

(f)   The action of a State in allowing its territory, which it has placed at the disposal of another State, to be used by that other State for perpetrating an act of aggression against a third State;

(g) The sending by or on behalf of a State of armed bands, groups, irregulars or mercenaries, which carry out acts of armed force against another State of such gravity as to amount to the acts listed above, or its substantial involvement therein.

Despite the apparent breadth of this prohibition, since 1946 there have been no domestic or international trials for alleged crimes of aggression—although the UN Security Council has, on occasion, determined that acts of aggression were committed by, for example, South Africa and Israel. Since amendments to the Rome Statute in 2010, new trials for alleged crimes of aggression on a domestic and international level are a possibility. Because of the difficult procedures for prosecuting the crime of aggression and the coming into force of the amendments, some commentators, such as Milanovic (2012: 166), and O'Connell and Niyazmatov (2012: 191), however, doubt whether any person will ever be prosecuted for the crime of aggression as defined in the Rome Statute.

Equally unlawful was the Trump administration's dropping of the 22,000 lb MOAB (referred to by the US military as the 'mother of all bombs'), supposedly on tunnels built by 'Islamic State [ISIS] forces' near the Afghanistan–Pakistan border.

In Afghanistan, the United States was able to operate militarily under the cloak of the fraudulent 'war on terror' that was rubber-stamped by the United Nations in 2001 following the 9/11 terrorist attacks. UN Security Council Resolution 1373 empowered states to combat terrorism 'by all means', effectively giving the United States a licence to pursue its predatory bid to take control of the resource-rich and strategically vital Middle East and Central Asia (Head 2012: 179–85).

Acting on the assertion that the Taliban government had assisted the 9/11 attacks, the Bush administration occupied Afghanistan and installed a series of puppet regimes. The latest such government was evidently informed of, and perfunctorily consented to, the bombing, as provided by the Security and Defence Cooperation Agreement that Afghanistan was prevailed upon to sign with the United States in 2014.

However, the use of the largest explosive device the United States has utilised since dropping atomic bombs on Hiroshima and Nagasaki in World War II was in blatant disregard for civilian casualties. It was the first time such a weapon, capable of killing people within a radius of up to 2 km, was used in combat. It was also disproportionate to any threat posed by the relatively small number of ISIS fighters said to be in the region. And it was designed to terrorise the people of Afghanistan and the world.

Under the norms of international humanitarian law (IHL), any military operations, even if sanctioned by the United Nations, must obey the rules of 'necessity' and 'proportionality'.

(1) The scale of the military force must be necessary to deal with the purported threat.

(2) The rule of proportionality prohibits any 'attack which may be expected to cause incidental loss of civilian life, injury to civilians, damage to civilian

objects, or a combination thereof, which would be excessive in relation to the concrete and direct military advantage anticipated' (Article 51(1)(b) of the Rome Statute).

(3) International humanitarian law forbids the use, or threat of use, of any weapon or tactic when the primary purpose of the operation is to terrorise the civilian population.

Article 8(2)(b) of the Rome Statute prohibits:

Other serious violations of the laws and customs applicable in international armed conflict, within the established framework of international law, namely, any of the following acts:

i   Intentionally directing attacks against the civilian population as such or against individual civilians not taking direct part in hostilities;

ii Intentionally directing attacks against civilian objects, that is, objects which are not military objectives;

iii Intentionally directing attacks against personnel, installations, material, units or vehicles involved in a humanitarian assistance or peacekeeping mission in accordance with the Charter of the United Nations, as long as they are entitled to the protection given to civilians or civilian objects under the international law of armed conflict;

iv Intentionally launching an attack in the knowledge that such attack will cause incidental loss of life or injury to civilians or damage to civilian objects or widespread, long-term and severe damage to the natural environment which would be clearly excessive in relation to the concrete and direct overall military advantage anticipated;

[. . .]

xx Employing weapons, projectiles and material and methods of warfare which are of a nature to cause superfluous injury or unnecessary suffering or which are inherently indiscriminate in violation of the international law of armed conflict, provided that such weapons, projectiles and material and methods of warfare are the subject of a comprehensive prohibition and are included in an annex to this Statute, by an amendment in accordance with the relevant provisions set forth in articles 121 and 123;

[. . .]

The International Criminal Court and the invasion of Iraq

The lack of any serious enforcement of any of these provisions has been illustrated by the record of the International Criminal Court (ICC), established in 2002, on the 2003 Iraq invasion and subsequent occupation of the country by the United States and its allies.

Then ICC Prosecutor Moreno-Ocampo reported in February 2006 that he had received 240 communications in connection with the invasion of Iraq in March 2003 alleging that various war crimes had been committed. The overwhelming majority of these communications came from individuals and groups within the United States and Britain. Many of these complaints concerned the British participation in the invasion, as well as the alleged responsibility for torture deaths while in detention in British-controlled areas (Norton-Taylor 2005).

Moreno-Ocampo (2006) explained that two sets of complaints were involved:

(1) complaints concerning the legality of the invasion itself; and
(2) complaints concerning the conduct of hostilities between March and May 2003, which included allegations in respect of:

(a) the targeting of civilians or clearly excessive attacks; and
(b) willful killing or inhumane treatment of civilians.

Three participants in the invasion—Australia, Poland and Britain—were state parties to the Rome Statute that established the ICC and therefore their nationals were liable to prosecution in the Court for the violation of any relevant international criminal laws. Because the United States was not a state party, it could not be prosecuted by the Court (except for crimes that took place in the territory of a state that had accepted the Court's jurisdiction, or situations referred to the Court by the UN Security Council, over which the United States has a veto). (Moreno-Ocampo 2006: 4) explained that, although the Rome Statute:

... includes the crime of aggression, it indicates that the Court may not exercise jurisdiction over the crime until a provision has been adopted which defines the crime and sets out the conditions under which the Court may exercise jurisdiction with respect to it (Article 5(2)).

Hence:

[T]he International Criminal Court has a mandate to examine the conduct during the conflict, but not whether the decision to engage in armed conflict was legal. As the Prosecutor of the International Criminal Court, I do not have the mandate to address the arguments on the legality of the use of force or the crime of aggression.

(Moreno-Ocampo 2006: 4)

The states parties to the ICC adopted such a definition at a review conference in 2010, but the Court was able to exercise jurisdiction only over acts of aggression committed after this amendment entered into force (Miley 2010).

In regards to the targeting of civilians or a possible excess of violence, Moreno-Ocampo (2006: 6) stated: 'The available information established that a considerable number of civilians died or were injured during the military operations.' The ICC estimated a range of approximately 3,750–6,900 people (Moreno-Ocampo 2006: 6, fn 12). However, he concluded: 'The available information did not indicate intentional attacks on a civilian population' (Moreno-Ocampo 2006: 8).

Moreno-Ocampo also considered whether there were incidents in which, even though civilians were not intentionally targeted, the attack was nonetheless clearly excessive to military necessity. For this, he bore in mind: (a) the anticipated civilian damage or injury; (b) the anticipated military advantage; and (c) whether the former was 'clearly excessive' in relation to the latter. He concluded that, while many facts remain to be determined, the available evidence 'did not allow for the conclusion that there was a reasonable basis to believe that a clearly excessive attack within the jurisdiction of the Court had been committed' (Moreno-Ocampo 2006: 7). As a result:

> After exhausting all measures appropriate during the analysis phase, the Office determined that, while many facts remained undetermined, the available information did not provide a reasonable basis to believe that a crime within the jurisdiction of the Court had been committed.
>
> (Moreno-Ocampo 2006: 7)

As far as the allegations of wilful killing or inhuman treatment of civilians, Moreno-Ocampo concluded that there was a reasonable basis to believe that crimes within the jurisdiction of the Court had been committed. He explained that the information available did support a reasonable basis for an estimated 4–12 victims of wilful killing and a limited number of victims of inhuman treatment, totalling in all fewer than 20 persons. He also reported that, in all of these cases, the national authorities had initiated proceedings (Moreno-Ocampo 2006: 7–9).

Moreno-Ocampo stated that this evidence on its own was not sufficient for the initiation of an investigation by the ICC, since the Rome Statute requires consideration of admissibility before the Court, in light of the gravity of the crimes. In examining this criterion, he explained:

> For war crimes, a specific gravity threshold is set down in Article 8(1), which states that 'the Court shall have jurisdiction in respect of war crimes in particular when committed as part of a plan or policy or as part of a large-scale commission of such crimes'. This threshold is not an element of the crime, and the words 'in particular' suggest that this is not a strict requirement. It does, however, provide Statute guidance that the Court is intended to focus on situations meeting these requirements. According to the available information, it did not appear that any of the criteria of Article 8(1) were satisfied. Even if one were to assume that Article 8(1) had been satisfied, it

would then be necessary to consider the general gravity requirement under Article 53(1)(b). The Office considers various factors in assessing gravity. A key consideration is the number of victims of particularly serious crimes, such as wilful killing or rape. The number of potential victims of crimes within the jurisdiction of the Court in this situation—4 to 12 victims of willful killing and a limited number of victims of inhuman treatment—was of a different order than the number of victims found in other situations under investigation or analysis by the Office . . . Taking into account all the considerations, the situation did not appear to meet the required threshold of the Statute.

(Moreno-Ocampo 2006: 9)

Moreno-Ocampo (2006: 3, fn 10) qualified this statement by noting that 'this conclusion can be reconsidered in the light of new facts or evidence'.

In 2014, then ICC Prosecutor Fatou Bensouda announced that the preliminary examination of the situation in Iraq, previously concluded in 2006, was to be reopened following submission of further information on alleged crimes (Office of the Prosecutor 2017: 40). Subsequently, in December 2017, Bensouda reported—once again—that war crimes had been committed:

On the basis of the information available, including some of the allegations brought to its attention since 2014 and considered credible, the Office reaffirms its previous conclusion that there is a reasonable basis to believe that in the period from 20 March 2003 through 28 July 2009 members of the UK armed forces committed the following war crimes in the context of the armed conflicts in Iraq against persons in their custody, including: wilful killing/murder (article 8(2)(a)(i) or article 8(2)(c)(i)), torture and inhuman/cruel treatment (article 8(2)(a)(ii) or article 8(2)(c)(i)), outrages upon personal dignity (article 8(2)(b)(xxi) or article 8(2)(c)(ii)), and rape or other forms of sexual violence (article 8(2)(b)(xxii) or article 8(2)(e)(vi)).

(Office of the Prosecutor 2017: 43)

Bensouda, however, followed her predecessor in dismissing allegations that British troops committed any war crimes on the battlefield:

The new information available does not alter the previous determination that, in the absence of information indicating intent to kill or target civilians or civilian objects, or cause clearly excessive civilian injuries, there is no reasonable basis to believe that war crimes within the jurisdiction of the Court were committed by British armed forces in the course of their military operations not related to the context of arrests and detentions. While additional incidents were brought to the Office's attention, the factual information provided does not constitute a reasonable basis to believe that the British armed forces intended to target civilians in these incidents.

(Office of the Prosecutor 2017: 44)

Even with regard to the initial finding of war crimes, nearly 15 years after the invasion began, there was still no definitive outcome, but only an ongoing 'admissibility assessment':

> Following a thorough factual and legal assessment of the information available, the Office has reached the conclusion that there is a reasonable basis to believe that members of the UK armed forces committed war crimes within the jurisdiction of the Court against persons in their custody. The Office's admissibility assessment is ongoing and is intended to be completed within a reasonable time frame.
>
> (Office of the Prosecutor 2017: 45)

Given this record, it is hardly surprising that British defence officials had previously said they were confident that the ICC would not move to the next stage and announce a formal investigation. This was supposedly because Britain had the capacity to investigate the allegations itself. A British government spokesperson said:

> We have a legal responsibility to investigate credible allegations of wrongdoing by UK forces, and that is what we are already doing as part of service police legacy investigations, which is reviewing the relatively small number of remaining cases after the closure of IHAT [the Iraq Historic Allegations Team], and through Operation Northmoor. We are confident that our existing efforts to investigate allegations preclude the need for any investigation by the ICC.
>
> (Bowcott 2017)

Bensouda's report itself referred to the fact that the British government had shut down its own Iraq Historic Allegations Team (IHAT) on 30 June 2017. Seven years earlier, in March 2010, confronted by a large volume of allegations of criminality by British forces in the Iraq War, the Ministry of Defence had established the unit, which comprised members of the Royal Navy Police (RNP) and ex-civilian police detectives. Its purpose was to channel the complaints into an official dead end, while officially serving to ensure that credible claims were properly investigated and the facts established.

Based on its official figures, IHAT received a total of around 3,400 allegations of unlawful killings and ill treatment between 2010 and the end of June 2017 (Office of the Prosecutor 2017: 41). Its case list included 52 allegations of 'unlawful death' involving 63 victims and 93 allegations of mistreatment involving 179 victims, including all but one of the cases referred to the ICC. Nearly four years after its establishment, IHAT has completed only a handful of the cases on its books, fining one soldier only £3,000 for badly beating an Iraqi, which was captured on video (Shaoul 2014).

By the time it was closed down, IHAT had forecast that its caseload was expected to reduce to around 20 investigations by summer 2017. Its remaining investigations were reintegrated into the military's own service police system and taken over by a new unit known as the Service Police Legacy Investigations (SPLI) (Office of the Prosecutor 2017: 42). Thus it is highly unlikely that any British war crime committed during the Iraq War will be seriously prosecuted, either in domestic or international courts.

Underscoring the impotence of the ICC is the refusal of the United States to recognise its authority. This has deep historical significance. The United States played a leading role in establishing the Nuremberg principles, but now refuses to submit to their enforcement—which amounts to an admission that if the United States were to be subject to an impartial application of the Nuremberg principles today, leading US officials would face trial.

References

Bowcott, O. 2017. 'The Hague says claims of war crimes by UK troops have "reasonable basis" ', *The Guardian*, 4 December, www.theguardian.com/law/2017/dec/04/icc-to-continue-investigation-into-claims-of-war-crimes-by-british-troops (accessed 10 February 2018).

Broomhall, B. 2003. *International Justice and the International Criminal Court: Between Sovereignty and the Rule of Law*. 2nd edn. Oxford: Oxford University Press.

Burnham, G., Lafta, R., Doocy, S., and Roberts, L. 2006. 'Mortality after the 2003 invasion of Iraq: a cross-sectional cluster sample survey', *The Lancet*, 368(9545): 1421–28.

Haas, M. 2008. *George W. Bush, War Criminal? The Bush Administration's Liability for 269 War Crimes*. New York: Praeger.

Head, M. 2012. 'Global governance implications of terrorism: using UN Resolutions to justify abuse of basic rights'. In M. Head, S. Mann, and S. Kozlina (eds), *Transnational Governance: Emerging Models of Global Legal Regulation*. London: Ashgate.

Hirsch, A. 2010. 'Iraq invasion violated international law, Dutch inquiry finds', *The Guardian*, 12 January, www.theguardian.com/world/2010/jan/12/iraq-invasion-violated-interational-law-dutch-inquiry-finds (accessed 11 January 2018).

Kristof, N. 2017. 'Trump was right to strike Syria', *The New York Times*, 7 April, https://kristof.blogs.nytimes.com/2017/04/07/trump-was-right-to-strike-syria/ (accessed 10 May 2017).

MacAskill, E., and Borger, J. 2004. 'Iraq war was illegal and breached UN Charter, says Annan', *The Guardian*, 16 September, www.theguardian.com/world/2004/sep/16/iraq.iraq (accessed 12 May 2018).

Milanovic, M. 2012. 'Aggression and legality: custom in Kampala', *Journal of International Criminal Justice*, 10(1): 165–87.

Miley, S. 2010. 'ICC nations define crime of aggression', *Jurist*, 12 June, www.jurist.org/news/2010/06/icc-nations-adopt-crime-of-aggression/ (accessed 10 November 2012).

Miller, R. 2013. 'Links to opinions on legality of war against Iraq', www.robincmiller.com/ir-legal.htm (accessed 11 May 2018).

Moreno-Ocampo, L. 2006. 'Letter concerning the situation in Iraq', 9 February, www.iccnow.org/documents/OTP_letter_to_senders_re_Iraq_9_February_2006.pdf (accessed 14 October 2017).

Norton-Taylor, R. 2005. 'International court hears anti-war claims', *The Guardian*, 6 May.

O'Connell, M., and Niyazmatov, M. 2012. 'What is aggression? Comparing the *jus ad bellum* and the ICC Statute', *Journal of International Criminal Justice*, 10(1): 189–207.

Office of the Prosecutor. 2017. *Report on Preliminary Examination Activities 2017*, 4 December, www.icc-cpi.int/itemsDocuments/2017-PE-rep/2017-otp-rep-PE_ENG. pdf (accessed 10 February 2018).

Sands, P. 2005. *Lawless World*. London: Penguin.

Shaoul, J. 2014. 'UK referred to International Criminal Court for war crimes in Iraq', *World Socialist Web Site*, 3 June, www.wsws.org/en/articles/2014/06/03/iraq-j03. html (accessed 11 February 2018).

Trotsky, L. 1934. *War and the Fourth International*. New York: Pioneer.

11 Would referenda provide any alternative?

Possibly the most democratic suggestions for war-making powers have been proposals for popular votes, or official referenda. Such propositions purport to address the incapacity or unwillingness of congressional or parliamentary mechanisms to act as a check on governments. No such referendum has ever taken place, however.

Proposals for referenda go back for centuries. Their proponents include prominent Enlightenment political theorists such as the Marquis de Condorcet and Immanuel Kant. At times, proposals have acquired popular support—most significantly, in the United States during the inter-war years. But in the face of entrenched and vehement opposition by ruling elites, none of these calls has ever succeeded in being implemented.

Some of these propositions have taken the issue to an international level. They have sought to introduce referenda as compulsory requirements in all countries, so that their populations could act in unison to stop their governments sending people off to kill each other along national lines. But no such global agreement has been reached, despite the horrors of two world wars. It has proven to be impossible under the current nation-state system, which is rooted in the antagonistic material interests of rival capitalist classes.

Even if such a world pact could be achieved, the question would remain as to how effective it would be. Could referenda, if ever permitted, actually be effective in halting or restraining drives to war? Could majority anti-war votes, even overwhelming ones, prevent wars? Or would the machinations, lies and deceptions of governments, and the underlying economic and political power of the ruling establishments, effectively lock countries into paths toward war, regardless of the wishes and fears of ordinary working people?

Moreover, most of the referenda proposals have contained exceptions—arguably, loopholes—permitting governments to go to war, without a popular vote, in cases in which the country is being actually invaded or attacked militarily. The history of warfare, however, as reviewed in earlier chapters, demonstrates that governments invariably go to war on the pretext of responding to an attack or forestalling an imminent one. Wars have generally been triggered by intrigues, alliances, blockades or provocations that have made wars virtually inevitable. Many examples could be cited, not least the Roosevelt administration's calculated moves to incite the Japanese attack on Pearl Harbor in

December 1941, which created the conditions for the United States to declare war on Japan despite widespread public anti-war sentiment. As discussed in this chapter, this oppositional sentiment had been partly reflected in opinion polls showing up to 75 per cent support for war referenda.

Enlightenment visions

War referenda were among the principles enunciated by some Enlightenment thinkers as part of their visions for human peace and progress. Among them were the Marquis de Condorcet, who proposed referenda in 1793, and Immanuel Kant, who did so in 1795. Their propositions expressed the hopes generated, in the dawning of the capitalist era, by the strivings to overturn the old despotic regimes, as seen the English, American and French revolutions of the 17th and 18th centuries (Bolt 1977: xii–xiii).

Condorcet, known as Nicolas de Condorcet, was a republican philosopher who initially sought to reform the French monarchy, serving in Jacques Turgot's short-lived administration from 1774 to 1776, then supported the early stages of the French Revolution that erupted in 1789. He ultimately died in 1794 while imprisoned for opposing the Jacobins and the execution of King Louis XVI. Condorcet is best remembered for his posthumously published final work of 1794, *Esquisse d'un tableau historique de l'esprit humain* [*Sketch for a Historical Picture of the Human Mind*], in which he diagnosed the stages of human progress and projected the progress yet to come.

On war, Kant, the great German philosopher, perhaps went further. He outlined the opposed interests of 'the citizens', who would pay a devastating price for any war, and the rulers, who would sacrifice little for the 'pleasure' of sending their subjects off to war. Kant expounded the idea that 'perpetual peace' could be secured through universal republics and international cooperation. He believed that this would be the outcome of universal history, even if not rationally planned.

In his 1795 *Perpetual Peace: A Philosophical Sketch*, Kant listed several conditions that he thought necessary for ending wars and creating a lasting peace. They included a world of constitutional republics. In Kant's view, inherent in these republics, flowing from their very nature, would be the need to obtain the consent of the citizens to declare war. His 'first definitive article for perpetual peace' was 'The Civil Constitution of Every State Should Be Republican'. Under that heading, he wrote:

The republican constitution, besides the purity of its origin (having sprung from the pure source of the concept of law), also gives a favorable prospect for the desired consequence, i.e., perpetual peace. The reason is this: if the consent of the citizens is required in order to decide that war should be declared (and in this constitution it cannot but be the case), nothing is more natural than that they would be very cautious in commencing such a poor game, decreeing for themselves all the calamities of war. Among the latter would be: having to fight, having to pay the costs of war from their own resources, having painfully to repair the devastation war leaves behind, and, to fill up the measure of evils, load themselves with a heavy national debt that would embitter peace itself and that can never be liquidated on account of constant wars in the future. But, on the other hand, in a constitution which is not republican, and under which the subjects are not citizens, a declaration of war is the easiest thing in the world to decide upon, because war does not require of the ruler, who is the proprietor and not a member of the state, the least sacrifice of the pleasures of his table, the chase, his country houses, his court functions, and the like. He may, therefore, resolve on war as on a pleasure party for the most trivial reasons, and with perfect indifference leave the justification which decency requires to the diplomatic corps who are ever ready to provide it.

(Beck 1963: 377)

Kant's vision was never actualised. By attributing war to the pleasure-seeking of rulers, Kant underestimated the predatory and commercial appetites of the emerging bourgeoisie. Nevertheless, he pointed incisively to the contrary interests of the exploited classes that were left to bear the human and economic burden of war. He also identified the readiness or rulers, with the help of the 'diplomatic corps', to concoct justifications for war.

World War I experiences

After 1914, amid the carnage of World War I, popular opposition to the United States joining the conflagration led to proposals for referenda as a means of keeping the country out of the war. Senate Joint Resolution 227, introduced by Senator Robert L. Owen of Oklahoma on 15 January 1915, stipulated:

No war of aggression shall be waged by the Army or Navy of the United States, except upon a declaration of war by the Congress of the United States, ratified and approved by a majority vote of the majority of the legal votes cast upon the question in a majority of the Congressional districts of the United States.

(Quoted in Patch 1938)

Such propositions won the support of liberal and pacifist sections of the ruling elite for a combination of reasons. On top of the fear of widespread anti-war sentiment were concerns that involvement in the costly conflict would drain the country's financial resources and undermine its emergence as a global force. Entering the war also risked tarnishing the image of pacificism, democracy and liberalism with which the United States was masking its increasingly imperialist operations, such as the occupations of the Philippines, Guam, Cuba and Puerto Rico, after the 1898 Spanish-American War. Finally, by refusing to come to Britain's aid, at least almost until the end of the war, the rising American capitalists could more readily supplant the British as the pre-eminent power.

Prominent figures in the political establishment took up the referendum call. 'Let the people rule', wrote former Secretary of State William Jennings Bryan in his weekly magazine, the *Commoner*. 'Nowhere is their rule more needed than in deciding upon war policies—nowhere would their influence be more salutary' (quoted in Patch 1938).

In 1916, Senator Robert La Follette, a Republican from Wisconsin, introduced a Bill for a referendum; in February 1917, after relations were severed with Germany, other Bills and resolutions were tabled in Congress calling for a referendum before a declaration of war. La Follette said that he had received 15,000 letters and telegrams, and that nine out of ten of them endorsed his stand in opposing war. He entered in the *Congressional Record* reports of the results of local straw votes, taken in various parts of the country, showing substantial majorities against war and he submitted a petition signed by more than 7,000 citizens of California asking for a referendum before war was declared (Patch 1938).

For all of the occasional invocation of popular rule, these proposals were extremely limited. Most were not constitutional amendments, but one-time Bills designed to address the immediate conflict, and were only advisory, based on the argument that if most voters opposed declaring war, then the government would have little choice but to pull back. The proposals also carved out broad exemptions for invasion or insurrection, when no referendum would be required to go to war.

In reality, these propositions helped to ease the way for war. They diverted anti-war hostility behind illusions that the public might halt entry by placing democratic pressure on the administration. Their proponents also pledged to support war if it became 'necessary' to defend the country, thus lending legitimacy to the ultimate decision to join the war.

Many in the growing socialist movement objected that the government could easily doctor evidence to invoke the invasion clauses, thereby permitting it to plunge the country into wars, just as it always had. Nevertheless, the Wilson administration and its allies rejected such schemes out of hand, branding them impractical and wanting to leave their hands free to enter the war to the United States' advantage.

In 1916, the Socialist Party, whose presidential candidate Eugene V. Debs had won almost 1 million votes in 1912, inserted the referendum call into its election manifesto, while opposing the war outright as a capitalist war for profit and plunder. The manifesto began:

> In the midst of the greatest crisis and bloodiest struggle of all history the Socialist Party of America reaffirms its steadfast adherence to the principles of international brotherhood, world peace, and industrial democracy.
>
> The Great War which has engulfed so much of civilization and destroyed millions of lives is one of the natural results of the capitalist system of production. Fundamentally it was the desire of competing national groups of capitalists to grasp and control the opportunities for profitable foreign investments and trade which brought about the war, and it is that same desire which prompts the present organized effort to fasten upon this country the crushing burdens of militarism. Not until the capitalist system of production is replaced by a system of industrial democracy will wars for markets cease and international peace be securely established.

> (Socialist Party 1916)

Later, the manifesto outlined a series of demands, the first three of which were as follows:

> The Socialist Party maintains its attitude of unalterable opposition to war. We reiterate the statement that the competitive nature of capitalism is the cause of modern war, and that the cooperative nature of Socialism is alone adapted to the task of ending war by removing its causes. We assert, however, that even under the present capitalist order, additional measures can be taken to safeguard peace, and to this end, we demand:
> Measures to Insure Peace.

(1) That all laws and appropriations for the increase of the military and naval forces of the United States shall be immediately repealed.

(2) That the power be taken from the President to lead the nation into a position which leaves no escape from war. No one man, however exalted in official station, should have the power to decide the question of peace or war for a nation of 100 million. To give one man such power is neither democratic or safe. Yet the President exercises such power when he determines what shall be the nation's foreign policies and what shall be the nature and tone of its diplomatic intercourse with other nations. We, therefore, demand that the power to fix foreign policies and conduct diplomatic negotiations shall be lodged in the Congress and shall be exercised publicly, the people reserving the right by referendum to order Congress, at any time, to change its foreign policy.

(3) That no war shall be declared or waged by the United States without a referendum vote of the entire people, except for the purpose of repelling invasion.

(Socialist Party 1916)

These demands, while said to be realisable even under the existing capitalist order, were met with implacable hostility on the part of the Wilson administration, Congress and the agencies of the state. Debs and other proponents of a referendum on war were among those quickly targeted for persecution once the administration entered the final stages of World War I in April 1917.

Less than three weeks after voting for war, the US Congress began debate on what became the Espionage Act of 1917. President Woodrow Wilson brushed aside objections that the intervention was motivated by mercenary commercial considerations and warnings that the introduction of conscription would provoke opposition that would have the streets of America 'running red with blood' (Stone 2004: 137). He declared that 'disloyalty' would be met with a 'firm hand of stern repression'—that so-called disloyal individuals had 'sacrificed their right to civil liberties' (Stone 2004: 137).

Once the nation was at war, the Espionage Act made it a crime, punishable by up to 20 years' imprisonment, for any person to wilfully (a) 'make or convey false reports or false statements with intent to interfere' with the military success of the United States; (b) 'cause or attempt to cause insubordination, disloyalty, mutiny, or refusal of duty' in the US military; or (c) 'obstruct the recruitment or enlistment service of the United States'.

These laws were applied in an atmosphere of war hysteria. At the government's direct instigation, vigilante groups accused thousands of people of disloyalty, often on the basis of hearsay, gossip and slander. The attorney general boasted that, with the assistance of these volunteer groups, the government had 'scores of thousands of persons under observation' (Stone 2004: 156–58). Altogether, more than 2,000 dissenters were prosecuted for allegedly disloyal, seditious or incendiary speech (Stone 2004: 170).

The US Supreme Court's embrace of the repression—particularly directed against socialists—was displayed in *Schenck v. United States* 249 US 47 (1919). Led by Justice Oliver Wendell Holmes, the Court unanimously upheld the conviction of Socialist Party supporters who had been charged with conspiring to obstruct the recruiting and enlistment service by circulating a pamphlet to men who had been conscripted. The pamphlet argued that the draft was unconstitutional and a 'monstrous wrong' designed to further the interests of Wall Street (Stone 2004: 192).

Justice Holmes dismissed arguments that the pamphlet was protected by the US Constitution's First Amendment guaranteeing free speech, declaring:.

When a nation is at war many things that might be said in time of peace are such a hindrance to its efforts that their utterance will not be endured so long as men fight and no Court could regard them as protected by any constitutional right . . .

(*Schenck v. United States* 249 US 47, 52 (1919))

Likewise, in *Debs v. United States* 249 US 211 (1919), Debs was sentenced to ten years in prison for making a speech near a prison after visiting three Socialist Party members who had been jailed for violating the Espionage Act.

Hearing the appeal in the Supreme Court, Holmes again roundly rejected the First Amendment argument. While acknowledging that the main theme of Debs' speech was to celebrate socialism, Holmes added, if 'one purpose of the speech, whether incidental or not does not matter, was to oppose [the] war, . . . and if, in all the circumstances, that would be its probable effect, it would not be protected' (*Debs*, at 212–15).

Holmes, one of America's most celebrated jurists, displayed with full force the role of the judiciary when facing a perceived threat to the political order. Debs defiantly ran his 1920 presidential campaign from prison, as 'Convict No. 9653', and again received nearly 1 million votes (Stone 2004: 198).

After the 'Great War'

Despite the repression, demands for votes on war did not disappear. Among the congressional supporters were prominent liberal senators such as La Follette, George Norris of Nebraska, William Borah of Idaho and Thomas Gore of Oklahoma. Winifred Mason Huck of Illinois, the third woman ever elected to

Congress, devoted much of her single term in the House of Representatives, from 1921 to 1923, to pressing unsuccessfully for two Bills: a constitutional amendment requiring a popular vote on involvement in any war that required US armed forces to be sent overseas; and a ban on US economic relations with any country that did not adopt similar referenda laws (Bolt 1977).

On the other side of the Atlantic, Wilhelm Cuno, a businessman who was chancellor of Weimar Republic from November 1922 to August 1923, included a Europe-wide war referendum requirement in a set of proposed peace plans meant to stave off a German economic collapse. Ironically, Cuno was no democrat. He had been appointed chancellor by Germany's Social Democrat President Friedrich Ebert via presidential decree and without a vote in the Reichstag.

US Secretary of State Charles Evans Hughes initially backed Cuno's proposals. It was reported at first that the United States had acted as an intermediary in the matter. However, the State Department announced that the Washington government had refused to transmit the proposal to the principal Allied powers. The fate of Cumo's peace plans was another lesson in major power politics and intrigue. France rejected the proposals after the United States refused to guarantee enforcement and France then occupied Germany's industry-rich Ruhr Valley as collateral for insufficient reparations payments. Unable to contain popular opposition to the French occupation, the Cuno government soon fell (Patch 1938).

Back in the United States, in 1924, both the Democrats, who nominated John Davis, and the Progressives, led by La Follette, endorsed a war referendum amendment to the US Constitution. International action on a war-referendum plan was suggested when the Democratic National Convention included in the party platform a plank, believed to have been written by William Jennings Bryan, advocating 'a joint agreement with all nations for world disarmament and also for a referendum of war, except in case of actual or threatened attack' (Patch 1938).

The platform stated, extremely cautiously, that 'those who must furnish the blood and bear the burdens imposed by war should, whenever possible, be consulted before this supreme sacrifice is required of them' (Patch 1938). The referendum plank was adopted unanimously by the platform committee and by the convention, which included prominent party leaders, among them future President Franklin D. Roosevelt. However, once in office, during the lead-up to World War II, Roosevelt vehemently opposed such a constitutional amendment, moved by Representative Louis Ludow (to whom we will return later in the chapter).

The Progressive platform on which Robert La Follette ran for the presidency in 1924 urged a constitutional amendment 'to insure a popular referendum for or against war except in cases of actual invasion'. In support of this plank, the campaign textbook said in part:

> The power to declare war is vested by the Constitution of the United States in Congress alone. As a matter of fact, the President declares war. There is no instance in our history when a President has asked Congress to declare war that Congress has failed to follow his suggestion. We maintain that the man does not live, and never will live, who is noble enough, high-minded enough,

or wise enough to lead one hundred and ten million people into war without the sanction and express demand of the people themselves . . . We maintain that in the hands of those who are compelled to fight wars should rest the war-making power. We hold that if those who make wars were compelled to fight wars, warfare would cease.

(Quoted in Patch 1938)

Administration spokesmen in Congress denounced the referendum proposal, which died when Calvin Coolidge retained the presidency.

The 1928 Kellogg–Briand Pact

Despite the defeat of referenda proposals, the losses of millions of lives in World War I made the idea of declaring war to be illegal immensely popular internationally. This prompted another bid to hold out the illusory promise that another world war could be prevented by agreements between the rival powers.

Negotiations that began between US Secretary of State Frank Kellogg and French Foreign Minister Ariste Briand were expanded to include 15 states, which signed a pact in Paris during August 1928 to outlaw war, except for in circumstances of self-defence. The final version of the Pact of Paris—officially, the General Treaty for Renunciation of War as an Instrument of National Policy—had two clauses: one prohibiting war as an instrument of national policy; the other calling upon signatories to settle their disputes by peaceful means. The signatory states promised not to use war to resolve 'disputes or conflicts of whatever nature or of whatever origin they may be, which may arise among them'.

Signatories included France, the United States, Britain, Ireland, Canada, Australia, New Zealand, South Africa, India, Belgium, Poland, Czechoslovakia, Germany, Italy and Japan. Later, an additional 47 nations followed suit, so the Pact was eventually signed by most of the world's established nations. The US Senate ratified the agreement by a vote of 85–1, but only after making reservations to note that US participation did not limit its right to self-defence or require it to take action to enforce the agreement against signatories breaking it (Quigley 1966: 294–95).

It did not take long for the Pact to break down. Its first major test came just a few years later in 1931, when Japan invaded Manchuria. Although Japan had signed the Pact, no action was taken to enforce it or to defend China. It soon became clear there was no way of policing the Pact, which also failed to clearly define 'self-defence'. The signatories, having renounced the use of war, began to wage wars without declaring them, as in the Japanese invasion of Manchuria, the Italian invasion of Abyssinia in 1935, the Spanish Civil War in 1936, the Soviet invasion of Finland in 1939, and the German and Soviet invasions of Poland in 1939 (Quigley 1966: 294–95). Thus, in the end, the Kellogg–Briand Pact proved incapable of preventing World War II, even though Kellogg was awarded the 1929 Nobel Peace Prize for his work on the agreement (Ellis 1961).

The Ludlow Amendment 'crusade'

A resurgence of isolationism in the United States during the 1930s, especially following the congressional investigation headed by North Dakota Senator Gerald Nye into the cause of US entry into World War I, generated new war referendum proposals. Many Americans were determined not to repeat the experience of World War I. The Nye Committee concluded that the US involvement had been caused by the influence of powerful munitions and banking interests and vicious foreign propaganda. The rekindled anti-war sentiment triggered mandatory neutrality legislation during the middle and late 1930s, and war referenda constitutional amendments from 1935 until 1941.

One of the foremost advocates of referenda was Representative Louis Ludlow, a former journalist. Ludlow became interested in the war referendum when he covered the neutrality debates in Washington, DC, during World War I, but was galvanised by the Nye investigation into wartime profiteering by arms manufacturers. The referendum was needed, Ludlow wrote to President Roosevelt, because there was a 'constant danger of the United States being forced into war by the rapacity and greed of the munitions makers'.

Ludlow's proposals, moved in various versions from 1935 to 1938, won the support of up to 75 per cent of the American population, as measured by opinion polls, but failed to ever achieve the congressional numbers needed to proceed with a constitutional amendment. Despite Ludlow's entreaties to Roosevelt, the administration ferociously opposed the proposals and worked hard to secure their defeat—clearing the way for Roosevelt to enter World War II after the 1941 Pearl Harbor attack. One study of Ludlow's efforts, which is dubbed a crusade, stated that '[t]hroughout his twenty years of congressional service, Louis Ludlow's political philosophy remained a unique blend of Christianity, Jeffersonian, and isolationism' (Griffin 1968: 269).

In a speech before the House, Ludlow explained the dual purpose of his measure:

> First, it gives to the rank and file of our citizenship who have to suffer and die and pay the awful costs of war the right to decide whether there shall be a war. Secondly, it takes the profits out of war, and by removing the incentive of those whose hellish business it is to foment wars minimizes the probability of wars in the future.
>
> (*New York Times* 1936)

Ludlow passionately argued for his measures, insisting that they could protect Americans from the suffering and grief produced by war. He pleaded:

> The amendment would do more to keep American boys out of slaughter pens in foreign countries than any other measure that could be passed. It is based on the philosophy that those who have to suffer and, if need be, to die and to bear the awful burdens and griefs of war shall have something to say as to whether war shall be declared.
>
> (*New York Times* 1936)

Ludlow also made an appeal to those who hoped to end war on a global scale: 'If the United States had such an anti-war provision in its Constitution, other countries would follow our example, and I believe wars would be brought to an end' (*New York Times* 1936).

Ludlow was acutely aware of the immense political pressures that were brought to bear on Congress to ensure that no presidential usurpation of the power to declare war was ever challenged by Congress, the body formally handed that power by the US Constitution. In a 1935 speech, he declared:

> To declare war is the highest act of sovereignty. It is a responsibility of such magnitude that it should rest on the people themselves and should not be delegated to any man or any body of men. Under the present system whoever happens to be President of the United States has it within his power so to coerce Congress that he can lead the Nation into any war, as President Polk led us into war with Mexico primarily for the purpose of gaining territory to the southwest. It is unfair to expect the Members of Congress, after all of the atmosphere of war has been created, to resist the terrific pressure and propaganda for war, thus subjecting themselves to the taunts and charges of treason that are always hurled at those who do not go along with the leaders in such circumstances.
>
> (Griffin 1968: 178–79)

Popular sentiment strongly backed referenda proposals. The American Institute of Public Opinion asked a representative cross-section of the US public: 'In order to declare war should Congress be required to obtain the approval of the people by means of a national vote?' The percentage responding affirmatively during the period 1935–38 varied as follows:

- November 1935—75 per cent;
- September 1936—71 per cent;
- October 1937—73 per cent; and
- October 1938—68 per cent (Griffin 1968).

Despite this seemingly overwhelming popular support for Ludlow's resolutions, the vast majority of American newspapers, controlled by media magnates, staunchly opposed and denounced them—particularly after it became clear that the House of Representatives would finally vote on his 1938 resolution. Between 1935 and 1938, Ludlow had himself tailored his resolutions to seek to appease the big business interests that he originally blamed for the war drive and to demonstrate his loyalty to the underlying cause of strengthening the geo-strategic power of US imperialism. But that did not stop the Roosevelt administration and the ruling elite from insisting on the defeat of his measures, because they potentially limited the White House's militarist machinations and opened the doors of popular anti-war feeling developing to further heights.

The text of Ludlow's proposed amendment, as originally proposed in January 1935, had two sections:

SEC. 1. Except in the event of an invasion of the United States or its Territorial possessions and attack upon its citizens residing therein, the authority of Congress to declare war shall not become effective until confirmed by a majority of all votes cast thereon in a nationwide referendum. Congress, when it deems a national crisis to exist, may by concurrent resolution refer the question of war or peace to the citizens of the States, the question to be voted on being, Shall the United States declare war on _____? Congress may otherwise by law provide for the enforcement of this section.

SEC. 2. Whenever war is declared the President shall immediately conscript and take for use by the Government all the public and private war properties, yards, factories, and supplies, together with employees necessary for their operation, fixing the compensation for private properties temporarily employed for the war period at a rate not in excess of 4 percent based on tax values assessed in the year preceding the war.

(Ludlow 1935)

Ludlow soon decided to eliminate the second section, which proposed trying to take the immediate profit motive out of warmongering by proposing the temporary nationalisation, with compensation, of war-related industries during periods of declared war. Such was the political and economic power of the industrial conglomerates involved.

After a number of interim rewrites, the final 1938 version further watered down the first section, rendering it effectively toothless. It read:

EXCEPT in case of *attack* by armed forces, *actual or immediately threatened*, upon the United States or its Territorial Possessions, or by any non-American nation against any country in the *Western Hemisphere*, the people shall have the sole power by a national referendum to declare war or to engage in warfare overseas. Congress, when it *deems* a national crisis to exist in conformance with this article, shall by concurrent resolution *refer* the question to the people. Congress shall by law provide for the *enforcement* of this section.

(Morrow 1939, emphasis added)

The critical word 'invasion' was changed to 'attack', creating a giant loophole for any administration to exploit by depicting any hostile military gesture as sufficient to commence armed warfare. The phrase 'immediately threatened' further widened the scope for aggression, prefiguring the 'pre-emptive self-defence' doctrine later invented by the George W. Bush administration. The reference to the Western Hemisphere embraced the Monroe doctrine, whereby the United States had, since 1823, asserted the right to dominant influence over both North and South America, to the exclusion of any other power.

Moreover, the proposal left in the hands of Congress the power to 'deem' whether to 'refer' a 'crisis' to the people for a vote and to determine the means for the 'enforcement' of the section. Given Congress's track record of acceding to executive war-making power, this was hardly a guarantee of any popular vote.

Notwithstanding these enormous concessions offered by Ludlow and his supporters, Roosevelt's administration was determined to block the resolution. For two years, the administration kept Ludlow's Bills buried in the House Judiciary Committee. At the end of 1937, however, the amendment got enough congressional support, including the signatures of nearly half the Democrats in the House, for a House vote on a discharge petition designed to permit debate on the proposed constitutional amendment (Schlesinger 2004: 97–98).

Congressional debate on the amendment was prompted by the 12 December 1937 bombing of the *USS Panay* by Japanese warplanes in the Yangtze River near Nanjing, China. Roosevelt discussed with his cabinet and military high command the possibility of economic or military retaliation against Japan. Roosevelt drew back, however, when he realised that there was no public outcry for retaliation and that, in fact, peace sentiment in the country had actually strengthened (Herring and Carroll 1996: 90; Kennedy 1999: 402).

A hysterical campaign was launched to defeat Ludlow's Bill. House Speaker William Bankhead and Representative Emanuel Celler, who had been chair of the judiciary subcommittee that had held hearings on the Ludlow resolution in 1935, intimated that alien influences supported Ludlow. Celler maintained that the German Nazis favoured the resolution because it would 'destroy all of our effectiveness, moral and otherwise, in any foreign difficulty' (quoted in Patch 1938).

Roosevelt arranged for Postmaster General James A. Farley, who was also chair of the Democratic National Committee, to telephone Democratic House members to enlist their support against Ludlow's amendment. Senator Key Pittman, chair of the Foreign Relations Committee, said 'it would be the first step and a fatal step in the destruction of our republican form of government'. Taking up an oft-repeated refrain, he insisted that the proposition would assist domestic 'subversives', as well as foreign enemies. Pittman claimed that, in a referendum campaign, the people would be influenced by 'misrepresentative propaganda, not only from foreign sources, but from subversive forces in our own country' (quoted in Patch 1938).

On 10 January 1938, Ludlow obtained recognition from Speaker Bankhead and called for a vote on the question of discharging the war referendum resolution from consideration by the judiciary committee. Before the balloting, Bankhead read a letter from Roosevelt, who branded the resolution 'impracticable in its application and incompatible with our representative form of government'. Roosevelt declared that 'such an amendment to the Constitution as that proposed would cripple any President in his conduct of our foreign relations, and it would encourage other nations to believe that they could violate American rights with impunity'.

In October 1937, the last opinion poll before the sinking of the *Panay* showed that 73 per cent of Americans supported the referendum amendment; around the same time, 95 per cent expressed opposition to future US involvement in European wars. Ludlow needed 218 votes in the House of Representatives to get the Bill out of the judiciary committee, where the chair had it stalled, and to the floor for debate. In the end, as a result of the efforts of Roosevelt and Farley, it was defeated in Congress by a vote of 209–188. This vote was far short of the two-thirds majority required by both Houses of Congress (290 in the House) for later passage of a constitutional amendment (Powaski 1991: 74).

Roosevelt's efforts to defeat Ludlow's referendum bill, combined with public approval of his handling of the *Panay* crisis and Hitler's invasion of Czechoslovakia in March 1939, led to a sharp decline in public approval of the idea, which Ludlow and others continued to introduce until the Pearl Harbor attack of December 1941. Because that attack occurred in a US territorial possession, the referendum requirement would not have applied anyway (Patch 1938).

Referenda and the Marxist movement

In 1938, the founding programme of the Fourth International, led by Leon Trotsky, exiled leader of the 1917 Russian Revolution, took up the demand for a referendum on war as one means of developing and mobilising the widespread anti-war sentiment of the working people. At the same time, it warned against illusions that a referendum, by itself, could actually halt the drive to war by the US ruling class. Under the heading, 'The struggle against imperialism and war', the document stated:

[T]he Fourth International supports every, even if insufficient, demand, if it can draw the masses to a certain extent into active politics, awaken their criticism and strengthen their control over the machinations of the bourgeoisie.

From this point of view, our American section, for example, entirely supports the proposal for establishing a referendum on the question of declaring war. No democratic reform, it is understood, can by itself prevent the rulers from provoking war when they wish it. It is necessary to give frank warning of this. But notwithstanding the illusions of the masses in regard to the proposed referendum, their support of it reflects the distrust felt by workers and farmers for bourgeois government and Congress. Without supporting and without sparing illusions, it is necessary to support with all possible strength the progressive distrust of the exploited toward the exploiters. The more widespread the movement for the referendum becomes, . . . the more acute will distrust of the imperialists become.

(Trotsky 1973: 130)

The demand for a referendum was not raised as an isolated slogan. It was one of a number of transitional demands advanced by the document with the aim of raising popular consciousness about the underlying capitalist nature of the war. The demands sought to lay out the necessity for a politically independent movement of the working class, against both the twin parties of big business—the

Republicans and Democrats—to overturn the entire socio-economic order responsible for once again plunging humanity into a world war.

The programme further raised the demand for electoral rights for men and women from the age of 18, saying that '[t]hose who will be called upon to die for the fatherland tomorrow should have the right to vote today' (Trotsky 1973: 130). It continued, taking up an issue that Ludlow raised, but quickly dropped:

> Light must be shed upon the problem of war from all angles, hinging upon the side from which it will confront the masses at a given moment. War is a gigantic commercial enterprise, especially for the war industry. The '60 Families' are therefore first-line patriots and the chief provocateurs of war. *Workers' control of war industries* is the first step in the struggle against the 'manufacturers' of war. To the slogan of the reformists: *a tax on military profit*, we counterpose the slogans: *confiscation of military profit* and *expropriation of the war industries*.
>
> (Trotsky 1973: 130–31, emphasis original)

Instead of an 'armaments programme', the document called for 'public works' (Trotsky 1973: 131). Further demands set out to expose the predatory machinations in ruling circles, conducted 'behind the backs of the people' under the slogans of going to war to defend democracy and liberty:

> Complete abolition of secret diplomacy; all treaties and agreements to be made accessible to all workers and farmers;

> Military training and arming of workers and farmers under direct control of workers' and farmers' committees;

> Creation of military schools for the training of commanders among the toilers, chosen by workers' organisations;

> Substitution for the standing army of a *people's militia*, indissolubly linked up with factories, mines, farms, etc.
>
> (Trotsky 1973: 131, emphasis original)

These demands followed the tradition of the Bolshevik-led Soviet Russian government that took power in October 1917 and set about ending World War I. One the first acts of that government had been to publish the secret treaties between the former Tsarist and capitalist governments of Russia and their British and other allies for the carve-up of the spoils of war against Germany and the Ottoman Empire. In doing so, the new government led by Lenin and Trotsky hoped to urge soldiers and workers from all the warring countries to refuse to keep fighting each other and to instead turn their hostility toward overthrowing the governments that were ordering them to continue the slaughter across the trenches of Europe.

The Fourth International's programme linked its demands to the basic slogan of the Marxist movement, enunciated in the Communist Manifesto: 'Workers of the World Unite!' It explained that the movement's transitional demands sought to raise, in the eyes of millions of working-class people world-wide, the unavoidable need to take political power into their own hands. To that end, the next section of the document advocated the formation of workers' and farmers' governments to overturn the capitalist governments and establish the democratic rule of the working class in the interests of the exploited and oppressed majority of the global population (Trotsky 1973: 133–35). In other words, while calling for a referendum on war in the United States, the Fourth International explained that the only way of ending war was to overturn the capitalist profit system itself.

This approach flowed from the basic prognosis and aim of the Transitional Program:

> It is necessary to help the masses in the process of the daily struggle to find the bridge between present demand and the socialist program of the revolu-tion. This bridge should include a system of transitional demands, stemming from today's conditions and from today's consciousness of wide layers of the working class and unalterably leading to one final conclusion: the conquest of power by the proletariat.
>
> (Trotsky 1973: 114)

In a discussion on the referendum demand with leaders of the Socialist Workers Party, the Trotskyist party in the United States, Trotsky advocated giving criti-cal support to the campaign for the Ludlow amendment, rather than opposing it. He emphasised that the Ludlow referendum could not stop the war drive of America's wealthiest '60 families', but it was necessary to join the fight for the proposal to clarify the illusions that existed among anti-war and pacifist-minded workers that a referendum could keep the United States out of the war.

Trotsky proposed the following approach in the Party's political campaigning:

> We say: The Ludlow referendum, like other democratic means, can't stop the criminal activities of the sixty families, who are incomparably stronger than all democratic institutions. This does not mean that I renounce democratic institutions, or the fight for the referendum, or the fight to give American citizens of the age of eighteen the right to vote.
>
> (Trotsky 1973: 93)

The '60 families' was a reference to *America's 60 Families*, a book by Ferdinand Lundberg in 1937 that became an influential analysis of wealth and class in the United States, showing how the fortunes of the rich were leveraged to exercise political and economic power. Specifically, the author documented a 'plutocratic circle' of a tightly interlinked group of 60 families (Lundberg 1937).

In the 21st century, the overwhelming power of the super-rich over major political and geo-strategic decisions, such as provoking and instigating wars, has reached new heights in the United States and globally. According to a report published in November 2017 by the Institute for Policy Studies, the three richest Americans— Jeff Bezos, Bill Gates and Warren Buffett—owned more wealth than the poorest half of the US population—some 160 million people. In effect, the '60 families' had been replaced by only three billionaires whose estimated combined wealth exceeded US$264 billion (Collins and Hoxie 2017).

Globally, too, the corporate concentration of wealth and power has only intensified since the 2008 global economic crisis. A study undertaken in 2011 by researchers at the Swiss Federal Institute of Technology found that, of 43,060 major transnational companies, only 1,318 collectively owned the majority of the world's large manufacturing firms, representing 60 per cent of global revenues. Of these, only 147 companies—overwhelmingly, the giant banks and investment funds headquartered in the United States, Western Europe and Japan—controlled 40 per cent of the total wealth in the network (Coghlan and MacKenzie 2011).

These processes have been accelerating in recent decades. An inaugural World Inequality Report published in December 2017 by economists Thomas Piketty, Emmanuel Saez, Gabriel Zucman, Facundo Alvaredo and Lucas Chancel, charted a rise in global income and wealth inequality between 1980 and 2016 (World Inequality Lab 2018).

The report, based on tax data and other financial information collected for the World Wealth and Income Database by more than 100 researchers in 70 countries, found that concentration of wealth in the hands of the richest 1 per cent rose sharply—particularly, in the United States, Russia and China. In the United States, the wealth share monopolised by the top 1 per cent rose from 22 per cent in 1980 to 39 per cent in 2016; in China, it doubled from 15 per cent to 30 per cent; and in Russia, it went from 22 per cent to 43 per cent (World Inequality Lab 2018: fig. E8).

The 1990–91 Gulf War

In January 1991, despite considerable popular opposition, a US-led coalition began a devastating aerial bombardment of Iraq. Washington claimed at the time that its actions were justified by Iraq's invasion of Kuwait in August 1990 and the need to uphold the 'right to self-determination' of this oil-rich sheikdom.

In reality, the United States had cynically encouraged Iraq's incursion into Kuwait to establish a pretext on the basis of which it could implement long-standing plans to seize control of the Persian Gulf and its vast oil reserves. Utilising its military and technological superiority, the United States sought to demonstrate its pre-eminent role in what President George H. Bush proclaimed the 'new world order' to be established in the wake of the dissolution of the Soviet bloc (Bush 1991).

What Bush meant by this phrase was that the United States was now free to restructure the world in the interests of the US capitalist class, unencumbered by the countervailing military power of the Soviet Union.

Over the course of 43 days, warplanes dropped 80,000 cluster bombs containing 16 million anti-personnel 'bomblets'. US forces fired an estimated 944,000 rounds of radioactive depleted uranium (DU) ammunition on Iraq and Kuwait. Iraq's schools, hospitals, industry and infrastructure were severely damaged, thousands of innocent civilians were killed, and air and water supplies were polluted (Workers League 1991: 228–30).

Iraq was crippled by UN sanctions, which caused immense human suffering, then falsely accused of violating the disarmament regime imposed on it, providing the pretext for the Second Gulf War—the even more devastating invasion by the United States and its allies in 2003, conducted under the false flag of eliminating 'weapons of mass destruction' (WMDs).

During the lead-up to the 1991 US-led assault, the Trotskyist party in the United States, then named the Workers League, raised the demand for a referendum as a means of seeking to galvanise anti-war sentiment and demonstrating the necessity for a socialist overturn of the underlying corporate profit system that drove Washington's aggressive militarism.

In a November 1990 statement, 'Demand a Referendum on the Gulf War', the party stated: 'This demand must be the first step in the mobilization of the entire working class against the imminent threat of imperialist war.' It said that tens of millions of people were opposed to the war policies of the White House and Pentagon, 'but their voices are being ignored'. No one had consulted the young soldiers who would be sent to conduct the slaughter, mostly aged 19–25, largely working class and 40 per cent black or Hispanic, nor had their families been granted a voice (Workers League 1991: 133).

The statement poured scorn on the role of Congress, indicting its complicity in the drumbeats for war. It pointed out that politicians from 'both big business parties'—the Democrats and Republicans—conspired to keep the issue of the Gulf War out of the 1990 congressional elections. None of the candidates had even mentioned the war preparations, yet White House officials later admitted that the decision to go to war was made in October 1990, before the elections (Workers League 1991: 137).

The statement characterised as 'phoney' a debate in the media and political elite over whether to have a formal declaration of war by the Congress, pointing toward the purely tactical nature of the questions raised:

> None of these representatives of big business challenges the basic premise of US intervention into the Persian Gulf. All agree that US imperialism has the unquestioned right invade the Middle East, seize control of the oil fields and impose its will on the Arab population.
>
> (Workers League 1991: 137–38)

Senator Sam Nunn, a leading Democrat, had told a Senate hearing: 'The question is not whether military action is justified; it is. The question is whether military action is wise at this time and in our national interest' (quoted in Workers League 1991: 138). While differences might have existed over timing and efficacy, there was no dissent from the underlying recourse to militarism and therefore no prospect that the Congress would stand in the way of the administration's decision, once made, to attack Iraq: 'The bosses' Congress is so cowardly it is incapable of even enforcing its own legislation, the War Powers Act, passed in 1973, supposedly to prevent future undeclared wars like the US aggression in Vietnam' (Workers League 1991: 138).

Congress spoke for the corporate bosses, bankers, billionaires and Pentagon generals; for Exxon, Mobil, Texaco and Chevron, which had carved up the Persian Gulf oil fields in the 1930s and reaped billions of dollars in profits from them every year; and for General Dynamics, McDonnell Douglas, Lockheed, Grumman and 'all the other manufacturers of advanced killing machines' (Workers League 1991: 139).

As for the exact timing of the war? That was being worked out in backroom negotiations at the UN Security Council, 'a den of thieves', where the United States was 'sparing no expense to bribe, threaten and cajole' other countries to rubber-stamp the planned attack. Thus every aspect of the war preparations was conducted behind the backs of the people of the United States and the world.

While calling for a referendum, the Workers League cautioned against any illusions about the demand being adopted by the administration or Congress. It said that the demand for a popular vote was not an appeal to Congress or the White House to legitimise war through a ballot; rather, it was directed to the labour movement to provide a means of freeing the working class from the political stranglehold of the Democratic Party and the trade unions, all of which backed the war:

> In calling for a referendum, the Workers League makes clear this cannot by itself stop the war . . . Even if the referendum were to pass, the working class would have to enforce it through its own independent strength, against the attempts of the capitalist government to ignore the outcome or engineer a pretext to overturn it.
>
> (Workers League 1991: 142)

To stop the war, it would be necessary to overturn the political order and establish a workers' government, based on elected workers' councils and committed to a socialist programme. This would start with seizing the oil and war industries, nationalising the banks and basic industries, and dismantling the military machine.

In the end, Congress voted overwhelmingly in January 1991 to authorise the assault on Iraq, without insisting on a formal congressional declaration of war. As the statement had predicted, there was no question of Congress blocking the attack, which began within days of the congressional votes. The roll call was 98–0 in the Senate and 399–6 in the House of Representatives (Workers League 1991: 181).

Conclusion

None of the schemes proposed by various scholars and commentators to prevent executive governments from taking their populations to war, via parliamentary or congressional votes or referenda, have proven feasible or effective.

While referenda theoretically provide a mechanism for popular hostility to war to be brought to bear, the forces driving toward war are deeply rooted in the socio-economic structure and social relations of capitalism itself.

Powerful consortia of capitalist banks and corporations utilise 'their' national states to wage a commercial and ultimately military struggle for control of the raw materials, oil and gas pipelines, trade routes, and access to the cheap labour and markets that are critical to the accumulation of profit.

As outlined in the Introduction to this book, the essential cause of militarism and war lies in the deep-seated contradictions of the world capitalist system: between a globally integrated and interdependent economy and its division into antagonistic national states; and between the socialised character of global production and its subordination, through the private ownership of the means of production, to the accumulation of private profit by the ruling capitalist class.

The most immediate danger of war derives from the escalating—increasingly unsuccessful and disastrous—efforts of US capitalism, through years of unending war, to counter its relative decline in relation to its major rivals and to establish the global hegemony it sought after emerging from World War II as the strongest capitalist power.

European and Japanese imperialism, facing the same underlying contradictions, are pursuing the no less predatory and reactionary interests of their own ruling classes. Junior imperialist powers, such as Canada and Australia, are aligning themselves with the United States as a means of asserting their own strategic and profiteering agendas.

What is required is a new international mass movement against war, uniting the working people and youth in opposition to capitalism and imperialism. There can be no serious struggle against war except in the fight to end the dictatorship of finance capital and the economic system that is the fundamental cause of militarism and war.

In opposing another global conflagration, in which millions of ordinary people would perish, the international working class is the social force that objectively constitutes the base for world socialist revolution, which signifies an end to the nation-state system as a whole and the establishment of a global economy based on equality and scientific planning. Only the abolition of the nation-state system and the establishment of a world socialist federation will make possible the rational, planned development of global resources. Only on this basis can be built the eradication of poverty and the raising of human culture to new heights that will render war unnecessary and obsolete.

References

Beck, L. 1963. 'Perpetual peace'. In *Kant on History*. Indianapolis, IN: Bobbs-Merrill.

Bolt, E. 1977. *Ballots before Bullets: The War Referendum Approach to Peace in America 1914–1941*. Charlottesville, VA: University Press of Virginia.

Bush, G. 1991. 'Address before a Joint Session of the Congress on the State of the Union', 29 January, www.presidency.ucsb.edu/ws/?pid=19253 (accessed 21 November 2017).

Coghlan, A., and MacKenzie, D. 2011. 'Revealed: the capitalist network that runs the world', *New Scientist*, 24 October, www.newscientist.com/article/mg21228354.500-revealed–the-capitalist-network-that-runs-the-world.html (accessed 10 January 2012).

Collins, C., and Hoxie, J. 2017. *Billionaire Bonanza*. Washington, DC: Institute for Policy Studies.

Ellis, L. 1961. *Frank B. Kellogg and American Foreign Relations, 1925–1929*. New Brunswick, NJ: Rutgers University Press.

Griffin, W. 1968. 'Louis Ludlow and the war referendum crusade, 1935–1941', *Indiana Magazine of History*, 64(4): 267–88.

Herring, G., and Carroll, J. 1996. *Modern American Diplomacy*. New York: Rowman & Littlefield.

Kennedy, D. 1999. *Freedom from Fear: The American People in Depression and War, 1929–1945*. Oxford: Oxford University Press.

Ludlow, L. 1935. 'The Ludlow Amendment', U.S. House of Representatives, H.J. Res. 199, 75th Congress, 1st Session.

Lundberg. 1937. *America's 60 Families*. New York. Vanguard.

Morrow, F. 1939. 'New hearings in Ludlow referendum', *Socialist Appeal*, 16 May.

New York Times. 1936. 'To seek war curb again; Ludlow will reintroduce plan calling for popular vote', 29 November.

Patch, B. 1938. 'The power to declare war', http://library.cqpress.com/cqresearcher/cqresrre1938010600 (accessed 20 November 2017).

Powaski, R. 1991. *Toward an Entangling Alliance: American Isolationism, Internationalism and Europe, 1901–1950*. New York: Greenwood Press.

Quigley, C. 1966. *Tragedy and Hope*. New York: Macmillan.

Schlesinger, A. 2004. *The Imperial Presidency*. New York: Houghton Mifflin Books.

Socialist Party. 1916. 'Our platform for the 1916 Campaign: as drafted by the National Executive of the Socialist Party', 29 July, www.marxisthistory.org/history/usa/parties/spusa/1916/0729-spa-draftplatform.pdf (accessed 10 October 2017).

Stone, G. 2004. *Perilous Times: Free Speech in Wartime*. New York: Norton.

Trotsky, L. 1973. *The Transitional Program for Socialist Revolution*. New York: Pathfinder.

Workers League. 1991. *Desert Slaughter: The Imperialist War against Iraq*. Detroit, MI: Labor.

World Inequality Lab. 2018. *World Inequality Report 2018*, https://wir2018.wid.world/ (accessed 1 February 2018).

12 Conclusions

Definite conclusions must be drawn from the questions raised in this book. Averting wars, and the danger of a global conflagration, has become a critical issue for the future of human civilisation. Leaving the war powers in the hands of executive cabals not only is an affront to democracy, but also escalates the risk of a third world war between the major powers for supremacy. Such a war would almost certainly involve the use of nuclear weapons on a scale that could imperil the planet's population.

What is at stake?

A decision to go to war, whether made by formal declaration or not, is probably the most grave and potentially catastrophic decision a government can take. Millions of lives may be lost as a result, both combatant and civilian, not to speak of the devastating consequences for the lives of many millions more people who are likely to lose loved ones or be forced to flee their homes and countries.

Another world war would almost certainly involve far more powerful nuclear weapons, endangering the lives of billions of people and the planet's entire environment.

Going to war also has far-reaching domestic political and legal consequences, including the extensive powers assumed by governments, the impact on the civil and political rights of their populations, and the implications for democracy.

In each of the countries examined in this book, the United States, Britain and Australia, governments largely ruled by decree or regulations during previous world wars, invoking emergency powers, interning thousands of people and laying serious charges against anti-war dissenters. Wartime powers can include the internal mobilisation of the armed forces to deal with social unrest or anti-war opposition.

Undemocratic war-making powers

The issue of war, whether formally declared or not, has become a major and critical political and legal issue internationally. Public, parliamentary and constitutional debates have erupted since the turn of the century in Western countries, particularly after the declaration and adoption by many governments of the 'war on terror' and the US-led intervention in Iraq in 2003.

Nevertheless, despite the human costs involved, the power to go to war is still exercised undemocratically, by 'the executive', with virtually no public, legislative or judicial scrutiny or accountability. Whether is it cloaked in the language of 'prerogative', 'presidential' or 'executive' powers, the legal authority to deploy armed forces for warfare is held in the hands of small cabals. The historical record shows that no parliamentary or congressional vote is necessary, let alone a public plebiscite, and no domestic court would uphold a legal challenge to a decision to launch a war.

In the three countries examined in this study, various efforts have been made to introduce forms of legislative control over war-making. Each has failed, underscoring the determination with which the ruling establishments insist that the power must remain free of limited or even token forms of democratic restraint.

A common problem with previous works on war-making and related powers is that they take as their starting point the continuation or re-establishment of the existing economic, political and legal order, and discuss how to accommodate the resort to war powers. They rarely examine the actual measures, including provocations and deception, adopted to prosecute war or the underlying implications for democracy.

War and democracy

Almost invariably, efforts to introduce parliamentary checks have been motivated by concerns to provide war-making decisions with a cloak of democratic legitimacy, to generate or bolster public support for the military mobilisation. Suggestions of mass popular participation in decisions to go to war, such as via referenda, generally have been dismissed out of hand.

Even such proposals, however, take no account of the underlying economic and political power held in the hands of the corporate, military and political elite, and the capacity of that elite to shape, poison or overwhelm public opinion, with the help of a complicit corporate media.

Far from becoming more democratically exercised, the war powers have become less so over the past four centuries, since the 17th- and 18th-century revolutions in England, France and the United States. Having overthrown the old monarchic and feudal orders, and consolidated economic and political power in its own hands, the capitalist classes have increasingly arrogated to themselves also the powers to go to war, overturning somewhat democratic constraints that were initially generated by those revolutions.

Who really decides on war?

Real doubts surround the formal exercise of war powers by the office formally endowed with those powers, whether it be a president, prime minister, cabinet or vice-regal representative.

In the United States, Congress and both of the major political parties serve as rubber stamps for the confluence of the military, the intelligence apparatus and Wall Street that really runs the country. The so-called Fourth Estate—the mass media—essentially functions as an arm of what President Dwight D. Eisenhower dubbed the 'military-industrial complex'.

Similar webs of economic, political and military-intelligence exist in Britain and Australia. Moreover, they are linked to the US establishment by formal alliances, informal networks, the hosting of US bases and the integration of their military forces. If the United States goes to war, these two allies are necessarily involved in many ways.

Intensifying war preparations

Amid escalating geo-strategic tensions, including trade war threats, preparations are being made for a new period of war, including by the major powers that fought World War II. The most aggressive in this planning is the United States. Its *2018 National Defense Strategy* publicly signalled preparations for direct military confrontation with nuclear-armed Russia and China.

The Pentagon document outlined an historic shift from the ostensible justification for US global military operations for nearly two decades—the so-called war on terror: 'Inter-state strategic competition, not terrorism, is now the primary concern in U.S. national security.'

What emerged from the document was a vision of US imperialism in mortal danger of losing global dominance and prepared to provoke new wars to restore it. The thrust of the strategy was a demand for an urgent build-up of the US war machine to win the coming wars.

The United States is not alone in preparing for war. Significantly, both the imperialist powers defeated in World War II, Germany and Japan, are rearming.

Rising military spending

Global military spending rose to more than US$1.7 trillion in 2017—the highest level since the Cold War. Yet just 13 per cent of the annual spending would be enough to end world poverty and hunger.

Expending more than $610 billion in 2017, the United States remained by far the world's biggest military spender, dedicating a greater amount to its military than the next seven countries combined. The 2018 defence budget signed by President Donald Trump would push this figure to $700 billion.

The United States still outspent China, the second largest spender globally, almost threefold, even though China increased its military spending by 5.6 per cent to $228 billion in 2017. China's spending, as a share of world military expenditure rose from 5.8 per cent in 2008 to 13 per cent in 2017, helping to produce an arms race with ominous implications.

Every major power is rearming, pushing international military spending up by nearly 10 per cent during the decade following the global financial crisis of 2008. An arms race is under way that finds its most acute expression in the arena of nuclear weaponry, delivery systems and associated technologies. Determined to maintain its supremacy in Asia and globally, the United States is planning to spend $1 trillion over the next three decades to develop a broader range of sophisticated nuclear weapons and the means of delivering them to their targets.

Warnings of another world war

Increasingly openly, the prospect of another global war is being discussed in reports by official and semi-official think tanks. At a certain point, such military fatalism becomes a significant contributing factor to the outbreak of war.

US officials have adopted the policy that a nuclear first strike against Russia could be 'successful', asserting that the environmental dangers posed by multiple atomic or thermonuclear detonations—a so-called nuclear winter—have been disproven.

The last world war ended with the use of nuclear weapons. One of the most barbaric decisions of the 20th century, the dropping of atomic bombs on Hiroshima and Nagasaki was presented to the American and global public on the basis of a lie: that the bombings were necessary to 'end the war' and to 'save lives'.

Likewise, decisions to go to war today, and to use nuclear weapons, will be based on fabrications designed to hide the truth about the causes of the war—both the immediate triggers and the underlying socio-economic driving forces. Any discussion about the war powers that ignores or brushes aside this historical record is falsely based.

What would a nuclear war look like?

For all the money and resources being poured into US nuclear dominance, the idea that a nuclear war against Russia or China is winnable, even with the most advanced weapons systems, is just as irrational as it was during the height of the Cold War. The use of low-yield 'tactical' nuclear weapons would likely escalate into a conflict in which many millions of people would die.

Given the vast numbers of mega-weapons held by the major powers, there is a strong chance that most large cities in combatant countries would be hit. By one estimate, 30 per cent of the US and Russian populations would be killed within the first hour. A few weeks later, radioactive fallout would kill another 50 per cent or more.

Because of the short missile-launch time frames involved, there would be no time for a formal declaration of war, let alone a parliamentary or popular vote.

Some fundamental problems of analysis

This book identifies common underlying problems of analysis. In general, examinations of war powers suffer because they:

- divorce the question of war powers from the underlying geo-strategic and economic causes of war, particularly in the present epoch, starting with World War I;
- take for granted the existence, and accept the legitimacy, of the current system of rival nation-states, based on competing economic interests;
- accept or understate the dominant role of major powers—above all, the United States—in seeking global hegemony;
- treat today's wars as a series of isolated events, each triggered by a separate incident, crisis or cause, rather than as part of an underlying pattern or trend;
- ahistorically examine wars in the abstract, without referring to the character of the warring parties, for example by making a distinction between a predatory or neo-colonial war waged by an imperialist power, such as the United States, and one fought by a country or population, such as Vietnam or Iraq, targeted by that aggression;
- suppose that countries referred to as 'modern liberal democracies' are inherently unable or unlikely to launch aggressive or expansionist military operations, and are likely to consider war only as a defensive necessity;
- assume that countries each make their own decisions to enter military conflict, when in fact they may be effectively compelled to do so by the demands or pressures imposed by other powers, or because their military forces or facilities are closely integrated into those of other powers;
- ignore the well-documented fact that every contemporary war has been launched on the basis of lies, such as 'coming to the aid of little Belgium' (World War I), responding to the attack on Pearl Harbour (World War II), the Gulf of Tonkin incident (the Vietnam War) or 'weapons of mass destruction' (the conquest of Iraq);
- brush aside the systematic whipping up of nationalist, patriotic, xenophobic and racist prejudices by governments and mass media to drum up support for war and to overcome prevailing anti-war sentiment among the population;
- bury the connection between war and the suppression of domestic opposition to war, including the accompanying sacrifices imposed on working people, such as the imprisonment of anti-war activists, the jailing or execution of resisters to conscription or deserters, and the mass internments of political opponents and 'aliens';
- fail to examine the domestic powers, usually of an authoritarian nature, assumed by governments during periods of war;
- whitewash the conflicting interests of the ruling financial, corporate and military elites, and the working-class members of society who invariably pay the highest price for war, not least by killing or being killed;
- dismiss the objective interests of the international working class, created by global capitalism, in unifying across national lines and overturning the nation-state system itself; and
- separate the 'legal' issues of war-making from all of these factors, as though law arises in a vacuum, guided by an 'internal' logic and history that is isolated from the political and economic driving forces and calculations involved.

Common political and socio-economic assumptions

Numerous such works appeared internationally in the wake of the 2003 US-led invasion of Iraq, in which both Britain and Australia played prominent supporting roles. That invasion defied massive anti-war demonstrations globally and that opposition was intensified by the subsequent exposure of the official lies that were perpetrated as pretexts for the military onslaught—most notably, the claims that the Iraqi government posed an imminent threat to the United States and its allies because it possessed 'weapons of mass destruction' and nuclear weapons capacity.

Many of the works that have appeared subsequently can be seen as attempts to restore public faith in government decisions to go to war by proposing some, invariably limited, form of legislative approval of war-making. What is ruled out is any conception of the population itself holding the power, or even having the right to know what decisions about war are being made. Among the common invalid political and socio-economic assumptions are the following.

First, countries such as Britain, the United States and Australia are described as 'liberal democracies', when in fact handfuls of billionaires monopolise society's wealth, giving them an extraordinary grip over the economic, political and military levers of power. Genuine democracy would require mass democratic participation in economic decision-making itself, including control over the transnational finance houses and corporations, as well as the military and state apparatuses.

Second, these 'democracies' have a record of supporting—and helping to impose—dictatorships in less-developed countries to further their own geostrategic and economic interests.

Third, the 'state' is said to be 'protecting' not only itself, but also 'its' citizens and their 'ways of life'. This takes no account of the social and class divisions wracking the political and legal order. A state based on yawning social inequality and domination of weaker and poorer countries does not represent the interests of people outside the wealthy elites. Whenever a whistleblower, such as Daniel Ellsberg, Chelsea Manning, Julian Assange or Edward Snowden, seeks to alert the mass of the population to the war crimes or mass surveillance being conducted in their names, the response of the state is invariably one of repression, intimidation and demonisation designed to block citizens from any access to the information.

Fourth, the word 'protecting' projects an image of defensive actions by the state, rather than aggressive military actions that plunder other countries, secure resources, dominate markets or otherwise pursue corporate profit.

Fifth, the terms 'national security' and 'welfare' are vague and laden with unstated political values.

Sixth, to insist that parliaments and courts must 'enable' the executive to 'deploy the armed forces and wage war when it is deemed necessary' reduces them to facilitators of war.

Finally, to propose that public deliberation be permitted only 'where possible' is to leave all decisions about public participation in the discretionary hands of the executive.

The driving forces of world wars

The history of the 20th century, during which two calamitous world wars were fought, suggests that the essential cause of militarism and war does not rest in the personalities of the political, corporate and military leaders involved nor even in the immediate profit calculations of the military-industrial complexes of the rival powers.

Rather, it lies in the deep-seated contradictions of the world capitalist system, none of which were resolved by two world wars—contradictions primarily between:

- a globally integrated and interdependent economy and its division into antagonistic national states; and
- the socialised character of global production and its subordination, through the private ownership of the means of production, to the accumulation of private profit by the ruling capitalist class.

Powerful capitalist banks and corporations utilise 'their' states to wage commercial and ultimately military struggles for control of the raw materials, oil and gas pipelines, trade routes, and access to cheap labour and markets that are critical to the accumulation of profit. They also regard such struggles—and war itself—as necessary to quell the social discontent generated by the ever-greater inequality produced by the capitalist accumulation of wealth, and they divert the disaffection along nationalistic, jingoist and patriotic channels.

A new period of contested hegemony

Today, the danger of another world war is centred in the efforts of the United States to maintain its position as the global hegemonic power—a position that it gained as a result of the defeat of Germany and Japan in World War II.

The Pentagon's *2018 National Defense Strategy* publicly accused Russia and China of seeking to establish regional hegemonies, thus displacing the United States as the dominant power.

However, the drive to war is not confined to the US ruling class; all of the major powers are pursuing the no less predatory and reactionary interests of their own ruling elites. All are attempting to secure their stakes in a ferocious battle for the global redivision of world economic and political power.

Escalating US-led wars

The United States has been at war on an almost continuous basis since the first Iraq War of 1990–91. The American ruling class saw the dissolution of the Soviet Union in December 1991, combined with the restoration of capitalism in China, as an opportunity to restructure global geo-politics, with the aim of establishing the unchallenged hegemony of the United States.

The *Defense Planning Guidance*, drafted by the US Department of Defense in 1992, outlined an 'American grand strategy' to 'discourage advanced industrial nations from challenging our leadership or even aspiring to a larger regional or global role'. This strategy committed the United States to the unceasing use of military power.

Legislatures as a legitimising factor in war-making

Following the eruption of widespread public opposition to the 2003 invasion of Iraq, numerous efforts were made to provide a more 'democratic' framework for war-making. Although appeals were made to democratic conceptions and claims were made that more parliamentary or congressional involvement in the process would lessen the likelihood of war itself, the thrust of many of these proposals was to provide political legitimacy to decisions to deploy military forces. Indeed, a veneer of democratic legitimacy may make military action more likely, not less.

In fact, in some instances, the arguments were directly linked to assisting the executive to overcome popular anti-war sentiment. Other arguments clearly assigned to the legislature the task of helping to build a constituency for war.

War and deception

Many instances can be cited of the systematic deception by governments and intelligence agencies of the populations whose interests they claimed to be defending, in order to create the conditions for war. Not only were legislators fed distortions and fabrications to ensure their approval of the military interventions, but also—and more importantly—the people were misled in concerted efforts to manipulate public opinion and to generate a pro-war atmosphere.

Two well-documented experiences of deceit, both of which had calamitous consequences for millions of people, are the long war in Vietnam, from the 1940s to the 1970s, and the 2003 invasion and ongoing military operations in Iraq. Both wars aroused intense popular opposition, leading to the ultimate exposure of many of the lies told to launch them, but this did not prevent the carnage from continuing for many years. In neither case have those responsible been held to account, despite irrefutable evidence of fraud and illegality.

Commissioned by then US Secretary of Defense Robert McNamara in 1967, a 7,000-page study, officially known as the *Report of the Office of the Secretary of Defense Vietnam Task Force*, represented an exhaustive internal study of the policies that led to the US war in Vietnam and its progressive escalation.

The principal impact of the report was its exposure of the systematic lying by successive administrations over the reasons for, and the conduct of, the US intervention in South East Asia.

In sum, the report showed that successive US governments had repeatedly lied to the American people, carried out secret illegal operations in Vietnam, militarily intervened on blatantly false pretences and killed tens of thousands of Vietnamese civilians. The report demonstrated that Washington had consistently violated international law and committed the most serious war crimes.

Invariably, official inquiries into such crimes have resulted in whitewashes that have been readily accepted by governments, the mass media and legislatures. In the case of Iraq, the British government's Chilcot Inquiry provided an example of how, even when documented evidence is produced of deliberate deception, those responsible are excused, depicted as unwitting and innocent, if willing, dupes of 'intelligence failures'.

Subsequent academic studies of the Iraq War, however, demonstrated the opposite: a campaign of intentional deception and propaganda designed to overcome widespread popular opposition to going to war, and to engineer the conditions for a parliamentary rubber stamp for a predetermined decision to join the US-led invasion of Iraq.

Broader conclusions about the 'war on terror'

There is comprehensive evidence that strategies of deception were pursued by the US and British governments during the year leading up to the March 2003 invasion of Iraq.

Under the false flags of fighting terrorism or defending their populations against 'weapons of mass destruction', the United States and Britain overthrew governments in Afghanistan, Iraq and Libya, while Syria and Yemen were engulfed in protracted and destructive battles and wars aiming at regime change. Hundreds of thousands of people have died or been maimed in these conflicts, millions have been uprooted and Europe faces its largest refugee crisis since World War II.

The outrages in New York and Washington, DC, of 11 September 2001 (9/11) provided the pretext for the implementation of plans prepared much earlier—during the 1990s—for the conquest of Afghanistan and Iraq for mercenary and geo-strategic reasons. The Middle East and Central Asia, as is well known, contain the largest proven concentrations of oil and natural gas reserves in the world.

Bitter lessons from the Iraq War

The material produced by the Chilcot report demonstrates the depths and lengths to which Western governments—supposedly the leading democracies of the world—are prepared to go to manipulate their populations into supporting wars about regional and global hegemony. The 'close-knit propaganda campaign' that British Prime Minister Tony Blair canvassed with US President George W. Bush in 2001 shows that deception as a political strategy is incompatible with democracy.

The very scale of the propaganda exercise undertaken to try to justify the Iraq War indicate the growing difficulties that the ruling elites are experiencing in overcoming popular opposition. Further rigorous research and greater circulation of its results to the world's people can contribute to the development of a mass global anti-war movement. In February 2003, despite the official campaign of lies and fabrications, millions of people around the world were already marching against the impending invasion of Iraq.

The bitter experiences in Vietnam and the Middle East demonstrate the necessity of developing an even stronger and more politically conscious movement that goes beyond mass protest to overturn the governments and the ruling establishments that are responsible for such barbaric military interventions and wars.

Increasingly unrestrained war powers in the United States

Despite the US Constitution explicitly vesting the power to declare war in the hands of Congress—as a result of the American Revolution—every US president since Harry Truman launched the three-year Korean War in 1950 has gone to war without congressional approval, let alone any popular vote.

The US experience also demonstrates the futility of any perspective based on legislative control, or even restraint, of executive war powers. The assertion of imperial presidential authority has been accompanied and facilitated by the complicit surrender by Congress of the war-making power.

After US forces had already killed millions of people in Korea and Indochina, Congress passed the 1973 War Powers Resolution, purporting to place some limits on presidential war-launching. Nonetheless, Congress has approved multibillion-dollar defence spending bills every year, permitting one president after another to assert congressional agreement with each US military intervention.

Since 2001, each administration has been permitted to rely on two Authorizations for the Use of Military Force (AUMFs), originally adopted in the wake of 9/11 to back the invasions of Afghanistan and Iraq, to initiate and extend a series of military interventions.

The judiciary too has proven complicit in this process, helping to clear the path for unfettered US militarism. No court has upheld a challenge to presidential war-making; rather, they have invariably upheld White House submissions to block or strike down suits for one reason or another.

The violation of the US Constitution reached new heights under President Barack Obama. Despite being at war for his entire two terms in office, including in Afghanistan, Iraq, Libya, Syria and Niger, Obama never once went to Congress for authorisation to use military force and he defended his orders for drone assassinations of US citizens as part of the prerogatives of the commander-in-chief.

Obama's White House not only sidelined Congress in its pursuit of US militarism, but also blocked every attempt by citizens to hold the government to account via the courts. In doing so, the Obama presidency cleared the path for the even greater unilateralism and aggression of Donald Trump's reign.

The Trump administration has exploited the precedents set by the Obama and George W. Bush administrations, with the complicity of Congress, to go even further in asserting executive war-making powers, starting with Syria. With regard to Syria itself, the White House asserted the right to expand the US military operations indefinitely—long past the defeat of so-called Islamic State, the ostensible reason for the intervention.

No discussion of US war powers can realistically ignore the power of the financial corporate elites, whose interests in waging war are bound up with two major factors.

First and foremost, the military supremacy of the United States since World War II has been an essential aspect of its global economic hegemony.

A secondary, but interrelated, factor is the inexorable rise of the war-related sections of the US capitalist elite. The 'military-industrial complex' that Eisenhower warned of in 1961 has magnified vastly since then, with Wall Street investing huge sums of money in the armaments industry.

Unrestrained war powers are today being asserted and exercised by US administrations, with serious and ominous implications both globally and domestically. With the complicity of Congress, the judiciary, the corporate media and academic commentators, the world's greatest military power is seeking to prevent its identified rivals—starting with Russia and China—from developing the capacity to obstruct or challenge the supremacy that the United States established as a result of World War II.

Britain's royal war prerogative reasserted

In Britain, as in the United States, successive governments have increasingly resorted to, and expanded, executive war-making powers—although in the seemingly peculiar and anachronistic form of a 'prerogative' inherited from Britain's pre-17th-century absolute monarchy. This royal mandate, once said to be derived from the 'divine right of kings', has morphed into an authoritarian power, said to be held in the personal hands of a prime minister, possibly in consultation with a formal council, or informal cabal, of ministers and military and intelligence chiefs.

Limited attempts to constrain the 'war prerogative' following the exposure of the lies told to invade Iraq in 2003 have ultimately come to nothing. Instead, the ancient and legally unchallengeable royal prerogative to go to war has been reasserted.

Following the exposure of the lies about 'weapons of mass destruction' and the threat of nuclear attack exploited by Blair's Labour government to join the US-led invasion of Iraq in 2003, a plethora of government and parliamentary reports sought to head off popular outrage by devising ways of pretending that the House of Commons is able to vote on any decision to enter a war.

Each proposal to legislate in the form of a US-style 'War Powers Act', however, has ultimately been killed off, leaving the war prerogative intact.

Nonetheless, claims were made, both official and academic, that Blair's decision to secure parliamentary approval of the Iraq operation established a 'convention' that a prime minister must allow the House of Commons to debate and vote on the deployment of forces. This convention supposedly obviated the need for legislation to ensure parliamentary consent.

Events since 2011, in which British military forces, including special forces, have conducted overt and covert operations in Libya, Syria, Mali and Yemen without any preceding parliamentary vote, have shattered these claims.

With one exception, governments effectively disregarded the supposed convention. In 2013, facing widespread public opposition to a war with Syria, Prime Minister Cameron moved a House of Commons resolution to authorise and politically legitimise military operations in Syria. But he suffered an embarrassing defeat. So no such vote was permitted five years later, in April 2018, when Prime Minister Theresa May and her cabinet ordered British forces to join a missile attack on Syria without a parliamentary vote, despite opinion polls showing even greater public opposition than in 2013.

May then went further, indicating that Britain's Parliament would never again be allowed to prevent a planned military intervention, as it had done when voting against an attack on Syria in 2013.

A shroud of secrecy surrounds who exactly exercises these powers, whom they consult, and what role is played by the military and intelligence chiefs, the royal palace and the governments of the United States and other allied powers in deciding to launch military operations.

No legislation authorises the National Security Council, which comprises ministers and military and intelligence chiefs; legally, the power remains in the hands of the prime minister, supposedly to exercise personally. This concentration of power in the realm of a shadowy and undefined ruling class circle is totally anti-democratic.

Some three centuries after the struggle for parliamentary and civilian supremacy over the British monarchy—and in a political system that professes to be democratic—the powers of the government to declare war, to call out the military domestically and to impose draconian emergency measures still rest on the vestiges of regal authority. Such power is incompatible with genuine democracy.

Successive British governments have deliberately left open recourse to prerogative powers. The only conclusion that can be drawn is that the ruling establishment in Britain is determined to retain unfettered powers to instigate or to join wars and to deal militarily with serious political, economic and social upheavals. For all of the references to 'rule of law' and 'democracy', great care has been taken to preserve the royal prerogative powers.

This insistence on the anti-democratic exercise of the war powers by an executive committee, not Parliament, intensified during the 20th century, which was marked by two horrific world wars in which Britain played a central role.

After the exposure of the lies underpinning the Iraq War, various reviews and proposals sought to formalise an enhanced role by the House of Commons—whether via legislation, a parliamentary resolution or a convention—in deploying the armed forces. In the end, however, regardless of how limited or qualified the recommendations were, these projects all came to naught.

In 2016, the British government abandoned plans to introduce a 'War Powers Act' that would enshrine into law a commitment—however limited and qualified—to seek parliamentary approval before deploying British troops in combat.

In Britain, as in the United States, people challenging war decisions, or affected by them, have found it almost impossible to prosecute or obtain redress for such conduct. Courts have dismissed legal actions on various grounds, including non-justiciability (that is, arguments that the issues are beyond the jurisdiction of the courts), a lack of legal standing among ordinary people in challenges to war-related actions and potential damage to 'national security' or 'international relations'.

Such rulings are an indication of the readiness of the courts to embrace and rubber-stamp war-related government activities, regardless of their apparent illegality, in the interests of 'national security' and military alliances. This has particular implications for decisions to join wars launched or triggered by allied powers, such as the United States.

In relation to the war prerogative, the courts have limited any consideration even of its existence and scope, instead broadly asserting the Crown's exclusive prerogative, exercised by a government, to declare war and deploy the armed forces. They have not examined its precise existence or scope; rather, war-related powers have been treated as axiomatic and as matters in which the courts should defer to the Crown.

The war power in Australia: from legal subordination to political subservience

In Australia, the executive exercise of the war power is completely unfettered by the Constitution. Additionally, the 'executive' that exercises the war power is very narrowly conceived, comprising only the prime minister and cabinet. The consequence is that, in Australia, a mere handful of people formally wield the war power.

Since Federation in 1901, this unfettered legal power has 'developed' in a circle in Australia, from the royal war power prerogative of the English monarch to the executive war power prerogative of the Australian prime minister.

The unconstrained character of the war power has been a key component in the participation of Australian troops in US military interventions since World War II, despite considerable popular opposition to such participation.

Any discussion of the development and exercise of the war power in Australia must recognise two crucial factors:

- the significance of Australia's colonial origins, which, although now legally transcended, played a pivotal role in the historical development and exercise of the war power in this country; and
- the crucial importance of Australia's close geo-strategic alliance with the United States, which now dominates the exercise of the Australian war power.

The Australian ruling establishment has always relied upon the military support of the predominant world power—a status once held by the British Empire, but achieved by the United States as a result of World War II.

Australia went to two world wars according to the dictates of the executive branch of a government of another nation, Britain. The decision to commit Australian blood and treasure to any conflict was made in Whitehall, not Canberra.

From 1951 onward, the prime minister and cabinet—that is, the elected, rather than appointed, members of the Executive—exercised the war power without vice-regal input.

In all of the major conflicts in which Australia has participated since 1945—Borneo, Malaya, Korea, Vietnam, Iraq (1991), Afghanistan, Iraq (2003), Iraq (2014) and Syria (2014–18)—the prime minister and cabinet made the decision to commit troops.

The legal subordination that was characteristic of the period known as the colonial hangover has continued to manifest in political subservience in circumstances in which the United States has replaced Britain as the world's greatest superpower.

Australia's increasingly close military alliance with the United States arguably renders Australian constitutional arrangements superfluous: decisions are made in the White House and the Australian executive in Canberra simply follows suit. At the very least, it can be argued that the current constitutional location of the Australian war power in the executive makes it much easier for Washington to garner Australia's agreement to, and participation in, its military actions across the globe.

There is no merit to the suggestion that the discretionary exercise by the Australian governor-general of 'reserve' powers could operate as political check on an authoritarian and/or war-minded Australian prime minister and cabinet. Not only is this unlikely, but also it is certainly less democratic.

Unfettered executive war power in combination with the other side of the coin—recently expanded domestic power of the executive branch to call out troops domestically—gives a dangerous, authoritarian, monopoly to the executive branch in relation to military actions.

Limiting the powers to go war?

Australia, where proposals to curb or modify the executive war-making have been moved for three decades, provides a telling example of the inadequacy and failure of such efforts. None of these proposals have suggested a referendum or a plebiscite as a means of trying to establish popular democratic control over war powers. Instead, they have involved highly problematic suggestions of restoring the war declaration powers of the governor general, inherited from the war prerogative of the British monarchy, or of limited reviewing roles for one or both Houses of Parliament.

The idea that Parliament should approve Australian commitments to engage in military activities first found political expression during the 1950–53 conflict in Korea in calls from Leader of the Opposition in the Senate William Ashley. For more than 30 years, minor political parties—first the Australian Democrats, then the Australian Greens—have been attempting to reform the executive war power prerogative in such a fashion via amendment of the Defence Act 1903 (Cth).

Their proposals still allowed for the government, via the governor general proclaiming an 'emergency', to initiate a military conflict. This left open the possibility that Parliament would, in effect, be reduced to the role of rubber-stamping, as a *fait accompli*, a war that had already been launched or provoked.

Nevertheless, since 1985, the Labor Party and the Liberal–National coalition have repeatedly resisted any move to broaden the exercise of the war power beyond a narrowly defined political executive.

War and dissent: sweeping domestic powers

Wars—whether formally declared or not—have serious domestic consequences, including losses of soldiers' and other victims' lives, the diversion of massive resources into the war effort, the channeling of funds from social spending into war expenditure and the development of anti-war opposition.

Both world wars and every major US-led war since—Korea, Vietnam, Afghanistan and Iraq—have been accompanied by draconian internal measures to enforce the war mobilisation and to suppress social unrest and dissent. Governments have invariably resorted to repressive provisions, including emergency powers, special legislation and regulations, detentions without trial, widespread surveillance and police harassment, particularly directed against opponents of the war.

To impose such sacrifices on a population necessarily entails extraordinary legal and punitive measures, going far beyond 'peacetime' provisions in their impact on basic democratic rights, including freedom of political opinion.

In the United States, a declaration of war automatically brings into effect a host of statutes that confer special powers on the president and the executive branch.

An authorisation for the use of military force (AUMF) does not automatically trigger these standby statutory authorities, but some can come into effect if a state of war in fact comes into being after an AUMF and most can be activated if a president proclaims a national emergency.

The AUMF in response to the 9/11 terrorist attacks has been asserted as legal authority for comprehensive executive actions in the domestic context. The Bush administration asserted that it permits detention without trial of persons arrested in the United States on suspicion of terrorism related to Al Qaeda. This was bolstered by the Supreme Court's decision in *Hamdi et al. v. Rumsfield* 542 US 507, 531 (2004) that the detention of enemy combatants captured in Afghanistan was authorised as 'a fundamental incident of waging war'.

In previous wars, the Alien Enemy Act of 1798 had provided the chief means of interning suspected enemies domestically. During both world wars, thousands of people were detained or forcibly displaced by US governments in supposed prosecution of the war efforts, overriding their most basic legal and democratic rights.

The George W. Bush administration deemed terrorist suspects to be neither prisoners of war nor enemy combatants, thus justifying their incarceration without trial. President Bush signed a military order that denied such suspsects access to civilian courts, allowed the military to hold them indefinitely anywhere in the world and instituted military commissions that could impose the death penalty. The government established a detention facility at Guantanamo Bay, believing it to be a legal quagmire because it was not US territory.

The National Defense Authorization Act (NDAA) of 2012 included provisions that appear to both codify and expand a purported executive power to hold individuals, including US citizens, in military detention, potentially indefinitely.

In Britain, potentially authoritarian powers can be activated during wartime, as they were in World War I and World War II. The courts have held that the government can imprison and deport British subjects and aliens in the exercise of its prerogative.

During World War I, the executive relied mainly upon statutory powers, imposed via the Defence of the Realm Act 1914 (DORA), for executive imprisonment and internment. This legislation conferred vast powers on the executive to make regulations, including to suppress opposition to the war.

World War II again saw resort to emergency powers. In *Liversedge v Anderson* [1942] AC 206, the House of Lords demonstrated the judiciary's willingness to accept a wide-ranging use of war powers, including for detentions without trial.

The Civil Contingencies Act 2004—the 'most powerful and extensive' peacetime emergency powers ever enacted—can also be invoked during times of war or military conflict. The Act, while itself containing vast powers, did not completely replace other far-reaching legislative provisions—notably, the Emergency Powers Act 1964—and provided for continued application of royal prerogative powers.

In Australia, emergency powers were adopted during both world wars, and were used to suppress socialist and anti-war opinion. The legislation provided almost boundless powers to make regulations outlawing anti-war activity and the Unlawful Associations Act 1916 authorised the government to declare any organisation illegal.

Wartime powers were invoked in World War II to ban communist organisations and to conduct police raids of offices and homes to enforce those proscriptions by seizing documents and arresting Party members.

Contemporary preparations for wartime measures

In each of the three countries reviewed in this book, plans and blueprints have been prepared for future major wars. These include proposals based on imposing the 'law of war', for both international and domestic use, and expanding powers to deploy military forces domestically to deal with anticipated civil disorder.

In the United States, the US Department of Defense's *Law of War Manual*, released in June 2015 and periodically updated since, insists that the law of war overrides other international and domestic law, as well as the US Constitution. In this pseudo-legal framework, the 'law of war' is an independent source of legal authority that overrides key democratic rights and sanctions arbitrary rule by the military.

This doctrine resembles that of German Weimar Republic theorist and Nazi 'crown jurist' Carl Schmitt. Under Schmitt's infamous 'state of exception' doctrine, in conditions of a national emergency, the executive is permitted to override democratic protections and disregard the rule of law. Under this doctrine, democratic rights are not formally abrogated; they are simply suspended indefinitely.

The *Manual* is chiefly concerned with asserting the US military's powers in war theatres and countries occupied by the United States. It says little about the domestic application of its doctrines. However, it insists that the law of war can also override domestic law and it proposes that any breach of a law of war obligation by a member of the armed forces would be dealt with by military institutions, not civilian courts.

Since the opening years of the 21st century, governments in the United States, Britain and Australia have adopted new powers to deploy the military internally, overturning long-standing precedents against the domestic mobilisation of the armed forces. Although mostly introduced under the cover of combating terrorism, the provisions permit wider use of the military to put down unrest.

In the United States, the Bush administration of 2001–09 initiated reviews of the Posse Comitatus Act of 1878, which restricts domestic use of the military. The British Civil Contingencies Act 2004 empowered the British government to deploy the defence forces in broadly defined 'emergencies'. In Australia, the Sydney Olympics Games in 2000 provided the initial rationale for legislation giving the federal government explicit and expanded powers to call-out troops to deal with 'domestic violence'.

Official lawlessness and judicial complicity

In the event of war, in addition to whatever wartime or other emergency or extraordinary legislation is in place and regardless of any limits placed on governments by that legislation, the English-derived common law provides considerable scope for dictatorial measures to suppress anti-war dissent or other forms of social or political discontent.

First, the common law has been prepared to support recourse to the imposition of martial law, which is, in essence, the suspension of law altogether. Martial law declarations can pave the way for extensive military powers, including the right to summarily try and execute individuals, to put down civil unrest. It cannot be assumed that resort to martial law is no longer possible. Such declarations were made during the 20th century by British authorities in India, Egypt and Ireland.

Second, courts have recognised indemnities—immunities from prosecution and defences—such as self-defence and 'reasonable use of force' that protect governments from legal liability or accountability for the use of state violence against political opponents during times of war or strife.

Third, courts have protected governments from punishment for official lawlessness—acts of surveillance, harassment, violence or intimidation undertaken in the name of defending the state. Such lawsuits have been defeated, almost without exception, since the launching of the 'war on terror' in 2001, setting ominous precedents for future wars.

Finally, governments have succeeded, with the assistance of the judiciary, in using various legal devices to block attempts to challenge decisions to undertake military action or to engage in war-related activities, such as rendering prisoners to be tortured as part of the 'war on terror'.

Numbers of case studies provide a further revealing picture of the lengths to which the US government, assisted by European governments, has gone to prevent any legal challenges to its assertion of far-reaching executive powers, including the assassination of alleged enemies of the country (including US citizens) or transporting detainees to other countries in which they can be tortured.

International law cannot stop wars of aggression

The international law of war or international human rights law provide for protection against illegal wars of aggression or accompanying human rights abuses. Yet, despite the post-war Nuremberg principles outlawing wars of aggression, there seems little prospect of any major power being held to account, let alone the United States, which has refused to even accept the jurisdiction of the International Criminal Court (ICC).

These realities were underscored by the 2006 decision of ICC Prosecutor Moreno-Ocampo on the 2003 invasion of Iraq, in which it was stated that the Court has a mandate to examine conduct during the conflict, but not whether the decision to engage in armed conflict was legal or a crime of aggression. Moreover, despite much evidence of war crimes committed by the invading allies, the ruling also declared that there was insufficient evidence of the targeting of civilians or of clearly excessive attacks. And although there was sufficient evidence of wilful killing or inhuman treatment of civilians, the instances were said to be too few to support an argument that they were committed as part of a plan or policy or as part of a large-scale commission of such crimes; hence the cases were outside the Court's jurisdiction.

Domestically, international law reserves to the national state the power to override even the most basic legal and democratic rights amid war and alleged emergencies. In the Universal Declaration of Human Rights, the International Covenant on Civil and Political Rights and other related instruments, the civil and legal rights listed are mostly subject to far-reaching exemptions, such as 'national security', 'public safety' or 'public emergency which threatens the life of the nation'.

Referenda would not, by themselves, prevent wars

Proposals for popular votes, or official referenda, on going to war purport to address the incapacity or unwillingness of congressional or parliamentary mechanisms to act as a check on governments. In the face of entrenched and vehement opposition by ruling elites, however, none of these calls has ever succeeded in being implemented.

Some of these propositions have sought to introduce referenda as compulsory requirements in all countries, so that their populations could act in unison to stop their governments sending people off to kill each other along national lines. But no such global agreement has been reached, despite the horrors of two world wars. It has proven to be impossible under the current nation-state system, which is rooted in the antagonistic material interests of rival capitalist classes.

Even if such a world pact could be achieved, such referenda could not prevent wars. The machinations, lies and deceptions of governments, and the underlying economic and political power of the ruling establishments, would effectively lock countries into paths toward war regardless of popular votes.

The modern history of warfare, as reviewed in this book, demonstrates that governments invariably go to war based on pretexts of responding to an attack or forestalling an imminent one. Wars have generally been triggered by intrigues, alliances, blockades or provocations that have made wars virtually inevitable.

Moreover, most of the referenda proposals have contained exceptions—arguably, loopholes—permitting governments to go to war, without a popular vote, in cases in which the country is being invaded or attacked militarily.

Overall conclusion

None of the schemes proposed by various scholars and commentators to prevent executive governments from taking their populations to war, via parliamentary or congressional votes or referenda, have proven feasible or effective. While referenda theoretically provide a mechanism for popular hostility to war to be brought to bear, the forces driving toward war are deeply rooted in the socio-economic structure and social relations of capitalism itself.

Powerful consortia of capitalist banks and corporations utilise 'their' national states to wage a commercial, and ultimately military, struggle for control of the raw materials, oil and gas pipelines, trade routes, and access to cheap labour and markets that are critical to the accumulation of profit.

As outlined in the Introduction to this book, the essential cause of militarism and war lies in the deep-seated contradictions of the world capitalist system: between a globally integrated and interdependent economy and its division into antagonistic national states; and between the socialised character of global production and its subordination, through the private ownership of the means of production, to the accumulation of private profit by the ruling capitalist class.

The most immediate danger of war derives from the escalating—increasingly unsuccessful and disastrous—efforts of US capitalism, through years of unending war, to counter its relative decline in relation to its major rivals and to establish the global hegemony it sought after emerging from World War II as the strongest capitalist power.

European and Japanese imperialism, facing the same underlying contradictions, are pursuing the no less predatory and reactionary interests of their own ruling classes. Junior imperialist powers, such as Canada and Australia, are aligning themselves with the United States as a means of asserting their own strategic and profiteering agendas.

What is required is a new international mass movement against war, uniting the working people and youth in opposition to capitalism and imperialism. There can be no serious struggle against war except in the fight to end the dictatorship of finance capital and the economic system that is the fundamental cause of militarism and war.

In opposing another global conflagration, in which millions of ordinary people would perish, the international working class is the social force that objectively constitutes the base for world socialist revolution, which signifies an end to the nation-state system as a whole and the establishment of a global economy based on equality and scientific planning. Only the abolition of the nation-state system and the establishment of a world socialist federation will make possible the rational, planned development of global resources. Only on this basis can be built the eradication of poverty and the raising of human culture to new heights that will render war unnecessary and obsolete.

The war powers must be taken out of the hands of the ruling capitalist establishments, but this is possible only as part of a fundamental reorganisation of economic and social life on a world scale to provide for the needs of all, not only the wealthy elites. It is the aim of this book to help to clarify the necessity of this alternative perspective—and thereby to prevent a catastrophic third world war.

Index